SITUATING FEDERALISM

MECHANISMS OF INTERGOVERNMENTAL RELATIONS IN CANADA AND INDIA

SITUATING FEDERALISM

Mechanisms of Intergovernmental Relations in Canada and India

REKHA SAXENA

Foreword by
M.P. SINGH

MANOHAR
2006

First published 2006

ISBN 81-7304-676-X

The publication has been partly financed by Indian Association for Canadian Studies

Published by

Ajay Kumar Jain for
Manohar Publishers & Distributors
4753/23 Ansari Road, Daryaganj
New Delhi 110 002

Typeset at

Digigrafics
New Delhi 110 049

Printed at

Lordson Publishers Pvt. Ltd.
Delhi 110 007

Distributed in South Asia by

FOUNDATION BOOKS

4381/4, Ansari Road
Daryaganj, New Delhi 110 002
and its branches at Mumbai, Hyderabad,
Bangalore, Chennai, Kolkata

To my parents
late Ram Babu Saxena
and Asha Saxena

Contents

Foreword

Canada in 1867 and India in 1949–50 pioneered, in North America and Asia respectively, a mixed constitution seeking to reconcile parliamentary and federal principles of government. The former constituted this device of governance in the era of dual-sovereignty federalism flagged by the US American and Swiss constitutions of 1787 and 1848 respectively. This may well be the cause, if not the reason, why the British North America Act/ Canada Constitution Act, 1867, did not provide for any formal intergovernmental forum for the two orders of government. India made its constitution in the post-World War II years by which time the era of cooperative federalism had already made intergovernmental forums a commonplace device in federal systems. Predictably, both the Government of India Act, 1935, and the Constitution of independent India formally provided for an Inter-Provincial / Inter-State Council.

Dr. Rekha Saxena has made the first qualitative book-length study in India at any rate, of the working of intergovernmental agencies in India and Canada. She covers more than a century of the Canadian experience and more than half-a-century of the Indian experience in these two Westminster-inspired federations. I wish someone would undertake a similar comparative study of India and Australia (since 1900–1). In fact, a comparative study of India and the USA is also very much needed. The USA is not a Westminster-inspired federation. Yet the American principle of separation of powers and checks and balances and judicial review is of late becoming part of the Canadian and Indian parliamentary federations in practice in some ways if not in theory.

There are several reasons why the importance of intergovernmental forums of what Canadian constitutionalists call 'executive federalism' has grown and is likely to continue to grow in both Canada and India. There is the bare necessity of bringing together the executive heads of two orders of government—first ministers, ministers, civil servants—to harmonize policy making and implementation in exclusive and concurrent jurisdictions of governments. Besides, the federal second chambers of Parliaments of Canada and India are ill-suited for intergovernmental policy making. This is even more so in the case of the Canadian Senate than the Indian Rajya Sabha. The former is neither elected nor equal to the House of Commons. The latter is elected, but not equal to the Lok Sabha except in terms of veto over federal constitutional amendments. In addition, both the popular and federal chambers in Canada and India are reflective of the varying sizes of population and do not give formal equality of representation to provinces/states, irrespective of their populations. So smaller federating units are outnumbered in both the Chambers, unlike the US Senate which allots two seats to each state, big or small. Intergovernmental forums are size-neutral; they decide by consensus, as sensed by the chair, rather than by majority.

There are other reasons why the importance of intergovernmental forums has been growing. Both India and Canada have moved into multi-partisan configurations and into neoliberal economic policy regimes. These paradigm shifts have increased the potentiality of jurisdictional conflicts among governments. Hence putting in place adequate regulatory mechanisms for de-bureaucratized sectors of the state and economy can hardly be exaggerated. If forums of intergovernmental relations and state-society interface are not activated and expanded, current compensatory response of judicial activism and overload would result in judicial delay, politicization, and ineffectiveness, particularly so in India.

Dr. Rekha Saxena's book is therefore a topical tract of the time, and as welcome as the Metro Rail in Delhi.

M.P. SINGH

Professor
Department of Political Science
University of Delhi, Delhi
17 January 2005

Preface

I have always been fascinated by Indian politics. The idea of India as an 'imagined political community' has continuously been rediscovered and reinvented by Indians as well as foreigners. Indian nationalism is in many ways a gigantic experiment in multicultural existence and governance. My first serious foray into Indian political studies began with my Masters and M.Phil. dissertations, both dealing with transformation in the party system and the elections that brought about this change.

In course of doing these works, I realized that the change in the Indian party system had brought about a wider cluster of institutional and cultural transformation that could broadly be subsumed under the rubric of 'federalization'. This is how I was gradually drawn to the study of Indian federalism. While exploring the process of federalization in India, I was deeply interested in the study of this problem in comparative perspective. My comparative inquiries led me to study the Canadian political model, which seems to have greatly influenced the design of the federal Constitution of India. As Ronald L. Watts was to tell me later, the British North America Act 1867 served as the model for the Government of India Act 1935; they were both originally the products of British Parliament. The striking similarities between the 1950 Indian Constitution, on the one hand, and the BNA Act and the 1935 Government of India Act, on the other, are thus not purely incidental. Against this background, my choice of a comparative study of India and Canada is only natural.

The specific topic of my research—mechanisms of intergovernmental relations—still needs some explaining. There are of course many aspects of federalization process that I could have selected for my study. The intergovernmental mechanisms struck me not only as entities whose salience was likely to improve in a more federalized context but also as the core institutions of a vigorous federal political system.

My comparative study suggests that as of now, intergovernmental mechanisms have already acquired a degree of institutionalization and effectiveness in Canada but in India the picture is not so rosy. What is certain is that their importance in both countries is likely to increase further in the years to come. This is evident not only from the agenda and action on constitutional reforms in Canada and India but also from the fact that the growing significance of regional and global integration of these two countries in their respective regions, demands intergovernmental negotiations and harmonization of policies at multiple levels of governments.

REKHA SAXENA

Acknowledgements

I have incurred the gratitude of many institutions and individuals while carrying out sustained research on this theme. Among the institutions, I would like to first mention the Political Science Department, University of Delhi, and the Shastri Indo-Canadian Institute (SICI). The former granted me registration as a Ph.D. candidate and the latter awarded me a doctoral fellowship to work in Canada. In Canada, I mainly worked at the Department of Political Studies and the Institute of Intergovernmental Relations, both at the Queen's University, with occasional visits to the Parliament Library and the Intergovernmental Conference Secretariat in Ottawa.

This book is based on my Ph.D. work. My largest scholarly debt is owed to my supervisor, Professor M.P. Singh, who was actively associated with this study in an advisory capacity right from its conception to its execution. His indefatigable and patient interest and guidance in this work kept me going in the positive direction. At times my perseverance would give up, but he constantly goaded me to a more perfect completion of this work.

Professor C.E.S. Franks was my contact person in Canada during my stay as a Shastri Fellow there. I cherish the care and concern for my welfare that he and his wife Daphne showed to me. I have immensely benefited from discussions with many other eminent scholars and friends in the field of political and federal studies in the two countries. I would particularly like to mention the names of Douglas Verney, Ronald L. Watts, Harvey Lazar, Hugh Thorburn, Peter Russell, J. Peter Meekison, David Cameron, Richard Simeon, Thomas Courchene, Keith Banting, Jayant Lele, Peter Leslie, Will Kymlicka, John Wood, B.D. Dua, Kathy Brock, Johnathan Rose, Douglas Brown, Hamish Telford, Alan Whitehorn, Ian Greene, Hugh Segal, Nelson Wiseman, Evert Lindquist, Jean Chotard, Paritosh Kumar, John Mclean, K.N. Kabra, Balveer Arora, George Mathew, Akhtar Majeed, C.P.

Bhambhri, Rajeev Dhavan, Imtiaz Ahmad, Bidyut Chakrabarty, Sandeep Shastri, Manoranjan Mohanty, Subrata Mukherjee, R.B. Jain, A.S. Narang and S.N. Mishra. They were not only generous with their time, but also provided me with useful insights, valuable references and reading materials. Some of them were also helpful in arranging my meetings with political and administrative functionaries. My discussion with Lawrence Saez on the theme was equally rewarding.

A number of Union and Federal officials in India and Canada were extremely helpful in course of my interviews with them on various aspects of the problem under study. They include S. Lakshminarayanan, Ravi Dhingra, S.K. Bagga, and Kamal Taori in the Inter-State Council, Naveen Verma and Rajeev Malhotra in the Planning Commission, Sayan Chatterji in the Election Commission, N. Vittal in the Central Vigilance Commission, Maxwell Pereira, Indian Police Service, B.P. Singh, former Home Secretary, A.R. Nanda, former Health Secretary in India. During my study tour in Canada, George Anderson, James Ross Hurley, Leslie Seidle in the Privy Council Office, and Stuart Mackinon, Secretary, Intergovernmental Conference Secretariat were extremely helpful and also provided me with very valuable documentary and scholarly sources.

The documentation centres at which the research for this study was mainly conducted were the Stauffer and Law libraries at the Queen's Campus and the Parliament Library in Ottawa, and the Indian Parliament Library, the Indian Institute of Public Administration library and the library of the Institute of Industrial Development in New Delhi. I also benefited from the personal collection of books and newspaper clippings of Professor M.P. Singh.

Anup Taneja, editor, ICHR and the in-house editor, Manohar Publishers, deserve special thanks for the meticulous copy editing of the text. I also wish to acknowledge the financial support given to me by the Indian Association for Canadian Studies (IACS) towards the publication of this book.

My sincere thanks are also due to V.K. Ohri, advocate in the Supreme Court of India, whose ever-willing and ready help in course of this study has been invaluable. He has been my standard reference for legal documentation and discussion. I am beholden to Cheryl Saunders, Professor at Law School, University of Melbourne, B.N. Tandon, Director, K.K. Birla Foundation, Sumit Chakravartty, Editor, *Mainstream*, Ash Narain Roy of the Institute of Social Sciences, Rupak Chattopadhayay of the Forum of Federations, Anil Kumar Singh of Star News for their kind help and encouragement as and when required.

I am deeply indebted to the Shastri Indo-Canadian Institute, Indian Association for Canadian Studies, Institute of Social Sciences, Centre for Federal Studies, Hamdard University, and Forum of Federations, Ottawa for associating me with their academic programmes and activities.

My several friends in Canada like Pauline, Stephanie, Carmen, Dinah, Kim, Tannu, Ali, Emebet and Jaya deserve special mention for their help and assistance during the completion of this project.

I owe a great deal of gratitude to late Professor M.M. Sankhdher and Mrs. Mandakini Sankhdher for having extended their whole-hearted cooperation to me both at the professional and personal levels. I am highly grateful to my uncle, R.B. Saxena and his family for their affection, care and support. My cousins Kavita, Mamta and Amita have constantly helped me in organizing the material. I have enormously benefited from their computer expertise. I want to express my appreciation for my other relatives and friends who cannot be singled out individually for their assistance.

I would also like to acknowledge the special affection showered on me by my sister and brother-in-law, Renu and Shailesh Srivastava, brother Deepak and late sister-in-law, Anuradha Saxena, and my nephews Abhishek, Shashank and Rishabh. I will be failing in my duty if I do not record my special gratitude to my late parents. Their fond memories and blessings are a constant source of inspiration to me.

Last, but not the least, I would like to thank M/s Manohar Publishers for their keen interest in the publication of this book.

REKHA SAXENA

CHAPTER 1

Introduction

This study explores and analyses patterns and trends in the relationship between the central and regional governments, known as the federal and provincial governments in Canada, and the union and state governments in India, the two Commonwealth countries. This problem has acquired special significance in recent decades as both these political systems have undergone an eventful process of transition from a predominantly parliamentary regime to more federalized governance.

Both Canada (in 1867) and India (in 1950) adopted a form of government broadly similar in principle to the Westminster model prevalent in England, but with the modification that they added on a federal component to a parliamentary framework. This combination of parliamentary and federal principles of government was necessitated by social and regional diversities characterizing the two countries. However, it was a combination marked by the predominance of the parliamentary principle over the federal component.

In working a parliamentary federal system in the rapidly changing social and political scenario, both Canada and India have been under great pressure internally as well as externally to adapt their constitutional theory and practice to the needs of the emergent global situation where divergent forces of globalism and localism are struggling for an equilibrium. While on the one hand, within the nation, regional and local forces are asserting their identities for recognition by the national state, on the other, forces of global and regional integration at the supranational level are impinging upon the national states to accommodate global capital and finance and join in the international division of labour. Given this broader global context, the federal states in the two countries are experiencing some limitations on their power and autonomy from pressures both global and local. Both countries in the early post-Second World War years put in place strong national developmental states based on a strategy of state-led industrialization.

Post-war Canada established a highly developed welfare state providing social and economic security to Canadians which, according to some observers, still constitutes one of the important bases of Canadian identity. This is now being replaced by a social union framework renegotiated by the federal and provincial governments in Canada. India could by no stretch of imagination be said to have developed a welfare state, yet Chapter IV of the Constitution on Directive Principles of State Policy contained the promise of a welfare state as and when the resources available to the state allowed the institution of a universal system of social and economic security. None the less, with limited resources, India was probably the first developing country to provide a reasonable degree of social assistance to the extremely needy sections of the population in particular and the middle classes in general. With a reasonably organized trade union movement at least in the formal sectors of the economy, Indian workers enjoyed significant collective bargaining rights and economic benefits. Reservation policy introduced a system of reverse discrimination in favour of those who had been historically disadvantaged. Urban consumers were supplied rationed food items through the Public Distribution System (PDS) at controlled prices. The union and state governments also set up a huge system of subsidies to farmers and consumers to give incentives for agrarian and social modernization.

All these political and economic structures and policies in these two countries came under a great strain following major distortions and policy shifts beginning in the 1970s. Subsequently, the Keynesian macroeconomic policy framework was replaced by a neo-liberal policy package in 1991 emanating from the so-called Washington Consensus. For over two decades, Canada and India have been adjusting to a paradigm shift from a state-centred strategy of development to one that emphasizes the market and the civil society.

The forces of economic liberalization thus have got amalgamated with forces of political federalization propelled by the growing assertions of regionalism and localism. Under the combined impact of these economic and political forces, federalism has become the new buzzword. The growing tempo of federalization demands new patterns of federal–provincial or union–state relations in these countries. The purpose of this study is to explore these changes in the patterns of federal politics, with special reference to the role of intergovernmental mechanisms. With the growing autonomy of provincial and state governments, the importance of these intergovernmental mechanisms has enlarged. Canada being an older federation has obviously moved ahead of India in the institutionalization of these mechanisms.

In the course of the evolution of political systems in Canada and India, the federal features of their respective societies have continuously clamoured for a greater recognition by the political establishment. In his revised edition of the classic entitled *Federal Government* published in the mid-1960s, K.C. Wheare made an interesting observation about Canada and India. On the basis of his study of the two constitutions, Wheare classified Canada and India as 'quasi-federal'. He proceeded to make an interesting distinction between the two countries on the basis of their actual governance. According to him, the Canadian Constitution was quasi-federal but the Canadian government was federal. As far as India was concerned, both its Constitution and Government were quasi-federal. By the 1990s, the Government of India, too, had become federal despite its Constitution.[1]

This leads one to factors promoting federalization that are specifically internal to the political system, in addition to the socio-economic factors elaborated earlier. Within the political system at least two major factors have significantly contributed to increasing federalization in Canada and India: party system transformation and judicial interpretation. Both these factors have operated in the two political systems in a rather reverse fashion in terms of their federalizing effects. For example, judicial interpretation favoured greater provincial autonomy fairly early in the evolution of the Canadian federation, while in India it initially favoured centralization. The Judicial Committee of the Privy Council, which was the highest court of appeal in Canada before the institution of the Supreme Court in 1949, interpreted the BNA Act to the advantage of the provinces.

In India, on the other hand, the Supreme Court initially interpreted the Constitution in a way that contributed to centralization (*State of West Bengal* vs *Union of India*, 1963).[2] Similarly, prior to *S.R. Bommai* vs *Union of India* (1994)[3] case, the Court gave the union executive practically a free hand in determining whether the constitutional machinery in a state had broken down in terms of Article 356 for proclaiming President's Rule there. It had reasoned that it was a political thicket best left to the union executive. For the first time, the Court reversed its earlier rulings in the Bommai judgement, saying that the power to declare President's Rule was, of course, to be exercised by the President on the advice of the union cabinet. This power, however, was not absolute; rather it was one which the union executive ought to exercise on the basis of certain determinable criteria that should bear relationship with the objective realities of the case concerned. The Court, in fact, went ahead to establish its power of judicial review in the matter and ruled that the assembly of the state in which a government is dismissed should not be dissolved until at least the approval of the Presidential Proclamation by Parliament. The Bommai judgement has in effect become the new constitution as far as President's Rule is concerned until the Supreme Court itself reverses that ruling.

With reference to the role of the party system in the federalization process in Canada and India, it may be mentioned that its effectiveness became evident in Canada much earlier than it did in India. There is a rather subtle difference between the two countries. Both countries started with one party dominance system—under the Conservatives in Canada and the Congress party in India. However, Canada gradually moved to an alternating two party system with the Liberals and Conservatives, with a minor presence of a third party in Parliament, the New Democratic Party. This has been the national pattern, while at the provincial level, a number of regional parties have always existed, some of them being the ruling parties in the provinces. An early development of this kind of competitive party system in Canada significantly contributed to the federalization process. The 1993 Canadian Parliamentary elections witnessed a major change in the party system. There was a further trend towards multiparty configuration with the emergence of two new parties, namely, the Reform Party and the Bloc Quebecois. The Reform Party, later called the Canadian Alliance, was aspirationally a national party, but for all practical purposes, it was a regional party largely confined to the Western Provinces. Feeding on right wing Christian evangelism, its rise weakened and fragmented the Progressive Conservative Party in the West. The Canadian Alliance subsequently merged with the Progressive Conservative Party to form the Conservative Party. Bloc Quebecois, a separatist Quebec party, emerged in the wake of the decline of the Liberal Party in that province whose ranks deserted the parent party to organize a separatist political force contesting only the federal elections and leaving the provincial electoral field for the pre-existing separatist Parti Quebecois.

In India, the Congress dominance in the early decades whittled down the federal forces in the country under a strong parliamentary centralism headed by Nehru and Indira Gandhi. Tendencies towards party pluralism at the state level in 1967 and at the centre in 1977 gave a freer play to the forces of federalism, but an irreversible phase of federalization set in only with the 1989 Lok Sabha elections. This was the turning point in party system configuration when India made a definite transition from one party dominance to a multiparty system. Since then, a series of minority and coalition governments have continued with a strong tendency towards governmental instability. None the less, in the period of over a decade since 1989, India has witnessed a strong spell of federal governance that is likely to continue in the foreseeable future.

Commenting on the new trends in the Indian federal system since the 1990s, Verney aptly observes:

> Assuming present trends continue, the national parties will play a decreasing role, and the state parties will continue to expand. A few years ago, it was possible to view this development as an indication that an overcentralized quasi-federal India was moving toward a genuine federation, a partnership of the national and state governments. Today, there is the possibility that the state parties could become the dominant parties in the national legislature. It would then be too late to bring about reform of the party system. The India that began as a highly centralized federation (often called a 'quasi-federation') would have

been transformed into a much looser federation (one that might be called a 'quasi-confederacy').[4]

The forms and trends of intergovernmental relations in Canada and India have undergone a reasonably long process of evolution. Canada, of course, has had a longer history and has developed a somewhat more evolved pattern. India, too, has an appreciable length of experience in working intergovernmental relations. Despite some similarities, the patterns have diverged to a considerable extent in the two countries. The Canadian Constitution made no mention of the need for any formal agency for intergovernmental contacts and policy-making. Yet, intergovernmental relations at the administrative level began informally very early after the founding of the federation in Canada. Deputy Ministerial meetings and First Ministers' Conferences were organized early in the twentieth century, again informally outside the framework of the Constitution. Following the expansion of the role of government and complexities of the economy, administrative, ministerial and first ministerial conferences grew enormously in frequency and importance. The extensive network of these meetings still exists largely outside the constitutional framework, though the First Ministers' Conference is now mentioned in passing in the 1982 Canada Constitution Act in the context of the amending formula. Wars, economic depression, cultural conflicts, constitutional reforms, increasing volume of interprovincial and international trade, and ecological challenges have combined to put intergovernmental relations in Canada in the top gear. This has increased their importance in the Canadian political system to an extent that they can be said to rival the Cabinet and Parliament in importance even though the constitutional supremacy of Parliament remains unquestioned, at least legally. In any case, decisions taken by intergovernmental mechanisms have no validity and sanction unless they are approved by Parliament and provincial legislatures. In practice, of course, this is not always done.

The Indian Constitution envisaged the necessity of intergovernmental relations and provided for the contingent creation of an Inter-State Council under Article 263. This Article in the 1950 Constitution was borrowed from a similar provision in the

Government of India Act, 1935, providing for the creation of an Inter-Provincial Council. However, Article 263 was rarely used before the President of India set up a regular Inter-State Council (ISC) in 1990. Since then the ISC and its sub-committees have met occasionally, made some recommendations and produced reports that have not been included on the active agenda of the governments for implementation. Despite an enabling constitutional provision, constitutionally entrenched intergovernmental mechanisms have not been all that important and functionally consequential in India.

However, another intergovernmental mechanism, i.e. the National Development Council (NDC) established outside the framework of the Constitution by a Cabinet Resolution of the Nehru government in 1952, has been more significant in many ways in the field of economic policy-making and planning than the ISC has been in the political sphere. Since its inception, the NDC has met regularly to approve five-year plans and annual plans on behalf of the union and state governments. The Sarkaria Commission Report on centre–state relations (1987-8) recommended constitutional entrenchment of the NDC, though it still awaits implementation. Consisting of the prime minister, key union ministers and chief ministers of the states and the executive heads of the union territories, the NDC is the grand economic council of the Indian Republic that in federal matters may appear to eclipse the Parliament in importance. Yet in constitutional and legal terms, the Parliament is supreme.

In India, as in Canada, intergovernmental mechanisms in substantial terms have largely operated outside the framework of the Constitution. Although the top level or first ministerial conferences in Canada and India are important in ultimate power terms, the actual details of intergovernmental negotiations and agreements are worked out in less publicized ministerial and bureaucratic conferences bringing representatives of the two levels of government together. However, the groundwork done by them must finally be approved and announced by the First Ministers. In the final analysis, they need parliamentary and legislative sanction at the federal and regional levels.

This study is the first book-length research of intergovernmental mechanisms in Canada and India. Despite their potential and growing importance in the working of the two federations, there has been no detailed and definitive research on them. This would appear to be an interesting example of political developments overtaking academic studies in the two countries. The approach followed in this work is comparative and historical with an empirical thrust. The empirical data and information used here have been collected from libraries and government departments as well as through direct interviews with academicians, bureaucrats, and eminent political personalities. Interviews were particularly useful in filling the gaps in information where no public documents or studies were available.

The choice of Canada for this comparative study originating in India was dictated by the consideration that Canada was the first country in the world to have combined the parliamentary and federal system in 1867. India was the first country in the Afro-Asian world to attempt a similar combination of parliamentarianism and federalism. Further, despite differences in their levels of economic development and demography, Canada and India are both multicultural societies with deep cultural cleavages and strong regional identities as well as economic disparities. With more or less comparable constitutional systems, these countries have interesting parallels in their ideological spectra, their party systems and their framework of public policies and development strategies. Moreover, both systems are working out a transition from a centralized federal system to a more decentralized one, and a shift from Keynesian economic policy paradigm to a neo-liberal policy paradigm.

This volume is divided into eight chapters. Chapter 2 provides a critical survey of theories of federalism and illustrates their applicability to Canada and India. This is done to lay an elevated theoretical ground from where a survey of the growth of intergovernmental relations in two more or less similar federal political systems could be conducted. Understandably, the more abstract federal theories are used here only as the backdrop of the federal theatre set up to script more limited episode focused on intergovernmental mechanisms in the two countries. Obviously, theories cast with a focus on total political systems cannot be used for analysing and explaining intergovernmental relations with a more delimited empirical concern. For this, a middle range model/theory of intergovernmental relations in Westminster-type parliamentary federal systems has been formulated and empirically elaborated in this study. The next two chapters deal with the structure and evolution of federal systems in Canada and India. Chapter 5 offers an overview of major intergovernmental and central mechanisms having implications for the regional governments in the two countries. Chapter 6 is a case study of the First Ministers' Conferences in Canada, the most important apex mechanism of intergovernmental relations. Chapter 7 is a case study of the Inter-State Council and the National Development Council in India. The last chapter presents the summary and conclusions of this study; and reviews the middle range theory of intergovernmental relations emerging from the case studies of Canada and India.

NOTES

1. For an early formulation of this argument in the Canadian and Indian contexts, see M.P. Singh, 'Accommodating Regionalism: Federal Constitutional Discourses in Canada and India', in *Regionalism in Canada: A Multidisciplinary Approach*, ed. Chandra Mohan, Delhi: Allied Publishers, 1995. This idea was subsequently elaborated in the earlier works of M.P. Singh and Rekha Saxena, eds., *Ideologies and Institutions in Indian Politics*, Delhi: Deep & Deep, 1998; Rekha Saxena, 'Political Regionalisation', *The Pioneer*, 26 February 1998; idem 'Federalization of Predominantly Parliamentary Regimes', in *Political Science Annual 1997*, guest eds., M.P. Singh and Rekha Saxena, Delhi: Deep & Deep, 1998; and M.P. Singh and Rekha Saxena, 'India Independent: The First Half Century of Political Development and Decay', *The Indian Historical Review*, vol. XXVI, July 1999.
2. Ravi Bhatia, 'Federalism in India and the Supreme Court Ruling', in B.D. Dua and M.P. Singh, eds., *Federalism in the New Millennium*, Delhi: Manohar, 2003.
3. *S.R. Bommai* vs *Union of India and Others*, *All India Reporter*, Supreme Court Section, 1994.
4. Douglas V. Verney, 'From Quasi-Federation to Quasi-Confederacy? The Transformation of India's Party System', *Publius*, vol. 33, no. 4, Fall 2003, p. 171.

CHAPTER 2

Theories of Federalism

Comparative federalism is an area of growing interest in the study of politics today. Federalism has been found to be an important device to accommodate diversities within a shared framework of unity and conflict resolution as an integral part of a political system as well as a mechanism for supranational regional integration in international economic and political relations. In a federal polity where at least two orders of government co-exist, the role of intergovernmental mechanisms can hardly be exaggerated. The network of intergovernmental mechanisms and their functioning cannot be adequately understood and analysed in the absence of a review of theories of federalism bequeathed by the variegated experience of federal polities around the world.

The concept of federation is older than the United States Constitution of 1787 which is regarded as the first modern instance of a federal polity. The federal idea can be traced back to ancient Indian, West Asian and Greek antiquities as well as the medieval times. In classical Indian texts, there are references to *mahajanpadas* or territorial proto-states in the sixth century BC, most of which were monarchies but some of them were republics and *ganasanghas* or proto-federations.[1]

Biblical sources refer to the federation of ancient Israelite tribes over 3,200 years ago.[2] Similarly, there were leagues of ancient Hellenic city-states in Greece which aimed at aggregating different communities and promoting trade and defence needs. Later, the Roman Republic also established asymmetrical federations of cities dominated by the central city, Rome.[3]

Medieval Europe witnessed the formation of confederations of self-governing cities in Germany, Italy and Switzerland for trade and defence.[4] The earliest confederations of Switzerland and the Netherlands belonged to the pre-history of federalism. Relatively modern instances of federal systems include those of America (1787), Switzerland (1848), Canada (1867), Australia (1901), India (1950), etc. A number of Latin American federations also date back to the late nineteenth and early twentieth centuries. Most Afro–Asian federal systems developed in the second half of the twentieth century.

The idea of federalism may be regarded as a genus subsuming a great variety of federal arrangements of which federation is only one such entity. Elazar (1994) and Watts (1999, 2001), for example, identified as many as seven different species of federal–political arrangements, each with a different nuance and emphasis:[5]

1. Decentralized union under which the constituent units are parts of a common structure of government rather than dual governmental structures, such as pre-1993 Belgium which since that date became a federation and Scotland and Wales in the United Kingdom prior to the recent devolution.
2. Federations in which strong constituent units of government are federated with a strong general government such as Canada, India and Australia.
3. Confederations whereby polities are joined together in a common government with certain limited jurisdictions such as defence or economic policy with units retaining larger and exclusive jurisdictions, e.g. Articles of the US Confederation of 1777 and the European Union.
4. Federacies where a large unit is linked to a smaller unit (units) with the latter retaining substantial autonomy to itself and playing a minimum role in the government of the larger unit, e.g. US–Puerto Rico and India–Kashmir.
5. Associated statehoods which are similar to federacies, but can be terminated by either of the units unilaterally on prearranged terms, e.g. Italy–San Marino and India–Bhutan.
6. Condominiums under which a political unit functions under the joint rule of two or more external states in a way that the people of the unit have substantial internal self-rule, e.g. Andorra–France and Spain (1278-1993).
7. Leagues linking politically independent polities for specific

purposes that work through a common secretariat and from which units may unilaterally withdraw, such as the Commonwealth of Nations and the South Asian Association for Regional Corporation (SAARC).

POLITICAL–INSTITUTIONAL APPROACH

The Political–Institutional Approach here subsumes legal-constitutional perspective as well as the norms and values underlying the organizations that guide the behaviour of political elites in particular as well as the members of the political community in general. J.G. March and J.P. Olsen have more recently used the word 'New Institutionalism' to characterize this theoretical perspective, although this approach is not all that new. Its origins go back to *The Federalist* by Alexander Hamilton, John Jay and James Madison in the field of practical constitution-making and to K.C. Wheare in the field of academic comparative study of federal governments.[6]

To define federalism, it is worthwhile to discuss some important conceptualizations appearing in political science literature. Federal principle, according to Wheare—probably the first modern scholar to make an attempt to formulate an academic theory of comparative federalism in the post-Second World War period—means the method of dividing powers so that the general and regional governments are each, within a sphere, coordinate and independent.[7] He added,

> if the federal principle is to operate not merely as a matter of strict law but also in practice, it follows that both general and regional governments must each have under its own independent control financial resources sufficient to perform its exclusive functions. Each must be financially co-ordinate with the other.[8]

Wheare's approach has generally and appropriately been regarded as essentially legalistic and static in the sense that his discussion focused more on the constitutions rather than on their actual working. He propounded the doctrine of dual sovereignty in a federal system which in behaviourally-oriented studies dissolves into a system of functional interdependence between the federal and regional governments.

Davis observed that what is notable in a federal political arrangement is that this 'inescapable federal principle of distributing functions' between national and regional governments is only a meaningful directive if there is a mode of knowing what is a 'national', 'common', 'local', or 'particular' matter for the members of a political community.[9] To him,

> . . . the federal constitution is essentially a political bargain, struck by political bargainers—the 'founding fathers'—who assemble from a variety of motives to create some degree of permanent union between communities. . . . It is founded on a particular set of assumptions and expectations as to who should make the law, over what territorial area, over what activities, in what relation the laws of the general and regional governments should stand to each other, what sort of government should prevail, and what benefits will flow from the bargain. . . .[10]

According to Geoffery Sawer, in a federal system the 'power to govern is distributed between the centre and the regions in such a way that each set of governmental institutions has a direct impact on the individual citizens and other legal persons within its area of competence'.[11] He hinted at some difference between federalism and nationalism such that people in a federal system are likely to be more attached to their regional identities than the national identity *per se*, though obviously they do value their federal affiliation to the extent that it contributes to their common well-being as a federal nation-state. In his words:

> If . . . an attempt is made to evaluate federalism in the range of constitutional systems, I would say that it is a prudential system best suited to the relatively stable, satisfied societies of squares such as abound in Canada, Australia, West Germany and Austria, and probably still constitute the majority in the USA. It is not a swinging system. People are not likely to go to the stake, or the barricades, to defend federalism as such. They may undertake heroic actions for the sake of some value which federalism happens at the minute to favour, and may then even inscribe federalism on their banner—'Liberty and Federalism'—'Equality and Federalism'—but never just 'Federalism'.[12]

Ronald L. Watts, an eminent student of Wheare, defined federalism in terms very similar to Wheare but aptly observed that this definition provides a general but not an exact test for classifying states as federal or not. When we move away from definitions limited purely to the consideration of constitutional law to definitions encompassing also political and administrative practice and social attitudes as aspects of a political system, inevitably less precision is possible.[13]

Watts added that federal systems may 'evolve by a complex process of both aggregation and devolution'.[14] He cited the examples of India, Pakistan, Nigeria and Canada which have been identified as federations which were the product of both 'devolution and aggregation'.[15] According to him, federalism by decentralization means 'a process of constitutional "devolution" from a formally unitary colonial administration to coincide with a social "aggregation" of culturally and historically distinct groups, the two processes meeting in a political federation'. He cited the examples of India and Pakistan where the achievement of provincial autonomy in 1935 was the 'culmination of a long history of increasing decentralization within British India'. These political systems bear evidence of federalism by aggregation. In Nigeria, 'the Constitutions of 1946, 1951, and 1954 progressively devolved authority to the regions until in 1954 when they became fully autonomous'. Watts argued that the process of devolution in Nigeria 'accounts for the relatively strong central powers assigned by the federal constitutions of Nigeria'.[16]

Variations of the political–institutional approach to federalism are found in the works of Donald Smiley and Preston King. In King's opinion, federations are distinctive forms of political organization by virtue of the coordinate powers of central and regional governments. He formulated his own definition: 'Basically we propose that any federation be regarded as an institutional arrangement, taking the form of a sovereign state, and distinguished from other such states solely by the fact that its central government incorporates regional units into its decision procedure on some constitutionally entrenched basis.'[17] In a federation, according to him, 'the regions (states, provinces, cantons) are constitutionally incorporated into the centre as an essential or entrenched aspect of the centre's decision-making procedure'.[18]

Donald V. Smiley defined a federation as a sovereign state in which

1. There is a constitution which distributes the power of government between central and regional governments and

which provides some protection for the people and/or the governments of these regional units in the structure and operation of the central government.

2. The elements of the constitution related to the respective powers of the centre and the regions are not subject to change by the action of the central or regional governments alone.
3. Individual citizens and private groups are subject to the laws and other authoritative exercises of power by both the central and regional governments.[19]

Elazar adopted a more functionally-oriented institutional perspective by pointing out that this political arrangement combines both 'self-rule' and 'shared rule'.[20] He related American federalism to the concept of partnership. In his first important work entitled *American Partnership*, he tried 'to demonstrate that the pattern of American federalism—the American partnership—has been a constant one since the early days of the Republic', that is, 'virtually all the activities of government in the nineteenth-century United States were cooperative endeavours, shared by federal and state agencies in much the same manner as government programmes are shared in the twentieth century'.[21] He referred to

> [r]adical states-righters in the early 1960s [who detested] what they call[ed] 'coerced federalism', 'that is, federalism involving' co-operation between the two levels [national and state] of government in the implementation of new programs in the United States in areas which, according to these states' autonomists, had previously [been] the sole responsibility of the states. . . .[22]

According to Elazar, coerced federalism was 'an inevitably sharing of the same functions, with arrangements for joint financing and generally, some type of federal supervision . . . '. Far from being harmless, in the view of the advocates of state rights, this essentially involuntary type of federalism signalled 'the destruction of the true constitutional system . . .'.[23]

Elazar affirmed that 'federalism in the United States, as practised, has traditionally been cooperative . . . dual federalism as demarcation of responsibilities has never worked in practice. . . . Governmental activities in the nineteenth century, as in the twentieth, were shared by the federal and state governments in collaboration despite formal pronouncements to the contrary'.[24] He argued:

> The American federal system has been fundamentally a co-operative partnership of federal, state and local governments since the early days of the Republic. Within a dualistic structural pattern, the governments of the United States have developed a broadly institutionalized system of collaboration based on the implicit premise that virtually all functions of government must be shared by virtually all governments. . . .[25]

In a similar vein, Morton Grodzins noted in 1960: 'The American form of government is often, but erroneously, symbolized by a three-layer cake'.[26] Grodzins along with his student Elazar argued: 'The American federal system has never been a system of separated governmental activities,' because '[t]here has never been a time when it was possible to put neat labels on discrete "federal", "state", and "local" functions.'[27]

Grodzins used the metaphor—marble cake or rainbow—as a 'far more accurate image' of the American federal system than the layer cake. The marble cake is 'characterized by an inseparable mingling of differently coloured ingredients, the colours appearing in vertical and diagonal strands and unexpected whirls'. Drawing an analogy, Grodzins noted: 'As colours are mixed in the marble cake, so functions are mixed in the American federal system'. He added, 'functions are not neatly parceled out among the many governments. They are shared functions. It is difficult to find any governmental activity which does not involve three of the so-called "levels" of the federal system.'[28]

A good explication of the political–institutional perspective on federalism can be found in the report of the Task Force on Canadian Unity appointed by the Prime Minister in July 1977. Entitled *Coming to Terms: The Words of the Debate* (February 1979), the report contains an analytical overview of commonalities among federal systems and permissible variations. The essential characteristics common to federal systems include:

1. Two orders of government existing in their own right under the Constitution and each acting directly upon the same citizens;

2. a central government directly elected by the electorate of the whole federation and exercising authority directly by legislation and taxation upon the country as a whole;
3. regional units of government, variously called 'provinces', 'states', 'cantons', or 'lander', each directly elected by and directly acting by legislation and taxation upon its own regional electorate;
4. a formal distribution of legislative and executive authority and of sources of revenue between the two orders of government;
5. a written Constitution defining the competence and resources of the two orders of government, and not unilaterally amendable in its fundamental provisions by only one order of government;
6. an umpire to rule upon disputes relating to respective governmental powers and to interpret the Constitution; it is usually the Supreme Court or a specialized constitutional court, but may sometimes take the form of the electorate acting through a referendum; and
7. processes and institutions to facilitate intergovernmental interaction.[29]

It discusses variations between the federal systems in terms of:

1. The organization of the central government, which can be parliamentary, presidential or collegial in form;
2. the provision of regional representation in the institutions for central policy-making, such as the executive, the second chamber, the bureaucracy and regulatory agencies;
3. the number and relative size and wealth of the regional (provincial) units;
4. the allocation of specific fields of legislative and executive competence and of spending authority and revenue sources between the two orders of government and among the regional (provincial) units, and the manner of distribution of 'exclusive', 'concurrent' and 'residual' authority;
5. the structure and jurisdiction of the judicial system, the Supreme Court or constitutional court, and the use of referenda and other devices for arbitrating and adjudicating

disputes related to respective governmental powers; and

6. the processes and institutions through which intergovernmental consultation and cooperation are facilitated.

Within each federation the particular blend of these variables will depend on the social, economic and political forces which the federal system attempts to express and channel. That is why there are important differences between the Canadian, the American, the Australian, the Swiss and the German federations.[30]

A significant variation among federations, affecting their operation, is the extent to which the principle of the 'separation of powers' has been applied within the central and state governments. The diffusion of authority within each order of government has enabled the development of many points of contact and interpretation between the orders of government. This model has been described as 'marble cake', examples of which are the United States and Switzerland. Those federations which have parliamentary systems and there is no separation of powers between the legislature and executive, the dominance of the parliamentary cabinets have made these executive bodies the focus of relations between the two levels of government. This executive federalism often seems to operate in a manner not unlike international diplomacy. The result is a 'layer cake' federalism such as Canada and Australia in contrast to the 'marble cake' character of non-parliamentary federations. One can also add India to this category, though India in actual working is more intermeshed and mixed than either Canada or Australia. In other words, though the union has its own central services for strictly central concerns, most federal policies are actually implemented at the state level by the state civil services.

The report goes on to describe the term 'asymmetrical federalism' which in theory is usually considered desirable for the constituent units (states or provinces) of a federation to be equal in constitutional status, in practice its inequality in size, power and character often leads to differences in the degree and areas of power exercised by the different units. It puts the Canadian federal system in this category since the BNA Act and subsequent constitutional acts have included provisions specific not only to Quebec but also to other provinces.[31]

In this study, this approach is applied to the discussion of the structure and evolution of federalism in Canada and India. This approach has been elaborated in the survey of major intergovernmental and central mechanisms in these two countries, and the detailed case studies of First Ministers' Conferences in Canada and the Inter-State Council and the National Development Council in India.

In both systems, these mechanisms have evolved in the institutional parameters of Westminster-influenced predominantly parliamentary system in combination with a certain extent of federalism. This institutional parameter is different from the US presidential federal system based on separation of powers and checks and balances. Mechanisms of this type are likely to be more salient and autonomous from both orders of government in the US than in Canada and India which are influenced by a fusion of powers between the executive and legislature, albeit within the framework of federalism with a parliamentary centre constitutionally vested with some overriding powers over the federating units.

A comparison of India and Canada reveals that these mechanisms are more active and powerful in Canada than in India. This difference is attributable mainly to two factors. First, Canada has become federally more decentralized with powerful Provincial Governments despite its Constitution than India where federal decentralization has made some headway only since the 1990s. Second, federal coalition governments have been non-existent in Canada whereas they have become the norm in India since 1989. Federal coalition governments having powerful regional parties as partners provide some state governments direct access to the federal cabinet. This partly eclipses the intergovernmental forum as the only or at least the major arena for intergovernmental representation.

SOCIO-CULTURAL APPROACH

The socio-cultural approach is another paradigmatic development in the study of federalism that focuses on a larger socio-cultural setting as a causal variable especially in the primary creation of a federal political system.[32]

Despite being an institutionalist, Vile recognized the importance of political–cultural and behavioural factors as is evident from his

> emphasis on 'human nature' to the exclusion of the mechanics of government, the underlying assumption that it is the relative power of 'groups' that provide the independent variables of the political system upon which all other factors depend, and the consequent belief that institutional structures can have little or no significant effect upon the outcome of political situations.[33]

> The expression of the behavioural approach . . . errs . . . in underestimating the requirement of order in the political system, and in taking for granted the institutionalized order of constitutional states like Britain and the United States. Behaviourists concentrate on what happens within the ordered system founded by the Constitution, ignoring the long-term stabilities which are the context of, and the prerequisites for, such behaviour.[34]

> The study of politics must, therefore, very largely consist of the ways in which constitutional and political institutions, and the social forces and movements in a particular society, interact with each other; of the limits upon the extent to which stable constitutional modes of behaviour can be developed and maintained; and the effects they can have in moulding behaviour.[35]

He was critical of behaviouralists who believe that formal structures are relatively unimportant.

Vile described federalism as 'a system of government in which central and regional governments are linked in a mutually interdependent political relationship'.[36] The essence of this relationship is bargaining since neither level of government can dictate the decision of the other. Vile added that while functions would be allocated initially by a constitutional document, thereafter the real working relationship would mainly be a product of the political process. This is not to deny the importance of the Constitution for it may have a continuing impact on the perceptions of the participants in the federal system and provide a basis for bargaining.[37]

Livingston pioneered the emphasis on the importance of sociocultural factors in the seminal introductory chapter of his work entitled *Federalism and Constitution Change* (1956), even though he himself did not systematically exploit this theoretical perspective in his book. According to him, federalism has to be understood as a 'sociological phenomenon'. Developing the concept of a federal society, he argued, 'federalism is a function not of government but of societies'.[38] In Livingston's opinion,

> . . . the essential nature of federalism is to be sought for, not in the shadings of legal and constitutional terminology, but in the forces—economic, social, political, cultural—that have made the outward forms of federalism necessary. Federalism, like most institutional forms, is a solution of or an attempt to solve a certain kind of problem of political organization. . . . [F]ederal governments and federal constitutions never grow simply and purely by accident. They arise in response to a definite set of stimuli; a federal system is consciously adopted as a means of solving the problems represented by these stimuli.[39]

Livingston differed from Wheare in two important respects. First, unlike Wheare, he conceptualized federalism as a continuum rather than a discreet category, defining it as 'an institutionalization of compromise' between the demands for federal recognition of territorially-based socio-cultural groups and the desire for integration.[40] Second, Livingston asserted that the (governmental) institutions themselves do not provide an accurate index of the federal nature of society which subtends them; they are only the external manifestations of the deeper federal quality which lies beneath the surface.[41] 'The essence of federalism lies not in the constitutional or institutional structure but in the society itself.'[42] He assumed that federalism is a response to certain societal needs; it is 'a device by which the federal qualities of the society are articulated and protected'.[43] Only federal societies, according to Livingston, would produce federal polities. Plural societies would give rise to some other constitutional system embodying milder forms of constitutional guarantees.

Livingston suggested that like a federal polity, a federal society, too, represents a continuum, and as one moves from the extreme of a purely unitary society to a purely federal one, the probability of adoption of a federal constitutional arrangement would gradually increase. However, given the imprecise measures at hand, it is difficult to specify the neat threshold point at which a federal solution would become inevitable. Notwithstanding the major limitation of Livingston's formulation which is inherent in most works on the topic, it is fair to credit him with implicitly suggesting that though federalism is in many ways comparable to the general phenomenon of integration, it deserves, by its peculiar nature, to be treated as a separate species within this genre. For it refers to a situation not only of socio-cultural cohesion leading to the desire for union, but also of socio-cultural diversity producing the opposite desire for federal recognition of that diversity.

Livingston's recognition of socio-cultural factors is apt. In a way, Watts refined his argument by pinpointing the federal solution to 'that segment of the spectrum [of societies] in which the pressures for unity and diversity are fairly closely balanced'.[44] He talked about equilibrium which was missing in Livingston's argument. He defined 'federal society as that kind of inclusive social system in which social forces making for diversity among differentiated communities are in approximate balance with forces making for unity'.[45] Further refining the argument, Michael Stein argued that Watts did not suggest indices which could permit an identification of the kind of society and the type of equilibrium which he envisaged. Nor did he make a distinction between 'federal societies' and other kinds of societies.

The importance of socio-cultural factors in federal political systems is further elaborated by Aaron Wildavasky (1967) who made a distinction between what he termed 'structural federalism' and 'social federalism'. This distinction draws attention to the fact that in some countries like Australia and the USA, a federal political solution was adopted in a societal context where diversities of language, religion and culture were not all that pronounced. In other societies such as Switzerland, Canada and India, federalism emerged as a political solution seeking to accommodate social and cultural diversities. According to Wildavasky, 'structural federalism' can be seen today in the first category of political system largely because a structural framework of federalism was originally adopted and has created vested interests which support its retention rather than because of the social make up of territorially-based groups. The political framework of federalism is no longer a minimum condition for the survival of these societies as a nation-state. However, it may be added that Wildavasky overlooked the fact that in what he called 'structural federalism' the absence of socio-cultural diversities does not really mean that there are no geographical or regional diversities that create a desire for a federal form of government.

A somewhat comparable formulation to Livingston's is found in the writings of Deutsch. Though Deutsch's primary concern was communication and nationalism rather than federalism *per se*, it is obvious that federalism is closely related to the phenomenon of national integration. Deutsch offered a list of nine necessary conditions for integration, or what he called 'amalgamated security community', of which class federation is a subset, either at the supranational or subnational level. In a subsequent publication, more directly connected to federation, he reduced this list to five 'social and economic pre-conditions' for federation: (*a*) compatibility of basic values; (*b*) predictability of behaviour; (*c*) unbroken links of social communications; (*d*) an expanding elite that is willing to broaden its base of recruitment; and (*e*) mobility of persons.[46] In brief, the basic theme of Deutsch's explanation of federalism rests on the causal variable of socio-cultural unities. Thus, the formation of a constitution, according to Deutsch, depends on the existence of background 'forces'. According to this approach, the relevant features of a political situation are social and economic, not political.[47]

Like Deutsch, Friedrich also made an attempt to elaborate the forces and conditions, mainly social and economic, which facilitate and stimulate the federalizing process rather than referring to it as a static pattern of government.[48] Friedrich summarized his approach in a paper entitled 'New Tendencies in Federal Theory and Practice'. He described a federation as 'a union of groups, united by one or more common objectives, but retaining their distinctive group character for other purposes'.[49] This description can be applied not only to a federal state but also to an alliance, a functional association of states, or a union of groups within a state (such as the Trade Union Congress). Federalism is said to be the process of federalizing, that is, the process of achieving a union of groups which retain their identity.[50] According to Friedrich, 'federalism may be operating in both the directions of integration and differentiation. For both the transformation of the British Empire into the Commonwealth of Nations and that of European States into a United States of Europe (as envisaged and initiated) are federalizing process'.[51] In Birch's opinion, this approach seeks to identify factors facilitating integration and those impending integration in a variety of situations, and has shown that the social and economic forces at work are often the same, even though in one context they contribute to nation-building, while in another they contribute to international integration. To approach federalism in this way is to view it in a broad perspective which helps one to understand some of its features and draws one's attention to what may appropriately (if inelegantly) be called its dynamics.[52]

William Riker took issue with Deutsch pointing out that the conditions mentioned by him were neither necessary nor sufficient for the emergence of federalism. Although Riker was overly critical of Deutsch, the example chosen by Riker to illustrate his point, particularly that of the nineteenth-century colonial empires, was not very apt. Riker's principal contribution lies in his conceptualization of the 'centralized/peripheralized' dimensions of the federal continuum, and in highlighting the role of 'political' factors in the origins and maintenance of federal bargain.

According to Riker, a constitution is federal if it provides for two levels of government, each of which has at least one area of action in which it is autonomous, and each of which has some guarantee (even though merely a statement in the constitution) of its 'contained autonomy' within its sphere.[53] He argued that this type of contribution is a consequence of a political bargain taking place in historically unique situations. He added that there are two conditions which have been responsible for it and described them as pre-eminent conditions for a federal bargain among politicians. Simply stated, Riker tried to explain the formation of federal union in terms of the so-called 'military' and 'expansion' conditions, and its maintenance in terms of the nature of the party system.[54]

Riker's sole conditions are:

> (1) A desire on the part of the politicians who offer the bargain to expand their area of influence by peaceful means, usually, either to meet an external military or diplomatic aggression and aggrandizement, (2) A willingness on the part of the politicians who accept the bargain to give up some independence for the sake of union, either because they desire protection from a military or diplomatic threat or because they desire to participate in the potential aggression of the federation.[55]

According to him, the bargains are initiated by relatively large and powerful states like Virginia, the province of Canada, or Bismarck's Prussia and are accepted by smaller states whose gains and losses are balanced. First, they have more to lose because they would be relatively less influential within the larger union, and second, more to gain because they could not hope to attain security, let alone expansion by themselves.[56]

Another dimension which Riker stressed is the condition for the maintenance of a federal system. He concluded,

> that whether or not a federal system survives depends on the nature of the party system that develops, i.e. it does not depend on the division of governmental powers, on the extent of governmental activities, or on the survival of provincial loyalties and a belief in states' rights: these factors influence the nature and working of the federal system, but it is the structure of the parties which determines how long the system is maintained.[57]

Riker's approach to federalism is somewhat different from the political–institutional approach discussed earlier, even though he emphasized political–situational and structural variables like military threat and the party system. He began with socio-cultural variables in society but laid stress on the military factor in explaining the origin of federalism and the nature of the party system in explaining the maintenance of the federal political arrangement. As he argued about the continued maintenance of the federal system in the USA, the centralizing features of American capitalism would have probably eroded the system of political federalism but for the continued federal character of the American party system with the state-based organizations of the two major American parties.

Disagreeing with Riker's strong emphasis on the military origins of federalism, Dikshit argued, 'an external military threat, which is in most cases an important agent in bringing discordant units together into a federation, is nevertheless (particularly in modern times) not a necessary condition for the origin of federal unions under all circumstances'.[58] He assumed is that no single factor can explain the formation of a federal union in every case. Even in a particular instance, a variety of factors may be responsible for the federal union. He focused on the evolution of federal unions and how they differ in the extent of powers conferred on the central government, and the reasons why some federations are more successful and maintain themselves longer than others. He divided them into two categories: (*a*) factors for overall union; and (*b*) factors giving rise to the desire for regional autonomy.[59] Factors which, according to Dikshit, lead to a union are:

1. sense of common military insecurity and the consequent need for common defence;
2. a community of 'race', language, and culture (including religion);
3. interdependent economies and expectations of greater economic benefits from union;
4. prior existence of communities as parts of a single overall politico–administrative set-up or common experience as parts of the same political system;
5. easy inter-regional transport and communication or a close geographical neighbourhood; and
6. the political communities involved in a federation should possess an overall compatibility in their social and political institutions.[60]

According to Dikshit, the conditions for the maintenance of regional autonomy are contrary to the ones leading to a federal union. These are as follows:

1. The existence of regionally grouped diversities in respect of language, religion or race as opposed to cultural homogeneity.
2. The existence of units with independent or competitive economies as opposed to the hope for economic benefits from union.
3. Prior existence of the political units as:

   (*a*) independent units or,
   (*b*) regionally autonomous provinces of a broader political system or empire;
   (*c*) a popular democracy;
   (*d*) popularly recognized hereditary kingship, etc., as opposed to common experiences as parts of the same political system;

(*e*) absence of a common external threat to the survival of the units concerned;
(*f*) presence of conflicting threats to the different units involved;
(*g*) existence of groups of units following contrasting and mutually incompatible social, economic, and political philosophies as opposed to the political communities possessing an overall compatibility in their social and political institutions.[61]

The prominence of factors included in list A, according to him, would lead to the formation of a unitary state and, conversely, the prominence of factors included in list B would preclude the formation of a union. Only when some factors of set 'A' and some of set 'B' are jointly present or there is a balance between the two would there be a federal union—that so-called 'halfway house between complete unity and complete separation'.[62] He further argued that the different factors of sets 'A' and 'B' (that is, those for unity and separation) may be present in different combinations. Accordingly, therefore, the nature of the resultant federation would also differ.[63]

Offering a modified explanation in 1975, Riker talked about the benefit analysis of federalism. While evaluating federalism, he argued, 'it is straightforward ideology in the sense that it is the justification of the advantage of some advantaged interest'. Then he posed the question: 'who benefits from federalism'?[64] According to him, the beneficiaries of federalism are those who want the continued existence of the system or who desired federalism in the first place. He continued, for instance, that those who seek defence against external or internal enemies or those who use the big government of federalism for aggression, can be called 'military beneficiaries' or 'nationalists'.[65]

He argued 'initial circumstances of federalism do not last forever. The changed circumstances also change the nature of political problems and lead people to reorder their priorities. With the change in issues, the continued existence of the federation becomes an accepted political premise.'[66] He believed that if the two levels of government do not behave the same way, then clearly a minority benefits. But, according to him, the beneficiaries of federalism vary with the degree of nationalism and the internal political structure of the federal system. When there is barely enough nationalism to keep a federation going, then the beneficiaries are nationalists. However, when national feeling is sufficiently strong to guarantee the continued survival of federalism, then the beneficiaries are those who can use constituent governments to enforce minority policies.

Riker's argument is basically sound. However, it may well be pointed out that even though federalism in general does promote individual freedom, yet it is more likely to tilt in favour of territorially grouped cultural communities that enjoy special provincial or regional rights and privileges under a federal constitution. Riker talked about the ideology of federalism which claims to be of universal benefit: federalism boosts democratic polity, democracy by promoting an interest in state autonomy; and maintains individual freedom.[67]

Federalism as a Strategy of Multinational State-Building

Both federalism and nationalism are features of modern and modernizing political systems. They are essentially products of the eighteenth and nineteenth centuries. Nationalism as a modern force is closely associated with national self-determination. Federalism also involves a union based on free will and consent at the historical moment of its formation. However, it is notable that a very strong sense of nationalism and federalism are not compatible because high-pitched nationalism would likely settle for a unitary government than one based on federalism. Federalism is preferred only when some territories with strong regional or ethnic identifications want to enjoy autonomy at one level and wish to unite in a federal union at the larger national level. Federalism thus becomes an ideal institutional solution for certain territories and/or nationalities desiring self-rule as well as shared rule in matters that are regional and those that are national.

Viewed from this perspective, federalism offers a strategy of multinational state-building. Federalism also significantly modifies the classical monistic doctrine of state sovereignty. This is because a federal political system is based on a division of sovereignty between at least two levels of government. In a multinational state, the regional communities would not accept a federal compact unless they have a meaningful share in governance. To be sure, federations are not only formed by a union of preciously sovereign states as in the case of the United States, but also by devolution of powers from the centre to provinces or states that were not previously sovereign as in the case of Canada. In India, the formation of a federal state combined both the foregoing processes inasmuch as the British provinces which joined the Indian Union after independence were non-sovereign but the princely states were notionally sovereign under British paramountcy. None the less, theories of federalism are premised on a meaningful division of powers between the federal and regional governments. Furthermore, it must be added that the classical doctrine of dual sovereignty in actual practice gets transformed into one of functional interdependence between two levels of government, each performing some functions assigned to it separately and concurrently.

Federalism is often regarded as a variant of liberalism or pluralism. King delineated at least seven varieties of pluralism: the doctrine of separation of powers; the doctrine of checks and balances; the argument of plural party system; the ideology of corporatism; the device of proportional representation; the doctrine of social pluralism (which encompasses the idea of cross-cutting cleavages or/of multiple affiliations); and the doctrine of federalism.[68]

It is, however, important to mention that despite cognate kinship, there can also be some measure of conflict between liberalism and federalism. Kymlicka rightly pointed out that federalism does provide some institutional protection to national minorities by recognizing them as provincial majorities, but the question arises: what really happens to the individual and the minority groups within the provinces? Kymlicka therefore cautioned that 'a liberal-democratic form of multi-nation federalism must ensure that all governments—whether at the central-state or sub-state level—respect basic rights. How best to protect the rights of such internal minorities is a fundamental challenge facing all multi-nation federations'.[69]

This approach has been adopted in this study to show how the federal institutional choice was influenced by socio-cultural and regional diversities in Canada and India. This approach is also reflected in the discussion on the way in which mechanisms of intergovernmental relations in these two countries are not only influenced by the parliamentary federal constitutions of Westminster lineage, but also by socio-cultural and regional cleavages that account for the growing federal decentralization of the predominantly parliamentary systems.

ECONOMIC INTERPRETATION OF FEDERALISM

Another important condition for the origin of federal unions is the prominence of economic benefits. Presenting a case for the prominence of economic motives, Beard opined that Americans adopted their present Constitution under the influence of merchant capitalists and the Constitution itself was drafted to safeguard their economic interests. According to him, American politics after the revolutionary war was swayed by the conflicting interests of merchant capitalists and farmers. For Beard, though the farmers were in great numbers, yet they were not very influential and opposed the Constitution. The interests of the merchant class were to have a strong central government to tranquillize revolutionary outbreaks by the agrarian radicals, such as Massachusetts in 1786-7; to impede non-payment of debts and printing of paper money; and to defend their commerce on the high seas. The choice of the Constitution marked the swing of the revolutionary pendulum back to the rights of the state and the restoration of 'order'.[70]

Davis referred to the role of finance in determining the nature and extent of the coordinate and independent status of both the general and regional governments. He selected four integral elements of fiscal independence: (*a*) the right to decide when to raise revenue; (*b*) the right to elect the purposes for which revenue is to be raised; (*c*) the right to determine the amount to be raised; and (*d*) the machinery to administer these decisions.[71] He observed that a model of fiscal independence would have all these elements, and where these elements are missing would be completely a dependent model. In reality, a variety of situations may be found depending upon the kind and degree of deviation between these two points of perfect fiscal independence and complete fiscal dependence.

Davis raised a question: 'Can a financial scheme be devised to satisfy the ideal ingredients of both "fiscal independence" and "fiscal sufficiency"?'. According to him, a standard financial arrangement cannot be devised for all federal systems. His findings are summarized as follows.[72]

First, it has been found impossible to frame a permanent fiscal settlement because of two reasons: (*a*) it is impossible to predict the cost of government for any long-term period unless the level of political demand and price movements can be predicted, and (*b*) it is equally impossible to predict for any long-term period the revenue yields from any tax fields.

Second, the increased demand for governmental spending—on welfare policies and war—has multiplied the scale of all governmental transactions, but federal governments, through their superior fiscal and monetary powers, have been better able to meet the increased demands than the states.

Third, the greater scope and hence manoeuvrability of federal financial powers—and in some cases the constitutional priority of federal tax claims—has placed federal governments in a favourable bargaining position in the choice of remedial measures.

Fourth, the remedial policies applied by each federal state have varied with the local circumstances—the degree of imbalance between federal and state revenues on the one hand, and among the states on the other; the degree of political forbearance by the federal government in the competition for revenues; and the priority attached to 'federal' solutions over 'logical' tax schemes, 'rational' economic policies, and administrative convenience.

In such a situation, regional governments became dependent on the general government for financial grants, thus adversely affecting their political independence. However, Davis' concern was how in this situation can Wheare's categories of 'federal', 'quasi-federal' and 'non-federal' be applied with accuracy and rigidity.

It is important to take into consideration the fact whether there is any correlation between fiscal and political dependence. Discussing this point, Sawer noted that the federal balance in

Australia is not towards but away from organic federalism; in spite of its financial strength the Commonwealth government is unable 'to turn its money power into effective policy control' and the regional governments persist in going their own way.[73]

May offered an interesting argument about the fiscal adjustments in the old as well as the new federations with special reference to inequalities between the rich and poor units. To quote him:

> This division between rich units and poor is reflected not only in that units support different principles for the determination of fiscal relations but also, further, in that financial inequalities produce different attitudes to 'federal encroachment'. While rich units may consider financial autonomy in terms of independence of revenue sources, poor units generally interpret it as the ability to satisfy the demands made on them for the provision of public services, irrespective of whether they derive such ability from the central government. Nor does this necessarily imply any real loss of political independence—to the extent that federal assistance meets demand that unit governments are anxious to satisfy, it is as sensible to talk of the central government losing power to the units as it is to talk of the units losing powers to the Centre, and perhaps more so. If revenue transfers are secured by the political bargaining power of unit governments (that is, if it is effectively impossible for the central government to withdraw its goodwill), then there would seem little doubt that the gain is to the units.[74]

It becomes amply clear from May's argument that financial dependence does not lead to loss of political independence.

An economic interpretation of the Indian Constitution like that of the American Constitution by Beard is still awaited.[75] However, the political economy approach to the study of Indian politics, in general, and federalism, in particular, is reflected in two forms: economic aspects of contemporary politics and federal politics in India, and the study of fiscal federalism in terms of policy focus.[76]

This study is primarily institutional and sociological. It does not aim at an economic interpretation of federalism in Canada and India nor does it offer an analysis of economic policies. However, economic and fiscal issues incidental to the working of intergovernmental mechanisms in the two countries are discussed.

BASES OF COMPARING FEDERAL SYSTEMS

Some political scientists proposed a useful distinction between federalism as an ideology and federation as a form of real world political system. This implied demarcation may be illustrated by referring to liberalism as an 'ism' and the Liberal Party in a country as an organization. The advantage of this distinction is that one can compare different instances of federal systems by arraying them on an ideological continuum ranging from, say, 10 to 100 on an equal interval scale. Thus, a system's position on this scale would indicate the extent to which it is federal.

This distinction between federalism and federation can be traced back to Preston King (1982). This theme has further been elaborated by several authors such as Burgess and Gagnon (1993), Douglas V. Verney (1995) and Ronald L. Watts (1998, 1999). Burgess and Gagnon approached the ideological basis of federalism and drew attention to distinct North American and European tradition of federal thought, the latter derived from foundations unrelated to the *Federalist*. For them, 'federalism' and 'federation' refer to a genus of political organization encompassing a variety of speeches, including federations, confederacies, associated statehoods, unions, leagues, condominiums, constitutional regionalization and constitutional 'home rule'. In a similar vein, Verney proposed three separate categories in this context: (*a*) federalism as a philosophical concept; (*b*) the federal political system of the United States marked by unique and dense configuration of federal institutions and agencies; and (*c*) federations such as Canada and India that include the federal principle in combination with principles of government other than federal, that is, parliamentary.[77]

Watts also distinguished three terms—federalism, federal political systems and federations—on a more or less similar basis. But he did not restrict the 'federal political systems' category to the US. He added,

> the term 'federal political systems' refers to a broad category of political systems in which, by contrast to the single central source of authority in unitary systems, there are two (or more) levels of government thus combining elements of shared rule through common institutions and regional self-rule for the governments of the constituent units.[78]

Given the complexity and diversity of federal systems, it is not easy to suggest succinct and parsimonious schemes for comparing such systems. Hueglin (1998) identified three bases of comparison: (*a*) autonomy, (*b*) self-sufficiency, and (*c*) identity. According to the classical theory, he asserted, the duplication of governments in federal systems means a vertical separation of powers. Neatly separated spheres of jurisdiction are designed to prevent the abuse of political power and to ensure the autonomy of the component member-states.[79] He added that given the rapid structural changes forced upon advanced industrial societies by the volatility of national and international markets, the content of formally decentralized political power becomes very much a measure of subnational economic self-sufficiency. For Hueglin, the capacity of provinces, states, or lander to adapt to these structural changes depends on various factors: the degree of industrial diversification, including the procurement of resources, infrastructure and know-how; the capacity to raise revenues; and a system of fiscal transfers routinely compensating for structural disparities.[80] He quoted Schattschneider's observation that all political systems have a specific 'bias in favour of the exploitation of some kinds of conflict and the suppression of others' and said that 'it is safe to say that while the formation of federal systems is usually based on the pre-existence of strong regional identities, the retention of such identities is reinforced by the federal organization of politics'.[81] Therefore, Hueglin considered political structures, political economies and political cultures of states and provinces as the basis for comparison.

A noted Canadian scholar of comparative federalism aptly observed:

> There is no single pure model of federation that is applicable everywhere. Rather the basic notion of involving the combination of shared rule for some purposes and regional self-rule for others within a single political system so that neither is subordinate to the other has been applied in different ways to fit different circumstances.[82]

Watts remarked:

> Federations are varied and continue to vary in many ways: in the character and significance of the underlined economic and social diversities; in the number of constituent units and the degree of symmetry

or asymmetry in their size, resources and constitutional status; in the scope of the allocation of legislative, executive and expenditure responsibilities; in the allocation of taxing power and resources; in the character of federal government institutions and the degree of regional input to federal policy-making; in the procedures for resolving conflicts and facilitating collaboration between inter-dependent governments; and in procedures for formal and informal adaptation and change.[83]

In an ambitious comparative scheme formulated by Elazar, an attempt has been made to locate selected federal and non-federal systems in the world of the mid-1970s in a diagram constructed on two intersecting axes: homogeneity–diversity and unity–disunity. As is clear from Figure 2.1, most federal systems are located in the two demarcated cells on the right side. These two cells are defined in terms of (*a*) unity–diversity and (*b*) diversity–disunity.[84] Federal or devolutionary systems such as the US, the UK, Switzerland, India, South Africa, Nigeria, Columbia and China are located in the first cell, and Canada, Belgium, Burma and Pakistan in the second.

In an insightful paper, Verney[85] presented a comprehensive sketch explaining a global comparison of federal systems. This comparative federal theory should take into account the following major dimensions:

1. Whether the distribution of powers is decentralized or centralized?
2. Whether the separation of powers and checks and balances among the three organs of government are as full-scale as in the Presidential American Constitution or else is there a fusion of powers between the legislature and the executive as in Canada and India with checks and balances via judicial review? The varying quantum of power of judicial review in Canada and India is gradually being reduced after the incorporation of the Charter of Rights and Freedoms into the Canada Constitution Act of 1982.
3. Whether the Constitution makers were primarily motivated to limit the powers of the government in order to preserve the liberty of the people as in the USA or whether they were more concerned about strengthening the federal state

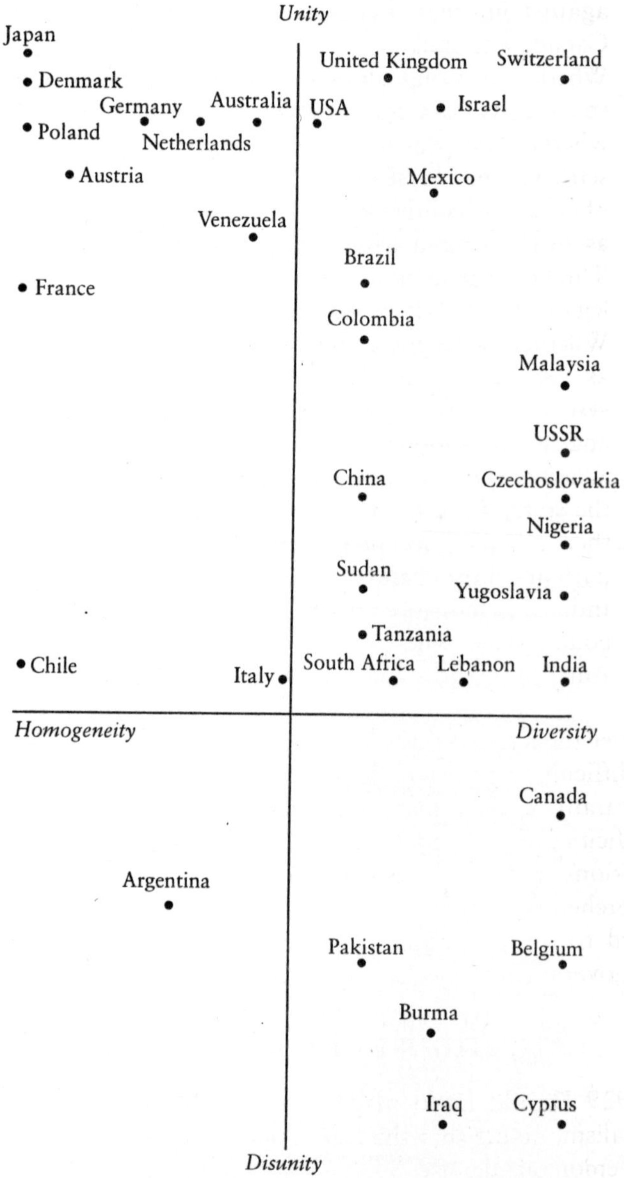

Source: Daniel J. Elazar, ed., *Federalism and Political Integration* (Ramat Gan, Israel: Turtledove Publishing, 1979), p. 65.

FIGURE 2.1: UNITY AND DIVERSITY IN SELECTED FEDERAL AND NONFEDERAL SYSTEMS (mid-1970s)

against internal divisiveness and external threat as in Canada and India?

4. Whether the Constitution was designed to recognize popular sovereignty as a revolutionary legacy like in the USA or whether the principle of parliamentary sovereignty was settled in the course of a constitutional evolution as a result of intra-elite conflict between the Crown and the Parliament as in the United Kingdom? About India, Verney noted: 'Unlike Canada, which has remained a monarchy, India is legally a Republic based on popular sovereignty'.[86]
5. Whether the federal system is worked by state-based parties as the major American political parties? 'None of the systems, based on "parliamentary federalism"—e.g. Canada and India—adopted this form of party organization'.[87]
6. Whether there is a powerful Second Chamber representing the states as in the United States and Germany or else is there a weaker Second Chamber partly eclipsed by popular parliamentary chamber as in Canada? Verney added that India's federation differs from the US and Canadian counterparts where the Rajya Sabha is weaker than the American Senate but stronger than the Canadian Senate.

Given the scope of this study, finding answers to these questions is a difficult proposition. For such an attempt demands a global comparative analysis that delves into the sociological and historical specificities of each federal system to explain the similarities and variations in federal systems around the world. However, a comprehensive comparative case study of Canada and India with regard to the evolution of federal structures and working of intergovernmental mechanisms is offered in detail here.

FUTURE OF FEDERALISM

In 1929 Harold Laski made a pessimistic observation about federalism, saying that the federal idea appeared doomed to an unceremonious demise. Such a statement from one of the most brilliant political scientists of his time would, in retrospect, seem to be rather surprising in view of the fact that federalism today is being revived both at the national and international levels. But it is not difficult to imagine why Laski said what he did. He lived in the United Kingdom, the classic land of unitary or parliamentary form of government. Besides, he wrote in the latter part of the interwar years which had witnessed such political upheavals as the rise of fascism in Italy, Nazism in Germany and militarism in Japan as well as the Great Economic Depression and the early straws in the wind of the impending Second World War. This was a period that saw the departure from the laissez-faire economy and the resultant tremendous expansion of the role of the state and enormous pressures for political, economic and technological centralization. Such an atmosphere did not augur well for federalism.

However, the future course of events were to prove Laski wrong. This was because the post-war period saw an unprecedented onrush of federal ideas and experiments. In the wake of the war a large number of colonies attained independence and Eastern Europe came under the Soviet influence. These boundaries created by colonial conquests and wars were generally arbitrary and included multiple cultural groups within their borders. The post-war international changes called for federal groupings of territories, though in some cases partitions also took place. Moreover, the new phase of democratization, international organizations, and the formation of new security blocs after the war necessitated federal principles and procedures to institutionalize all these changes.

The paradigm shift to neo-liberal economic reforms that followed the fiscal crisis of the welfare states in the West and the deepening crisis of the developmental states in the Third World also provided a new avenue for the revival of federalism. In the context of state failure, the emphasis on marketization and the building of civil society has created a new climate in which there is a spurt of activities at the local, provincial, national, supranational, regional and global levels that are finding expression in a variety of institutional experiments premised on the federal idea. Thus, federal managements all over the world are increasingly finding favour in relations within as well as among nations. Nationally, the revival of the civil society with an accent on identity and communitarian politics has propelled neo-federal patterns of political states' organizations. The localities are clamouring for power-sharing and renegotiating the terms of politics as well as economic relations. Such trends are evident in the Americas, Europe and the Third World. Watts observed, 'at the turn of the century, among some 180 politically sovereign states in the world there are 24 countries that fit the criteria of federations. These federations contain nearly two billion people representing about 10 per cent of the world population, and they encompass about 480 constituent units of federated states'.[88]

Internationally, trade and security considerations are prompting similar developments. Supranational experiments in integration are somewhat limited, the most advanced among them being the European Union with a common European Parliament and a common currency. Moreover, at the regional level, efforts at integration are evident in all parts of the world such as SAARC (aiming at economic cooperation in the South Asian region), BIMSTEC (five Bay of Bengal States—Bangladesh, India, Myanmar, Sri Lanka and Thailand), ASEAN (Association of South and East Asian Nations), and NAFTA (North American Free Trade Agreement). Available indications reveal that federalism has a great future. Even existing federal states such as India are experimenting with sub-state federal institutions like Regional Development Councils (as in Jammu & Kashmir and Assam), and are forming groups of states in some regions with strong interlinkages such as the North-Eastern States Council. In addition, some unitary states are going through the process of non-federal devolution of powers (the United Kingdom, for example, has been devolving powers to Scotland), or negotiating some kind of federal arrangement in an area where separatism has led to recurrent war (such as Singhalese–Tamil relations in Sri Lanka).

To conclude with Watts who, quoting Elazar (1996), remarked: 'We appear to be in the midst of a paradigm shift which is taking us from a world of sovereign nation-states to a world of diminished state sovereignty and increased interstate linkages of a constitutionally federal character'.[89]

Among specialists in the area of Indian federalism, Lawrence Saez[90] and M.P. Singh[91] have pioneered research on the impact of economic liberalization, globalization and regional integration on India. In the course of this study, new policy areas have emerged with the increasing importance of Canada's continental and global integration and India's growing association with global capitalism (such as environment and ecology, treaty making power of the federal government in a world that is rapidly becoming globalized). Global trade, ecological protocols, terrorism, etc., demand concerted action on the part of federal and state governments as well as global and regional economic groupings. These treaties often impinge on the exclusive jurisdiction of provincial or state governments that are increasingly demanding consultation and participation in the negotiation and implementation of these federal, regional and global agreements.

NOTES

1. Romila Thapar, *From Lineage to State: Social Formations in the Mid-First Millennium B.C. in the Ganga Valley*, Bombay: OUP, 1984; R.S. Sharma, *Aspects of Political Ideas and Institutions in Ancient India*, Delhi: Motilal Banarsidass, 1991.
2. Daniel J. Elazar, *Federalism: An Overview*, Pretoria: HSRC, 1995, p. 19.
3. Ronald L. Watts, *Comparing Federal Systems*, 2nd edn., Montreal and Kingston: McGill-Queen's University Press, 1999, p. 2.
4. Ibid.
5. Ronald L. Watts, 'Models of Federal Power Sharing', *International Social Science Journal* (Federalism), vol. 167, UNESCO: Blackwell Publishers, March 2001, pp. 24-7; Daniel J. Elazar, ed., *Federal Systems of the World: A Handbook of Federal, Confederal and Autonomy Arrangements*, 2nd edn., Harlow: Longman Group Ltd., 1994; Ronald L. Watts, *Comparing Federal Systems*, op. cit.
6. See J.G. March and J.P. Olsen, 'The New Institutionalism: Organizational factors in Political Life', *American Political Science Review*, vol. 78, 1984; and March and Olsen, *Rediscovering Institutions*, New York: Free Press, 1989. Also see Robert E. Goodin and Hans Dieter Klingemann eds., *A New Handbook of Political Science*, New York: Oxford University Press, 1966; Alexander Hamilton, John Jay and James Madison, *The Federalist* (with an Introduction by Edward Mead Earle, dated 14 May 1937), New York: The Modern Library College Editions; and K.C. Wheare, *Federal Government*, London: Oxford University Press, 1963.

   The chief academic proponents of this approach are K.C. Wheare, Ronald L. Watts, Daniel Elazar, Douglas Verney, Hamish Telford among comparativists. Works on India using this approach are those by M.V. Pylee, M. Venkatarangaiya, M. Shiviah, Amal Ray, K.R. Bombwall, Balveer Arora, Nirmal Mukherjee, B.D. Dua, M.P. Singh, George Mathew, Rajeev Dhavan, Ajit Moozomdar, Bidyut Chakrabarty, Sandeep Shastri and others. Canadianists who use this approach are J. Peter Meekison, Richard Simeon, David Cameron, Thomas Hueglin, Kathy Brock, Jonathan Rose, etc.

7. K.C. Wheare, *Federal Government*, London: Oxford University Press, 1963, p. 10.
8. Ibid., p. 97.
9. Rufus Davis, 'The Federal Principle Reconsidered', in *American Federalism in Perspective*, ed. Aaron Wildavsky, Boston: Little Brown and Company, 1967, p. 3.
10. Ibid., pp. 9-10.
11. S. Geoffery Sawer, *Modern Federalism*, London: C.A. Watts and Co. Ltd., 1969, pp. 1-2.
12. Ibid., pp. 186-7.
13. Ronald L. Watts, *New Federations: Experiments in the Commonwealth*, Oxford: Clarendon Press, 1966, p. 14.
14. Ibid., p. 115.
15. Ibid., p. 116.
16. Ibid., pp. 116-17.
17. Preston King, *Federalism and Federation*, London: Croom Helm Ltd., 1982, p. 77.
18. Ibid., pp. 142-3.
19. Donald V. Smiley, *The Federal Condition in Canada*, Toronto: McGraw-Hill Ryerson Ltd., 1987, p. 2.
20. Daniel J. Elazar, *American Partnership: Intergovernmental Cooperation in the Nineteenth Century United States*, Chicago: University of Chicago Press, 1962, pp. 5-6.
21. Ibid., p. 1.
22. Ibid., p. 23.
23. Ibid.
24. Ibid., p. 24.
25. Ibid., p. 297.
26. Morton Grodzins, *U.S. President, Commission on National Goals, Goals for Americans*, p. 265.
27. Ibid., p. 268.
28. Ibid., pp. 265-6.
29. Task Force on Canadian Unity, *Coming to Terms: The Words of the Debate*, February 1979, p. 24.
30. Ibid., pp. 24-5.
31. Ibid., p. 25.
32. Among Indian analysts of federal politics who have focused much attention on sociological and ethnic factors are Rasheeduddin Khan, A.S. Narang, Akhtar Majeed and others. Canadianists using this perspective are Kenneath McRoberts, Alan Gagnon and others.

33. M.J.C. Vile, *Constitutionalism and the Separation of Powers*, Oxford: Clarendon Press, 1969, p. 297.
34. Ibid., p. 302.
35. Ibid., p. 314.
36. M.J.C. Vile, *The Structure of American Federalism*, London: OUP, 1961, p. 199.
37. Robert F. Adie and Paul G. Thomas, 'Federalism and the Administrative State', in *Canadian Public Administration, Problematical Perspectives*, ed. Robert F. Adie and Paul E. Thomas, Scarborough: Prentice Hall, Canada Inc., 1987, p. 427.
38. William S. Livingston, *Federalism and Constitutional Change*, Oxford: Clarendon Press, 1956, p. 4.
39. William S. Livingston, 'A Note on the Nature of Federalism', *Political Science Quarterly*, vol. LXVII, no. 1, March 1952, pp. 83-4.
40. Livingston, *Federalism and Constitutional Change*, op. cit., pp. 5-6.
41. Ibid.
42. Ibid., p. 2.
43. Ibid.
44. Watts, *New Federations, Experiments in the Commonwealth*, op. cit., p. 95.
45. Michael Stein, 'Federal Political Systems and Federal Societies', *World Politics*, vol. XX, July 1968, pp. 721-47 or J. Peter Meekison, ed., *Canadian Federalism: Myth or Reality*, Toronto: Methuen, 1968, p. 40.
46. Karl W. Deutsch, *Nationalism and Alternatives*, New York: Alfred A. Knopf, 1969, pp. 108-12.
47. Karl W. Deutsch, et al., *Political Community and the North Atlantic Area*, Princeton: Princeton University Press, 1957, p. 58.
48. A.H. Birch, 'Approaches to the Study of Federalism', *Political Studies*, vol. XIV, no. 1, February 1966, p. 18.
49. C.J. Friedrich, 'New Tendencies in Federal Theory and Practice', mimeograph, 1964, p. 2. Also see his paper in *Systems of Integrating the International Community*, ed. Elmor Plischke, 1964.
50. Birch, 'Approaches to the Study of Federalism', op. cit., p. 18.
51. Friedrich, *New Tendencies in Federal Theory and Practice*, op. cit., p. 2.
52. Birch, 'Approaches to the Study of Federalism', op. cit., p. 19.
53. William H. Riker, *Federalism: Origin, Operation, Significance*, Boston: Little, Brown and Co., 1964, p. 11.
54. Ibid., pp. 5-6, 12.
55. Ibid., p. 12.
56. Ibid., pp. 12-13.
57. Birch, 'Approaches to the Study of Federalism', op. cit., pp. 20-1.
58. Ramesh Dutta Dikshit, 'Military Interpretations of Federal Constitu-

tions: A Critique', *Journal of Politics*, vol. XXXIII, February 1971, pp. 188-9.

59. Ramesh Dutta Dikshit, *Political Geography of Federation*, Delhi: Macmillan, 1975, pp. 226-7.
60. Ibid.
61. Ibid., pp. 227-8.
62. Ibid., pp. 228-9.
63. Ibid., p. 229.
64. William H. Riker, 'Federalism', in *Handbook of Political Science: Governmental Institutions and Processes*, vol. 5, ed. Fried I. Greenstein and Nelson W. Polsby, Reading, Massachusetts: Addison-Wesley Publishing Company, 1975, pp. 151-2.
65. Ibid., p. 152.
66. Ibid., p. 153.
67. Ibid., pp. 156-7.
68. Preston King, *Federalism and Federation*, London and Canberra: Croom Helm, 1982, p. 19.
69. Will Kymlicka, 'Federalism and Nationalism in Canada: A Comparative Perspective', in *Mapping Canadian Federalism for India*, ed. Rekha Saxena, Delhi: Konark, 2002.
70. Charles Beard, *An Economic Interpretation of the Constitution of the United States*, New York: Free Press, 1965.
71. Davis, 'The Federal Principle Reconsidered', in Aaron Wildavsky, op. cit., p. 17.
72. Ibid., p. 22.
73. Geoffrey Sawer, *Modern Federalism*, London: Watts and Company, 1969, p. 181.
74. Ronald J. May, *Federalism and Fiscal Adjustment*, Oxford: Oxford University Press, 1969, p. 162.
75. For an economic interpretation of Canadian Federalism, see the works of Harold Innis.
76. The emphasis on economic dimension of federalism can be illustrated by the works of Rudolphs, Francine Frankel, Lawrence Saez among the foreign scholars. Focus on fiscal federalism is exemplified in the writings of Govinda Rao, K.N. Kabra, Amaresh Bagchi, Hemlata Rao and others. Writers on fiscal federalism in Canada include Thomas Courchene, Peter Leslie, Harvey Lazar, Douglas Brown, Keith Banting, etc.
77. Douglas V. Verney, 'Are All Federations Federal? The United States, Canada and India', in *Multiple Identities in a Single State: Indian Federalism in Comparative Perspectiv*, ed. Balveer Arora and Douglas V. Verney, Delhi: Konark, 1995, p. 20.
78. Ronald L. Watts, *Comparing Federal Systems*, op. cit.
79. Thomas O. Hueglin, 'Federalism in Comparative Perspective', in

Perspectives on Canadian Federalism, ed. R.D. Olling and M.W. Westmacott, Scarborough: Prentice Hall Canada Inc., 1988, p. 19.

80. Ibid., p. 24.
81. Ibid., p. 27.
82. Ronald L. Watts, 'Federalism, Federal Political System and Federations', *Annual Review of Political Science*, no. 1, 1998, pp. 117-37.
83. Watts, *Comparing Federal Systems*, op. cit., p. 1.
84. Daniel J. Elazar, *Exploring Federalism*, Tucaloosa: University of Alabama Press, 1987, p. 65.
85. Verney, 'Are All Federations Federal? The United States, Canada and India', in Balveer Arora and Douglas V. Verney, op. cit., pp. 22-44.
86. Ibid., p. 33.
87. Ibid., p. 41.
88. Ronald L. Watts, 'Intro: Federalism in an Era of Globalization', *International Social Science Journal*, no. 167, UNESCO: Blackwell Publishers, March 2001, p. 9.
89. Ibid.
90. Lawrence Saez, *Federalism Without a Centre*, New Delhi: Sage, 2002.
91. M.P. Singh, 'Economic Liberalization and Political Federalization in India: Mutually Reinforcing Responses to Global Integration', in *The Impact of Global and Regional Integration on Federal Systems: A Comparative Analysis*, ed. Harvey Lazar, Hamish Telford and Ronald L. Watts, Montreal: McGill–Queen's University Press, 2003, Chap. 6.

CHAPTER 3

Structure and Evolution of the Federation: Canada

THE FOUNDING PROCESS

In 1867 Canada ushered in a new kind of federation in the history of modern governments. Its novelty lies in continuities as well as departures. The continuities can be seen in Canada's adherence to the Westminster parliamentary tradition with some federal modifications. The departure can be seen in Canada's modernity of tradition as well as in charting out on the course of a new kind of federation as distinguished from the pre-existing presidential federalism with separation of powers and checks and balances earlier established in the United States (1787) and later with certain modifications in Switzerland (1848).

This chapter briefly unravels the process of founding a parliamentary federal system in Canada in an attempt, to outline its basic structure and to trace its phases of evolution from quasi-federalism in 1867 to a cooperative and double image federalism today. It provides a fascinating description of the heroic efforts of Canadians at constitutional renewal during the last two decades. These endeavours are aimed at adapting the Canadian Constitution that was in existence around the mid-nineteenth century to the prevailing conditions marked by regional economic integration in North America and elsewhere and globalization of culture and capitalist economy in the world.

The development of the parliamentary federal system of government in Canada was more an outcome of practical considerations than a theoretical exercise. The founding parties that included some British North American colonies and the imperial government in the United Kingdom formed a first government of its kind. The novelty of this system lay in forming a government that was in principle similar to the British

Constitution but one that was constrained to incorporate some federal principle to accommodate diversities of economic and cultural aspirations centred around the states and regions.

The origins of Canada are shrouded in early French, English and Dutch exploratory, fishing, and trade activities along the Atlantic coast and their interactions and encounters with the aboriginal Indian tribes. A series of wars, treaties with Indian tribal chiefs, diplomatic and trade intrigues eventually led to the ascendancy of the English and the French and the subsequent victory of the former over the latter by 1759 when Quebec City fell into the hands of the English. The configuration of European settlements in North America developed in such a way that in the north the French set up in St. Lawrence Valley, a colony of New France; the British loyalists established themselves in Upper Canada; and the British colonies that rebelled against the British Crown set up New England in the south. The threat of war from the thirteen rebellious American colonies also contributed to the growth of Canadian nationalism in the years following the English conquest of Quebec. The colony of Canada thus founded included present-day Ontario and Quebec. Settlers from the United Kingdom also established British colonies in the Maritime provinces, some of whom joined hands with the colony of Canada in founding the Confederation, while others joined the Union later.

Between 1763 and 1860, the British colonial rulers alternately tried to bring about assimilative absorbtion of the French and recognition of Quebec's distinct French and Roman Catholic culture. By the Royal Proclamation of 1763, they tried to impose British laws and institutions on the French. The Quebec Act of 1774, however, reversed this policy by granting official status to Roman Catholic religion and restoring the French civil law and social system. This was done in response to the French resistance as well as with a motive to win over the French so that they did not join the American War of Independence and make common cause with the English colonies to the south. Another major development was the Constitution Act of 1791 which was a response to the sizeable migration of the 'Loyalists' from the United States who did not support the American War of Independence. This Act bifurcated the colony of Canada into Upper

Canada in the high reaches of the St. Lawrence basin and Lower Canada further down the valley. The English-speaking settlers dominated the former and the French-speaking, the latter. Both were granted their own representative institutions. Simultaneously, other British colonies in the Maritime provinces—Nova Scotia, New Brunswick, Prince Edward Island and Newfoundland—were also given their own representative institutions.

However, relations between the English and the French continued to remain tense in the two provinces of Canada, especially with the influx of Scot and Irish migrants from Britain. On the recommendation of Lord Durham, the British government decided to unite the two Canadas by the Act of Union of 1840. In a way, it was a return to the policy of assimilation. The affairs of the unitary province continued to be fraught with conflicts that led to a movement in favour of a federal solution. This movement culminated in the 'Confederation' established by the British North America Act which was an enactment by the British Parliament on the recommendation of the colonial leaders in Canada with only minor modifications.

The original founders of the Canadian federation were the united provinces of Ontario and Quebec called Canada, New Brunswick and Nova Scotia. It has been debated whether the original impulse for the union came from the Canadians or from the imperial British rulers. In Watts' considered opinion:

> A significant feature of the creation of the federation in 1867 was that it was the localities in the British North American colonies and not the imperial government that provided the driving force and negotiated the new federation. These local colonial elites held meetings in Charlottetown in 1864 and Quebec City in 1865 where agreements were reached on the shape of the proposed new federal structure. They then travelled to London in 1866 to persuade the Imperial Government to enact the new Constitution in British Law.[1]

He added:

> It should also be noted that it was almost totally negotiations among the political and commercial elite in the colonies and not the public at large that produced the federation. There was no extensive public debate about federation. The resulting federation was thus a product of elite compromises and accommodation in which John A. Macdonald and

Etienne Cartier were the key English and French Canadian leaders.[2]

A complex set of motivations relating to cultural, regional, economic and diplomatic–military factors contributed to the formalization of the Canadian Federal Union. For the two major founding units—Ontario and Quebec—the federation would put an end to their recurrent conflicts and provide a framework for shared as well as self-rule. Federal autonomy was in some ways a desperate measure of protecting the cultural distinctiveness of the people of Quebec, but for those in Ontario, too, it would provide respite from having to live in a common province despite nagging hostilities. For the Atlantic colonies of New Brunswick and Nova Scotia, provincial autonomy saved them from the domination of more populous Ontario and Quebec in a unitary legislative union that was initially proposed by the centralists. Moreover, the defence and trade needs of the founding units aided in the process. The fear of attack from the United States was underlined by the earlier experience of hostilities in the war of 1812-14 and an armed raid during the 1860s. The end of the Civil War in the United States over the question of slavery could signal a shift in American focus on the north with the aim of absorbing Canada, especially at a time when the imperial British Government withdrew its troops from Canada for economic reasons.

Moreover, an important reason for formalizing the federal union was the interests of capitalist entrepreneurs. The decision of the United States to allow the Reciprocity Treaty of 1854 (premised on free trade) to expire in 1864 increased the importance of inter-colonial trade among the British colonies to the north of the United States. To quote Stevenson:

> George Brown, the spokesman for Toronto business, joined forces with John A. Macdonald, whose political allies included Cartier and Galt, the spokesmen for Montreal business. Macdonald's genius, symbolized by the location of his Kingston constituency midway between the two major cities, lay in his ability to represent the interests of the whole ruling class, or at least the lowest common denominator of such interests. Brown accepted expansion to the east, Cartier accepted expansion to the west, and Macdonald accepted federalism, about which he had serious reservations even though he had been a long-time supporter of uniting the colonies.[3]

Besides, technological factors also propelled a move in the direction of a federal union as the shift from sailing boat to steamboat and from waterways to railways combined with the strong advocacy by commercial and railway interests for intensifying east–west trade to the decline of north–south trade.

From the four founding provinces, Canada of 1867 gradually expanded into a subcontinental country. Over the years, six new provinces and three northern territories joined the federation. The new provinces were Manitoba (1870), British Columbia (1871), Prince Edward Island (1873), Saskatchewan (1905), Alberta (1905) and Newfoundland (1949).

The enlargement of the Canadian federation from four to ten provinces also contained a fascinating account of the process of federalization in the northern half of the North American continent that joined the federation in 1867 but had second thoughts later. The newly elected legislators in the province for the local legislature as well as the Federal House of Commons were opposed to the Union, and Premier Joseph Howe sought to approach London for its repeal. But the repeal movement gradually petered out and as a part of a bargain the Federal Government enhanced its annual subsidies to Nova Scotia and Macdonald inducted Joseph Howe into the Federal Cabinet, of which New Brunswick's Leonard Tilley was already a member. By 1876, Prince Edward Island also bargained for 'better terms' and joined the union. With the completion of the inter-colonial railway by 1876 to the satisfaction of the Maritimes, the dangers which emanated from the isolation or withdrawal of the Atlantic Provinces from the federation had ceased to exist.

Macdonald next turned his attention to the westward expansion of the Canadian federal state, eyeing the prospect of a nation with continental dimensions. The Federal Government negotiated with the Hudson Bay Company offering it a staggering £ 300,000 to withdraw its claim to vast tracts of land and trading monopoly in the Northwest Territory as part of its ancient Rupert's Land Charter granted by the British Crown. The Hudson Bay Company and the Grand Trunk Railway, both managed by an interlocking directorate, tried to capitalize to the maximum on the Canadian expansion into the western wilderness. The vast potential farmlands in the Prairies were eyed with greed by Ontario farmers. Farmers as well as commercial interests in the province believed that the shifting western frontier would be a predominantly English-speaking settlement whose metropolis would naturally be Toronto rather than Montreal.

The French-speaking Quebeckers, on the other hand, were disturbed by this prospect. They were naturally pleased when Louis Riel, a native French Metis, born of mixed Indian and white parents, mobilized a full-fledged rebellion against the newly appointed Governor of the Western Outport Red River area, William McDougall, a Toronto expansionist. Through a combination of reconciliation and military action the crisis was diffused. Riel was executed. The new province of Manitoba was established by an Act of Parliament in 1870, which guaranteed the same system of government as in other Canadian provinces (in all respects), except for the fact that it ensured Quebec-like constitutional protection to the equality of French and English as official languages and of Protestant and Roman Catholic schools. The Act also granted the federal government the authority over unsettled lands, which it could administer to encourage immigration and subsidization of railways.

Further west of the Prairies, the Pacific coast was also in private control of the Hudson Bay Company. Fearing American expansion in the area, the British Government had created the colonies of Vancouver island and British Columbia in 1849 and 1850 respectively. Inspired by central Canadians, a pro-Canada federalization movement surfaced in British Columbia in 1869. It culminated in British Columbia's entry into the Canadian federation on the condition that Ottawa would assume the accumulated debt of the new province and build a railway to the Pacific linking it to the rest of Canada. Commenting on this act of the Union, Kenneth McNaught observed: 'Railway planning in Canada, then, as in Bismarck's Germany, Cavour's Italy or U.S. Grant's America, seemed essential to nation-building.'[4]

STRUCTURE OF GOVERNMENT

The text of the Canadian Constitution and conventions of the Constitution set up parliamentary forms of government at the federal as well as provincial levels. According to Sections 17 and

18 of the Constitution Act 1867, the Canadian Parliament comprises three institutions—the Queen of the United Kingdom who is also the Queen of Canada, the appointed Senate and an elected House of Commons. All three are important for the legislative process. Statutes are passed by the House of Commons and the Senate and then approved the Queen through her representative, the Governor-General, who is appointed by the Queen on the advice of the Canadian cabinet. The monarchy is thus a symbolic element of the Constitution without any real powers.

The 105 members of the Senate are appointed by the Governor-General-in-Council (which effectively means the Cabinet). The Senators are supposed to represent the provinces they come from, but for all practical purposes they are patronage appointees of the prime minister and therefore lack democratic legitimacy. The Senate seats are constitutionally distributed: Ontario and Quebec, twenty-four each; the four provinces west of Ontario and Newfoundland in the Maritime region, six each; Nova Scotia and New Brunswick, ten each; Prince Edward Island, four, and one each for the three Territories. Legislation ought to be passed by both the houses and in this respect the Senate has a veto, though in practice it has sparingly used its power. The Senate, however, is the target of much reformist demand and debate due to its unelected character. The reformists aim at making it a triple 'e'—elected, equal and effective—Federal Second Chamber (this demand has been especially strong in the Western Provinces).

The House of Commons, being the parliamentary chamber popularly elected by the people, is the real locus of power. The cabinet is conventionally formed from the elected members of the political party (or parties in the case of a coalition government), holding the majority of seats in the House of Commons. The prime minister is the head of the government and forms and chairs the Cabinet. The Governor-General as the Queen's representative in Canada is the head of the State.

A similar structure of legislative and governmental system is seen in the provinces, except for the fact that the Lieutenant Governor of the province, appointed by the federal government, performs functions similar to those of the Governor-General at the federal level. The role of these monarchic offices is strictly formal or constitutional. The provincial legislatures are unicameral. The principle of responsible government is also fundamental to provincial political framework.

The Canadian Constitution establishes an integrated hierarchy of federal and provincial courts appointed and administered by the federal government. At the apex, the federal government appoints two main courts—the Supreme Court of Canada and the Federal Court—and a number of minor courts such as Court Martial Appeal Court, Tax Appeal Board, and the territorial courts for the Territories. Besides, two broad categories of provincial courts—Provincial Superior Courts and District or County Courts—are also federally appointed. A third category of Provincial Inferior Courts is appointed by the provincial governments.

Before the enactment of the Supreme Court Act by the Canadian Parliament in 1949, the final court of appeal in Canada was the Judicial Committee of the Privy Council in the United Kingdom (a part of the British House of Lords). The Supreme Court is based on a federal legislation rather than a constitutional provision. The judges are appointed solely by the Government of Canada with the provincial government having no formal role. However, there is a federal dimension in the composition of the Supreme Court and the Federal Court in the sense that at least three judges of the former and four of the latter must be appointed from the Bar or Bench of Quebec. The Supreme Court hears appeals in civil or criminal cases from the provincial courts on matters it considers of legal importance and is also required to give advisory opinion on matters referred to it by the federal government. The Federal Court deals with appeals from judicial or quasi-judicial orders of federal tribunals, boards and agencies. The inclusion of the Charter of Rights and Freedoms in the Constitution in 1982 has added a new jurisdiction to the courts. Indeed, the Charter cases concerning the relationship between the states and citizens comprise the bulk of the work of the Supreme Court! The system of judicial review is an integral part of the Canadian system of government, grounded primarily in the federal nature of the Constitution coupled with the Charter of Rights and Freedoms.

The administration of the affairs of the federal state and the execution of government policy are carried out by a professional bureaucracy. The vast majority of federal public servants are appointed on the basis of merit through competitions held by the Public Service Commission, a body independent of the government which reports directly to the Parliament. Provincial Public Services are entirely independent of the federal government being fully appointed by the provincial governments and financed by the provincial treasuries. Until as late as the 1960s or 1970s, the provincial governments appointed civil servants largely on the basis of the Spoils System under which friends of the governments in power were rewarded in a manner that smacked of a partisan attitude. Pioneered by the Cooperative Commonwealth Federation (CCF) government of Saskatchewan in the 1940s and followed by Ontario and Quebec in the 1960s, the first modern Provincial Public Services in Canada (based on merit) were instituted through the instrumentality of the Provincial Public Service Commissions. Other provinces joined the bandwagon by the 1970s.

Reflecting the classical approach to dual federalism, the 1867 Constitution Act did not provide for any forum for intergovernmental relations. However, the need for such forums was realized very early and within a year of the establishment of the federation, civil servants from the two levels of government found themselves meeting at conferences for negotiating matters of common interest. By 1906, the prime minister of Canada and the provincial premiers met for the first time in a forum which has come to be known as the First Ministers' Conference (FMC) and this has become an annual feature.

One of the major paradoxes of the British North America (BNA) Act, 1867, was that originally being a legislation by the British Parliament (which Canadian nationalists choose to underplay), it lacked any formal procedure for constitutional amendment. Amendments had to be obtained by the circuitous process of the Canadian Parliament formally resolving to request the British Parliament to enact the derived legislation. This was obviously a thorn in the flesh of Canadian nationalism. The Liberal Prime Minister, Pierre Elliott Trudeau, took the initiative to patriate the Constitution from London to Ottawa. Trudeau had to make compromises, the most important of which was recognizing provincial rights. Although an ardent votary of the authority of the federal state, Trudeau, much like Macdonald, defended central authority in the name of protection of minorities, including provincial minorities as well as for national purpose.

The Constitution Act, 1982, thus resulted in the patriation of the Constitution to Canada and entrenched the Charter of Rights and Freedoms to which all governments and legislatures are subject, with an overriding clause that a legislature can put the Charter under abeyance for a maximum period of five years. Commenting on the inclusion of the Charter of Rights and Freedoms in the 1982 Constitution, Russell observed that there were two broad political purposes which inspired the Canadian politicians, especially the federalists:

> The first has to do with national unity and the Charter's capacity to offset, if not reverse, the centrifugal forces which some believe threatens the survival of Canada as a unified country. This national unity function of the Charter is most relevant to explaining why politicians, especially those who led the Federal Government, pushed so hard for a Charter. The second kind of purpose is the conviction that a Charter will better protect, indeed will even 'guarantee', fundamental rights and freedoms.[5]

The Charter includes a set of justifiable fundamental freedoms such as freedom of conscience and religion, freedom of thought, belief, opinion and expression, freedom of peaceful assembly and freedom of association (Section 2); a series of democratic rights such as right to vote, to have legislative bodies elected for five years subject only to their extension under special circumstances, and to have annual meetings of legislative bodies (Sections 3-5); mobility rights guaranteeing the right to move and earn a livelihood anywhere in Canada (Section 6); legal rights such as right to life, liberty and security of person, right against unreasonable search or seizure, and right against arbitrary arrest and detention (Sections 7-14); and equality rights such as equality before and under law and equal protection and benefit of law (Section 15). In addition, Sections 16-23 of the Charter validate English and French as the official languages of Canada, besides guaranteeing certain minority, language and educational rights in Canada and in certain provinces with linguistic minority populations. Moreover, Section 24 of the Charter confers on every Canadian citizen the right to move a court of law for the enforcement of rights and freedoms under due procedure for obtaining evidence.

Finally, there are a number of interpretative provisions relating to aboriginals, multicultural groups, women and advocates of separate, dissentient and denominational schools that ensure the Charter does not affect them adversely. Further, Section 33 of the Charter contains the 'notwithstanding clause' that allows the Parliament or provincial legislatures to override some of the Charter Rights, namely, fundamental freedoms and legal rights, by a special law for a period not extending beyond five years. The inclusion of the Charter has enormously expanded the role of the courts as an interpretative and enforcement agency.

By way of comparison, it is interesting to note that the application of the Bill of Rights to the states in the American presidential federal system was made by the Supreme Court. But in Canada, the Charter of Rights and Freedoms was grafted on the Canadian parliamentary federal system by negotiation among political leaders. Another comparative comment that can be made here is that even though the fundamental rights under the Indian Constitution are also subject to reasonable legislative restrictions, yet the overriding clause added to the Canadian Charter appears to be more limiting.[6]

Part V of the Constitution Act, 1982, introduced an amending formula. According to Section 38, most of the amendments must be approved by both houses of Parliament and two-thirds of the legislative assemblies of the provinces, 'that have, in the aggregate, according to the then latest general census, at least 50 per cent of the population of all the provinces.' An amendment made under this general formula—if it affects legislative powers, proprietary rights or any other rights or privileges of a provincial government—shall additionally require majority resolutions of the Senate, the House of Commons and the legislative assemblies concerned. Such a resolution of dissent may be revoked by the provincial legislative assembly concerned prior to the proclamation of the amendment. The amending formula also lays down that some parts of the Constitution may be amended by the general formula in Section 38(1), irrespective of the dissenting provinces. These subjects include proportionate provincial representation in the House of Commons, composition and powers of the Senate, provincial representation in the Senate, residential requirements of the Senator, the Supreme Court of Canada, establishment of new provinces and extension of provincial boundaries into the territories (Section 42). Section 41 enshrines that certain parts of the Constitution may be amended by the unanimous consent of all the eleven governments in Canada. These parts include the monarchy and other monarchic offices in Canada, representation in the House of Commons, the use of English and French as official languages, the composition of the Supreme Court of Canada, and the amending formula itself.

Finally, amendments that affect some but not all the provinces can be made with the consent of Parliament and the concerned provincial legislatures (Section 43). Section 44 deals with amendments affecting the structure of the executive of Canada, the Senate and the House of Commons. These parts can be amended by Parliament alone, if they do not affect the provinces. Parts of the Constitution relating to the provincial government require only the consent of the province concerned (Section 45). Additionally, Section 49 stipulates the convening of a constitutional conference, which in effect means a First Ministers' Conference, to review the 1982 Constitution within fifteen years of its coming into effect.

According to Brock:

> The amending formula is very rigid in some instances requiring a significant degree of consensus while it is very flexible in other instances. A final point of interest about the amending formula is that the Senate may not kill an amendment. It can only delay an amendment for 180 days. If the Senate rejects an amendment, the House of Commons must wait 180 sitting days of the House and then it may pass it again. The amendment may then be proclaimed by the Governor-General without Senate's approval.[7]

Section 91(24) of the 1867 Constitution confers on the Parliament of Canada jurisdiction over 'Indians and lands reserved for Indians'. This concerns the policy of settling Indians on reserves and imposing a form of local government with elected chiefs and band councils. According to a Supreme Court judgement, the northern Inuits are also included in this category. However, the Indian Act, the main federal Act under the authority of Section

91(24), excludes Inuit, Metis and other categories of aboriginals. Though Parliament has exclusive jurisdiction, the judiciary has made the provincial laws applicable to Indians and on Indian reserves for long.

An important area calling for federal–provincial cooperation is the aboriginal land claims. Since most of the land rich in natural resources is provincially owned public land, it is essential that provinces are involved in discussions leading to any agreement. The first such agreement took place in Quebec between the federal government, the Quebec government and the Inuit and Cree people. Another tripartite agreement was reached in British Columbia seeking to address the land claims.

In 1995, the federal government introduced a new policy framework for delegating authority to aboriginals for self-government based on a pilot project conducted in Manitoba in late 1994. The emergence of autonomous aboriginal governments calls for their fusion and co-existence with the prevailing federal system, which would then have three orders of government—federal, provincial and aboriginal. The legislative authority exercised by the aboriginal self-governments would be subject to negotiation among the three orders of government.

DISTRIBUTION OF LEGISLATIVE POWERS

The distribution of legislative powers in Canada was specified in the British North America (BNA) Act of 1867. This ensures that both orders of governments have authority to legislate on the subjects mentioned in their exclusive jurisdiction and that they are not dependent on each other as both derive their power from the Constitution which is the supreme law of the land. The enumerated 'exclusive powers' are mentioned in Sections 91-5 of the Constitution Act of 1867. Most of the powers mentioned in this section are awarded exclusively to the federal government or the provincial governments. The exclusive legislative powers accorded to the federal government total twenty-nine and are mentioned in Section 91. These are powers of national importance like foreign affairs, defence, trade and commerce, transport and communication, banking and currency.

Section 92 mentions the exclusive powers assigned to the

provincial legislatures. It lists sixteen subjects including natural resources, administration of justice, prisons, municipalities, hospitals, management and sale of public lands, local works, etc. In addition, a separate Section 93 assigns education to the provincial governments. Besides, as in other federations, there is another category of 'concurrent powers' that is allotted to both orders of government, but in the case of a conflict between the federal and provincial legislation, the federal legislation prevails. Thus, it becomes a 'federal paramountcy'. Section 95 of the original BNA Act had designated only two areas of such concurrence: agriculture and immigration. Another area, old age pensions, was added to this a century later by Section 94A. However, in the event of a conflict, the provincial law would prevail, that is, 'provincial paramountcy' prevails. Section 92A was also added in 1982 that set in certain areas of non-renewable natural resources under this list with federal paramountcy in the event of a conflict.

The general residual powers or the remainder are allotted to the federal government by Section 91 that says '. . . to make laws for the peace, order and head government of Canada (POGG) in relation to all matters not coming within the classes of subjects by this Act assigned exclusively to the Legislatures of the Provinces'. Consequent upon the formation of the federation, the courts have refused to conform to the broad interpretation of POGG power. Rather they have restricted themselves to three key areas:[8]

1. Areas where the issues fall into a 'gap' that has not been covered by allocation of federal/provincial powers, e.g. official language matters in relation to Parliament and the Federal Public Service.
2. An area of national importance which is not covered by an enumerated federal power, e.g. marine pollution.
3. An area that is categorized as a national emergency and is not covered by an enumerated head of power, e.g. situations of acute economic inflation.

The provinces also enjoy mini residual powers under Section

92(16) that lays down 'generally all matters of merely local or private nature in the provinces'. The Constitution mentions some emergency provisions that are assigned to the federal government to be exercised in times of emergency.

Besides, there are certain provisions that empower the Federal Parliament to act unilaterally and override a provincial legislation. For example, Section 90 gives power of reservation and disallowance of provincial legislation and Sections 91(29) and 92(10)(*c*) empower the Federal Parliament to bring a local work under federal jurisdiction by declaring it to be 'for the general advantage of Canada or for the advantage of two or more of the provinces'. These powers were used often in the early decades of the federation but have now fallen into disuse. The last instance when any bill was reserved for the Governor-General's assent was in 1961 and the last time when any such bill was rejected was in 1943. Therefore, these powers appear to be dormant. Section 93 also empowers the federal government to look into the appeals from provincial decision affecting minority education rights and to take action—but this, too, has not been used in reality. Therefore, by convention, they have become inoperative.

DISTRIBUTION OF TAXING POWER

In the field of taxation, Section 91(*b*) of the BNA Act empowers the Federal Parliament to raise money 'by any mode or system of taxation', whereas under Section 92(2) the provincial governments are restricted to 'direct taxation within the province . . . for provincial purposes'. This means that both orders can levy direct taxation which may result in double taxation. Section 92(9) grants licensing power to the provinces to issue a permit. Over the years, however, the courts have recognized similar powers for the Parliament in their respective areas of jurisdiction. Further, Section 109 makes provision for royalties for the provinces for exploitation of their lands, mines and minerals. The federal government may also levy royalties on natural resources coming under areas of its jurisdiction like the Northern Territories.

Sections 92(3) and 91(4) of the BNA Act grant independent authority to both levels of government to borrow money. The most controversial areas in Canadian federalism are the federal spending power and the shared-cost programmes which are a result of the vast taxation system.

> By far the largest programmes relate to health care, social assistance and post-secondary education, which are now combined in the Canada Health and Social Transfer Program. This programme involves cash and tax transfers in the order of $25 (Cdn) billion annually. The federal government's authority to do this—its 'spending power'—derives not from an explicit head of power in Section 91, but is inferred from several provisions of the *Constitution Act, 1867* relating to the authority to tax and spend.[9]

When the federal government transfers funds to the provinces to help reduce regional disparities or makes equalization payments, it is not disputed by most provinces. However, when it is used in areas that fall under provincial jurisdiction, many provinces see it as an 'intrusion' and also contrary to the spirit of federalism. The premiers have repeatedly demanded that the spending power of the federal government should be curtailed. This can be realized by submitting federal shared-cost programmes in areas of provincial jurisdiction as per the wishes of the provinces or on the basis of voting in a reformed upper house, with the provinces having the option of withdrawing from a proposed programme after financial compensation. Since equalization of payments is an important issue, many provinces have suggested that the principle of equalization should be constitutionally entrenched.

Pelletier, a leader of the Quebec Liberal Party and a federal minister of Intergovernmental Affairs, observed: 'Increasingly, the Federal Government is eager to intervene in fields of provincial jurisdiction and in no way seems willing to truly limit its alleged spending power.'[10]

Since the Second World War, there has been a system of transfer of payments from the federal government to provincial governments. First, there are conditional grants given to a few or all provinces subject to agreement on the use to be made of the funds. Most typical of such grants are the 'shared-cost' programmes in which the federal government matches provincial expenditures on a percentage basis. Second, there are unconditional grants given by the federal government to provincial governments with 'no strings' as to how the money is spent. One form of this is the equalization grant where money is transferred unconditionally to the poorer provinces to offer services at levels comparable to those of richer provinces without imposing a heavier tax burden.

THE PHASES OF EVOLUTION

Federalism in Canada has evolved through a series of stages which enable one to understand the contemporary state of affairs in federal–provincial relations. Adie and Thomas delineated seven such phases.[11]

PHASE I: QUASI-FEDERALISM

The first phase—termed as the quasi-federal one—spanned the first twenty years after the establishment of the 'Confederation' in 1867. The period coincides with the major part of the Prime Ministership of Sir John A. Macdonald.

The quasi-federal nature of federal–provincial relations was influenced to a certain extent by the provisions of the constitution that assigned the bulk of revenues and granted several overriding powers to the federal government. Moreover, this was also the period of the dominance of one party, the Conservatives, in Canadian politics. Besides, the Canadians were sceptical of the excesses of the states' rights and secession that they read into the US Constitution and politics. Furthermore, the early federal cabinets were an assemblage of talents that exposed provincial politics to some kind of brain drain. In addition, the federal government initially controlled the natural resources of the Western Provinces that for this reason stood in a colonial relationship with Ottawa.[12] Mallory described it as one of quasi-federalism while Cody called it the 'Confederation Era (1867-83)'.[13]

PHASE II: POWER TO THE PROVINCES

Adie and Thomas demarcated the second phase between 1896 and 1914 and labelled it 'the power to the provinces' period. This phase witnessed the development of a more genuine federal state in which there was a greater balance of power between the two levels of government. J.A. Corry described this phase as a classic type of federalism in which powers were allocated to the two orders of government each enjoying an exclusive jurisdiction with emergent disputes arising on the margins being settled by the courts.[14] In the shift towards classic federalism, also called 'dual federalism' by Cody,[15] the judiciary played an important role. During this period, the Judicial Committee of the Privy Council (JCPC) interpreted the Constitution in such a way that it favoured the cause of provincial autonomy.[16] Another factor that led to the development of dual federalism was the emergence of strong and demanding premiers in various provinces who challenged the dominance of the federal government. The JCPC went to the extent of interpreting the BNA Act as an international treaty rather than a founding constitutional document.[17] Powerful premiers like Oliver Mowat of Ontario and Honore Mercier of Quebec fought for provincial rights and succeeded in holding the first ever provincial conference in 1887 where the provinces demanded the renegotiation of the financial arrangements of the Confederation. As a result, forty years after the BNA Act was passed, the First Ministers' Conference was held in 1906, agreeing to greater financial subsidies for the provinces. The federal government realized that there was no need for strict economic direction and control from Ottawa as Canada was on the path to prosperity. The use of power to disallow provincial legislation also declined considerably. The federal government under the Liberal prime ministership of Wilfrid Laurier electorally committed itself to ensure provincial autonomy. An era of mutual consultation set in. It was in these pre-war years that the federal government introduced grants-in-aid and shared-cost programmes in areas like agriculture, technology, education and transportation.

Although the British JCPC is commended by some authors for interpreting the Canadian Constitution in a federal way with a pro-provincial slant to meet emergent ground realities, Stevenson was critical of this extraneous influence on the Canadian political system:

> This peculiar situation, which even the Australians largely had the foresight to avoid, had the effect that for almost a century the most influential concepts of Canadian federalism were mainly defined by outsiders, men who had no practical knowledge of Canada, or of

federalism, and who were not even required to live in the society that to a large degree was shaped by their opinions.[18]

Phase III: Emergency Federalism

The First World War ushered in a period of 'Emergency Federalism' in Canada when Parliament delegated authority to the executive to make regulations for 'Peace, Order and Good Government' of Canada. The federal government assumed enormous powers relating to matters of civil rights and property which in peacetime belonged to the provinces. The courts also declared that the division of power was a peacetime luxury which must be forgone in wartime.[19] During the period of hostility, the pendulum swung back towards a centralized unitary state. Further, the federal government, for the first time, introduced direct personal and corporate taxes. It also imposed wage and price controls and proscribed strikes in industries important for the war.

Phase IV: Provincial Power

Once the war was over, the courts reverted to their earlier stance, interpreting the Constitution in favour of the provinces. By the 1920s, there was an upturn in provincial powers. From a marginal role, provincial governments assumed greater responsibility for health, education and welfare. The advent of the automobile led to the demand for the construction of provincial highway systems. Provincial governments also tapped personal and corporate income taxes. There were new sources of revenue in automobile licensing, gasoline taxes, resource royalties and liquor excise. Statutory subsidies from the federal government, which were earlier a major source of provincial income, declined in importance (approximately around 10 per cent) in provincial budgets as the provinces began to mobilize their own sources of revenue.

Phase V: Return to Emergency Federalism Due to the Depression and the Second World War

The Great Economic Depression of the 1930s and the Second World War reversed the earlier trend and led to the centralization of powers in the federal government. The provincial finances, particularly those of the Prairies and the Maritimes, suffered a major setback forcing the federal government to step in to rescue them. The Great Depression necessitated joint action by the federal and provincial governments giving rise to increased consultations and intergovernmental relations. A chaotic tax structure developed with all levels of government scrambling to explore additional sources of revenue. This led to a situation often described as 'tax jungle' with the government levying double or even triple taxation. In its search for solutions to these problems, the Rowell-Sirois Commission on Dominion Provincial Relations was appointed by the federal government. The Commission submitted its report in 1940. Its recommendations favoured centralization of powers in the federal government. It was generally opposed to collaborative ventures: 'Where legislative power over a particular subject is divided, it is ordinarily desirable that these powers should be pooled under the control of a single government in order to secure a unified effort in administration.'[20]

The report of the Commission in any case remained unimplemented partly due to war conditions and partly due to opposition of the wealthier provinces to the centralized fiscal scheme recommended by it.

Phase VI: Paternalist Federalism

Beginning from the late 1940s and continuing through the 1950s and 1960s, the Canadian federal system entered the phase of paternalistic federalism. During this period Canada developed a welfare state under which the federal government assumed a leading role. The dominant economic ideology of this period was Keynesian which prescribed that the national state must guarantee economic growth, employment and a tolerable rate of inflation through efficient management of the economic environment. This policy framework as applied to Canada meant a leading role for the federal state, the organization of national pressure groups, belief in the greater competence of the federal government and continued dominance of the Liberal Party in Ottawa. Several provinces also contributed to the greater manoeuvrability of the federal government in the economic field. The fiscal dominance of the federal government during this period may be gauged from the fact that by 1955 Ottawa netted 75 per cent of all taxes whereas the provinces and municipalities together collected only 25 per cent of the total revenue. This dominance was realized largely through two mechanisms: one, a series of five-year rental/tax sharing agreements signed with the provinces whereby the federal government acquired the power to collect personal and corporate income tax for both levels of government; and two, conditional federal grants-in-aid to support certain shared-cost programmes launched by the two levels of government. These developments extended federal involvement in areas of provincial jurisdiction. However, Quebec remained aloof from these federal–provincial ventures but without any alternative schemes of its own.

Summing up the developments in this era, Adie and Thomas observed:

> The relationships among officials under the mantle of many shared-cost programmes became symbiotic. They shared common outlooks, met frequently, created programmes that expanded their authority, developed client and special interest-group support and often appeared to circumvent control by elected policy-makers. In the United States this model of intergovernmental relations has been described as *picket fence federalism* because the main competition is between the 'pickets' or programme areas within governments, not between the two levels of government.[21]

PHASE VII: COOPERATIVE AND DOUBLE IMAGE FEDERALISM

Since the 1970s, Canadian federalism has entered a phase which is marked by two rather divergent trends. This period witnessed the emergence of a less unequal partnership between the federal and provincial governments in English Canada and increasing assertion of separatism in Quebec. A number of factors contributed to the declining importance of Ottawa in federal–provincial relations. The shared federal tutelage of provinces in the developmental spheres gradually increased provincial competence and self-confidence. Moreover, the 1967 Royal Commission Report underlined the fact that the post-war national fiscal and monetary policies were in some ways unsuited to the prevailing economic scenario. In addition, the incidence of minority government formations in Ottawa from 1962 to 1968 weakened the leading role of the federal government.

Developments in Quebec since the 1960s highlighted the provincial governments' resolution to encourage the programme of province-building on a large scale. The Liberal government of Jean Lesage elected in 1960 used the instrument of the provincial state to develop the economy and society of Quebec so that French-Canadians did not remain backward. Quebec's success in this regard encouraged other provinces to adopt similar strategies of province-building. The trends outlined earlier have generally been referred to by scholars as 'cooperative federalism'.

The phrase 'double-vision' applied to the period under review points to the growing trend of separatism in Quebec, especially after the Separatist Parti Quebecois was voted to power in 1976. Its government held a referendum in 1980 seeking a mandate for the Government of Quebec to negotiate Quebec's separation from Canada. The mandate was rejected by nearly 60 per cent of the Quebeckers who voted in the referendum.

THE CONSTITUTIONAL RENEWAL

Canada's recent federal politics illustrates a paradigm shift from a state centred approach to federalism towards a civil society-oriented approach to federal relations.[22] Canada witnessed a gradual shift from statist versions of federal relations encapsulated in English–French biculturalism to a more variegated federal politics which is sensitive to intra-English Canada divisions such as the Western and Maritimes' alienations and multiculturalism that also reaches out to immigrants such as 'visible minorities' from around the world.

Watts surveyed five major issues in modern federal politics in Canada, three of which pertain to promises for decentralization and two relate to laying the framework for a 'shared community' with uniform patterns of constitutionally entrenched rights and freedoms for all Canadians and fiscal federalism for all provincial governments as well as more representative structures of parliamentary government.

The three issues that exerted cumulative pressure for greater decentralization related to Quebec, regionalism elsewhere in

Canada and the aboriginals. Quebec witnessed a 'Quiet Revolution' in the 1960s which led to a political–economic and cultural transformation. A newly emergent class of French–Canadian bourgeoisie and the transformed political class of the province committed itself to expand and use the role of the provincial state in promoting the aspirations of the Quebeckers.

The 1867 Canadian Constitution had recognized Quebec's position not as a province (like other provinces) in two ways. First, it included a section guaranteeing the use of French and English languages in the Quebec legislature and in national institutions such as the Parliament and courts. Second, it contained a clause ensuring the preservation of the civil law system in Quebec based on Napoleonic code and a common law system in the rest of the country based on English law and customs. This dualism has greatly influenced Canadian federalism. For instance, there is a convention that the position of the Chief Justice of Canada would alternate between judges from Quebec and from the rest of the country. Likewise, in the appointment of the Governor-General, the convention of rotation is in vogue.

The language issue has been a recurrent bone of contention between Quebec and the rest of Canada. The Official Languages Act enacted by Parliament in 1969 established English and French as the two official languages of Canada, thus making available federal government services in English as well as in French throughout the country. The Act aims at making the francophones comfortable in the whole country rather than in Quebec alone. Besides, the provinces of Manitoba, Ontario and New Brunswick with significant French-speaking minorities have enacted language policies for the minorities.

In 1977, the Separatist Parti Quebecois Government exacerbated the language situation in Canada by enacting the so-called 'Bill 101' or the 'Charter of the French Language' which made the province unilingual in French. This was obviously aimed at encouraging separatist sentiments in the province in preparation for the provincial referendum on separating Quebec from Canada.

The second pressure for decentralization came from 'the increased salience of regionalism throughout Canada exemplified by the impact of a century of "province-building" efforts by the provincial communities and governments'.[23] Besides, differences in ethnic and cultural composition of the population in numerous regions of Canada, the factors of history, geography and divergent economic relations with different parts of the world have all contributed to the persistence and assertion of regional identities in Canada. The Western Provinces as well as Maritimes have particularly made strong assertions of regionalism in federal–provincial relations. For example, a survey conducted by Canada West Foundation during the 1979-85 period revealed that four out of every five Western Canadians perceived that the Canadian political system favoured Ontario and Quebec. This alienation has spread to such an extent that nearly one in every twenty Western Canadians advocates separation from Canada and union with the United States.[24] Similarly, many Maritimers believe that they form a pocket of dependent economy in Canada and that it is in the long-term interest of the region to undo this situation.[25]

As far as Western alienation is concerned, it was mitigated to some extent when Brian Mulroney (after he won the 1984 general elections) formalized the Western Accord which dismantled the National Energy Programme and Trudeau's marketing restrictions on the sale of oil and natural gas. As Jackson and Jackson commented on regional alienation:

> In the Maritimes, there have always been a fierce pride and independence, but they have been mitigated by the area's need for federal financial assistance. In the West, alienation combines economic discontent and antipathy toward French Canada in particular with a demand for a stronger role for the West in the federation.[26]

The aboriginal issue is the third important political issue in Canada because of the rising consciousness of natives about maintaining their own way of life. They believed that since they had never surrendered their sovereignty to the European settlers, they had an inherent right to self-government. The federal government is constitutionally, politically, and legally answerable to First Nations. It has a government department that looks after Indian Affairs and Northern Development (DIAND). This department ensures that Status Indians (those recorded in the Indian Act register) living on reserves have access to the same basic services that other Canadians are entitled to receive from provincial and municipal governments. In December 1996, there were around 611,000 Status Indians, 331,000 of whom lived on reserves.[27] The department has been increasingly funding First Nations to enable them to provide services for themselves. In 1997-8, federal expenditures by DIAND and twelve other federal departments and agencies for aboriginal peoples totalled $ 6 billion. Of a total of $ 4.3 billion disbursed by DIAND, the largest share ($ 983 million) was for building schools, infrastructure (roads, water and sewage systems) and housing, followed by education ($ 899 million) and social assistance ($ 671 million). Funding to the tune of $ 39 million was used to promote self-government.[28] Aboriginal peoples' inherent right to self-government is acknowledged and protected by the Constitution. The DIAND negotiates and implements self-government agreements with First Nations and provincial and territorial governments. More than eighty negotiations involving about a half of all First Nations and Inuit communities were under process in 1997-8. In 1991, a Royal Commission on Aboriginal Peoples was established with four aboriginal and three non-aboriginal commissioners. Its task was to help restore justice to the relationship between aboriginal and non-aboriginal people in Canada, and to provide practical solutions to problems. For example, at the time when the Commission was set up, Canadian leaders were discussing the place of aboriginal peoples in the Constitution; there was anguish and upheaval among First Nations peoples; and disturbing facts about poverty, ill health, family breakdown and suicide among aboriginal communities came to light.[29] In 1996, the Commission in its final report proposed recommendations on a number of issues from treaties, economic development and health to housing and Metis perspectives. The report said: 'Canada is a test case for a grand notion—the notion that dissimilar peoples can share lands, resources, power and dreams while respecting and sustaining their differences.' The commissioners' central conclusion, however, was to declare that Canadians need to understand that aboriginal peoples are political and cultural groups with values and ways of life distinct from those of other Canadians.[30]

The other two issues in recent federal politics mentioned earlier lead to what in the words of Peter Russell may be called the 'mega constitutional politics'.[31] Between 1963 and 1971, conflict between the Quebeckers and the federalists led to various meetings culminating in the Victoria Charter in 1971. There was near agreement on the Charter for a formula for amending the Constitution, the Charter of Rights and Freedoms, and arrangements for entrenching the composition of and the method of appointment to the Supreme Court. In the end, however, the Governments of Quebec and Saskatchewan did not endorse it.

The rounds of deliberations between 1976 and 1982 were followed by the 1976 elections in which the first Sovereignist Parti Quebecois (PQ) formed the government. In this phase, the dominant issues were intensification of regionalism in the provinces of 'outer Canada', especially the Western Provinces and sovereignty association, as the condition for Quebec's association with Canada. In 1980, Trudeau returned to office. In May 1980, the PQ government led by Rene Levesque called a referendum on 'sovereignty association', with the rest of Canada requiring the voters to say *Oui* or *Non* to the question whether they would like the Quebec government to negotiate 'sovereignty association' with Canada. The mandate was denied by six out of ten voters. The federalists achieved a large majority in Quebec because of Trudeau's promise of 'renewed federalism'. Following the referendum, Quebec and seven other provinces (out of nine) pressed for the devolution of powers. On the other hand, Trudeau's government attached more importance to entrenchment in the Constitution, a Charter of Rights against provincial and federal encroachment and to the assumption of greater control by the federal government over the economy.

In the summer of 1980, negotiations were held between the federal and provincial governments behind closed doors on a 12-item agenda. When the first ministers failed to arrive at a consensus in September 1980, Trudeau decided to seek unilateral patriation of the Constitution and constitutional change on the basis of a 'people's package'. This was supported by Ontario and New Brunswick. However, all the other eight provinces challenged the decision. As it happened, the highest court in Manitoba and Quebec ruled in favour of the federal government, but the Newfoundland Court gave a contrary judgement. On appeal of the federal government, the Supreme Court in its judgement on 28 September 1981 ruled that the unilateral patriation was legal but contradictory to the conventions of the Constitution which required 'substantial' consent of the provinces—the endorsement of more than two provinces but less than ten.[32] Commenting on this judgement of the Supreme Court of Canada, Russell et al. observed:

> Both the Federal Government and the eight provinces that opposed its unilateral approach found support in this decision. By undermining the legitimacy of the Federal Government's unilateralism, the Court's decisions greatly increased the political costs of proceeding without substantial provincial consent. On the other hand, provincial leaders realized now that there was no legal bar to the federal initiative. Consequently the decision had the immediate effect of reviewing interest in reaching a Federal-Provincial agreement on the terms for patriating the Canadian Constitution.[33]

In deference to the conventions of the Constitution, a First Ministers' Conference was held on 2 November 1981 to seek support of provincial governments for the terms of patriation. All governments with the exception of the Government of Quebec agreed to sign a document to resolve the constitutional issue. On 1 December 1981 Quebec's National Assembly adopted a resolution rejecting the patriation package. The Supreme Court ruled that Quebec had no veto in law or practice to exercise over the patriation of the Constitution and it was legally bound by the Constitution of 1982. The delicate judicial balancing act of the Supreme Court has been aptly explained by Russell et al.

> In dealing with this reference case, the Supreme Court was in a peculiar position. Since the question at issue was entirely one of convention, the Court's answer could have no legal consequences. But it would have been a political bombshell for the Supreme Court to find that Canada's so-called 'new constitution' had been obtained in a manner that violates a convention of the Canadian Constitution. Such a ruling would certainly detract from the 'new constitution's' legitimacy and bolster the political fortunes of Rene Levesque's Parti Quebecois Government. To nobody's great surprise, the Supreme Court did not render such a decision.[34]

The Government of Quebec said that though it was legal yet politically illegitimate because it restricted the legislative jurisdiction of the National Assembly without its consent and decided not to participate in any further constitutional discussion. Rene Levesque opposed both the process and the content of the constitutional deal. He protested to the process which did not recognize Quebec's veto and objections to the Charter which now limited Quebec's constitutional authority over property and civil rights. In any case, nine of the provinces and the federal government were in agreement. The delegation from Quebec thus faced a *fait accompli*.

As to the content, his first objection was that the amending formula did not contain a specific Quebec veto over constitutional amendments. Second, there was no modification in the division of powers between the federal and provincial governments. Third, the Charter posed a threat to Quebec's ability to shape its society and laws as it chose. For instance, mobility rights restricted Quebec's laws designed to control the movement of unwanted people to the province. Further, protection of minority language rights by the Charter undermined the unilingual obsession of Bill 101 of the province of Quebec. Fourth, the 1981 deal did not recognize Quebec as a 'distinct society' within Canada.

For the federalists the situation changed in December 1985 when the Parti Quebecois lost to the Liberals under Robert Bourassa. The victory of Brian Mulroney in the 1984 federal elections also contributed to this changed environment. The federalist Quebec Liberal Party tried to reconcile the province to the 1982 constitutional revision by advancing five conditions for accepting the 1982 changes. These five points included recognition of Quebec as a 'distinct society', restoration of a Quebec veto over all constitutional amendments, expansion of Quebec's role over immigration which was a concurrent subject since 1867, excluding the federal spending power in areas of select provincial jurisdiction, and entrenchment of Quebec's say in the appointment of three judges from Quebec to the Supreme Court. In the fall of 1986, Mulroney and the provincial premiers entered into constitutional negotiations and on 30 April 1987, they agreed in principle on the Accord at Meech Lake. The Accord included five points which Quebec had been demanding with slight modifications to broaden its application to all the provinces. The consensus also included the agreement on further First Ministers' Conferences on Senate reform and annual conferences on economy. On 3 June, Quebec signed the constitutional document for the first time in five years and thus the Meech Lake Accord was born. Its greatest achievement was Quebec's return to the constitutional family.

Despite the unanimous agreement, the Accord did not receive ratification within the three-year deadline prescribed in the constitutional amending formula. In the meantime, new premiers were voted to office in New Brunswick, Manitoba and Newfoundland. The Meech Lake Accord thus fell due to the failure of Manitoba and New Brunswick to ratify it by the fall of 1988. The rest of Canada was, in reality, unwilling to recognize the 'distinct society' status of Quebec in the Constitution. On the other hand, the non-ratification of the accord aroused a strong emotional reaction in Quebec based on the perception that Quebec had been humiliated by the rest of Canada. Public opinion surveys in the late 1990s revealed that support for separation in Quebec increased to as high as around 65 per cent.[35]

After the failure of the Meech Lake Accord, the fourth round of constitutional deliberations in 1991-2 convened the next round of constitutional reforms culminating in the Charlottetown Accord of 1992. In contrast to the Meech Lake Accord which focused on Quebec, the new Accord was designed to be a 'Canada round'. The Charlottetown Accord included with some modifications most of the provisions of the Meech Lake Accord regarding Quebec but it also addressed the concerns of the other provinces. It discussed Senate reforms demanded by western Canada, the concerns of less affluent provinces of the Atlantic region as well as the demands of Manitoba and Saskatchewan for a commitment to federal equalization and national and economic objectives. It also catered to the interests of the aboriginals for self-government and those advocating the Charter and other social and economic objectives. The major thrust of the Charlottetown Accord was, in the words of Watts, 'inclusiveness—emphasis upon the inclusion of all the various interests and elements that make up Canada'.[36]

On 28 August 1992, the federal Prime Minister, the premiers of the ten provinces and the two territories, and leaders of all four national aboriginal organizations in Charlettetown unanimously agreed on the text of the Consensus Report on the Constitution which came to be known as the Charlottetown Accord. They also agreed to hold two referenda—one in the whole of Canada, excepting Quebec—under the auspices of the federal government and the other in Quebec under provincial jurisdiction. Negotiations between all the four governments led to the decision to put the following question to the people in both referenda: 'Do you agree that the Constitution of Canada should be renewed on the basis of the agreement reached on 28 August 1988?'. The referendum was supported by only 46 per cent of the electorate. Hence, a decision against further ratification was taken. The percentage of 'No Vote' was 54. Six provinces, including Quebec, and one of the territories, were opposed to it.

The Charlottetown Accord failed due to several reasons. As Hurley observed, it was more 'an honourable compromise that would avoid the unhappy consequences of failure, rather than a stirring vision of the future'.[37] In some quarters, the 25 per cent guarantee of seats in the House of Commons for Quebec was resented by voters in the rest of the country. It was seen as a departure from democratic liberalism. Besides, some people wanted to know what aboriginal self-government really meant. Some were of the view that an equal and elected Senate was sought to be secured at the cost of effectiveness of Parliament with supremacy of the Commons. Also, some women's groups believed that gender equality issues were not adequately addressed. The aboriginal leaders were dissatisfied that they did not get enough time to study the legal drafts. Preston Manning, the Reform Party leader, was critical of this 'Mulroney deal' among the group of 17 foisted on the nation. The Accord was rejected in most of the provinces by a majority of Canadians, including a majority in Quebec and by Indians living on reserves. The failure of the people to ratify the Accord left many important issues unresolved from the past many years of 'mega constitutional politics', particularly Quebec's place in Canada.

In the September 1994 Quebec elections, the Sovereignist Parti Quebecois returned to office after a decade. It was committed to working for Quebec's independence and holding a referendum on the subject within a year of coming to power. Premier Parizeau espoused separation. Public opinion polls revealed that a consistent majority of Quebeckers opposed an outright separation of Quebec from Canada. Hence, the Parti Quebecois government modified the question put to referendum: 'Do you agree that Quebec should become sovereign, after having made a formal offer to Canada for a new economic and political partnership, within the scope of the Bill respecting the future of Quebec and the agreement signed on 12 June 1995?'. In the referendum held on 30 October 1995, the sovereignists were rejected by a narrow margin of 50.6 per cent. Commenting on the mood of the Quebeckers, Maurice Pinard observed even before the declaration of referendum results: 'They are tempted by the option but afraid of the cost, torn by the attraction to independence and fear about the consequence.'[38]

In response to these developments, in September 1996 the federal government referred to the Supreme Court of Canada some fundamental legal questions relating to Quebec's separation from Canada. In the Court's unanimous opinion, there was no foundation under Canadian law or international law upon which the Government of Quebec could claim a legal right to secede from Canada. It opined that in order to legally secure it, secession must be undertaken through the means of a constitutional amendment. The Court declined to go into the question as to which amending procedure would be applicable in this context as there was no precedent available. It did, however, clarify that Quebec's secession could not be accomplished unilaterally by the National Assembly of the province. The Court's ruling on the question was guided by the four principles that it identified as integral to the Canadian Constitution: (*a*) federalism, (*b*) democracy, (*c*) constitutionalism and the rule of law, and (*d*) the protection of minorities. In the Court's estimation, no single principle could override the others. In a lucid and concise discussion of the judgement, Mary Dawson commented:

> The four principles are part of the rationale of why unilateralism is not appropriate, even if one group democratically determines that it wishes to act in a particular way. The different majorities represented in a federal system must be accommodated, as must be protection of minorities. In order for a democracy to function it must do within the framework of the rule of law and the Constitution. The four principles are particularly important to what the Court has to say about the duty to negotiate. . . .[39]

Elaborating on the relationship between the four principles, the Court deduced that it was the duty of the federal government to negotiate if the people of Quebec clearly expressed a desire to secede from Canada. The negotiation ought to reconcile 'the interests of the Federal Government of Quebec and the other provinces, and other participants, as well as the rights of all Canadians both within and outside Quebec'.[40]

In the opinion of the Court, a 'clear majority' on a 'clear question' would be required to entail the duty to negotiate the details of secession. The conduct of a party in the course of negotiations would have a bearing on the *legitimacy* of the stand of that party in the eyes of the international community. Thus, the question of 'unreasonable intransigence' is ultimately a political one in the domain of international law of recognition. The federal government introduced a legislation in the House of Commons on 10 December 1999 setting the terms of negotiation after a referendum on secession. The draft bill was described as a measure 'to give effect to the requirement for clarity' in the Supreme Court's advisory opinion on Quebec's secession.

Bill C-20 provides that the Government of Canada shall not enter into negotiations with a province on the question of secession unless the House of Commons determines that a referendum question as well as the verdict of the people are clear. In determining the clarity, the House of Commons shall take into account:

1. The size of the majority of valid votes cast in favour of the secessionist option.
2. The per cent of eligible voters voting in the referendum.
3. Any other matter or circumstances it considers to be relevant.[41]

The Commons

> shall take into account the views of all political parties represented in the Legislative Assembly of the province whose government proposed the referendum on secession, any formal statements or resolutions by the government or Legislative Assembly of any province or territory of Canada, any formal statements or resolutions by the Senate, any formal statements or resolutions by the representatives of the Aboriginal Peoples of Canada, especially those in the province whose government proposed the referendum on secession, and any other views it considers to be relevant.[42]

As a counter offensive, the Quebec National Assembly adopted its own bill that would reassert Quebec's right to decide its own future without any outside interference. Bill 99 passed by the Quebec National Assembly asserted the right of self-determination exercisable by the Quebec people 'alone' under a Referendum Act under which the winning option would be 'a majority of the valid votes cast, namely 50 per cent of the valid votes cast plus one'.[43]

In the parliamentary elections held in November 2000, the Liberals won 173 seats, the Canadian Alliance 66, the Bloc Quebecois 37, the New Democrats 13 and the Progressive Conservatives 12. Prime Minister Chretien was pleased that the Liberals had been elected in every province and territory. He declared that even in Quebec despite a low voter turnout, the convincing Liberal win should serve as a warning to sovereignist forces that Quebeckers did not want another referendum on separation. However, he refused to declare that separatism had become a dead issue. He said, 'it will never be dead and buried. There will always be people who want to separate Quebec from Canada. But I think Quebeckers do not want another referendum—I'm convinced of that'.[44]

In the House of Commons' election in 2004, the Liberals under Paul Martin with 135 seats lost power but managed to form a minority government with the support of the New Democratic Party (NDP) with 19 MPs from the parliamentary floor. The Conservatives, despite the unification of the right wing forces (Progressive Conservatives and Canadian Alliance), could secure only 99 seats. The separatist Bloc Quebecois (BQ) swept the polls in Quebec winning 54 seats far above its rally in 2000 and matching its high performance in 1993 when the sovereignists' mood was at its height. The Liberals' success in Quebec dipped to 21 out of 75 seats.[45] However, since the Liberals are still in power in Quebec (and will continue to be so till 2008), the sovereignists' calculations on a new referendum in Quebec appeared dampened on their own admission. As the BQ leader, Duceppe, told newsmen: 'You can't have a referendum in Quebec as long as the Parti Quebecois is not in power. Step by step we will see what happens'. He added that his party would fight for the province's interests issue by issue, with more money for health care and employment insurance reforms as priorities. It seems that even the separatists perceive that the Quebeckers are not in favour of an outright separation.[46]

In a bid to strengthen federalist forces in Quebec and to review themselves, the ruling Liberals in Quebec have released an important document prepared by a special committee headed by Benoit Pelletier entitled 'A Project for Quebec: Affirmation, Autonomy and Leadership—Final Report' (October 2001). The report underlines the fact that the majority of Quebeckers in every opinion poll since 1995 have preferred the federal option. The report suggests administrative measures supplemented by constitutional reforms to affirm Quebec's commitment to the people of Quebec and Canada. It seeks to balance the objective of promoting 'Canada's diversity' and 'Quebec's specificity' within the federation. It aims to build bridges with other provinces as well as with Canada. The constitutional changes that it proposes include, among others, granting Quebec and the other provinces a right of veto in accordance with the 'regional veto' formula; measures to curb federal spending power without affecting the equalization formula; reforming the Senate; a more federal procedure for appointing justices to the Supreme Court; financial compensation to provinces that dissent from or opt out of constitutional amendments; etc.[47]

May be Canada in all probability has turned the corner on the question of Quebec's separatism. As Cameron surmises:

> With the concomitant turnover of political leadership in many of the other provinces as well, there is reason to believe that intergovernmental relations in Canada will assume a different character. While the ascension to office of a new Prime Minister is likely to foster a degree of cooperative federalism not seen for some time, it is not to be expected that all will be sweetness and light. However, the issues in contention and the style in which they are addressed may very well alter.[48]

This general improvement in cooperative federalism cannot leave Quebec untouched.

NOTES

1. Ronald L. Watts, 'Federalism in Canada', typescript, Kingston: Queen's University, Institute of Intergovernmental Relations, March 1997, p. 13.

2. Ibid.
3. Garth Stevenson, *Unfulfilled Union: Canadian Federalism and National Unity*, Toronto: Gage Publishing Limited, 1982, pp. 26-7.
4. Kenneth McNaught, *The Penguin History of Canada*, London: Penguin Books, 1988, p. 147.
5. Peter Russell, 'The Political Purposes of the Canadian Charter of Rights and Freedoms', *The Canadian Bar Review*, vol. 61, no. 1, March 1983, p. 31.
6. *The Canadian Charter of Rights and Freedoms*, Ottawa: Ministry of Supply and Services, 1987.
7. Kathy L. Brock, *A Mandate Fulfilled: Constitutional Reform and the Manitoba Task Force on Meech Lake*, a project sponsored by the University of Outreach Fund, December 1990, p. 18.
8. Watts, *Federalism in Canada*, op. cit., p. 26.
9. David R. Cameron, 'Canada', *The Federal Idea*, the Centre for Policy Alternatives and the Forum of Federations with the Support of the Canadian International Development Agency and Foreign Affairs Canada, Browns Beach Hotel, Negombo, Sri Lanka, April 3-5, 2005, p. 23.
10. Benoit Pelletier, 'A Call into Question of the Foundations of the Federal Spending Power', speech delivered at the conference on Redistribution within the Canadian Federation, University of Toronto, Faculty of Law, 6 February 2004. Internet: http.//www.mce.gouv.qc.ca/v/html/v4061001.html.
11. Robert F. Adie and Paul G. Thomas, *Canadian Public Administration: Problematical Perspectives*, Scarborough, Ontario: Prentice Hall, 1987, Chapter 11.
12. J.R. Mallory, 'The Five Faces of Federalism', in *Canadian Federalism: Myth or Reality*, ed. J. Peter Meekison, 3rd edn. Toronto: Methuen, 1977, pp. 19-20.
13. Robert J. Jackson and Doreen Jackson, *Politics in Canada: Culture, Institutions, Behaviour and Public Policy*, Scarborough: Prentice Hall Allyn and Bacon, 1999, pp. 204-6.
14. Quoted in Mallory, 'The Five Faces of Federalism', op. cit., p. 22.
15. Howard Cody, 'Evolution of Federal Provincial Relations in Canada', *American Review of Canadian Studies*, vol. VII, no. 1, 1977, pp. 55-83.
16. Alan C. Cairns, 'The Judicial Committee and Its Critics', *Canadian Journal of Political Science*, vol. IV, no. 3, September 1971, pp. 301-45. Peter Russell, *Leading Constitutional Decisions: Cases on the BNA Act*, Toronto: McClelland and Stewart, 1973; Martha Fletcher, 'Judicial Review and the Division of Powers in Canada', in *Canadian Federalism*, ed. Meekison, pp. 100-23.
17. Bruce W. Hodgins, 'Disagreement at the Commencement: Divergent

Ontarian Views of Federalism, 1867-1871', in *Oliver Mowat's Ontario*, ed. Donald Swainson, Toronto: Macmillan, 1972, pp. 52-68.

18. Garth Stevenson, *Unfilled Union: Canadian Federalism and National Unity*, Toronto: Gage Publishing Limited, 1982, p. 43.
19. Mallory, 'The Five Faces of Federalism', op. cit., p. 23.
20. Adie and Thomas, *Canadian Public Administration*, op. cit., p. 432.
21. Ibid., pp. 436-7.
22. Daniel J. Elazar, 'Using Federalism Today', *International Political Science Review*, vol. XVII, no. 4, 1996, p. 349.
23. Ronald L. Watts, 'Canada: Three Decades of Periodic Crises', *International Political Science Review*, vol. XVII, no. 4, 1996, p. 355.
24. David Elton, 'Federalism and the Canadian West', in *Perspectives on Canadian Federalism*, ed. R.D. Olling and M.W. Westmacott, Ontario: Prentice-Hall Inc., 1988, p. 350.
25. Savoie, 'The Atlantic Region: The Politics of Dependency', in ibid., p. 291.
26. Jackson and Jackson, *Politics in Canada*, op. cit., p. 253.
27. The Government 3, *Canada Year Book 1999* on CD-ROM Statistics, Canada, 1999.
28. Ibid.
29. Ibid.
30. Ibid. For a detailed discussion, see the Royal Commission on Aboriginal Peoples, *Report of the Royal Commission on Aboriginal Peoples*, vols. 5, Ottawa: The Commission, 1996.
31. Peter Russell, 'The End of Mega-constitutional Politics in Canada?', *Political Science and Politics*, vol. XXVI, no. 1, 1993, pp. 32-7.
32. James Ross Hurley, *The Canadian Constitutional Debate: From the Death of the Meech Lake Accord of 1987 to the 1992 Referendum*, Canada: Ministry of Supply and Services, 1994, p. 4.
33. Peter H. Russell et al., *Federalism and the Charter*, Ottawa: Carleton University Press, 1990, p. 710.
34. Ibid., p. 760.
35. S. Dion, cited in Ronald L. Watts, 'Canada: Three Decades of Periodic Crises', *International Political Science Review*, 1996, p. 359.
36. Ibid., p. 360.
37. James Ross Hurley, 'The Canadian Constitutional Debate', op. cit., p. 23.
38. *The Ottawa Citizen*, 24 December 1994.
39. Mary Dawson, 'The Quebec Secession Reference', n.d., typescript, Library of Intergovernmental Relations, Queen's University, Kingston.
40. *The Quebec Reference Judgement*, 1998, para. 92.
41. Bill C-20, Section 2[2].
42. Bill C-20, Section 2[3].
43. Bill 99, Chap. 1, Section 4.

44. *The Globe and Mail*, 29 November 2000, p. A6.
45. Internet : www.theglobeandmail.com
46. 'Referendum years away: BQ', *Canadian Press*, 29 June 2004, Internet: http://www.canada.com/national/features/decisioncanada/story.html?id=67bf3111-21ef-448b-92cc-703a4981896b.
47. *A Project for Quebec: Affirmation Autonomy and Leadership—Final Report*, Montreal, Quebec: Quebec Liberal Party, October 2001.
48. David R. Cameron, 'Canada', op. cit., pp. 28-9.

CHAPTER 4

Structure and Evolution of the Federation: India

This chapter traces the evolution of the federal political system as a context for an analysis of intergovernmental relations in modern India. Historical and contemporary structures and habits of mind significantly influence the political culture and behaviour in a system. It is argued that the federal denouement in contemporary India has evolved through a long process of development. This evolution has been possible because of the nature of Indian society and culture, the patterns of state systems in Indian history from the ancient to the modern times, and the nature of the Constitution adopted after India's independence that has passed through several stages of development marked by centralizing and subsequently decentralizing trends. The significant changes in the process have been formalized by legislations, constitutional amendments, judicial interpretation and use of executive power. Today, federalism has a specific conceptual and theoretical meaning, and therefore caution should be exercised while using it in Indian history. It has a definite historical beginning. From this perspective, even though rudimentary beginnings of a federation-like political system are often traced back to classical periods, yet a federal polity in the modern sense of the term can be dated back to no earlier than the Government of India Act, 1935.

A brief survey of state systems in Indian history suggests that these entities were either centralized bureaucratic monarchies or feudal states. They are, therefore, not relevant for a discussion on the evolution of federalism in India. Yet, a brief review shows how at least some features of these states, even though not strictly federal, had certain traits that facilitated their transition into a federal polity. For example, almost all significant periods in Indian history were marked by at least a three level structure: central, regional and local. Mere demarcation of these levels do not of course make them federal. For these levels may be used for devolution of powers from the centre to the regions which is different from a federation based on contractually demarcated jurisdictions which cannot be obliterated at will by the central authorities. However, devolutionary decentralization may gradually develop into a federal decentralization, as has been seen in India.

The history of India reveals a recurring trend of competing regional kingdoms and subcontinental states. The first subcontinental state that integrated a number of kingdoms and republics was the Mauryan state in Magadha between 321 and 185 BC. Romila Thapar observed: 'The economic condition of the time and its own requirements gave to the Mauryan government the form of a centralized bureaucracy. The nucleus of the Mauryan system was the king whose powers had by now increased tremendously.'[1] The geographical extent of the Mauryan state can be inferred from the fact that Asokan inscriptions have been found as far and wide as Kandhar and Shahbazgarhi in the north-west, Kalsi and Nigali Sagar in the north, Mahasthan and Kalinga in the east, Girnar and Sopara in the west and Jatinga-Rameshwar in the south. It, therefore, appears that the entire subcontinent, with the sole exception of the southern peninsular tip, was ruled by the Mauryas.[2] There is some disagreement among historians of the Mauryan state about its centralized character. For example, V.R. Dikshitar[3] viewed it as a federal state and J.C. Heesterman,[4] on the basis of the *Arthashastra*, argued that its author may have intended to prepare a blueprint for a centralized bureaucratic monarchy, but did not really succeed in this respect, as the accounting and audit system prescribed in it shows that the king and the *mahamattas* were co-sharers in power. However, recent Indian scholarship continues to adhere to the interpretation that considers the Mauryan state as a highly centralized bureaucratic empire.[5]

After the disintegration of the Mauryan state around 200 BC, political fragmentation set in and continued for centuries. The division of the subcontinent into smaller regional kingdoms could only be partly arrested by the Guptas and Harshavardhan. The southern part of the subcontinent was dotted by smaller regional kingdoms. The process of fragmentation was partly stemmed by the Delhi Sultanate in the north and the Vijayanagara State in the south.

The post-Mauryan period also witnessed the rise of the feudal pattern of political and economic organization, especially in the north. Feudalism was based on parcellization of sovereignty by the central state to its regional vassals. Thus, sovereignty came to be shared between the monarch and the feudal lords who enjoyed considerable autonomy within their territorial jurisdictions on the condition of paying tribute and supplying army to the monarch either regularly or in times of need.

Feudalism in India developed into a very complex system. In conceptualizing Indian feudalism, D.D. Kosambi suggested two related aspects—feudalism from above and feudalism from below. Feudalism from above refers to a state in which the king collected a tribute from subordinates who independently ruled in their own territories, whereas feudalism from below denotes the second stage where a class of landowners was interposed in the village between the state and the peasants.[6]

Feudalism may be regarded as the historical predecessor of federalism, the difference between the two being that the former was essentially a traditional pattern of authority whereas the latter presupposes a democratic authority structure. To quote Thapar:

> The relationship of the vassal to the king was thus close but subordinate and the precise terms depended largely on how the relationship originated. Feudatories conquered in war were allowed little scope for independent action. On the other hand, some of the more powerful feudatories were permitted to grant land in their turn, without first obtaining permission from the king. Such feudatories often had their own sub-feudatories, thus building up a hierarchy.[7]

Another major subcontinental state in Indian history was the Mughal state. Even though it was feudal in character, it succeeded in establishing a fairly centralized monarchical system supported by a vast patrimonial military and civil bureaucracy. The Mughal state has often been described as a war state but it managed to institutionalize a fairly regular set of standardized rules and procedures of administration at the apex of which stood the monarch who acted as a powerful chief executive. Richards described the Mughal system as an 'autocratic centralism'.[8] He added:

The division of functions established at the Centre was duplicated in the provinces. At each provincial capital a governor, responsible directly to the emperor, shared power with a fiscal officer or *diwan* reporting to a *wazir*; military pay master and intelligence officer or *bakshi*, reporting to the central inspector-general of the army; and a *sadr*, reporting to the minister for religious and charitable patronage. The governor was responsible for the overall peace, security, and tranquility of his province. In this capacity, he supervised the military intendants or *faujdars* and the commandos of military check points (*thanas*) who were deployed with contingents of heavy cavalry and musketeers throughout each province. The provincial *diwan* managed imperial revenues, expenditures, and the provincial treasuries. The separation of powers between the governor and *diwan* was especially significant operating principle of imperial administration.[9]

These features of the Mughal administration, differentiated in terms of imperial and provincial levels, may be seen as historical antecedents of the federal division of functions and authorities between the centre and the states. Of course, the Mughal system was essentially feudal rather than federal.

The decline and disintegration of the Mughal state witnessed the rise of a number of regional kingdoms in various parts of the country. Besides the truncated Mughal state, there emerged successor states ruled by rebellious Marathas, Sikhs, Jats and Afghans. In addition, there were some states ruled by Nawabs. Most of these states continued the Mughal pattern of administration on a smaller scale. It was British intervention that reversed the trend of fragmentation and tried to consolidate another subcontinental state, probably the largest in Indian history.

The British colonial state evolved in two different phases. In the first phase, the East India Company adopted a policy of conquest and centralization of power. This phase extended from 1773 to 1857. In 1857, the administration of the Company was terminated by the rule under the British Crown. This phase witnessed direct rule by the Crown in the British Indian provinces and the rule of Indian princes in the so-called Indian states under the paramountcy of the British Crown. The Indian states numbering nearly 600 were brought under the system of subsidiary alliances following the treaties signed between the British Crown and the Indian rulers. By 1861, the British had created seven Indian provinces—Bombay, Madras, Bengal, North-West, Punjab, Oudh and Central Provinces. At the time of the Company rule there were only three Presidencies—Bengal, Bombay and Madras. The British proceeded to establish a fairly centralized system of bureaucratic administration in the provinces under the chain of command reaching the Viceroy in India and the Secretary of State for India in the British Cabinet ultimately responsible to the British Parliament.

The foregoing survey of the historical evolution of the state and administration reveals that there were structures and tendencies in the past which could be regarded as conducive to the transformation of India into a federal polity in modern times. As Singh aptly observed:

> Sovereignty in Indian history was crystallized in the main but was also partly diffused. Strong states were appreciably centralized but with some decentralizing features in parts. This pattern of sovereignty not only allowed appreciable autonomies to groups and regions within the state but also visualized a complex inter-state alliance system in the sub-continent in which the allies were the constituents of the subcontinental state. This was true of even strong sub-continental states like the Mauryas, the Mughals and the British. Feudal autonomies of the past as well as the earlier tradition of *ganasanghas* may be seen as precursors of the autonomy of state governments under the Parliamentary Federal Constitutional System in India today.[10]

GROWTH OF REPRESENTATIVE AND FEDERAL GOVERNMENT DURING THE BRITISH RAJ

The first phase of British rule in India under the East India Company was marked by growing centralization of administration. The Regulating Act of 1773 was the first step towards the creation of a central authority under the auspices of the Governor-General at Fort William in Calcutta and placed the Presidencies of Madras and Bombay under his control in respect of initiating war, peace and treaty with the Indian princely states. The subsequent Acts of 1786, 1793 and 1813 had nothing to do with centralization or provincial authority. The process of centralization reached its climax with the Charter Act of 1833 which divested the provincial governments of their autonomy in legislation and financial management and vested the 'superintendence, direction and control of the whole civil and military government of all territories and revenues' of India in the Governor-General-in-Council.[11] This Act also created a new Presidency of Agra. The Indian Councils Act of 1861 made it clear that the policy of centralization was not viable in a vast country like India marked by great regional diversities and local specificities. This Act set in motion the process of decentralization in Indian administration. It initiated the policy of legislative devolution to the provinces, besides giving some limited representation by nomination to Indians in the process of legislation. The Governor General was conferred with the power to create new provinces and appoint lieutenant governors for administering them. The impact of the great Indian Mutiny of 1857 is clearly seen in the recognition of the Act of 1861 of the need for a decentralized administration in India. Sir Charles Wood, the Secretary of State for India, in a speech underlined 'the extraordinary and inherent difficulties in devising a system applicable to the whole of India', and the serious anomaly in a single body at Calcutta legislating for the entire British possessions in India.[12] The Indian Councils Act of 1892 did not introduce any innovation from the point of devolution of powers to the provinces; it only empowered the Governor General to introduce 'a half-hearted system of elective principle'.[13]

The Government of India Act, 1909 made some progress in expanding the Councils including the representative elements in them, at the centre and in the provinces. However, it offended Indian nationalist opinion not only by limited advance towards representative government, but also by introducing religion-based separate communal electorate for Muslims. From the point of view of this study, the Act cannot be regarded as a step either in the direction of a responsible government or a federal government.

The next important landmark was the Act of 1919 in which for the first time central subjects were separated from provincial subjects. It also introduced dyarchy at the provincial level under which reserved subjects continued to be administered bureaucratically by the Governor but certain subjects relating to public health, education and local self-government were transferred to be administered by elected ministers. Sir Friedrich Whyte described the reform of 1919 as 'federalism in embryo'.[14]

The persistent nationalist demand for constitutional reforms in India led to the appointment of the Simon Commission by the British Government to consider the next package of reforms. The Simon Commission appointed in 1927 visited India and was greeted with nationwide protests. In 1930 the Commission reported in favour of dominion status for India. Its report was tabled at a Round Table Conference convened by the British government and attended by political representatives of British Indian Provinces and the rulers of the Indian states. A white paper prepared on the basis of these consultations was examined by a joint select committee of the British Parliament. This exercise resulted in the enactment of the Government of India Act, 1935.

The nationalist thought regarding the future government of India was expressed in the All-Party Nehru Committee Report, 1928. It broadly supported a centralized federal system with devolution of powers to the provinces.[15]

The Government of India Act, 1935 went beyond a system of devolution of powers from the centre to the provinces and, for the first time, envisaged a kind of federal system for India. Under all the preceding Acts, the Government of India was essentially unitary. The 1935 Act envisaged a federation of British Indian provinces and the princely states with constitutionally demarcated jurisdictions of the centre and the units. 'The federal system which the Act of 1935', noted Pylee, 'aimed to establish was perhaps the most complex ever known in the history of federalism'.[16] The Instrument of Accession devised to facilitate the princely states' joining the federation was so variable from case to case that it would preclude uniformity of administrative relations between them and the centre. In any case, these states never joined the federation due to the reluctance of their rulers. Ultimately it amounted to a federation of British Indian provinces only.

Among the important features of the Act were: (*a*) its highly centralized nature with the provision of the centre taking over the administration of the provinces under certain contingencies, (*b*) the division of legislative subjects into central, provincial, and concurrent lists, and (*c*) the assigning of demarcated sources of revenue to the centre and the provinces. Elected ministries came to be formed under the Act in the provinces but the Congress ministries resigned abruptly in 1939 when the British government dragged India into the Second World War without consulting the Indian National Congress.

As far as nationalist opinion in India was concerned, the Constitution of 1935 was inadequate even before it was implemented. This Act of the Parliament was of great historical importance as well as consequential for later developments. What was clear was that the Indian nationalists would not accept an Act of the British Parliament as the basis for their independent nationhood as the Canadians and Australians had done earlier. As early as in 1922 Mahatma Gandhi had argued in favour of a constitution for India framed by a Constituent Assembly elected by the people of India. This idea was officially stated in a resolution of the Indian National Congress in 1936.[17]

In the midst of the Second World War with the Japanese army advancing towards India, the Secretary of State for India proposed the formation of an Indian Council of Defence consisting of Indian representatives elected on the basis of proportional representation by the lower houses of provincial legislatures and nominees of the princely states in due proportion. It was intended to be used for mobilizing support for the war effort and for deliberating and framing a constitution for India in the future. The Viceroy's Executive Council presumably with expanded membership would continue to function as usual. But even before the Indian political parties and groups came into the picture, the idea was rejected by the Viceroy himself on the ground that 'his Executive Council would either be subservient to or in the dangerous conflict with, the new body it proposed to set up'. Moreover, 'it would precipitate the whole constitutional and communal controversy into the conduct of the war and the day-to-day government' and 'infect the army with the communal fever of the most catastrophic kind'.[18]

Sensing the mood of the public in India, the Cripps Mission that visited India in 1942 categorically announced that the new Indian Constitution 'should be framed by the elected representatives of the Indian people themselves'.[19] The terms of the declaration made by the Cripps Mission were that at the end of the war the British Government would take steps to form a constitution making body consisting of representatives from the British Indian provinces and the Indian states through a process to be decided in consultation with the Indian political opinion. The declaration contained two crucial clauses having a direct bearing on the proposed process of federalization:

> (i) The right of any province of British India that is not prepared to accept the new Constitution to retain its present constitutional position, provision being made for its subsequent accession, if it so decides. With such non-acceding provinces, should they so desire, His Majesty's Government will be prepared to agree upon a new Constitution giving them the same full status as the Indian Union and arrive at by a procedure analogous to that here laid down.
>
> (ii) The signing of a treaty which shall be negotiated between His Majesty's Government and the Constitution-making body. This treaty will cover all necessary matters arising out of the complete transfer of responsibility from British to Indian hands; it will make provision, in accordance with the undertakings given by His Majesty's Government, for the protection of racial and religious minorities, but will not impose any restriction on the power of the Indian Union to decide in future its relationship to other member States of the British Commonwealth whether or not an Indian State elects to adhere to the Constitution, it will be necessary to negotiate a revision of its treaty arrangements so far as this may be required in the new situation.[20]

The Muslim League adopted a policy of wait and see as Sir Stafford Cripps negotiated with the Congress leaders who rejected the proposal. The Cripps Mission was virtually a non-starter.

The Cabinet Mission's proposal (1946) for independent India envisaged a loose federation with a weak centre of British Indian provinces, including Muslim majority ones, and the Indian states. The centre was kept weak mainly to appease the separatist Muslim political opinion and the Indian princes. The Mission proposed a constitution making body to be formed through indirect election by each Provincial Legislature in the number of seats proportional to the population of the province roughly to the ratio of one to a million. The total number of seats estimated through this procedure was to be apportioned among the main communities—General, Muslim and Sikh—in proportion to their population.

The number of representatives from these communities was to be decided by the members of the same community in the legislative assembly already elected under the Government of India Act, 1935. This would form the Constituent Assembly of India that would frame the Constitution for the independent federal dominion of India.[21] This proposal was initially rejected by the Congress because of its reservations concerning a weak central authority. But it subsequently accepted it. The Muslim League initially accepted it but later, reacting against the Congress, turned it down.

In terms of the Cabinet Mission Plan, a Constituent Assembly of India was elected and an interim Congress–Muslim League Coalition government headed by Nehru was formed. Because of the Muslim League's persisting intransigence, the success of the Cabinet Mission's scheme of a loose federation for India was doomed. The deadlock was finally resolved by the Mountbatten Plan announced by the new Viceroy, Lord Mountbatten. On 3 June 1947, the plan for the Partition of India was announced with the acquiescence of the leaders of the three main political parties in India: the Indian National Congress, the Muslim League and the Akali Dal.

Dr Rajendra Prasad, the President of the Constituent Assembly, declared in the House:

> While we have accepted the Cabinet Mission statement of 16 May which contemplated a Union of the different provinces and the States within the country, it may be that the Union may not comprise all the provinces. If that unfortunately comes to pass, we shall have to be content with a Constitution, for a part of it. In that case we can and should insist that one principle will apply to all parts of the country and no Constitution will be forced upon any unwilling part of it. This may mean not only a division of India but a division of some provinces. For this we must be prepared and the Assembly may have to draw up a Constitution based on such division.[22]

Thus the Congress party negotiated with the British government in India to modify its plan of Partition on the basis of provinces taking into account intra-provincial regional diversities. In effect, it meant that the provinces of Bengal and Punjab would be further subdivided into Hindu majority and Muslim majority districts.

VISION OF THE CONSTITUENT ASSEMBLY AND THE NATURE OF INDIAN FEDERALISM

Due to uncertain future of the Cabinet Mission Plan, the Constituent Assembly debates reflect two perspectives on Indian federalism. The Objectives Resolution moved by Nehru at the outset on 13 December 1946 envisaged a confederation wherein the confederating states 'shall possess and retain the status of autonomous units, together with residuary power, and exercise all powers and functions of government and administration, save and except such powers and functions as are vested in or assigned to the Union, or as are inherent or implied in the Union or resulting therefrom'.[23] This entire trajectory changed overnight when Partition became inevitable and the Muslim League members from Muslim majority areas left to join the deliberations of the rump assembly in Pakistan.

At its second meeting on 6 June 1947, the Union Constitution Committee headed by Nehru came to the decision that 'the Constitution should be a Federal structure with a strong Centre'.[24] Subsequently, presenting the Draft Constitution as settled by the Drafting Committee to the Assembly for debate, its chairman, Dr B.R. Ambedkar, pointed out: 'The Draft Constitution has sought to forge means and methods whereby India will have Federation and at the same time will have uniformity in all the basic matters which are essential to maintain the unity of the country.'[25]

Thus, the dominant official view in the Constituent Assembly favoured a federation with a strong parliamentary centre. This did not, however, preclude the murmur of dissenting voices on the assembly floor. There were those like Brajeshwar Prasad and K.M. Panikkar who strongly pleaded for a straightforward unitary Constitution. Prasad (Bihar: General) rejected federalism because it was in his view 'a conservative force in politics' that 'perpetuates economic inequality between one province and another', and 'will weaken the hands of the nation on all fronts'.[26] In a note dated May 1947 submitted to the Union Constitution Committee, Panikkar strongly asserted,

> the Demarcation of Union and provincial powers which federalism involves, is to my mind a dead issue, and the idea which has gained

prevalence that the Indian Constitution must be of a federal type is definitely dangerous, to the strength, prosperity and welfare of India. Federation is a fair-weather Constitution and in the circumstances of India, it is likely to be a dangerous experiment leaving the national government with but limited powers, weak and consequently incapable of dealing with national problems.[27]

There is a misconception among some scholars that there were no strong advocates of state autonomy on the floor of the Constituent Assembly. On the contrary, a number of members strongly supported a greater degree of state autonomy in the federation being contemplated, prominent among these were Lokanath Misra (Orissa: General) Mahboob Ali Baig Sahib Bahadur (Madras: Muslim), Mohammad Ismail Sahib (Madras: Muslim), Lakshminarayan Sahu (Orissa: General) and B.M. Gupte (Bombay: General). Misra lamented the departure from the Objectives Resolution in the Draft Constitution which in his opinion 'was a magnificent product which represented the mind and spirit of India not only for the moment, but for the distant future too'.[28] Ismail Sahib was of the opinion that the Draft Constitution was 'not conducive to the happiness and prosperity of the country.' He added,

ours is a vast country of great distances and huge population. However much the Centre may be anxious to accord uniform treatment to the various parts of the country, still, in the very nature of things, there will be drawbacks and shortcomings. This will naturally lead to discontent and conflict . . . a federal type of government is more suitable than anything else for such a country as ours.[29]

Gupte deplored that in the Draft Constitution 'Units are kept completely dependent in financial matters on the good graces of the Centre and it is this kind of semblance of independence with complete dependence upon the Centre for finances that is in my opinion the most objectionable feature'.[30] According to Sahu, 'The ideals on which this Draft Constitution is framed has no manifest relation to the fundamental spirit of India'.[31]

The kind of Constitution adopted by independent India was dictated by its history, socio-cultural cleavages and contemporary challenges confronting it. To quote Austin:

Indians produced a Constitution with a unitary tone and strong centralizing features—taking much from the British imperial model, the 1935 Government of India Act. There would be single citizenship, not dual, state and national, citizenships as in the United States. There would be a single system for a higher judiciary and single national civil and police services, although the states also would have their own services. The great 'Anglo-Indian Codes' of the nineteenth century, nationwide in their reach, would be continued in force. The Fundamental Rights and the Directive Principles of State Policy would be national in reach, and the Rights were part of the original jurisdiction of the Supreme Court. The states would have a uniform Constitution embodied in the nation's Constitution. The heads of government in the states, the governors, would be appointed by the President, i.e. by the Prime Minister and the Council of Ministers. Under the Constitution's 'Emergency Provisions' the Central Government could legislate for and administer governments in the states. Other provisions for Centre-State relations clearly gave the Central Government strong influence or dominance.[32]

'Indian Constitution', observed Paul Brass, 'was born more in fear and trepidation than in hope and inspiration'.[33] This may sound somewhat more pessimistic than warranted especially to those who have heard Nehru's 'Tryst with Destiny' speech in the Constituent Assembly at the midnight hour of India's independence. Nehru's ringing words were infused more with optimism than pessimism. None the less, Brass is more realistic and balanced in his observation as revealed in the following quote:

> India's Constitution-makers thought they had good reasons to be fearful of disorder, even chaos, in the subcontinent as a consequence of the actions of a multiplicity of dangerous forces arising out of political movements associated with Muslim communalism, secessionism and revolutionary communism. Moreover, some of those forces were associated with acts of violence, revolutionary insurrection, extensive communal killings and war. The response of India's Constitution-makers to these threats and dangers was to use them as a basis for framing a Constitution with numerous provisions designed to deal effectively with the threat of disorder through the creation of a strong, centralized state.[34]

The framers of the Constitution did realize that the ethnic, cultural and linguistic conflicts were of a very complex nature and were not amenable to any simplistic solution, and second, that the process of modernization and socio-economic changes that would inevitably follow India's independence would generate new tensions which would require to go beyond the Act of 1935, even though being patterned partly on it, which was devised by the erstwhile rulers to solve the problems of a colony as viewed by them. It was not unnatural, therefore, that discontent surfaced immediately after the implementation of the new Constitution forcing the centre to appoint a commission for the purpose of reorganizing the units of the union (States Reorganization Commission, 1953, report submitted in 1955).

This kind of territorial reorganization was necessary in view of the unfinished process of creation of states along major cultural cleavages in India. It was also easy because Article 3 of the Constitution empowers Parliament to reorganize the states of the union through a process of legislation (as distinguished from constitutional amendment). Some consider this provision a patently unfederal feature of the Constitution. For it only requires the union to consult the concerned state(s) and proceed with the reorganization anyway as consultation does not necessarily mean consent.

The States' Reorganization Commission (SRC) report adopted a pragmatic rather than a consistent approach to the problem. It reflected the wishes of Nehru and other national leaders who were opposed to the creation of states either on the basis of religion or language, which could be decisive or destructive of national unity. The SRC report recommended the creation of linguistic states where it was necessary to do so in view of political agitation but otherwise advised retention of multilingual states to promote a composite culture.

The 1950s witnessed the reorganization of south India followed by the reorganization of western and northern Indian states in the 1960s and of the north-east in the 1970s. Three new states were created as late as in 2000. There are outstanding demands for the creation of other new states, e.g. Telangana in Andhra Pradesh and Vidarbha in Maharashtra. In the case of these and some other demands, the Union has experimented with sub-state regional developmental councils to satisfy regional, ethnic and tribal aspirations, e.g. Gorkhas in West Bengal, Bodos in Assam and Ladakhis in Jammu & Kashmir. What the final internal boundaries will be remains a debatable issue. At present there are 28 states and 7 union territories (see Table 4.1).

TABLE 4.1: STATES AND UNION TERRITORIES IN INDIA

States

1. Andhra Pradesh (1953, 1956, 1959)
2. Assam (1951, 1962, 1971)
3. Bihar (1950, 1956, 1968, 2000)
4. Gujarat (1960)
5. Kerala (1956)
6. Madhya Pradesh (1950, 1956, 2000)
7. Tamil Nadu (1950, 1953, 1959)
8. Maharashtra (1950, 1960)
9. Karnataka (1950, 1956, 1968)
10. Orissa (1950, 1960)
11. Punjab (1950, 1956, 1960, 1966)
12. Rajasthan (1950, 1956, 1959)
13. Uttar Pradesh (1950, 1968, 1979, 2000)
14. West Bengal (1950, 1954, 1956)
15. Jammu & Kashmir (1950)
16. Nagaland (1962)
17. Haryana (1966, 1979)
18. Himachal Pradesh (1966)
19. Manipur (1971)
20. Tripura (1950)
21. Meghalaya (1971)
22. Sikkim (1975)
23. Mizoram (1971)
24. Arunachal Pradesh (1971)
25. Goa (1987)
26. Uttaranchal (2000)
27. Jharkhand (2000)
28. Chattisgarh (2000)

Union Territories

1. Delhi (1950, 1956)
2. Andaman and Nicobar (1950, 1956)
3. Lakshadweep (1956)
4. Dadra and Nagar Haveli (1961)
5. Daman and Diu (1987)
6. Pondicherry (1962)
7. Chandigarh (1966)

Note: The years denote the dates of creation of the Units and changes in boundaries or status. The boundaries of various states have been continually altered. Some union territories (e.g. Goa) have become full-fledged states. Some new States have been created out of the boundaries of old ones.

Source: Rajeev Dhavan, 'Indian Federalism and Its Discontents: A Review', 1996, typescript (updated by Rekha Saxena).

Though at the formal level states in India are generally treated on a par with each other in most matters, yet the Constitution represents states on the basis of population not only in the popular Parliamentary Chamber but also in the Federal Second Chamber. Also, while there is a single Constitution both for the union and the states, the case of Jammu & Kashmir is an exception since it has its own Constitution framed in conformity with the Constitution of India in 1957. This asymmetry reflects the special historical conditions under which the Government of Jammu & Kashmir signed the Instrument of Accession with India in the face of veiled military invasion by Pakistan in 1947.

There are other notable asymmetries in the Indian federation, prominent among them being 'weighted' or 'preferential' equality granted to Nagaland and Mizoram whereby tribal, social and land relations regulated by customary laws in these states cannot be unilaterally changed by the Parliament of India without the concurrence of their respective state legislatures (371A and G). The remaining clauses in Articles 371, 371B, 371C, 371D, 371E, 371F, 371H and 371I make special provisions in respect of some states in matters of administration of tribal areas, intra-state regional disparities, law and order situation and fixation of number of seats in the legislative assembly, etc. Examples in this context are Maharashtra, Gujarat, Assam, Manipur, Andhra Pradesh, Sikkim, Arunachal Pradesh and Goa. Besides the foregoing, the Fifth and the Sixth Schedules of the Constitution make special provisions for the administration and control of Scheduled Areas and Scheduled Tribes, mostly in the north-eastern states.

Another asymmetrical feature of Indian federation is the creation of several autonomous regional development councils within some states. These include Darjeeling Gorkha Hill Council (1988), Bodoland Autonomous Council (1993), Jharkhand Area Autonomous Council (1994), and Autonomous Hill District Council for Ladakh (1995). According to Mathew, 'These are new decentralizing units, which gave further impetus and meaning to a multi-level federal system and a boost to the multi-layered institutional arrangement within the Indian federal framework.'[35]

Yet another kind of asymmetry in Indian federalism relates to a special kind of federating units that are called the union territories (UT). The seven UTs have been created on various points in time. The reasons for their creation were varied. These areas were either too small to be states or too difficult to merge with a neighbouring state on account of cultural differences, inter-state disputes, the specific needs of the National Capital Territory, or their far flung isolated location on the coasts. Originally, they were all administered directly by the union through a centrally appointed administrator. None of these has a legislature but all are represented by at least one seat in the lower house of the Parliament. The Parliament can either extend the jurisdiction of a neighbouring state to such territories or create a separate High Court for it (Article 241 [1] and [4]).

Subsequently, two new types of UTs were created, namely, Pondicherry (Fourteenth Amendment Act, 1962) and Delhi (Sixty-ninth Amendment Act, 1991). A common feature of these two territories is that they have been granted unicameral legislatures whose members are directly elected by the people. The Pondicherry legislature is partly elected and partly nominated. There is also a council of ministers responsible to the legislature in both the territories. The head of the state in both Delhi and Pondicherry is a Lieutenant Governor appointed by the union to perform formal executive functions of the government. Both the territories also have governments headed by chief ministers accountable to their respective legislatures. However, the Chief Minister of Delhi is appointed by the President of India on the recommendation of the Lieutenant Governor. This is presumably in view of the fact that Delhi is the National Capital Territory. The legislature of Delhi enjoys only concurrent jurisdiction as in case of conflict in regard to laws made by it and those made by the Parliament of India, the latter prevails, Pondicherry is represented by one seat each in the Lok Sabha and the Rajya Sabha. Delhi has seven Lok Sabha and three Rajya Sabha seats. Despite being called a state, Delhi is really a semi-state as some vital subjects like land, police and civil services are vested in the union government. The government of Delhi enjoys only concurrent jurisdiction in other subjects. Hence, there has been a long standing demand of full statehood for Delhi. In case of Pondicherry, land, police and civil services are under the jurisdiction of the state government.[36]

GOVERNMENTAL STRUCTURE AND PROCESSES

There was a long debate in the Constituent Assembly about the form of democratic government to be adopted for India. The architects of the Constitution were of the view that under the recommendations of the Acts of 1919 and 1935, India already had an experience of functioning as a limited parliamentary government. Dr Ambedkar stated, 'Draft Constitution in recommending the Parliamentary system of Executive has preferred more responsibility to more stability'.[37]

He further stated:

> The American and the Swiss systems give more stability but less responsibility. The British system, on the other hand, gives you more responsibility but less stability. The reason for this is obvious. The American Executive is a non-Parliamentary Executive which means that it is not dependent for its existence upon a majority in the Congress, while the British system is a Parliamentary Executive which means that it is dependent upon a majority in Parliament.[38]

It was thus a deliberate choice by the architects of the Constitution to adopt a parliamentary form of government both at the centre and in the states. This system differs from the presidential system in the sense that it does not adhere to the principle of separation of powers. On the contrary, it makes the executive responsible to the Legislature. Under this system, there is a President who is the head of the State. Much like the British monarch, he is only a constitutional head of the State. Ambedkar referred to him in the Constituent Assembly as the 'symbol' of the nation, not its ruler. However, the executive power of the union government is exercised in his name by the council of ministers headed by the prime minister who is the head of the parliamentary government and, therefore, collectively responsible to the Lok Sabha.

A qualitatively new phase in Indian politics was ushered in with the advent of the multiparty system in 1989 elections which has continued ever since. With no clear majority for any one party during this phase, the system of coalition and minority governments has been the dominant feature, with a decisive role played by some major regional parties. This complex set of developments has brought about a sea change in the political system. The prime ministerial system has dissolved into a kind of cabinet system that has gone beyond recognition in comparison to the classical Westminster system based on collective responsibility of the cabinet to the popular Chamber of the Parliament. The Indian cabinet system today is fragmented into segments nominated and controlled by participating parties, some of which are led by powerful chief ministers. Legally, the prime minister is still the kingpin of the system in the sense that the ultimate power rests in his hands. But the ministers are imposed upon him by coalition partners and withdrawn from his Cabinet sometimes against his will. Thus, the principle of collective responsibility is considerably strained which goes beyond the Parliament to the party bosses and the chief ministers. This is perhaps inevitable in a federal coalition cabinet but alien to the Westminster system.

With the decline of prime ministerial power, the presidential role has acquired more leeway, though this does not tantamount to an independent role for the President. However, Presidents in recent times have shown greater initiative and drive under coalition situations, particularly in the formation of governments and dissolution of the Lok Sabha in cases of uncertain majorities, than in the past. The phase of coalition and minority governments has also increased the autonomy of the Parliament as well as that of state governments than was ever the case under one party majority governments.

In the states, the structure of government is largely a replica of the structure of government at the union level. The Constitution enshrines the Executive Power of a state in the hands of the Governor whose position is almost the same in relation to the state council of ministers as that of the President to the union council of ministers. Theoretically, like the President, the Governor is the source of all Executive Power but, in practice, he is only a nominal head who has to act on the advice of his ministers. The council of ministers with the chief minister as its head enjoys the real Executive Power in a state. The Constitution makes them collectively responsible to the legislative assembly of the state. The powers and functions of the chief minister are similar to those of the prime minister in the union government.

Apart from being a parliamentary government, India is also a federation. This is reflected in a series of constitutional provisions relating to the structure of the government. The head of the state at the union level and in the states is either elected or appointed through a federal process. The President of India is elected by a federal electoral college consisting of the elected members of both houses of parliament and the elected members of the legislative assemblies of the states. The Governor is appointed by the Union Executive to serve as a federal link between the Government of India and the state concerned. Although not stated in the Constitution, expectation has gradually grown that the chief minister of the concerned state should be consulted in making such appointments. The prime minister heads the parliamentary component of the government, but there is a federal dimension to his Cabinet in the sense that its composition is supposed to reflect the regional diversities of the country as far as possible.

The Rajya Sabha is the Federal Second Chamber of the Indian Parliament. The form of government at the centre being parliamentary, the council of ministers is collectively responsible to the Lok Sabha. This accords a special position to the Lok Sabha in the scheme of the government. As a Federal Second Chamber, the Rajya Sabha is armed with two special powers: authorizing the Parliament (under Article 249) to legislate on an item in the state list and to create an All-India Service. The Rajya Sabha authorized the creation of a new All-India Service—the Indian Forest Service—in 1966. The other special power is related to an Emergency situation. If an Emergency is declared at the time when the Lok Sabha is dissolved, the formality of parliamentary approval of the proclamation is made by the Rajya Sabha. An Emergency so approved can be in operation for a maximum period of thirty days from the date on which the reconstituted Lok Sabha meets.

However, its federal character has been diluted by the absence of the principle of equal representation for each federating unit as in the United States of America but on the basis of their population (Articles 4[1] and 80[2] read with the Fourth Schedule). Thus, the state of Uttar Pradesh has 31 seats whereas states of north-east (like Meghalaya, Mizoram, Manipur), Pondicherry, and Goa have just one seat each in the Rajya Sabha. A constitutional amendment in 2003 abolished the domiciliary requirement for a member of the Rajya Sabha elected from a particular state. Another change that was given effect to was that voting in the Rajya Sabha be done openly rather than by secret ballot so that the party leadership could more effectively ensure that the state legislators did not transgress party lines in voting. This amendment led to the election of some business magnates and film actors from states where they were not residents. There is a case pending in the Supreme Court arguing that this is destructive of the Rajya Sabha's representative credentials as a Federal Second Chamber.

Two rationale underlie the composition of the Rajya Sabha: (*a*) federal representation of states on a territorial basis, and (*b*) ensuring review/revision of Bills received from the Lok Sabha. However, the Constituent Assembly debates suggest that the consideration of federal representation weighed more heavily in the minds of the framers of the Constitution than the revising role. In fact, some members advocated equal representation to each state (Lokanath Misra, Orissa: General) or at least proportionately larger representation to smaller states, if not equal (Shibban Lal Saksena, United Provinces: General).[39]

The impact of federalism on the working of the Rajya Sabha was not that evident in the era of Congress dominance as both Houses were more or less similar in terms of their membership. In the phase of multiparty system, the federal features of the Rajya Sabha have become increasingly evident. For, the Rajya Sabha has been under the control of an opposition stronger in state legislatures. The ruling party with a coalitional majority in the Lok Sabha must, therefore, work in cooperation with the opposition majority in the Rajya Sabha in the passage of legislation and constitutional amendment.

As a federal house, it was expected to represent the states. Initially, this role was rather insignificant. Its increasing federal relevance may be further strengthened by expanding its electoral college to include local bodies in addition to state legislatures. This would be consistent with the current efforts to put the local self-governing institutions on a constitutional footing. The pattern of membership is reflective of the party system as in the case of the Lok Sabha.

The powers of the Rajya Sabha are similar to those of the Lok Sabha except for the money bills that can originate only in the Lok Sabha and cannot be finally rejected by the Rajya Sabha beyond sending these back for reconsideration to the Lok Sabha, something which can be done only once. Deadlocks between the two chambers are resolved at a joint sitting, in which the Lok Sabha may have its way due to its numerical strength. In constitutional amendments, since there is no provision for a joint sitting for resolving a deadlock, the Rajya Sabha has a veto.

An independent judiciary is an integral organ of the federal government *par excellence*. Under the Indian Constitution, the rationale for this kind of judiciary is underlined by at least three major considerations. First, the Constitution includes the division of legislative subjects and revenue resources between the two levels of government in the Seventh Schedule which consists of the union, state and concurrent lists. Second, the demarcation of powers and functions of different organs of the government can also result in disputes as to alleged encroachments by one over the jurisdictions of others. Third, the fundamental rights guaranteed to citizens are equally binding on the governments both at the centre and in the states. On all these three counts, conflicts of jurisdiction and rights may arise that can be finally settled only by a federal judiciary. The Indian Constitution, much like its Canadian counterpart, established a common hierarchy of judicial structure consisting of the Supreme Court, High Courts and subordinate courts appointed by the federal functionaries but enjoying considerable autonomy and independence from the governments at both the levels.

Under the Constitution, the Union Executive is the appointing authority for courts, but under a series of case laws laid down by the Supreme Court in the 1980s and the 1990s, the advice of a collegium of judges is binding on the government in the appointment of judges (*S.P. Gupta* vs *Union of India* [1982]; *SC Advocates Association* vs *Union of India* [1993]). The NCRWC report 2002 recommended the establishment of a National Judicial Commission under the chairmanship of the Chief Justice of India. In addition, it consists of two other seniormost judges, the Minister of Law and a jurist appointed by the President of India to advise the Union Executive on the appointment of judges. In May 2002, the National Democratic Alliance (NDA) Cabinet took a decision to move a draft constitutional amendment to this effect but nothing has been done so far in this direction.

Moreover, there are a number of federal agencies created by the Constitution which work both for the centre and the states. The All-India Services are perhaps a unique feature of the Indian federal system. Both IAS and IPS officers are recruited by an independent Union Public Service Commission (UPSC), trained in the central academies of administration, and allocated to the state governments to man the highest ranking administrative and police posts. For all practical purposes, they serve under the disciplinary jurisdiction of the state government to whose cadre they belong, except for the ultimate disciplinary action of dismissal which must be referred to the Union Home Ministry. These officers are also deputed to serve as Secretaries in the centre for some years but they continue to belong to their respective state cadres to which they must return.

The Constitution also provides for the appointment of a Comptroller and Auditor General of India (CAG) who is empowered to audit 'the accounts of the Union and of the States and of any other authority or body as may be prescribed by or under any law made by Parliament' (Article 149). The office enjoys a good deal of constitutional security and autonomy. The CAG's reports pertaining to the accounts of the union are submitted to the President of India who 'shall cause them to be laid before each House of Parliament'. His reports relating to the accounts of a state are submitted to the Governor who 'shall cause them to be laid before the legislature of the state' (Article 151).

The Election Commission of India is also an independent federal agency with considerable constitutional autonomy, which is entrusted with 'the superintendence, direction and control of the preparation of the electoral rolls for, and the conduct of, all elections to Parliament and to the Legislature of every state and of elections to the offices of President and Vice-President held under this Constitution' (Article 324).

UNION–STATE RELATIONS

LEGISLATIVE RELATIONS

The federal division of power and revenues between the centre and the states is set out in the three lists in the Seventh Schedule. The union list as amended consists of 96 entries that include matters of national importance, such as defence, foreign affairs, banking, insurance, currency and coinage, citizenship, railways and airways, inter-state trade and commerce, census, All-India Services, audit and accounts of the union and the states, taxes on income other than agricultural income, customs and export duties, corporation tax, union excise duties, and any other matter not enumerated in the other lists. The Parliament has the exclusive authority to formulate laws in these matters. The state list includes 62 entries relating to matters of importance to the states such as public order and police, local government, public health and sanitation, agriculture, fisheries, land revenue and agricultural income tax, state excise duties and sales taxes, over which the state legislature has exclusive authority. The concurrent list comprises 47 entries which pertain to matters of common concern such as criminal law and procedure, civil procedure, marriage, contracts, torts, trusts, labour, planning and education. On these matters, both the union and the states can legislate but in the case of a conflict, the union law prevails. Residual powers—like in Canada, but unlike the USA, Australia and Switzerland—are vested in the Parliament. However, the Union Government can legislate on any subject included in the state list, under certain specific circumstances:

1. If the Rajya Sabha recommends by a two-third majority that such legislation is in national interest.
2. If two or more states mutually agree that such a legislation should be made for them.
3. In order to implement treaties or international agreements or connections.
4. In the case of failure of constitutional machinery in a State resulting in the proclamation of Emergency.

A major anomaly, according to Kabra, is that the term 'concurrent' is a misnomer as despite being legally correct, it may be undemocratically exercised by a centre that enjoys overwhelming concentration of fiscal and economic powers at the union level and the states' virtual dependence on the union in discharging only such functions which are leftover by and are permitted and tolerated by the latter. This makes for excessive and dysfunctional centralization which is not conducive to socio-economic change and materialization of democratic aspirations which can be articulated in India's uneven society in a decentralized framework.[40]

The original Constitution included 97 items in the union list, 66 in the state list and 47 in the concurrent list. Over the last half a century, some of the items in the state list have been included in the concurrent/union list. Between 1950 and 2001, 27 changes were introduced by constitutional amendments: 9 in the union list, 11 in the state list and 7 in the concurrent list. Four out of nine changes in the union list have enlarged the executive, cultural and coercive powers of the union *vis-à-vis* the states (for example, the 6th Amendment, 1956, added a new tax to the union list, namely, on the sale and purchase of goods other than newspapers of the scope of interstate trade and commerce). These changes are mirrored in the state list as the items gained by other lists were lost by the state list.

The concurrent list has not lost any item; it has only gained (for example, 42nd Amendment, 1976, added four new items to this list, namely, administration of justice in a state and formation of lower courts, forests, education, and population control and family planning). Of the 27 amendments introduced, 13 were made in the Nehru era, 14 during Indira Gandhi's regime and none in the post-1989 multiparty coalition government phase.[41]

Article 200 of the Constitution grants the union the Executive Power to intervene in the legislative process of states. A Bill presented to the Governor for his assent may be reserved for consideration by the union executive with its power to either approve it or disallow it. There is a similar provision in the Canadian Constitution, which over the years has fallen into disuse under conventions of the Constitution. However, in India this has been a major irritant in union–state relations as is amply documented by the Sarkaria Commission report. The report shows that out of 15 state legislations so reserved between 10 November 1969 and 7 June 1984, the union government withheld its assent in nine cases. In six cases, the decision was taken after one and a half years; in five, after three years; in three, after six years; and in one case after twelve years (Annexure, V. I, p. 159). The Commission recommended that normally the Governor must abide by the advice of the Council of Ministers. In its view, the discretion of reservation of a State Legislation by the Governor should be exercised in 'rare and exceptional cases' when such a legislation is 'patently unconstitutional'. The Commission also recommended that a State Bill so reserved should be disposed of within four months from the date of its receipt.

ADMINISTRATIVE RELATIONS

Article 256 of the Constitution provides that the executive power of every state shall be so exercised as to ensure compliance with the laws made by Parliament. The same Article goes on to say that the executive power of the union shall extend to issuing of such directions to a state as may appear to the Government of India to be necessary for such purposes as the construction and maintenance of means of communication and transportation of national and military importance and the protection of railways within the state, etc.

The major contentious issues that have a bearing on union executive power, administrative and political relations between the union and the states are treaty-making power of the union (Article 253), President's Rule (Article 356), the role of the Governor and the use of paramilitary forces.

Power of the Union Executive to Enter into International Treaties (Article 253): The Power to enter into any international treaty or convention is vested exclusively in the union executive. However, Article 253 of the Constitution requires a Parliamentary Legislation for giving effect to such agreements. This provision of the Constitution has acquired a somewhat controversial dimension in the context of globalization. For example, the Union of India signed the WTO treaty in 1995 which entailed obligations for the federating states as well even in their exclusive jurisdictions, for example, agriculture. The state of Tamil Nadu followed by Orissa, Rajasthan and Punjab filed cases in the Supreme Court precisely on this issue, which were subsequently withdrawn presumably after suitable assurances from the union government for such occasions in the future. In all probability, the Union of India would be more cautious in the exercise of its power relating to the execution of treaties in view of the likely responses and reactions from Parliament as well as from the state governments.

Imposition of President's Rule under Article 356: Emergency provisions contained in Part XVIII of the Constitution are among the most important provisions with a profound influence on the development of India's federal polity. Article 356 provides that if the President is satisfied that a situation has arisen in which a state cannot be governed in accordance with the provisions of the Constitution, he may promulgate an emergency resulting in the imposition of President's Rule. In the Constituent Assembly, Dr Ambedkar referred to these provisions as 'safety valves' and expressed the hope that there would be no occasion to use them. Unfortunately, this has often been misused by political parties to topple state governments which failed to promote the interest of the ruling parties at the centre.

An example of the blatant misuse of this Article was when the Janata Party came to power in 1977 and dissolved the assemblies of all states where the Congress party was in power and ordered fresh elections in as many as nine state assemblies. In the 1980 mid-term poll when Indira Gandhi returned to power, she also dismissed nine state assemblies where non-Congress governments were in power. The most controversial cases of partisan toppling of opposition governments in states were reported during the Congress dominance under Indira Gandhi. The transformation of the party system from one party dominance to a multiparty configuration coupled with judicial interventions in the matter has appreciably reduced the misuse of Article 356. Some political parties and state governments had earlier demanded the repeal of Article 356 and the abolition of the office of the Governor. In the changed context, however, such demands are seldom voiced. Neither the Sarkaria Commission report nor the deliberations in the Inter-State Council have supported such extreme views. A faithful adherence to the letter and spirit of the Constitution has been reiterated by all these authorities. A landmark judicial verdict in this context is the *S.R. Bommai case* (1994) in which the Supreme Court departed from the past practice of its reticence to judicially review Presidential Proclamations and declared the actions of the centre under Article 356 subject to judicial review. To circumvent the constitutional provision barring judicial inquiry into the advice received by the President from his Cabinet, the Supreme Court ingeniously argued that it was not scrutinizing the merit of such advice but only examining whether the reasons given for dismissal of a state government bore any relationship with the factual situation. In the opinion of the Court, while the 'satisfaction' of the President regarding the 'breakdown of constitutional machinery' in a state as visualized in Article 356 is 'subjective in nature', it is 'conditional' rather than 'absolute' power to be exercised on Cabinet advice on the ground of some 'relevant material'.[42] This judgement was a milestone in the sense that on previous occasions—for example, the *State of Rajasthan* vs *Union of India* (1977)—the Supreme Court had ruled that the determination of constitutional emergency in a state was a 'political thicket' best left by courts to the union executive.

The formation of coalition or minority government in New Delhi after 1989 has added a new dimension to the controversy surrounding President's Rule in states. The political parties, especially regional parties, extending support to the union government from the Parliamentary Floor without joining the Cabinet have often resorted to putting pressure on the union government for dismissing a state government to which these parties may be opposed to in their respective states. For example, between 1998 and 1999, the regional allies of the BJP minority government—the AIADMK, the Trinamool Congress and the Samata Party—had demanded the dismissal of the DMK, the Left Front and the RJD governments in Tamil Nadu, West Bengal and Bihar respectively. The Vajpayee government had resisted these pressures due to: (*a*) the criss-cross pattern of coalitional politics in the country; (*b*) lack of majority of the ruling coalition in the Rajya Sabha; and (*c*) the fear of judicial review. The central administrative and political teams dispatched to observe the law and order situation in these states were well received in Tamil Nadu, given a lukewarm reception in Bihar and openly opposed in West Bengal. Making a belated move, the centre dismissed the RJD government in Bihar headed by Rabri Devi in 1999 in the wake of persistent violence based on caste–class cleavages. However, the centre had to beat a hasty retreat as its action, though approved by the Lok Sabha, got a beating in the Rajya Sabha where the opposition forces led by the Congress (RJD's ally), had a majority. In 2002, the opposition parties in Parliament including the regional allies of the NDA government such as the TDP, the DMK and the Samata Party, persistently demanded the dismissal of the BJP government in Gujarat headed by Narendra Modi in the wake of recurrent communal riots triggered by the Godhra carnage. The Vajpayee government, however, resisted such pressures using the Bommai judgement as a shield. Such a dismissal would have exposed the Gujarat government as well as the presidential order of the NDA government to judicial scrutiny which the government and its allies did not want to risk. The Inter-State Council at Srinagar in 2003 had reached a consensus to incorporate the rules laid down in the Bommai judgement into the Constitution by an amendment. Though in principle this is a good idea (for if it becomes a part of the Constitution, even the Supreme Court cannot reverse its Bommai judgement), yet it still awaits implementation.

Role of the Governor: The institution of the Governor, with its dual role—as the constitutional head of the state and the representative of the centre—occupies a significant place in India's federal polity. As the constitutional head of the state he, unlike the President of India, has certain discretionary powers, taken almost verbatim from the Government of India Act of 1935, which are immune from judicial scrutiny.[43] As the representative of the centre, it is his duty to apprise the central government of developments in the state and he has to always keep in mind the conflicting claims of the centre and the state in a given situation and to balance them in accordance with the Constitution. This dual role makes the Governor's position crucial to the maintenance of cordial centre–state relations. After 1967, when non-Congress governments were formed in many states, tension began to mount as the central government attempted to make use of the prestigious office of the Governor for partisan ends.

The role of the Governor in this context became a highly contentious issue in centre–state relations. The main issues of contention were related to the appointment of the Governor by the centre and his partisan role in the formation and dismissal of a state government at the behest of the centre. Governorship is now viewed as a reward for political loyalists (who could not be accommodated in the cabinet) and pliable bureaucrats seeking post-retirement employment. This has reduced the office of the Governor to that of a mere rubber stamp or agent of the centre. Often even the normal courtesy of consulting the state government before the appointment of a new Governor is not observed by the centre. An important instrument of centre–state relations has thus been seriously undermined.

Both the Administrative Reforms Commission and the Sarkaria Commission in their reports underlined the indispensability of the office of the Governor but were highly critical of the appointments made and of the role of the incumbents. The Sarkaria Commission in its survey found that the appointments made after Independence till October 1984 were misplaced as over 60 per cent of the Governors had played an active role in politics, many of them immediately prior to their appointment.[44] The Commission made a series of recommendations pertaining to the appointment and conduct of Governors. Regarding appointment, it was recommended that the appointee should have attained eminence in some walk of life; should be from outside the state; should be detached and not be too intimately involved in state politics; and should not have been actively involved in politics in the recent past. It was also recommended that the appointment should always be made after consultation with the chief minister of the state. The Commission cited the Constituent Assembly debates that clearly expressed this expectation. With respect to the role of the Governor, the Sarkaria Commission observed that in the submissions made before it, the state governments were unanimous in suggesting that the matter relating to the loss of majority support (by the ministry) in the legislative assembly should be decided on the floor of the House rather than in the Raj Bhavan, and that the chief minister should be given a reasonable opportunity to establish such majority.[45] The Commission lent its wholehearted support to this view in its recommendations.

In recent decades, there has been a perceptible decline in the misuse of Article 356 by the centre. However, some recent cases of the exercise of governmental power have brought to light different kinds of problems, the full implications of which have not yet crystallized. A Governor of one of the north-eastern states was dismissed on account of his differences with the centre. In Tamil Nadu, the Governor resigned in protest against the dismissal of the DMK government in 1991 by the Congress-supported SJP minority government headed by Chandrashekhar. Also, Romesh Bhandari, one of the Governors of Uttar Pradesh installed an all-defector government headed by Jagdambika Pal, summarily dismissing the BJP government of which Kalyan Singh was the chief minister. He did this in violation of all constitutional and conventional norms on the pretext of arresting horse-trading in the assembly by the BJP government, which incidentally rode back to power, for Pal could not muster the support of the majority. Ironically, the Gujral government at the centre adopted an ostrich-like attitude towards the whole episode. In the absence of any advice from his Cabinet, President K.R. Narayanan faxed an advice (not directive) to the Uttar Pradesh Governor to exercise restraint in precipitating the dismissal of the BJP government, which went unheeded by the Governor. However, the matter was referred to the Supreme Court which undid the Governor's act and reinstated the dismissed government. In 2004, the Congress-led UPA government selectively dismissed most BJP-appointed Governors with RSS background with the exception of the Rajasthan Governor, Madan Lal Khurana, and the Karnataka Governor, T.N. Chaturvedi. This again created controversies regarding the appointment of Governors who are normally expected to be non-partisan.

Use of Central Paramilitary Police Forces: The maintenance of law and order is primarily a state subject and to perform this task the states have set up their own agencies and organizations. In addition to these, there are agencies of the central government (such as the CRPF, the BSF and the CISF) whose basic purpose is to ensure that the law and order situation in different parts of the country does not get out of control.[46] The maintenance of 'parallel' agencies by the central government is a very 'unusual' feature of the Indian federal system. The states argue that since public order is a subject included under the state list in the Constitution, the setting up of central police forces is an encroachment on their jurisdiction. The centre, however, argues that these forces are required to protect properties and installations of the central government. In the late 1960s, a serious conflict arose between the centre and the states on the issue of deployment of CRPF units. However, in recent times Kerala and West Bengal have got accustomed to deploying the central police forces even for basic law and order functions, not to speak of special occasions such as election duty, natural disaster, and communal riots. The clamour of the states against the deployment of these forces in their respective territories has considerably reduced. The states, however, continue to demand a greater share in the divisible tax resources for more effectively exercising the responsibilities and obligations that the Constitution has entrusted them with. However, in 2004 Manipur witnessed a persistent popular protest movement against taking recourse to the Armed Forces Special Powers Act applicable in the north-eastern states in the event a state government declares the state a disturbed area under the Disturbed Areas Act. Both these Acts and a Central Act require endorsement of the state government concerned.

FINANCIAL RELATIONS

A major problem facing a system with multiple fiscal authorities relates to the integration of financial policies, which is one of the objectives of a planned economy. The net result is that there are surpluses at the union and deficits in the states. 'The outstanding feature of the financial relationship between the union and the states consequently is that the former is always the giver and the latter the receiver.'[47] The difference in levels of economic development leads to an imbalance among states in terms of income and wealth disparities. This, in turn, becomes a perennial source of tension for the union.

Within the present structure of union–state relations, all state governments have to cope with a paucity of financial resources.

On the one hand, the financial requirements of the states are vastly increasing, while on the other, the union has over the years cornered a major chunk of the country's national resources and has even gone to the extent of encroaching on the states' domain as far as financial powers are concerned. Another observable tendency is the increasing indebtedness of the states to the union—the states find it difficult to repay the instalments or interests on the debts without taking recourse to further central assistance.[48] The extent of indebtedness rose from Rs. 239 crore in 1952 to Rs. 4,094 crore in 1966. This is primarily due to increased public spending by the states for developmental purposes.

The Seventh Schedule of the Constitution vests taxing powers both in the union list and the state list. But there is a contradiction between the elastic sources of revenue earmarked for the centre and the expansive developmental expenditure of the states. The items embodied in the state list include land revenue, taxes on agricultural income, excise duties on alcoholic drinks and narcotic drugs, general sales tax and sales tax on motor spirits, tax on motor vehicles, stamps and registration, entertainment taxes and electricity duties. The exclusive rights for raising the most elastic taxes such as general income tax, corporate tax, excise duties (except on liquors and narcotics), customs duties are vested in the union government by the Constitution. On the one hand, the sources of revenue placed at the disposal of the states are not commensurate with the huge expenditure which they are expected to incur on various developmental activities, while on the other the union has access to expansive sources of revenue.[49] The concurrent list does not include any item pertaining to taxation. Proceeds of the taxes from the state list are retained by the states, while proceeds of some of the taxes of the union list are partially or wholly allocated to the states to rectify the imbalance between the functions and resources of the states. Such taxes are of four types: (*a*) those levied by the union but collected and appropriated by the states; (*b*) those levied and collected by the union but assigned to the states; (*c*) those levied and collected by the union but distributed between the union and the states; and (*d*) those union excise duties which are levied and collected by the union but whose proceeds are shared between the union and the concerned states.

Another attempt to rectify this imbalance is made by the provision of grants-in-aid in the Constitution (Article 275) whereby the union as a guardian may extend financial assistance to various units in times of need and for their all round development. The scheme defining financial relations between the union and the states is flexible and adaptable to varying needs depending on the situation. On the basis of periodical reviews (of resources available and needs of the states) made by the Finance Commission, necessary changes are suggested with regard to the distribution of finances between the union and the states. This is a unique feature of the Indian Constitution. In fact, by providing for the establishment of the Finance Commission (Article 280) for the purpose of allocating and readjusting the receipts from certain sources, the Constitution has made a pioneering contribution in this extremely complicated aspect of federal relationship. The union and states 'are mutually dependent' and this coordinate nature has given stability to the working of the Indian federation.

The Constitution has considered it more desirable to have a constitutionally entrenched Finance Commission to advise on a fair distribution and allocation of fiscal resources between the union and the states. Successive Finance Commissions have made valuable contributions to the federal system. Every state wants more resources, and a larger share of the divisible pool. The onus of ensuring that justice is done in the matter of allocation of funds by the union to different states rests on the Finance Commission. It aims to ensure that the states get funds commensurate with their requirements. The allocations made by the Finance Commission are accorded greater legitimacy by the states than those made by the Planning Commission. It may be noted that the total dispensation of fiscal transfers through the Finance Commission and plan allocations through the Planning Commission have increased, rather than bridged regional imbalances; to arrest this trend a radical change in the pattern of financial assistance to the states is called for.[50]

Plan as well as non-Plan resources are transferred to the states on the advice of both the Finance Commission and the Planning Commission. Another category of transfer in these areas, called discretionary grants (Article 282), is made on the advice of the

Planning Commission for any specific purpose/subject falling under the union, state or concurrent jurisdiction, for example, centrally-sponsored schemes (CSS), including the Pradhan Mantri Gramodaya Yojna (PMGY) introduced by the NDA government. The PMGY was launched in the 2000-1 annual plan in all the states and union territories to achieve the objective of sustainable human development at the village level.[51] The NDC meeting in 1999 set up a committee on the transfer of centrally-sponsored schemes under the chairmanship of deputy chairman of the Planning Commission with members from both the union and the states to identify the CSS for retention by the union and those for transfer to the states/union territories. The committee suggested the modalities of transfer and funding of the identified CSS.[52]

The state governments generally prefer allocation of fiscal resources through the Finance Commission as compared to the Planning Commission. This is because the former is a constitutionally mandated and more objective body, while the latter is a creation of the union government through an ordinary executive order.

The Sarkaria Commission had recommended an amendment to the Constitution so as to enable the Parliament to provide for the sharing of the corporate tax along with suitable adjustments in sharing income tax and excise duties between the union and the states. It had also recommended the appointment of an expert body with appropriate representation from the states by the union government to suggest reforms in taxation and resource mobilization by the union and the states.[53] However, it did not favour the transfer of more subjects to the states and pleaded for a strong union to preserve the unity and integrity of India. It suggested that the Finance Commission, which is appointed every five years, should be made a permanent body, and that the Planning Commission be made a constitutional body with a secretariat.[54] According to scholars like Kabra, 'the practice of the centre appointing the members of the Planning Commission must be replaced by a system by which they are jointly appointed by the centre and the states'.[55]

The regional parties have demanded greater devolution of fiscal powers to the states. Under the guise of centralized planning, the union over the years had deprived the states of their rightful due of the fiscal resources. Since 1991 there has been a major reorientation in the economic ideology of the Indian aggregate state in favour of economic liberalization. One, therefore, hopes that in keeping with this ideology the union decentralizes the planning process.

The various Finance Commissions have generally adhered to the criteria of grants-in-aid to the states that has popularly been referred to as the Gadgil formula (named after a former deputy chairman of the Planning Commission). It takes into account in variable proportions the population of the state, developmental performance, budgetary deficit, etc.

The Ninth Finance Commission in its first report for 1989-90 recommended a modified Gadgil formula whereby income tax and union excise duties may be distributed among states in accordance with the following ratio: (*a*) 20 per cent on the basis of population; (*b*) 50 per cent on the basis of the gap between the per capita income of a state and the highest per capita income of a state multiplied by its population; (*c*) 12.5 per cent on the basis of a state's per capita income multiplied by its population; and (*d*) 12.5 per cent on the proportion of poor in the state to the total poor population nationally.[56] However, in the formula for central assistance to the states recommended by the Planning Commission and approved by the NDC in December 1991, population (60 per cent) continues to be given more weightage, beside, of course, some other criteria like per capita income (25 per cent) and performance (7.5 per cent). Moreover, the criterion of 25 per cent weightage given to per capita income was made to conform to the 'deviation method' such that higher the allocation of central assistance, lower the per capita income of a state than the national average.[57] At the meeting of the Inter-State Council held in Delhi in July 1997 a decision was taken that 29 per cent share in union taxes be given to states as suggested by the Tenth Finance Commission. As per the Commission's recommendation, this arrangement should suitably be provided for in the Constitution and reviewed once in fifteen years. The Commission also recommended that the union should continue to be vested with the power to levy surcharges (for the purposes of the union) and these should be excluded from the sharing arrangements with the states.[58] On the recommendation of the

Tenth Finance Commission, the Constitution (80th) Amendment Act, 2000 provided that the entire revenue receipt of the union must now be shared with the states.[59]

The Eleventh Finance Commission (2000) recommended a 'fresh look' at the Gadgil formula 'with a view to evolving a suitable alternative'. This is because it believed that revenue deficits 'are inherent in the practice of giving Central Assistance for States' plans in the form of grants and loans in the proportion of 30:70 as is the case with non-special category states, while their planned revenue expenditure constitutes nearly 60 per cent of the plan outlay.' Following economic liberalization in 1991, the states are 'now free to attract private investments from domestic as well as foreign sources'. This changed context must be taken into account by the centre. Moreover, the Commission also reiterated the recommendations of some earlier Finance Commissions for transferring centrally-sponsored schemes and their funds to the states which can plan and administer their own schemes with flexibility and autonomy.[60]

On the submission of the report of the Eleventh Finance Commission, economically more prosperous states led by Andhra Pradesh chief minister, N. Chandrababu Naidu (TDP) met the prime minister and expressed dissatisfaction with its recommendations. The Finance Commission reports have consistently given greater weightage to backwardness and population in decisions regarding federal fiscal transfers to states. Although the criteria of economic performance has been given more weightage in recent Finance Commission reports, poorer states receive proportionately more than richer states. Any drastic change in the pattern of transfers is likely to increase economic disparities at the regional level.

The Twelfth Finance Commission Report submitted in 2005 has recommended increase in the share of states in the total divisible pool of federal resources from the existing 29.5 per cent to 30.5 per cent. However, this slight gain to the states may be cancelled out because of the neo-liberal economic policies that have put a strain on union as well as state finances. In a view from the perspective of states on the Twelfth Finance Commission Report, V. Sridhar has commented:

Although the Constitution prescribed that the main task of the Finance Commission is to perform its role as an agency for setting the modalities for the transfer of resources from the centre to the states, the terms of reference of the TFC were expanded by asking it to suggest 'a plan by which the (state) governments, collectively and severally, may bring about a restructuring of the public finances, restoring budgetary balance, achieving macro-economic stability and debt reduction along with equitable growth'. In specific terms, there were fears that this was, apart from being a violation of the principles of federalism, an attempt by the centre to straitjacket the states in the liberal reform mode with all its harsh implications for the already financially beleaguered states.[61]

An important development in union–state relations is the setting up of the National Commission to Review the Working of the Constitution (NCRWC) in 2000 that submitted its report in 2002. This eleven-member Commission chaired by Justice M.N. Venkatachaliah has by and large endorsed the recommendations of the Sarkaria Commission. It does, however, break some new ground and travels some distance in meeting the demands of the states and functional requirements of the federation. For instance, it recommends a new look at fiscal federalism to allocate taxation of the expanding service sector of the economy to the concurrent list rather than settling the matter in a serendipitous way through residuary mechanism. It also suggests earmarking some service sector tax bases for state governments so as to augment their resources. Another important recommendation is the establishment of an 'Inter-State Trade and Commerce Commission' under Article 307 read with Entry 42 of the Union List. It seems to rely on the strengthening of judicial settlement of interstate river-water treaty, presumably in the background of its failure to arrive at a political settlement. Besides, it would like to see more effective utilization of the Inter-State Council and 'the desirability of prior consultation by the union government with the Inter-State Council may be considered before signing any treaty vitally affecting the interests of the states regarding matters in the state list'.[62] Regarding the role of the constitutional heads of the Federal and Provincial states, the NCRWC report has generally reiterated the well considered views of the Sarkaria Commission. Finally, the report has also underlined the importance of decentralization and devolution of powers to the local self-governing institutions and made suggestions for strengthening unique institutions of governance in north-east India.

Paradigm shifts in economic policies and union–state relations on account of growing federalization of the Indian polity have occurred since the 1990s. Economic liberalization has augmented the autonomy of the private sector as well as of state governments. Federalization has accentuated the tendency towards political as well as economic regionalism. While greater decentralized planning is still in place, public investment in the economy has considerably declined. This has opened up opportunities for economically more developed states to chart out their own strategies of development, but backward states have been put in a disadvantageous position on account of lack of resources and declining public investment on the part of the federal government. None the less, with the coming to power in 2004 of the Congress-led UPA, which relies on a sizeable parliamentary support of Communist Parties, there is likely to be greater emphasis on public investment, distributive justice and the planning process, even though the new liberal economic reforms are not likely to be reversed.

AMENDING FORMULA

A discussion of the structure of government would not be complete without the mention of the amendment procedure of the Constitution which lays down the basic structure of the government. The amending formula in the Constitution is variegated and complex. To start with, there are some provisions of the Constitution that can be amended by simple legislative process, e.g. admission or establishment of new states (Article 2). This category also includes the formation of new states by alteration of boundaries or names of the existing states under Article 3. However, this Article goes on to say,

> no Bill for the purpose shall be introduced in either House of Parliament except on the recommendation of the President and unless, where the proposal contained in the Bill affects the areas, boundaries or name of any of the States, the Bill has been referred by the President to the Legislature of that State for expressing its views thereon within such period as may be specified in the reference or within such further period

as the President may allow and the period so specified or allowed has expired.

Obviously this is a matter of concern to the states but the Constitution merely guarantees to them the right to be consulted. This departure from the federal principle was perhaps dictated by the fact that state boundaries in colonial India did not coincide with cultural boundaries and any procedure that granted veto to the states in this matter could result in unresolvable conflicts. However, other matters of federal concern relating to the structure and powers of the two levels of government cannot be unilaterally amended by the Parliament. Such an amendment requires two-thirds majority of the two houses of Parliament and a ratification by legislatures of at least half of the states of the union (Article 368).

Between June 1951 and January 2004, a total of 92 amendments to the Constitution were made. Of these, 37 (40.22 per cent) were related to federalism. The federal amendments cover a wide range of aspects of varying significance to centre–state relations. The largest number of federal amendments (35.14 per cent) concerned the reorganization of states. This clearly reveals the unsettled nature of interstate boundaries that resulted more from accidental factors of history rather than natural socio-cultural cleavages in Indian society. Against this background, it is easy to understand why the Constituent Assembly left the process of amending the Constitution for the purpose of reorganization of states without any strong federal entrenchment. If the power of amendment for this purpose had not been left to Parliament, and had been subject to the consent of the states, the question of territorial reorganization would not have arisen. States that would stand to lose territories would never consent to such an act. The Constitution enjoins the union government to consult the states but not necessarily be bound by their refusal. The second largest category of federal amendments (8 or 21.62 per cent) related to proclamation of President's Rule, the addition of the state of Delhi to the Presidential electoral college. Article 256 which relates to President's Rule has been the most vilified provision of the Constitution from the perspective of state governments as well as from that of federal theorists. However, it must be added that these constitutional amendments pertained mostly to extended spells of President's Rule in the insurgency infested Punjab in the 1980s.

The run of the mill abuse of this Article for partisan purposes did not call for a constitutional amendment, but the sheer frequency with which it has been misused led to the demand in some quarters for the wholesale repeal of this provision. The invocation of President's Rule in only genuine constitutional emergencies would have attested the claims of the framers of the Constitution that the union would intervene in state administration as a rescuer of a beleaguered state rather than as a destroyer of its autonomy. The third largest category (6 or 16.21 per cent) concerned sub-state autonomy or local self-government in a state. These were taken recourse to grant autonomous Regional Development Councils or to strengthen local bodies to satisfy intra-state demands for autonomy. The fourth largest category (5 or 13.51 per cent) related to the three lists of division of powers and taxes. The rather small number of amendments in this category suggests that constitutional division of powers and revenues has by and large been sound and stood the test of time. Three federal amendments related to linguistic federalism, i.e. recognition of new languages in the Eighth Schedule of the Constitution, and one amendment concerned the princely states (abolition of Privy Purses).[63]

Constitutional law imposes a limitation on the amending power of Parliament under Article 368 in terms of the unamendability of the 'basic structure' of the Constitution ingeniously devised by the Supreme Court in its judgements in the *Keshavananda Bharati* (1973) and the *Minerva Mills* (1980) cases.

LOCAL GOVERNMENTS

The local governments fall under the jurisdiction of state governments which establish them through legislation. They do not have any direct structural link with the union government. Any links between the top and bottom levels of the government are informal. Uneven, and in some cases irregular state of affairs at this level prompted the 73rd and 74th Constitutional Amendments in 1992-3 for rural and urban areas respectively. By virtue of these amendments, the Constitution includes a model local government legislation and distribution of responsibilities which the state legislatures are prompted to adopt or enact.

There is generally a three-tier structure of local government in rural areas at the village, mandal and district levels. In urban areas, there are municipalities—municipal corporations in cities. These local bodies are directly elected. In rural areas, panchayats at the village level are directly elected whereas mandal panchayats and zilla parishads are composed of the heads of the Panchayati Raj bodies at the next lower level. The structure of local government reflects population diversity in practice. Reserved representation is available for Scheduled Castes and Scheduled Tribes proportionate to their population and for women to the extent of 33 per cent by the 73rd Constitutional Amendment Act, 1992. The Eleventh Finance Commission for the first time devoted a full chapter to the finances of the local self-governing institutions.

A 1996 Parliamentary Act extended the Panchayati Raj provisions to the Scheduled Areas (some backward and tribal areas covered by the Vth and VIth Schedules of the Constitution). It provides, among other things, that every village must have a *gram sabha* (village assembly) for the purpose of approval of programmes and projects for social and economic development, identification of the target groups, and prevention of alienation of tribal lands. These institutions are regulated by central legislation which is a departure from the general pattern in the country where such institutions are governed by state legislation.

The NCRWC report (2002) recommended that the panchayats should categorically be declared to be 'institutions of self-government' and exclusive functions should be assigned to them even if this requires a further amendment of the Constitution. The Commission recommended major fiscal restructuring to enable the panchayats to function as viable local government institutions. Further, the Commission also suggested that all local authorities be allowed to borrow funds from their respective state governments and financial institutions. A new ministry of Panchayati Raj—earlier a part of the Ministry of Rural Development—has been set up by the UPA government.

PHASES OF EVOLUTION

Politics in India since Independence has evolved through several phases which from one point of view can be broadly divided into the parliamentary phase (until before the 1989 Lok Sabha elections) and the federal phase after that date. However, this broad periodization is further divisible into several phases within each in terms of nuances and emphasis with regard to tendencies relevant from the federal angle. Until the fourth general elections in 1967, the dominance of the Congress party was more or less complete at the centre as well as in most states. This factor submerged federal features of the polity and gave it the appearance of a parliamentary system to an extent. However, there were two factors, besides the constitutional text, that ensured that the federal features remained intact at least during the Nehru era. First, there were some chief ministers who had the political stature since the days of the nationalist movement and regional support base after Independence that Nehru could not ignore, e.g. C. Rajagopalachari in Madras, B.C. Roy in West Bengal and Morarji Desai in Bombay. Second, mass agitations in some states for the creation of unilingual states put pressure and in some cases forced the centre to concede their demands.

From 1971 to 1977, during the ascendancy of Indira Gandhi, the foregoing pattern changed considerably. The internal plurality and federality of the Congress government as well as the party was greatly whittled down by her centralizing drive and Congress chief ministers during this period came to be virtually appointed by the prime minister herself and mass political pressures were sought to be forcefully resisted by populist mass mobilization through slogans like *garibi hatao* and making a direct appeal to the people over the regional power structures to undercut them. Yet during this period, some old factors continued to operate and new ones emerged that restrained the centralizing trends of the period. These were the autonomy of the judiciary (albeit under great pressure); anti-Congress mass agitation that started in Gujarat and gathered momentum in Bihar and subsequently spread to the whole of north India under the leadership of Jayaprakash Narayan, and the continuing hold of the DMK government in Tamil Nadu and the one elected in the wake of the

Navnirman movement in Gujarat led by Morarji Desai. The Emergency proclaimed to suppress the JP movement was the culmination of the process of centralization and it was ended by the combined effect of judicial decisions, legacy of the JP movement and the electoral verdict of 1977.

The impact of an economic factor is also noticeable in this context. Sustained opposition to the Congress regime is correlated with the success of agrarian modernization or the so-called Green Revolution, cooperative movements in cash crops, dairy farming, as well as the rise of regional bourgeoisie. Relatively stable non-Congress governments were largely elected in areas marked by these developments in the late 1970s and the 1980s. Moreover, on the pattern of the success of the Dravidian parties, the left wing parties of West Bengal and later Tripura consolidated their political power by making an ingenious appeal to Bengali sub-nationalism in eastern India. In addition, the creation of new states through the 1960s to the 1970s based on linguistic, tribal and sub-regional considerations contributed to political forces strengthening the federal features of the Indian polity.

Thus, despite the return to power of Indira Gandhi in 1980, the political centralization of the 1970s could not be restored. This was largely due to two reasons. First, beginning with 1983, non-Congress governments were for the first time elected in Karnataka and Andhra Pradesh and this trend continued in Punjab, Assam and other states. By the end of the 1980s, there were non-Congress governments in almost half of the states. Second, state autonomy movements in Punjab and Assam gathered momentum in the 1980s and by the 1990s, Jammu & Kashmir had also joined this trend. Insurgencies continued to rock not only Assam, but other states of the north-east as well. New regional parties that emerged in Andhra Pradesh, Assam and some north-eastern states also contributed to the strengthening of this trend. It was under these pressures that Indira Gandhi appointed the Commission on centre–state relations chaired by Justice R.S. Sarkaria which submitted its monumental two-part report in 1987-8. Moreover, her successor Rajiv Gandhi signed regional accords with the Akali Dal (in Punjab), the Asom Gana Parishad (in Assam) and some other tribal parties in the north-east making peace with them.

The most marked phase of federalization which continues to be irreversible was heralded by the party system transformation in 1989 from one party dominance to a multiparty system in a formal as well as sustained way. It ranks as the most important factor contributing to the greater federalization of the political system. The 1989-2004 parliamentary elections may be said to have been held in a federal phase in the sense that their outcomes are marked by a regional segmentation of support for various parties as distinct from those of the previous decades which were typically characterized by uniform electoral response over large parts of the country either for the Congress or the Janata Party. Since the 1990s, parliamentary elections in India have demonstrated that even under the plurality electoral system, the expected effects of proportional representation to an extent are evident in the extreme fragmentation of the party system due to the division of votes along cleavages of caste and community. Of course, under a formal proportional electoral system, this fragmentation would become even more aggravated.[64]

Elections were held in an emotionally charged environment aroused by the anti-corruption campaign in the trail of the Bofors disclosures and the rising frustration fuelled by the belied expectations generated by Rajiv Gandhi's youth and idealism. However, rapidly growing restlessness among the people and factors like poor leadership, sycophancy, personality cult and abuse of the media for highlighting the sacrifices of the Gandhi dynasty aroused anti-government sentiments among the masses.

The 1989 elections were reminiscent of the 1977 polls, except for the fact that the latter were more extensive in regional spread than the former. The Janata Party victory was by and large a north Indian phenomenon, the region that had experienced the excesses of the Emergency more grievously. The Janata Dal-led National Front was practically a national phenomenon covering almost all the regions of the country. This federal coalition also included the Left parties influential in West Bengal and Kerala which Prime Minister V.P. Singh regarded as his 'natural allies', though they extended support to the coalition from outside—without joining the cabinet. Besides, there were major regional parties represented in the Front, e.g. the DMK in Tamil Nadu, the TDP in Andhra Pradesh, the AGP in Assam, and the Congress

(Secular). In addition, the National Conference of Jammu & Kashmir was a part of it and so was the Akali Dal in Punjab. The National Front minority government was also propped up by the Left as also by the BJP, a strange partner by virtue of it being an ardent votary of the Hindutva ideology, which was an anathema to the Janata Dal and the Left. Yet, this unlikely coalition materialized because of their common objective of keeping the Congress out of power.

During its eleven-month rule at the head of the National Front government (November 1989-November 1990), the JD was rocked by intense factionalism between its Jan Morcha (a Congress splinter) and Lok Dal constituents, the former led by V.P. Singh and the latter by the Devi Lal clan, leader of the prosperous Jat farmers and peasants of Haryana. The clash of egos between V.P. Singh and Devi Lal served as a major motivating factor for the former to unilaterally announce the decision to reserve the central government and public sector employment for 'Other Backward Classes' (OBC) to project himself as the messiah of the OBCs.

The Mandalization of the electorate was sought to be counteracted by Hindu mobilization launched by the BJP. The National Front government tried to talk the BJP out of its plan to undertake its Hindu revivalist Rath Yatra from Somnath to Ayodhya but failed in its endeavour. Finally, the journey was brought to a halt in Samastipur (Bihar) by the National Front government in New Delhi and the JD government in Bihar. This was provocation enough for the BJP to withdraw its support to the National Front government and, as a consequence, the latter fell in a no-confidence vote in the Lok Sabha.

To add to the woes of the National Front, Chandrashekhar, who was upset as he was ignored for prime ministership in favour of V.P. Singh, walked out of the parent JD along with the JD state chief ministers in Uttar Pradesh, Haryana and Gujarat and formed a separate party, the Samajwadi Janata Party (SJP). With the support of the Congress, Chandrashekhar formed a minority government. The SJP government in New Delhi resigned in early March 1991 (but continued as the caretaker government until mid-term elections in May-June), following the Congress boycott of the parliamentary session for several days in protest against the detection of two Haryana constables supposedly spying at the residence of Rajiv Gandhi.

The mid-term elections in 1991 were held in two phases—in May and June—separated by almost a month due to the assassination of Rajiv Gandhi. In Punjab, due to terrorist violence, polls were postponed and rescheduled for February 1992. The Tenth Lok Sabha, like its predecessor, also remained a Hung Parliament with no possibility of one-party government. The Congress regained plurality both in terms of votes and seats, and unlike its reluctance in 1989 to stake its claim to form the government as the largest single party, it promptly went ahead and formed a minority government headed by the veteran P.V. Narasimha Rao. The percentage of the Congress vote dropped but its seat share increased; but for Rajiv Gandhi's assassination and the consequent tremors of sympathy, the Congress vote would have probably dropped to lower levels, as 'between the two phases of polling, there was a swing in favour of the Congress varying between 3.5 and 11.9 percentage points'.[65]

The Congress government led by Rao happened to be the only government since 1989 to have completed its full mandated term of five years—half of it as a one-party minority government supported from the parliamentary floor by the heterogeneous assortment of opposition majority, and half of it as a one-party majority government made possible by an accretion of parliamentary support through splits and mergers in parties, the electoral success of the Congress in Punjab elections, and bribing of Jharkhand Mukti Morcha (JMM) MPs to buy their support in the confidence vote in the Lok Sabha.

The most important event of the Rao administration was a turnaround in the economy following the introduction of a major phase of economic liberalization premised on bureaucratic decontrol and partial disinvestment of public sector undertakings. This shift in economic policy considerably freed the private sector as well as state governments from the kind of centralized bureaucratic control that existed in the past. On the other hand, his government incurred the displeasure of the Muslim minority throughout the country consequent upon the demolition of the Babri Masjid in Ayodhya by a frenzied mob of Hindu fanatics in the BJP-ruled state of Uttar Pradesh on 6 December 1992. The event terminated the Congress honeymoon with the BJP opposition in Parliament. The Rao government promptly dismissed the BJP governments in Uttar Pradesh, Madhya Pradesh, Rajasthan and Himachal Pradesh. The proclamation of President's Rule in these states (along with some earlier cases in other states) came to be adjudicated by the Supreme Court, which delivered its momentous judgement in *S.R. Bommai* vs *Union of India* in 1994. While the Supreme Court validated the dismissal of the BJP governments under Article 356 of the Constitution, the proclamation in some earlier instances in other states was for the first time judicially reviewed and declared unconstitutional. This judgement greatly strengthened the federal autonomy of state governments.

As far as Rao's position in his own party during his tenure in the government is concerned, it may be mentioned that the sailing was not very smooth for him as he faced a stiff challenge from the loyalists of the Nehru–Gandhi dynasty and some senior party leaders. To silence them and to consolidate his position, Rao went through the motions of organizational elections in his party in 1992. Backed by the power enjoyed by him by virtue of his being the prime minister, the meek inheritor gradually revealed a Kautilyan shrewdness in weeding out challenges within the party and manipulating splits in the ranks of the opposition.[66]

The 1996 Lok Sabha elections witnessed the emergence of the BJP as the largest single party in another hung Parliament, followed by the Congress and the Janata Dal—in that order. The systemic relevance of some other smaller parties for government formation reached a new critical threshold as anti-Congressism of yore was supplemented by anti-BJPism. A United Front of over a dozen non-BJP and non-Congress parties came into existence after the elections which formed a minority government led by H.D. Deve Gowda (JD) in the trail of the failure of the two-week BJP Minority government led by Vajpayee to gain parliamentary allies and thus forcing the latter to resign just before the confidence vote after a valiant, if essentially a campaign, speech on the Parliamentary Floor. The United Front minority government included, among others, the AGP, the TDP, the DMK and the TMC, that split from the Congress just before the elections when the national leadership decided to resume the party's alliance with the All

India Anna Dravida Munnetra Kazhagam (AIADMK) led by Chief Minister Jayalalitha after a period of strained relations between the two parties in disregard of overwhelmingly expressed opposition of the Tamil Nadu unit of the Congress. The four regional parties promptly formed a federal front within the United Front. Another regional party, the National Conference of Jammu & Kashmir, subsequently joined the United Front government following elections in the state and resumption of political processes after nearly a decade-long terrorist violence. The Congress and the CPI(M) extended parliamentary support to the United Front minority government without joining the cabinet. The latter, however, joined the Steering Committee of the Front, while the former was content with an apex committee between the prime minister and the Congress president. Developments in the Congress party did threaten the stability of the United Front government but there was no cause for serious concern. These developments related to the replacement of Rao under the thickening clouds of corruption and criminal charges, first from the leadership of the Congress Parliamentary Party and subsequently from the presidentship of the party. He was replaced by Sitaram Kesri. Following Kesri's appeal to the former Congressmen (who had left the party in protest against the acts of omission and commission by Rao) to come back to the Congress fold, the Madhya Pradesh Vikas Party led by Madhavrao Scindia and the Indira Congress led by Narayan Dutt Tewari and Arjun Singh in Uttar Pradesh and Madhya Pradesh respectively, rejoined the parent party. This did not, however, affect the stability of the United Front government.

The United Front handled its internal policy and regional differences reasonably well. Neither the Cauvery water dispute between Karnataka and Tamil Nadu nor the Alamatty Dam dispute between Karnataka and Andhra Pradesh proved to be unsettling for the Front. Similarly, the perceptibly left leaning policy options of the Communist Parties in the Front on the issues of economic and media policies were consensually accommodated by a process of give and take through the meditation of the Steering Committee. However, the Front's relationship with the Congress became more unsteady. In the spring of 1995, the Congress appeared to be keen to replace the

United Front government by a government of its own, in coalition with a different set of like-minded allies. Having failed in the gambit, it sought a face-saving device in dictating the change in the leadership of the United Front from H.D. Deve Gowda to I.K. Gujral (both from the JD) on the plea of the insensitivity of the former to the interests and perceptions of the Congress. The fate of the United Front hung in balance in November 1997 in the wake of the leaked Jain Commission inquiry interim report on Rajiv Gandhi's assassination. The Congress insisted on the removal of the indicted DMK government from the Front. The Front, however, remained firm in its support to the DMK ministers and its ties with the ruling party in Tamil Nadu. Gujral finally resigned at the end of November and refused to yield to the pressure of the Congress.

The 1998 mid-term Lok Sabha elections took place in the backdrop of continuing governmental instability and the trend of party system fragmentation. One of the most notable features—in some ways new—in the heat of the pre-election politicking was the most complex patterns of inter-party alliances in 1998 that often varied in crazy quilt patchworks at the national and state levels. The BJP allies included the TDP (Lakshmiparvathi) in Andhra Pradesh; the Samata Party in Bihar; the Haryana Vikas Party in Haryana; the Lok Shakti in Karnataka; the Shiv Sena in Maharashtra; the Biju Janata Dal in Orissa; the Shiromani Akali Dal (B) and the Bahujan Samaj Party in Punjab; the AIADMK, the MDMK, the JP, the PMK and the Rajiv Tamil Nadu Congress in Tamil Nadu; the Samata Party and the BSP(J) in Uttar Pradesh; and the Trinamool Congress in West Bengal. The Congress alliance consisted of the UMF in Assam; the Rashtriya Janata Dal, the Jharkhand Mukti Morcha, the RJP and the Samajwadi Janata Party in Bihar; the UDF including the IUML and the Kerala Congress (M) in Kerala; the RPI and the Samajwadi Party in Maharashtra; the BSP and the CPI in Punjab; the BKPP in Uttar Pradesh, and the SFB and Jharkhand Party in West Bengal. The United Front allies comprised the TDP, the CPI, the CPI(M) and the Janata Dal in Andhra Pradesh; the Asom Gana Parishad, the CPI, the CPI(M) and the JD in Assam; the JD, the CPI and the CPM in Bihar; the HLD(R) and the BSP in Haryana; the JD and the CPI(M) in Karnataka; the CPI(M), the CPI, the JD, the RSP, the Congress (S), the Kerala Congress (J) together forming the LDF in Kerala; the JD, the CPI, the CPI(M), the PWP and the Bhartiya Panther Party in Maharashtra; the JD, the CPI and the CPI(M) in Orissa; the CPI(M) in Punjab; the DMK, the TMC and the CPI in Tamil Nadu; the Samajwadi Party in UP; and the CPI(M), the CPI, the FBL and the RSP forming the Left Front in West Bengal. Most of these smaller parties were negligibly marginal, further aggravating the extreme fragmentation of the party system in 1998.

The fragmentation and atomization of the party system after the 1998 mid-term polls is evident from a broadly tripartite configuration of parliamentary parties into the BJP and its allies (consisting of seventeen parties), the Congress and its allies (consisting of seven parties), and the United Front (an assortment of eight parties). Encircling these configurations was a marginal halo of eight unattached parties plus five independents, four of whom defected to the post-poll alliance with the BJP. The two parties of major pluralities stood at 179 (BJP) and 140 (Congress-I), while the decisive magic figure in the House of 543 in which elections were held for 539 seats happened to be 272. The Janata Dal—the third major party of plurality in the previous elections—this time with only six seats, trailed behind its erstwhile junior partners in the United Front—the TDP, the CPI(M) and the Samajwadi Party (SP).

The regional spread of the three major groups of parties clearly reflected the dispersal and fragmentation of the party system. The BJP and allies had over 40 per cent of votes in only eight states and 40 per cent of seats in ten states. A comparable position was held by the Congress and its allies in eight states in terms of percentage of votes and in seven states in terms of percentage of seats. The corresponding figures for the United Front were three states (percentage of votes) and four states (percentage of seats).

The post-poll allies to join the BJP alliance were the TDP (Naidu), the National Conference, the Haryana Lok Dal (R) and the Arunachal Congress. Out of seventeen parties and four independents in the alliance, only ten parties and three independents had joined the government. The Trinamool Congress, the TDP, the HVP, the MDMK, the JP, the National Conference and the Haryana Lok Dal (R) decided to extend outside support to the government from the Parliamentary Floor without joining the Council of Ministers.

The BJP-led coalition government was constantly under pressure from its regional allies like Jayalalitha of the AIADMK, Mamta Banerjee of the Trinamool Congress and the relatively more reasonable Samata Party led by Nitish Kumar and George Fernandes. All of them clamoured for the dismissal (by the centre) of their regional adversaries, namely, the DMK government in Tamil Nadu, the Left Front government in West Bengal and the RJD government in Bihar. Thanks to the *Bommai judgement* of the Supreme Court, the centre desisted from intervention under Article 356. Finally, Jayalalitha dramatically withdrew the AIADMK's support to the coalition government on 17 April 1999 after months of lobbying for the reinstatement of Admiral Vishnu Bhagwat—earlier sacked by the government for allegedly defying the principle of Cabinet control of the armed forces. Her real grudge, however, was the reluctance of the government to slow down judicial proceedings in corruption cases against her.

The 1999 mid-term elections were delayed by a few months due to the Kargil war during which the Vajpayee government continued in a caretaker capacity. The electoral campaign as well as the outcome of the 1999 elections marked the continuity with federal coalitional governance within the framework of a multiparty system that emerged in 1989. The electoral arena remained divided but instead of a tripartite configuration, there was a trend towards bipolar concentration of political forces between the NDA led by the BJP and the Congress-led alliance. The Third Force did not carry much weight due to fragmentation and decimation of the Janata Dal. The fourteen-party BJP-led alliance at the time of elections maintained its cohesion reasonably well despite the fall of its government. The loss suffered by the NDA due to the withdrawal of support by the AIADMK was made good by its main rival in Tamil Nadu politics—the DMK—that joined it. The NDA had the support of major regional parties like the National Conference, the Akali Dal (Badal), the Indian National Lok Dal, the Trinamool Congress, the Samata Party, the Biju Janata Dal and the Janata Dal (United) that comprised the J.H. Patel and the Sharad Yadav factions as also the Lok Shakti of R.K. Hegde. The six-party Congress-led alliance included, among others, two major regional parties—the AIADMK and the RJD. The so-called Third Force in 1999 was a misnomer inasmuch as it was a divided lot. The National Front, the Federal Front, the Rashtriya Loktantrik Morcha had all by now disintegrated and passed into oblivion. The only surviving front was the Left Front consisting of five parties, led by the CPI(M). On the eve of elections, the Congress suffered a major split that resulted in the formation of the National Congress Party (NCP) led by Sharad Pawar, P.A. Sangma and Tariq Anwar. A belated attempt to unite the Third Force was made by the NCP and the Samajwadi Party led by Mulayam Singh Yadav but to no effect. Pawar and Yadav, besides bringing their parties closer, also tried to form a common front with some other like-minded parties including the left parties and the RJD. However, the exercise of reviving a Third Front of non-BJP and non-Congress parties proved to be a futile one.

The electoral outcome in 1999 marked a continuity as well as a departure from the political patterns established in 1998. The continuity related to the return to power of a right-centrist coalition led by the BJP. The departure was that for the first time in the decade, a coalition government was voted to power that was no longer dependent on support from 'outside'. All the coalition partners joined the Cabinet with the exception of the TDP whose representative (G.M.G. Balayogi) became the Speaker of the Lok Sabha. In the previous governments, the division of its supporters between an Executive or Cabinet coalition and a Legislative coalition had proved to be the most destabilizing factor. This gain was bargained by the BJP by accommodating its regional allies even at the cost of remaining content with maintaining its parliamentary seats at the same level as in the previous house.

The NDA government was the first coalitional dispensation to have completed a full five-year term. Anticipating electoral victory on the basis of this remarkable success, it called a snap election more than six months ahead of schedule which proved to be a miscalculation. The Congress and its allies fared unexpectedly well on account of an electoral realignment by virtue of which it managed to regain the votes of Muslims, the Scheduled Castes and the Scheduled Tribes. In most of the regions, though not in all states, they emerged victorious. In these polls, the Communist parties also registered their best electoral performance since 1952, presumably because of the adverse effects of privatization and globalization of the economy. In the aftermath of the 2004 elections, the Congress (and its pre-poll allies) and the Communist parties formed the United Progressive Alliance and its government with the outside support of the Left. The formation of government signalled an ideological shift in the sense that the UPA formed a left of centre coalition replacing the previous right of centre coalition led by the BJP. The continuation of coalitional governance with persisting importance of some regional parties has maintained the federal tenor of Indian politics. However, in contrast to the NDA, not only the leading party, the Indian National Congress, but also its most sizeable ally, the CPI(M), is a national rather than a regional party.[67]

To sum up, the Indian federation has gradually evolved from the feudal and colonial phases of history to a parliamentary federal political system under the 1950 Constitution. The working of the system has gradually become more federal under the impact of growing politicization in society, regionalization of the party system, the belated judicial activism favouring state autonomy, and the liberalization of the economy in the 1990s. Under the cumulative impact of these causal factors, a new institutional functioning has become possible which is reflected in greater autonomy of state governments, the President and Governors. This effect is reflected in more autonomous constitutional mechanisms like the Election Commission, and the Finance Commission, as also the growing salience of the Inter-State Council (ISC) and the National Development Council (NDC).

NOTES

1. Romila Thapar, *A History of India*, vol. 1, Harmondsworth: Penguin, 1966, p. 82.
2. Ibid., pp. 80-1.
3. V.R. Dikshitar, *Mauryan Polity*, Madras: University of Madras, 1932.
4. J.C. Heesterman, *The Inner Conflict of Tradition: Essays in Indian Ritual, Kingship, and Society*, Delhi: OUP, 1985.
5. Romila Thapar, *Asoka and the Decline of the Mauryas*, Delhi: Oxford University Press, 1997, R.S. Sharma, *Aspects of Political Ideas and*

Institutions in Ancient India, Delhi: Motilal Banarsidass, 3rd revd. edn., 1991, Chap. XXIII.
6. Hermann Kulke, ed., *The State in India 1000-1700*, Delhi: Oxford University Press, 1995, p. 7, fn. 6.
7. Thapar, *A History of India*, op. cit., p. 242.
8. John F. Richards, *The Mughal Empire: The New Cambridge History of India*, Delhi: Foundation Books, 1993, p. 58.
9. Ibid., p. 59.
10. M.P. Singh, 'Indian State: Historical Context and Change', *The Indian Historical Review*, vol. XXI, nos. 1-2, January 1995, p. 52.
11. K.R. Bombwall, *Foundations of Indian Federalism*, Bombay: Asia Publishing House, 1967, p. 38.
12. Ibid., pp. 68-9.
13. M.V. Pylee, *Constitutional History of India (1600-1950)*, Delhi: S. Chand, 1984, p. 43.
14. Bombwall, *Foundations of Indian Federalism*, op. cit., p. 120.
15. Granville Austin, *The Indian Constitution: Cornerstone of a Nation*, Bombay: Oxford University Press, 1966, p. 190.
16. Pylee, *Constitutional History of India (1600-1950)*, op. cit., p. 82.
17. Meera Verma, Mrinal Mehta and Rumki Basu, eds., *Essays on Indian Government and Politics: A Continuing Review*, Delhi: Jawahar, 1999, p. 13.
18. V.P. Menon, *The Transfer of Power in India*, Bombay: Orient Longman, 1957, pp. 116-17.
19. Maurice Gwyer and A. Appadorai, eds., *Speeches and Documents on the Indian Constitution 1921-27*, vol. 2, London: Oxford University Press, 1957, pp. 521-32.
20. Menon, *The Transfer of Power in India*, op. cit., p. 124.
21. Pylee, *Constitutional History of India (1600-1950)*, op. cit., pp. 114-15.
22. *Constituent Assembly Debates (CAD)*, Book 1, vols. I-VI, 9 December 1946 to 27 January 1948, New Delhi: Lok Sabha Secretariat, 3rd rpt, 1999, pp. 366-7.
23. Ibid., p. 59.
24. B. Shiva Rao, ed., *The Framing of India's Constitution: Select Document*, New Delhi: Indian Institute of Public Administration, 1967, vol. 2, p. 553.
25. *CAD*, Book 2, vol. VII, 4 November 1948 to 8 January 1949, pp. 36-7.
26. Ibid., p. 372.
27. Shiva Rao, ed., *The Framing of India's Constitution: Select Document*, op. cit., vol. 2, Clause 3, p. 534.
28. *CAD*, Book 2, vol. VII, p. 241.
29. Ibid., p. 330.

30. *CAD*, Book 5, vols. X-XII, 6 October 1949 to 24 January 1950, p. 844.
31. Ibid., p. 613.
32. Granville Austin, *Working a Democratic Constitution: The Indian Experience*, Delhi: Oxford University Press, 1999, p. 560.
33. Paul R. Brass, 'The Strong State and the Fear of Disorder', paper presented at the conference on Democracy and Transformation: India Fifty Years After Independence, sponsored by UPIASI, New Delhi, 16-19 November 1997, p. 2.
34. Ibid., p. 3.
35. George Mathew, 'India: Republic of India', *The federal Idea*, Centre for Policy Alternatives and the Forum of Federations with the support of the Canadian International Development Agency and Foreign Affairs Canada, Browns Beach Hotel, Negombo, 3-5 April 2005, p. 53.
36. Rekha Saxena, 'Indian Model of Federalism', *The Federal Idea*, Centre for Policy Alternatives and the Forum of Federations with the support of the Canadian Development Agency—Foreign Affairs Canada, Browns Beach Hotel, Negombo, 3-5 April 2005, pp. 36-7.
37. *CAD*, Book 2, vol. VII, p. 33.
38. Ibid., p. 32.
39. *CAD*, Book 2, vol. VII, pp. 1195-1231.
40. K.N. Kabra, 'Towards a Participative Union-State Relations', *Mainstream*, 27 January 1996, p. 34.
41. M.P. Singh, 'Federal Division of Responsibilities in India', *Indian Journal of Federal Studies*, vol. 1, January 2004, pp. 109-11.
42. *S.R. Bommai* vs *Union of India and others, All India Reporter*, Supreme Court Section, 1994.
43. Ansal Ray, *Tension Areas in India's Federal System*, Calcutta: World Press, 1970, p. 84.
44. *Commission on Centre-State Relations, Report*, Nasik: Government of India Press, 1987-8, Part I, Chap. V, p. 122.
45. Ibid., pp. 135-7.
46. Ministry of Home Affairs, *Administrative Reforms Commission Centre-State Relations*, New Delhi: Ministry of Home Affairs, 1969, p. 36.
47. Ibid.
48. K. Mathew Kurian and P.N. Verghese, eds., *Centre-State Relations*, Delhi: Macmillan India Ltd., 1981, pp. 17-18.
49. Kurian, 'Financial Relations in Federal Set-up', in Mathew Kurian and P.N. Verghese, ibid., p. 131.
50. K.A. Ramasubramaniam, 'State Autonomy and National Integration', in *Centre-State Relations in India*, ed. Bidyut Chakrabarty, Delhi: Segment Book Distributors, 1990, pp. 78-9.
51. Information obtained from the Rural Development Division, Planning Commission, New Delhi, August 2001.

52. Government of India, Planning Commission, *Annual Report 2000-2001*, New Delhi: Yojna Bhawan, 2001, p. 21.
53. *Commission on Centre-State Relations, Report, Part I*, Chap. 10, pp. 315-18.
54. Ibid., p. 285.
55. K.N. Kabra, 'Federating the Planning Commission', *The Hindu*, 2 July 1996.
56. Ministry of Finance, Government of India, *First Report of the Ninth Finance Commission (for 1989-90)*, New Delhi: Ministry of Finance Press, July 1988, p. 29.
57. *Asian Recorder*, vol. XXXVIII, no. 4, 22-28 January 1992, pp. 22113-14.
58. Ministry of Finance, Government of India, *Report of the Tenth Finance Commission (For 1995-2000)*, New Delhi: Ministry of Finance Press, 2000.
59. M. Govinda Rao, 'Incentivising Fiscal Transfers in the Indian Federation', *Publics*, vol. 33, no. 4, Fall 2003.
60. Ministry of Finance, Government of India, *Report of the Eleventh Finance Commission (For 2000-2005)*, New Delhi: Ministry of Finance Press, 1994, Chap. III.
61. V. Sridhar, 'Short-Changing the States', *Frontline*, 8 April 2005, pp. 34-5.
62. *Report of the National Commission to Review the Working of the Constitution*, NCRWC, 2002, 159, Para 8.13.3, Chap. 11.
63. M.V. Pylee, *Constitutional Amendments in India*, Delhi: Universal Law Publishing Co., 2003.
64. For details, see M.P. Singh and Rekha Saxena, *India at Polls: Parliamentary Elections in the Federal Phase*, Delhi: Orient Longman, 2003.
65. Abhijit Sen and C.P. Chandra Shekhar, 'Election Analysis: Verdict '91', *Frontline* (Madras), vol. VIII, no. 14, 6-19 July 1991, p. 106.
66. Rekha Saxena, 'Against All Odds', *The Pioneer*, 9 April 1996.
67. On 2004 elections, see, Lawrence Saez and Rekha Saxena, 'Mandate 2004', *Mainstream*, Annual No., Jan. 2005; and M.P. Singh and Rekha Saxena, 'Lok Sabha Elections 2004: Change with Continuity', *Think India*, vol. 8, no. 1, Jan.-March 2005.

CHAPTER 5

Major Intergovernmental and Central Mechanisms in the Two Federations

Federal–provincial relations in Canada and union–state relations in India have over the years expanded into a sprawling network of organizations and mechanisms. An important feature of this structural growth is that they largely developed outside the framework of the Constitution, or were barely mentioned therein or were subsequently referred to in passing. For instance, the First Ministers' Conference, which has become the most important apex intergovernmental forum in Canada, was first mentioned in the Constitution in 1982, notwithstanding the fact that the first meeting was convened as early as in 1906. Similarly, the Inter-State Council (ISC) was provided for in the Indian Constitution since the beginning but it was only constituted in 1990. The convening of ministerial and official level intergovernmental meetings on a regular basis in both countries is neither mentioned in the Constitution nor in any parliamentary enactments. Yet, at these conferences significant federal–provincial or union–state negotiations or decisions are made.

The mechanisms that underlie the two federations may be classified into four categories on the basis of the insightful conceptualization of David Cameron:[1]

1. Intra-jurisdictional Intergovernmental Relations (IGR).
2. Inter-jurisdictional Intergovernmental Relations (IGR).
3. The Role of judiciary in IGR.
4. International and other forms of IGR in the context of the growing impact of global and regional economic integration on federal systems.

The most common example of an Intra-jurisdictional IGR is a Federal Second Chamber if it is so designed that the regions are brought under the domain of Federal Parliament. The Canadian Senate is deficient in this representative function as the Senate, even though notionally representing the provinces, is unilaterally appointed by the federal government of the day as a patronage to party faithfuls. The Indian Rajya Sabha has better federal representative credentials as its members are elected by members of the state legislature. Inter-jurisdictional IGR mechanisms may be of two types: (*a*) those that bring some or all regional units and the central government on a common forum; and (*b*) those that bring only some or all regional units on a common forum in the absence of the central government. These are the most common mechanisms of what Canadians call 'Executive Federalism'[2] (the term is applicable to India as well) and are illustrated by the FMC, ministerial and deputy ministerial conferences in Canada and the National Development Council (NDC), the Inter-State Council (ISC), conferences of the Prime Minister and Chief Ministers, Speakers and Presiding Officers, President and Governors, Ministers and Secretaries in India.[3] Only the ISC is a formal intergovernmental mechanism in the sense that it is established by a Presidential Order under Article 263 of the Constitution. The FMC is only partly so because it is now mentioned in passing in the Constitution Act, 1982 in the amending formula. The other mechanisms in both countries are informal in the sense that they are set up explicitly under a constitutional provision by an Executive Order or an Act of Parliament. However, it must be added that these mechanisms have become fairly institutionalized both in convention and practice.

Approaching the court to resolve an intergovernmental dispute is the last resort. Cameron aptly remarked 'The effect of judicial interpretation can be significant and long-lasting, which is why, in areas of genuine ambiguity, one often finds among the participants a mutual disinclination to force the matter to a court-imposed conclusion.'[4] Judicial recourse in this regard is far more frequent in India than in Canada. The most striking instances of international ramifications of IGR are the North American Free Trade Agreement (NAFTA) in Canada and the South Asian Association for Regional Cooperation (SAARC) in India and the World Trade Organization (WTO) in both countries.

Moreover, India has a forum, the National Integration Council, created by Jawaharlal Nehru, in the backdrop of the Chinese aggression in 1962 which goes beyond intergovernmental scope and encompasses non-governmental mechanisms like newspaper editors, vice-chancellors and important personalities from all walks of life.

Since Canada and India have successfully adapted the parliamentary federal model into their political systems, Executive Federalism emerges in both countries as the dominant mode of intergovernmental relations. An attempt has been made here to present the entire gamut of Executive Federalism in Canada and India. The intent is not to offer an exhaustive analysis of the working of these mechanisms but to present an illustrative discussion on the basis of some of their past and more recent meetings, mostly the latter. It may be noted that there are some mechanisms in both countries that are exclusively central in organization but have significant implications for provincial/state governments.

INTERGOVERNMENTAL EXECUTIVE RELATIONS IN CANADA

Canada is a country marked by subcontinental cultural complexity and diversity. This characteristic of Canadian society necessitated that a system of government, that could simultaneously fulfil the motivations and needs of a very diverse set of political elites in Canada and the imperial metropolis in London, be devised. The Canadian political leadership had to frame a Constitution that could take into account the competing regional interests, the emergent national interests, as well as the imperial interests. This balancing act had to constantly be on guard in view of the pressures from the newly established American republic to the south of the Canadian border. The nature of the BNA Act cannot be adequately explained without reference to this complex internal and external context. The founding fathers of the confederation framed a Constitution that was essentially parliamentary in character but added a federal feature almost as an afterthought. The Constitution was to be, as Hamish Telford aptly put it, 'federal if necessary, but not necessarily federal'.[5]

In contrast to the US, Canada is not a revolutionary polity with a ringing declaration of abstract ideals. In the overall milieu of continuity and conservatism of the classical British parliamentary tradition, the two elements that moved hesitantly and grudgingly towards some sort of novelty were federalism and extension of social rights and economic securities. Of these two, federalism was a subsidiary founding myth that has tended to grow over a period of time. As Porter observed:

> The one aspect of Canadian political structure which has received more attention than any other from historians, political scientists, and constitutional lawyers is the federal system. All the rationalizing on the part of royal commissions, politicians, and judges in Canada and the United Kingdom that has gone into constructing theories of Canadian federalism provides an unlimited field for scholarly activity.[6]

The federal feature of the Canadian Constitution was intended to correspond to the distinct cultural identities and the vertical mosaic that Canada contains within its bosom. Cultural diversities, political processes and judicial interpretations have all united to make the Canadian political system more sensitive to the federal features of Canadian society. Federalism and national unity are Canada's dominant obsessions that have been used to promote or hinder all sorts of interests and ideas, actions or inactions. To quote Porter, 'When Canadian politicians make pronouncements about Canadian federalism it is difficult to tell whether they are prisoners of a social mentality about federalism, or whether, in a Machiavellian fashion, they are using federalism as an instrument of power or as an excuse not to exercise power.'[7]

The Canadian Constitution was drafted in the era of classical federalism that believed in some sort of dual sovereignty. Therefore, the BNA Act did not make any formal provision for an intergovernmental mechanism. Moreover, there was much less emphasis on intergovernmental relations.

Despite all efforts at avoiding ambiguity while drafting a constitution, it is not possible to have a clear-cut demarcation (of jurisdictions) in terms of exclusive federal and provincial jurisdictions. In other words, there can be no watertight compartments. Some degree of interdependence between the two levels of government is inevitable.

Another reason why the need for intergovernmental mechanisms was felt was the emergence of new policy areas which had no relevance at the time when the Constitution was drafted. For example, no one at that time had any inkling about the kind of environmental and energy policies that would have to be tackled in the future. As Stevenson aptly demonstrated, way back in the 1870s and the 1880s, the need for intergovernmental mechanisms had already been felt in Canada.[8]

Forums that bring together the top political executives or bureaucrats from the two levels of government in Canada have been referred to by Canadian political scientists as an exercise in 'Executive Federalism'. In Canada, forums of 'Executive Federalism' are more important than those of 'Legislative Federalism' via the Senate. Given the weak position of the Senate in constitutional and representative terms, legislative federalism is much more efficacious in Germany and the USA.

Executive federalism in Canada is practised in different types of forums. Watts listed the following illustrations of this kind of intergovernmental relations: first, formal meetings can involve a diverse rank of officials such as meetings of First Ministers, Cabinet Ministers, Deputy Ministers, and other less senior appointed officials. Second, the meetings vary according to the scope of representation—federal–provincial involving leaders of eleven governments; federal–provincial–territorial consisting of leaders of thirteen governments; federal–provincial–territorial plus aboriginal peoples including leaders of the four major pan-Canadian aboriginal organizations; interprovincial meetings alone; federal and some, but not all, provinces/territories; and interprovincial–regional involving some, but not all, provinces on a regional basis.[9]

Among the forums mentioned earlier, the most significant mechanism of intergovernmental relations at the apex of the Canadian political system is the First Ministers' Conference. Launched almost forty years after the founding of the Federation, it has today become an indispensable organization, by virtue of having acquired some degree of institutionalization and finding a passing reference in the Constitution. This, however, does not suggest that this forum is the most frequently used one. Other intergovernmental mechanisms below this level hold meetings more regularly where much of the groundwork for negotiations and policy harmonization is done. According to some observers, the ministerial and deputy ministerial/official meetings are the ones at which substantive work is done for formal acceptance and announcement by the first ministers. Each of these major forums is discussed here.

First Ministers' Conferences

In a Parliamentary Federal system like the one in Canada, the requirement for intergovernmental relations is fulfilled by the executive organ of the government. Therefore, the prime minister and premiers in Canada inevitably became the natural forum for intergovernmental relations. The First Ministers' Conferences have two aims. First, when there is a growing political momentum on some issue on which the two levels of government need to work together, the item is put on the agenda of the FMCs. Second, the forum is used to finalize, confirm and announce decisions made on particular issues on the basis of work already done by ministers and senior officials; the first ministers are, therefore, instrumental in framing the items of agenda and confirming the final decisions. This forum is responsive to the needs of new situations and is useful not only at times when the federal and provincial governments are unanimous in their agreement, but also when they differ on a particular issue. It also plays a significant role in the formulation of policies.

In recent years, the FMCs have declined in frequency. First, they are convened only when a decision has to be taken on major issues such as the signing of the Meech Lake and Charlottetown Accords on constitutional reforms. Second, the FMCs project the image of premiers as decision makers at the national level. This is something that Chretien, the former liberal prime minister, did not want to encourage. (By implication, the federal government would concede the provincial governments the status of equal partners only when they cannot do without such meetings due to constitutional provisions.) But the best ongoing intergovernmental process takes place at a level below that of the FMCs, i.e. at the ministerial level. Meetings at this level are held on a more regular basis—annually—with common items of agenda concerning both governments. They have been more productive than the FMCs in sheer magnitude of their coordinated policy outputs.[10]

Apart from federal–provincial intergovernmental meetings, another forum of interprovincial relations (excluding the federal government) of considerable importance is the Provincial Premiers' Conference (PPC). Meetings of the PPCs have become a more regular phenomenon than even the FMCs in recent years when the provincial inputs into federal processes and policies have increased. The PPC is held on a fixed date in August every year. Considerable time is available for deciding on the items to be included in the agenda and preparing the background papers. Since 1995, it has tended to rare more substance than being merely a show. Premiers have developed a Pan-Canadian vision as is evident from the fact that they prepared an important report on social policies which became the precursor of the Social Union Framework Agreement of 1999. This is one example where a policy or programme proposed by provinces became an important federal programme.[11] In Crouchene's assessment, the PPCs—which have become an important forum for the representation of provincial perspectives—are doing much better than the FMCs. In some ways, a comparison can be drawn between the PPCs and the German Second Chamber in which are included the povincial Chancellors. The difference, of course, is that the PPCs operate at an informal level, devoid of any legal status, while the German Bundesrat is a constitutional body.[12]

Ministerial Meetings

A variety of federal–provincial conferences are held at the ministerial level. Most federal portfolios have a corresponding portfolio at the provincial level and the ministers occupying these offices meet at regular intervals, at least once a year. Ministers of agriculture also meet every year to define federal and provincial roles and exchange ideas in view of the fact that agriculture is a concurrent subject under the Constitution. Discussing the importance of these meetings, David Cameron noted, 'these workhorses of the system now operate in fields such as social policy renewal, forestry, transportation, education, and the environment'.[13]

A recent development was the convening of tri-level conferences involving the federal government, provinces and municipalities, but this was later scrapped. These conferences were sponsored by the National Ministry of State for Urban Affairs (MSUA) which was created in 1971 and disbanded seven years later.[14]

The MSUA and the federation of Mayors and municipalities were more enthusiastic about these tri-level conferences than the provincial governments. The first such conference was held in November 1972 during the course of which the participants agreed to convene further meetings but rejected the idea of setting up a tri-level secretariat. The second meeting commissioned a study of the financing of all three levels of government; however, the third planned meeting never took place.[15] Though formal and informal contacts between the provinces and their municipalities have continued, yet tri-level conferences have become less frequent because of the strong assertion of their statutory prerogatives in this area by the provincial governments.

Sectoral meetings of ministers, deputy ministers, senior appointed officials and other not so senior appointed officials—assistant deputy ministers and directors-general of ministries—began in the 1960s and have continued ever since. The aim of some of these meetings is purely to exchange information (for example, the meetings of federal–provincial statisticians), while others have become an ongoing review process. Yet others have become part of a hierarchical decision-making process. For instance, if the first ministers have to negotiate new fiscal arrangements, meetings are held at the level of officials, the decisions of which are reported in the meetings held at the deputy ministerial level. These in turn provide the basis for the ministerial meetings which finally prepare reports for presentation to the first ministers.[16]

Meetings of the Deputy Ministers/Officials

Below the ministerial level, therefore, there are a set of administrative committees involving officials from the two orders of government. According to Richard Simeon, the 'greatest number of conferences—about 90 per cent—take place at the official level. Most are concerned with relatively minor technical coordination, but some play a vital role in negotiations on broader policy areas'.[17] Illustrating the significance of officials' meetings, Simeon cited the example of the role played by the Continuing Committee on Fiscal and Economic Matters in financial negotiations.[18] These committees have registered tremendous growth—both in terms of numbers and role played—with the expansion of shared policy areas of governments and it is difficult to categorize them. While some of the committees are constituted formally and meet at regular intervals, others are set up on an ad hoc basis (as and when needed) and are not permanent consultative bodies.[19] Most of these committees are concerned with technical co-ordination of shared-cost programmes. They involve public servants at times for policy formulation, monitoring and adjustment of continuing programmes and the exchange of technical information. The Continuing Committee on Fiscal and Economic Matters consisting of deputy ministers plays an important role by undertaking studies on behalf of the Ministers of Finance.[20] Langford listed more than thirty federal–provincial committees in transportation and almost the same number for agriculture.[21]

The Constitutional Conference set up a Continuing Committee of officials to do preparatory work for the first ministers. In 1968, it met four times and each meeting lasted 2 to 3 days; the main aim of these meetings was to discuss the propositions submitted by the various governments. Again in 1969, the federal position papers on taxing and spending powers were first discussed at a Continuing Committee meeting allowing the federal government to make some modifications and the other governments to formulate their respective positions before the June Constitutional Conference.[22]

Interprovincial Conferences: Annual Premiers' Conference (APC)

At the interprovincial level, the most important conference is the APC which can be held independently of the FMC or simultaneously with it, say, a day before. These interprovincial meetings are held both at the political and administrative levels. The APCs have evolved from an occasional get-together to a working meeting. In 1960, Premier Lesage advocated that interprovincial conferences that had been held in the past occasionally be reinstituted on a regular basis. The first such conference was convened in 1887 in Quebec City. The second APC was held in 1902, also in Quebec City. Thereafter, the premiers met thrice in 1910, 1913 and 1926. At the end of the conference in 1926, despite the decision to meet at least once a year, the premiers did not meet for the next thirty-four years. It was in 1960, at the initiative of the Quebec Premier Lesage (who wanted to set up a permanent mechanism for interprovincial relations), that the premiers met in Quebec City where they discussed the objectives and procedures for an ongoing interprovincial conference of premiers, and decided to convene meetings on a regular basis.[23] It would be appropriate to mention here that a federal officer also attends the conference as an observer.

The statement released after the first conference in 1960 stressed that the APC should not be construed as being hostile to Ottawa. Though at the 1887 conference the premiers expressed a desire to solve the problems that existed between the federal and provincial governments, yet at the 1960 conference, they resolved to discuss only 'subjects which are purely provincial and interprovincial in their effects and which would in no way impinge on the area of Federal-Provincial collaboration and action'.[24]

The agenda of these meetings covers a wide variety of issues related to the provinces. For instance,

> in 1966, the agenda included twenty-three items, comprising such matters as regulation of mutual funds and investments, interprovincial competition in incentives to industry, consumer protection legislation, university financing, and uniform legislation for road safety and trucking. Some important legislations including regulation of private pension plans and securities legislation—have largely been the product of interprovincial discussions.[25]

These interprovincial conferences are becoming increasingly important in federal-provincial bargaining. For example, at the 1966 conference the delegates reported a 'frank exchange of views' on equalization, medicare, shared-cost programmes, tax sharing, and other federal–provincial matters. They were unanimous in their opinion that high priority should be accorded to federal assistance in educational financing.[26] At the 1967 and 1968 conferences, delegates discussed the federal medicare proposals and other federal-provincial issues in detail. In 1968, they passed resolutions urging Ottawa to consult the provinces before introducing tax reforms; to reopen financial discussions; and to permit provincial variations in the medicare scheme. Thus, the non-federal–provincial character of interprovincial conferences has somewhat changed.[27]

A review of agendas since 1975 reveals that at least three major issues have dominated these meetings: the economy and economic development; federal–provincial fiscal relations like shared-cost programmes; and issues related to the Constitution. In contrast to the broad themes discussed at the FMCs, the premiers concentrated on more specific issues such as the Young Offenders Act, DREE and grain handling.[28]

In recent years, these conferences have extended beyond the provincial spheres. 'The Annual Premiers' Conference has been used in part by the provinces to prepare their positions and, where possible, a common stance for the federal–provincial FMC.'[29]

Besides the ten premiers, the APC also includes ministers selected by their respective premiers, and senior officials who attend as advisors. Till 1975, government leaders representing particular territories as well as federal officials attended the APC as observers. But this practice has now been discontinued. The agenda of the conference is different every year as each province hosts the conference on a rotation basis. The meeting is chaired by the premier of the host province and he also acts as the spokesman for the premiers in matters of common interest that involve the federal government. Since 1960 the meetings have been held in camera. The premiers, however, issue communiques elaborating on their discussions of the agenda, which is followed by a press conference held by the chairman. Documents relating to the agenda items are coded and circulated to the delegations by the Canadian Intergovernmental Conference Secretariat (CICS), that also provides administrative services to the annual conference.

On 5 December 2003, the APC was formalized at Charlottetown into the Council of Federation by the premiers and territorial leaders aimed at forging strong unity among the federating units on issues of common concern, notably healthcare.

This unity was considered necessary to present a more concerted bargaining posture *vis-à-vis* Ottawa which with its overwhelming fiscal resources and surpluses enjoys enormous clout through its spending power. David McLaughlin, Deputy Minister, Commission on Legislative Democracy in Canada, expects it to 'remain a coordination or meeting organization body rather than a substantive policymaking or lobbying body'.[30] In other words, he expects that the substantive policymaking role would still remain with the First Ministers' Conferences. The objectives of the Council of Federation are promotion of interprovincial–territorial co-operation with the recognition of the diversity within the federation to ultimately strengthen Canada.[31]

Interprovincial ministerial conferences are generally common in almost all important policy areas such as health, agriculture, education, and environment. Among these, two intergovernmental bodies have been incorporated under the federal letters of patent. These are the Council of Ministers of Education Canada (CMEC) and the Canadian Council of Ministers of the Environment (CCME). The former received its letters of patent as a limited not-for-profit company in 1967 and the latter in 1964. The budget of the CCME is shared with the federal government contributing one-third and the remaining two-thirds provided by the provincial government on a pro rata basis in accordance with the population. The council works on the basis of consensus. If there is no consensus, the President can direct that the question be decided by at least a two-thirds vote of the membership. Each member has one vote.[32] For instance, in 1998 the CCME ratified a Canada-wide accord on Environmental Policy Harmonization which called for retention of the existing authorities, improved coordination in assessment, inspection and standards, and improved public reporting on results by all governments.[33]

Interprovincial Regional Meetings

The premiers also meet in regional groupings or bilaterally on a continuous basis. For example, the Council of Maritime Premiers comprising three provinces—Nova Scotia, New Brunswick and Prince Edward Island—was created in 1971 and meets every quarter. The council is actively associated with various economic, social and cultural programmes and coordination of public policies. It is also associated with various institutions like the Higher Education Commission, the Industrial Research Council, a municipal training board, and an energy corporation.[34] It is supported by a small secretariat and has been successful in functional collaboration in areas like regulation of highway transportation.

The Western Premiers' Conference comprising British Columbia, Alberta, Saskatchewan and Manitoba meets less frequently, once a year in spring. It has no bureaucracy of its own and no joint ventures to direct. But,

> it has become increasingly aggressive and successful in promoting regional concerns in relation to national policies. At one point, the Conference established a task force on constitutional trends, which was able to produce a list (the so-called 'Intrusions Report') of 61 intrusions by the Federal Government into provincial jurisdictions.[35]

Another unique supranational regional meeting is the Annual Conference of New England Governors and Eastern Canadian Premiers, bringing together the political leaders of the six New England states (Connecticut, Maine, Massachusetts, New Hampshire, Rhode Island and Vermont) and five eastern Canadian provinces (Nova Scotia, Quebec, New Brunswick, Prince Edward Island and New Foundland). The meeting is held every year in June and the venue alternates between Canada and the US.[36]

Some bilateral negotiations also take place. For instance, when Quebec and Ottawa negotiated a solution to the pension impasse after the Quebec Conference, the other provinces were not included in the negotiations. Likewise, the discussion on Quebec's opting out proposals went a long way before the other provinces were brought in. There was some resentment over the bilateral Quebec–Ottawa negotiations in April 1964, but it died down as the outcome benefited everyone.[37]

A synoptic view of the federal–provincial–territorial conferences of various types held during the 1990s is presented in Table 5.1. It is clear that in terms of sheer frequency of meetings, the federal–provincial–territorial ministers' meetings and the federal–provincial–territorial deputy ministers' meetings far exceed any other category of intergovernmental conferences, the former account for 32.78 per cent and the latter for 36.75 per cent of the

TABLE 5.1: CONFERENCES SERVED BY CICS
FROM 1 JANUARY 1990 TO 31 DECEMBER 1999

Year	*First Ministers (800)*	*FPT Ministers (830)*	*FPT Deputy Ministers (840)*	*Premiers (850)*	*P-T Ministers (860)*	*P-T Deputy Ministers (870)*	*Total*
1 Jan.–31 Dec. 1990	1	26	33	2	14	10	86
1 Jan.–31 Dec. 1991	0	33	20	2	12	8	75
1 Jan.–31 Dec. 1992	3 (2*)	40 (9*)	75 (56*)	4 (2*)	10	5	206
1 Jan.–31 Dec. 1993	1	22	20	3	14	11	71
1 Jan.–31 Dec. 1994	1	32	25	2	11	6	77
1 Jan.–31 Dec. 1995	0	17	16	3	12	3	51
1 Jan.–31 Dec. 1996	1	24	18	3	15	3	64
1 Jan.–31 Dec. 1997	1	24	16	6	17	6	70
1 Jan.–31 Dec. 1998	0	38	35	3	21	5	102
1 Jan.–31 Dec. 1999	1	32	37	4	16	14	104
Total	11 (1.21)	297 (32.78)	333 (36.75)	34 (3.75)	142 (15.67)	71 (7.83)	906

Note: *Number of meetings related to the 1992 Constitutional talks (Canada Round). These numbers are included in the total.

Source: Canadian Inter-Governmental Conference Secretariat, Ottawa.

total meetings. That the First Ministers' Conferences account for only 1.21 per cent of the total is understandable because this apex body specifically meets with the purpose of putting its stamp of approval on the groundwork done by the conferences below this level. Besides, only very important issues get referred to the first ministers. However, what is revealing is that intergovernmental relations below the level of the province do not take place as frequently as one would have expected. For instance, provincial and territorial ministers' meetings account for 15.67 per cent and provincial and territorial deputy ministers' meetings for 7.83 per cent of the total. Moreover, inter-provincial premiers' meetings are more frequent (3.75 per cent) than the first ministers' meetings (1.21 per cent). Provincial premiers meet less frequently than provincial and territorial ministers and provincial and territorial deputy ministers. Thus, the frequency of intergovernmental relations in Canada gravitates at the middle level, that is, federal–provincial decisions are taken by ministers and deputy ministers of the two major orders of government (Federal–Provincial meetings).

Central Mechanisms with Provincial Implications

Besides intergovernmental mechanisms, there are some central mechanisms which have provincial implications. For example, the Privy Council Office, the Treasury Board, the Department of Finance, the Bank of Canada, the Auditor General of Canada, the Solicitor General of Canada, the Royal Canadian Mounted Police (RCMP) and the Canadian Broadcasting Corporation (CBC).

Privy Council Office (PCO): The Privy Council consisting of the present and all former Prime Ministers seldom meets except on formal occasions such as the Queen's visit or centennial celebrations in 1967 when the Queen appointed all the present and former premiers as well to this Council. The PCO works regularly and directly supports the prime minister across the full range of his responsibilities as head of the government. It offers advice on such matters as the broad organization of government, the appointment of individuals to key positions and the mandates of those occupying high offices. It also extends support to the cabinet and its committees which is essential for the preparation for convening meetings. The Privy Council Office is headed by the prime minister who is assisted by the clerk attached to the PCO and secretary to the cabinet. Its membership includes deputy ministers and assistant secretaries to practically all sensitive departments relating to the economy, intelligence and intergovernmental affairs.

Treasury Board: The Treasury Board is a committee of the cabinet established by law and comprises six ministers responsible for the management of government expenditure and human resources in public service. While the Department of Finance is responsible for formulating a general policy on government revenues and expenditures, the Treasury Board oversees the management of the budget and credits. It plays a coordinating role in the preparation of the expenditure budget. According to the Financial Administration Act, the Treasury Board can deal with any question concerning financial management, giving it authority over departmental budgets, expenditure, financial commitments, revenue, accounts, personnel management, and all principles governing the administration of public service.

Department of Finance: This is an important central agency which plays a coordinating role within the decision-making process. It is concerned with all aspects of performance of the Canadian economy. It oversees all government actions affecting the economy to ensure harmony, keeps a watch on external factors having a bearing on domestic economic performance, and examines the actions taken by other orders of government at the economic level.[38] The minister of finance is responsible for the government's macroeconomic policy, including tax policy and tax expenditures. It is through the budget exercise that the minister of finance establishes a fiscal framework within which the government's expenditure management system can operate effectively.

Through close collaboration and coordination the Department of Finance and the Treasury Board Secretariat ensure that the decision-making process is cohesive and effective. These two mechanisms, through the Privy Council Office, counsel the prime minister and cabinet committees on policy related funding issues and the economic impact of proposals placed before the cabinet.

Bank of Canada: In the initial fifty years of the Confederation, Canada evinced little interest in the establishment of a central bank. It was only in 1913 that the subject was tabled in Parliament. The idea was initiated by W.F. MacLean, MP for South York, who called for a privately owned national bank subject to government control. The proposal was dismissed as Prime Minister R.L. Borden saw 'no present necessity' for such a bank. There was hardly any need for central banking in Canada in view of its mainly rural economy up to the Great Depression. Moreover, British influence continued to be reflected in the preference for a limited number of banks with multiple branches. In the years preceding the formation of the Confederation, small rural settlements spread over an extended area made branch banking a viable proposition. This network was sufficient to meet the basic needs of the nation for almost a century. The changed political climate of the early 1930s coupled with the deepening impact of the Great Depression and increasing criticism of the country's financial structure coincided with Prime Minister R.B. Bennett's specific concern over the lack of direct means in Canada for settling international accounts. Consequently, he set up a Royal Commission to study 'the organization and working of our entire banking and monetary system [and] to consider the arguments for or against a central banking institution'.[39] The Commission in its report suggested that the time was appropriate for the establishment of a central bank. The appendix to the report, entitled 'Suggestions as to Some of the Main Features of the Constitution of a Central Bank for Canada', became the framework for the Bank of Canada Act, which received royal assent on 3 July 1934. In March 1935, the Bank of Canada opened its doors as a privately owned institution, with shares sold to the public. Soon the new government introduced an amendment to the Bank of Canada Act, nationalizing the institution. In 1938, the Bank came to be owned by the public and it continues to be so even today.

The organization of the Bank integrated new functions with those that had already existed elsewhere. With the opening of the Bank, banknote operations were transferred from the Department of Finance and the offices of the Receiver General across the country became the agencies of the Bank. The Bank of Canada

Act, which defines the Bank's functions, has been amended many times since 1934. But the Preamble to the Act has remained unaltered. The Bank still exists 'to regulate credit and currency in the best interests of the economic life of the nation'.[40] Above all, it is responsible for the conduct of monetary policy in Canada: issuing banknotes; providing the means of final settlement of cheques and other items of payment cleared daily through financial institutions; and acting as a banker and fiscal agent of the Government of Canada.[41]

The Government of Canada also proposes to amend the Bank of Canada Act so as to specify that the Bank is entrusted with the mandate to achieve and preserve price stability. To ensure regional representation on the Board of Directors of the Bank of Canada, the government intends to solicit the views of provincial and territorial governments and make appointments to the Board after consultation with the former. In addition, it proposes to create regional consultative panels to counsel the directors of the Bank on regional economic conditions. It also intends to solicit the views of provincial and territorial governments with respect to the membership of the regional panels. Moreover, the appointment of the Governor of the Bank of Canada would be subject to Senate ratification.[42]

Auditor General of Canada: The office of the Auditor General provides appropriate audit information for use by the House of Commons in its scrutiny of government programmes and financial activities. The Auditor General is an independent officer of Parliament. He is appointed for a period of ten-years. He has the right to recruit his own staff and set the terms of their employment. The office of the Auditor General has three branches: Audit Operations, Professional and Administrative Services branch and Executive Office. It is the prerogative of the Auditor General to decide as to the type of inquiries and examination that are to be conducted for incorporation in his report to Parliament. The basic function of this office is legislative auditing which includes auditing the public accounts of Canada, of certain Crown corporations and other entities to meet legislative reporting requirements. Apart from this, it also performs some other less important functions.[43]

Solicitor General of Canada: This body lays down the overall policy directions for all programmes of the department and performs review functions related to departmental agencies. The department to which the Solicitor General belongs comprises the Secretariat; the office of the Inspector General of CSIS; four major agencies—the Canadian Security Intelligence Service, the Correctional Service of Canada, the National Parole Board and the Royal Canadian Mounted Police—and two review agencies whose work is directly related to the RCMP, and the office of the Correctional Investigator. Each agency head reports directly to and is accountable to the Solicitor General.[44]

Canadian Broadcasting Corporation (CBC): The Canadian Broadcasting Corporation is the national broadcasting service belonging to all Canadians and accountable to them through Parliament. It is judged by its mandate which is defined in the Broadcasting Act. It enjoys administrative and programming independence in carrying out the duties assigned to it within the Canadian broadcasting system without any political or governmental interference. The Corporation's autonomy is guaranteed through the authority conferred by Parliament upon its Board of Directors who act as Parliament's 'trustees' on behalf of the public to define and guard public interest and to ensure that the CBC's mandate is carried out. 'This principle of "arm's length" relationship between the CBC and government is critical to the Corporation's independence. But there can never be autonomy without responsibility, freedom without restraint.'[45]

The Board of Directors lays down broad corporate objectives and policies so as to ensure that the CBC programming, regardless of language (used for communication) or location, meets the desired standards (as per the stipulations of the Board) which are in consonance with common sense and fundamental journalistic principles.[46] In the process, the broadcaster is also able to carry out his duties without any fear of external pressures.

In the field of broadcasting policy area the Government of Canada proposes to:

1. Consult with the provinces on the issuance of new licences.
2. Provide provincial governments and their agents with the

opportunity to evolve into full public broadcasting undertaking with varied programming, subject to Canadian Radio-television and Telecommunications Commission (CRTC) regulation.
3. Further regionalize the operations of the CRTC and expand the roles of its regional offices.
4. Allow for provincial participation in the nomination of regional commissioners of the CRTC.[47]

While exercising their authority, the prime minister and the cabinet are supported both by line departments and central agencies. These central agencies play a key role in the successful formulation and implementation of government policies and programmes by overseeing interdepartmental mechanisms of information sharing, consultation and coordination. They are expected to provide integrated advice and support to the prime minister and the cabinet on important matters crucial to the interests of the government.

Public Service Commission (PSC): The PSC, a politically independent agency, is responsible for the administration of the Public Service Employment Act. The Commission ensures that recruitment to the public service is done on merit and fairness, without discrimination. In performing its duty to ensure that qualified candidates are appointed, the Public Service Commission reports to Parliament through the Minister of Canadian Heritage. The Public Service Commission consists of a President and two other Commissioners appointed by the Governor-in-Council.

The Commission is exclusively responsible for the recruitment, selection and appointment of qualified persons to and within the public service. In order to meet the personnel needs of government departments and agencies, the Commission conducts active recruitment programmes across Canada. It also takes the initiative in imparting training to the staff and evolving developmental programmes.[48]

An important part of the Privy Council Office (PCO) is the Federal–Provincial Relations Office (FPRO). It has been entrusted the specific responsibility for the coordination of the Government of Canada's policies in the area of intergovernmental affairs. The mandate of the FPRO is extensive and consists of overseeing constitutional reform initiatives, planning for FMCs, monitoring events in different provinces and participating in meetings convened by programme ministries.[49] While the FPRO is the central federal coordinating agency, a number of programme departments also contain units devoted to intergovernmental affairs.

Royal Canadian Mounted Police (RCMP): Yet another central agency impinging on federal–provincial relations is the RCMP. The mounted police force was the brainchild of Sir John A. Macdonald. Eruption of violence consequent upon the westward expansion in the United States led Macdonald to set up a force of mounted police. The rationale underlying this was to establish friendly relations with the aboriginal peoples and to ensure that an atmosphere of peace and harmony prevailed in the wake of arrival of hordes of new settlers. The North-West Mounted Police (NWMP) was organized in 1873 and dispatched west the following year. Its first and foremost task was to purge the area of traders (dealing in whisky) who conducted themselves in a most unbecoming and undignified manner which was against the spirit of the traditional and cultural values of the aboriginal peoples. The force soon adopted the fitting motto 'Maintien le Droit'.[50] In the 1890s, the presence of several hundred mounted policemen succeeded in thwarting the inroad of invaders in the Yukon Territory. The forces ensured the orderly development of the Western Arctic and Arctic Islands and managed to avert disaster by maintaining a constant vigil against the anticipated encroachment by infiltrators from the south and establishing close and cordial relations with the aboriginal peoples.

In 1904, the force was conferred the title 'royal' for its accomplishments by King Edward VII. In 1920, the government extended its jurisdiction across Canada, making it a truly national police force. The new force absorbed the Dominion Police that had enforced federal law in eastern Canada, and was renamed the Royal Canadian Mounted Police. It was vested with the power to maintain law and order (policing) throughout Canada in matters of exclusive federal jurisdiction such as customs and excise, Indian affairs, narcotics, merchant marine, internal security and protection of federal property. Besides, provincial governments which felt the need to supplement their own limited police forces entered into contracts with the federal government. The basic purpose was to entrust the RCMP with the responsibility of maintaining law and order in their respective provincial jurisdictions. Thus, the RCMP also served as a provincial police force in certain respects. Such agreements have been signed by eight Provinces; only Ontario and Quebec maintain their own police forces along with the territorial police in the Yukon and the Northwest Territories, as well as the local police force for about 200 municipalities.[51]

The RCMP may be perceived as an indicator of centralization of police power in Canada, but it is an instance in which certain provinces have voluntarily opted to allow the federal police force to encroach upon their provincial jurisdiction under the Constitution. J.R. Mallory commented that while 'there are great advantages of efficiency and economy' in this federal–provincial cooperation in policing, the apprehension is that these encroachments 'may have gone too far'. Mallory added, '. . . they not only impose a great strain on the resources of the force, but place too much responsibility for law and order in a single federal agency. It is likely today that all but the smaller provinces could support provincial forces large enough to operate at a high level of efficiency.'[52]

The most significant political, administrative and fiscal intergovernmental arrangements in Canada have generally developed informally outside the framework of the Constitution. On the basis of intergovernmental negotiations and agreements, many of them have now become part of the conventional or practical framework, and some have even been incorporated and mentioned in the Constitution.

The following observation of Cameron aptly concludes this section:

> The processes and arrangements that have been put in place to permit collaborative federalism may move IGR closer to an actual decision-making model, although the constraints on moving seriously in that direction are severe. But to the extent that intergovernmental forums develop a decision-making capability, they drift further out of the reach

of democratic control and processes of parliamentary accountability upon which our system is based. Finding a way of applying the principles of responsible government to an executive-dominated federal system continues to be a central democratic challenge for India.[53]

INTERGOVERNMENTAL EXECUTIVE RELATIONS IN INDIA

In contrast to the architects of the Canadian Constitution, the Constituent Assembly of India showed greater awareness about the relevance and role of intergovernmental mechanisms in the working of the federal system. Apart from Article 263 of the Constitution, this awareness is also reflected in the observation made by Dr Rajendra Prasad, President of the Constituent Assembly, in his final address on the text of the Constitution 'as settled by the Assembly' (though he mentioned here only central mechanisms having implications for the states as well): 'Our Constitution has adopted certain independent agencies to deal with particular matters.' He continued to mention in this context the Public Service Commissions (for the union and the states), the Comptroller and Auditor General (for the union and the states), the Election Commissioner, etc. In particular, he underlined the special care taken by the Constitution in 'giving additional safeguards about their independence'.[54]

In India, as in Canada, intergovernmental relations in their broadest sense include at least three kinds of interactions between the two orders of government or among federating states. To begin with, there are intergovernmental mechanisms bringing together representatives from the two levels of government, the most important among which are the National Development Council (NDC) and the Inter-State Council (ISC). Then there are central mechanisms created by the union government that work for the state governments as well and affect their working, the most prominent example of which is the Election Commission of India. Third, there is rather a rare category of meetings consisting exclusively of representatives from the state governments. Besides being rare, such meetings have never included all chief ministers in a comprehensive way. An occasion when chief ministers or state ministers have met on their own without the initiative or presence of the prime minister or respective union ministers seldom arises.

National Development Council (NDC)

First set up in 1952, the NDC is an intergovernmental forum which meets frequently with a certain degree of procedural regularity in the context of launching the strategy of planned economic development. It was established by the Union Executive through an administrative decision in preference to establishing it under Article 263 of the Constitution. It has since been an apex intergovernmental forum which plays an important role by way of according approval to the five-year plans. (An indepth study is given in the next chapter.)

Inter-State Council (ISC)

The framers of the Constitution seem to have shown greater awareness for the need for such a forum for centre–state consultation and deliberation. This is evident from the legal status bestowed upon it under Article 263 (more appropriately called the Intergovernmental Council as it not only includes the states but also the centre). Ironically, however, the ISC was never set up until the National Front government headed by V.P. Singh took the initiative in 1990.

This body, which does not meet on a regular basis, was set up as an instrument for cooperation, coordination and evolution of common policies. It consists of a general body comprising the prime minister as chairman and all chief ministers and union cabinet ministers as members. The Sarkaria Commission also recommended that the Council should be assisted by a small Standing Committee of Ministers and an Advisory Committee of Experts. It is expected to discuss all major problems, other than economic and developmental, among the union, the state and local governments. It would, however, be appropriate that zonal councils first consider zonal interstate problems before they are discussed by the ISC. (A detailed case study is offered in the next chapter.)

UNION–STATE PREMIERS' CONFERENCE (USPC)

The origin of the Chief Ministers' Conference (CMC)[55] can be traced back to 1946 when Vallabhbhai Patel who was the home minister in the interim central government called the Premiers' Conference to ensure that there was consensus on the idea of forming the 'Central Administrative', that is, the Indian Administrative Service (IAS) and the Indian Police Service (IPS). The frequency with which the USPC is concerned depends upon the 'gravity of issues warranting notice of chief executives as well as the predilections of the central leadership'.[56] It is convened when a problem of wider importance arises so as to draw the attention of the chief ministers. The prime minister presides over the Conference. It is also attended by some central ministers depending on the agenda. Both the union and the states submit the items for inclusion in the agenda, though in practice it is the union which takes the initiative. In the words of S.R. Maheswari, 'the chief ministers' conference is potentially an important forum for the discussion of issues and harmonization of relationship between the centre and the states'.[57]

Though there may not always be unanimity on decisions in the USPC, it does help in allaying misunderstandings and tensions between the union and the states. It has become a very powerful forum especially since the decline of the 'one party dominance' system in India to resolve union–state and interstate issues. Thus, the USPCs came to be imbued with renewed importance.

The crucial role of 'Executive Federalism'—ISC under Article 263 or what in journalism is referred to as the 'Chief Ministers' Conference' convened by the prime minister outside the framework of this Article is clearly evident in the policy area of power sector reforms. As Dubash and Rajan aptly observed in this context:

> One important manifestation of the central government's coordinating role has been a regular series of chief ministers' meetings to come up with a common agenda on power sector reforms. Such a meeting in 1996 is repeatedly invoked as a turning point. Chief ministers agreed to a common minimum action plan which included handling over retail tariffs to state electricity regulatory commissions and a determination that while cross subsidies cross sectors were to continue, they were to be restricted.[58]

A conference exclusively of chief ministers of states has never really been held. This is in contrast to the federal system of Canada where an Annual Provincial Premiers' Conference has become fairly institutionalized and is held on a fixed date. In India, a Council of southern chief ministers was convened by the Janata Dal chief minister of Karnataka, R.K. Hegde, in the early 1980s. However, the Congress chief ministers of the coalition government in Kerala did not attend it. The TDP chief minister of Andhra Pradesh, N. Chandrababu Naidu, took the initiative in convening a meeting of chief ministers to articulate their critical assessments of the Eleventh Finance Commission Report (EFCR) (2000) in New Delhi on 21 August 2000. They described this report as being 'against the interests of the better developing states that are already stifled by additional fiscal responsibilities'. Apart from Naidu, the TDP-sponsored meeting was only attended by six of the seventeen chief ministers invited. They rejected most of the recommendations made by the Eleventh Finance Commission headed by A.M. Khushro and approved by the union cabinet.

The chief ministers met Vajpayee with their long list of demands but failed to extract any tangible commitment from him. According to sources, the prime minister merely promised that their demands would be evaluated and duly considered by the finance panel. The states wanted 33.5 per cent of the new taxes that accrued to the centre. The Finance Commission in its interim report recommended 29.5 per cent conditional devolution on a pro rata basis. As for the aggregate transfer of funds to the states, between 1990 and 1995, they ranged between 38.72 and 44.06 per cent. It was, however, pointed out that imposing an upper ceiling at a much lower level was unfair.[59]

Conference of Constitutional Heads of the Union and States (CCHUS)[60]

The CCHUS owes its origin to the colonial period when 'the Governor-General used to call the Conference of Governors who, under the earlier dispensation, were the real, not nominal, executives'.[61] The President of India is the Chairman of the Conference. The Vice-President and the prime minister also attend the Conference, besides other central ministers depending on the agenda. The agenda includes items suggested by the central government as well as those proposed by individual Governors. According to Maheshwari,

> The rationale of the Governors' Conference lies in its being a source of information to the central government on matters concerning the states, which is independent of the state-governmental machinery. Like the USPC, this is a forum where the President-appointed Governors apprise the President frankly and directly with the political, social and economic situation in their respective states.[62]

Like the USPC, this body was defunct until the 1967 elections. But the situation changed after the fourth general elections. Maheswari succinctly described this in the following words:

> The political fluidity resulting from the Fourth General Election (1967) reflecting in and, in turn, getting aggravated by, the spectacle of 'Ayachands' and 'Gayachands' caught the Governors napping, as it was, swinging them in the mainstream of political decision-making who was to be invited to form the government in the state; how was majority in the state legislative assembly to be tested; how claims and counter-claims of different political parties in the state legislature were to be examined were only some of the questions demanding almost instant answers from the Governors. These are among the questions that the Governors' Conference has been discussing since 1967 and has, therefore, become a forum useful to the bewildered Governors, codifying gubernatorial responses towards questions like the above.[63]

After the 1989 Lok Sabha elections, there was a sea change in the political scenario in New Delhi as well. Congress dominance was decisively ended with the introduction of a multiparty system and the necessity to form a coalition or minority government. This suddenly magnified the role of the President as an active constitutional umpire in the context of uncertain verdicts and unclear majorities for any party or coalition of parties. It was in this context that President Shankar Dayal Sharma convened a two-day conference of Governors in New Delhi in December 1995. At the concluding day of the conference, he announced the formation of two committees of state Governors. One would examine minorities' welfare and the other would review the role of a Governor as Chancellor of universities.

Earlier in the meeting, Prime Minister Narasimha Rao made a

detailed presentation of the security environment in India's neighbourhood and reiterated his government's commitment to hold elections in Jammu & Kashmir. The panel responsible for the welfare of minorities was to suggest 'ways of ensuring that the position of minorities is safeguarded (to) enable their continued contribution . . . as equal citizens'. The other committee reviewing the Governor's role as Chancellor was to function with the purpose of improving the quality of higher education. The President stated that Governors served as a bridge between students and teachers and the state governments. K.V. Krishna Rao, Governor of Jammu & Kashmir, was hopeful of an early restoration of peace and democratic processes in the state, and remarked that the spate of violence unleashed by terrorists would not pose a major difficulty in the conduct of elections. Finance Minister Manmohan Singh threw light on the economic situation of the country (and answered various queries relating to the unabated inflationary spiral and development of backward areas), while the late Madhav Rao Scindia elaborated on the educational policy in his capacity as Minister for Human Resource Development.

The President also discussed the role that the Governor was supposed to play in the changing scenario. He stressed that Governors ought to act in a non-partisan manner, without being influenced by parochial considerations of party loyalties and affiliations. They should act as true 'representatives' of the people as a whole and of the state in particular so that the dignity and prestige of the office of Governor is maintained and also enhanced. Though the constitutional arrangement enjoins the Governor to defer the advice of the Council of Ministers to a later date, the President said, 'Governors have to arrange to keep themselves properly informed—particularly by touring the state intelligently and being in touch with the people and public opinion in different spheres, and interacting suitably with the central and state governments.' The President reminded the Governors of the role they were supposed to play during 'exceptional cases' for which they must 'equip themselves'. He did not, however, elaborate on those 'exceptional cases'. Even in normal times, he delineated two important roles for Governors: '(1) to ensure that the Rules of Business are followed properly and that deviations are brought promptly to the attention of the chief minister for correction; and

(2) to protect the morale of the civil service in the state, particularly that of members of the All India Services.' The President noted, 'it is in the national interest that those services function efficiently, that officers of outstanding merit received due recognition and encouragement, and that witch-hunting does not take place'.[64]

Intergovernmental Ministerial Conferences (IGMC)

In addition to the intergovernmental conferences already discussed, there is another category which brings together ministers of the two orders of government in particular policy areas. For instance, a conference of state education ministers (and secretaries) which was held on 22-4 October 1998 in New Delhi. The agenda papers circulated to state education ministers by the Union Ministry of Human Resource Development before the conference reiterated certain priority areas of action in the area of education. An annexure to the agenda papers specified certain goals (to be achieved) and priorities that the non-BJP ministers participating in the conference strongly objected to. The West Bengal Education Minister Kanti Biswas drew the attention of his counterparts in other states to the unwarranted intrusions into the agenda which transgressed the domain of the conference.

The Madhya Pradesh Chief Minister Digvijay Singh was among the first to take up the issue and question Vajpayee about the propriety of 'thrusting' the recommendations of the Vidya Bharti on the Union–State Education Conference when it was known that the views of the former were 'to say the least, highly controversial'. He said that the educational policy, as laid down in the 1986 statement and subsequently amended in 1992, had evolved through national debate and it was 'unfair to the country to stifle such a debate'.

Before the conference, education ministers from various states announced that they would not be party to the proceedings unless the conference took due cognizance of the reservations expressed by them. The HRD Minister (M.M. Joshi), however, remained unperturbed by these outbursts. When the conference began, as many as 15 ministers threatened to walk out in protest rather than be party to the proceedings to legitimize the intrusion of the divisive ideology of Hindutva into formal educational systems. Joshi was forced to retreat when half of the quorum chose either to boycott or abstain (from attending the conference) as the fitting option. The recommendations of the Vidya Bharti (for consideration in the conference agenda) were withdrawn, Chittalangia's speech was cancelled and Saraswati Vandana was substituted by the National Anthem as the invocatory theme of the conference. At the end of the conference, Kanti Biswas briefed the press that Joshi, by retreating on a number of fronts, showed that he was committed to a secular vision of India.[65] However, subsequent events revealed that the controversy surrounding the NDA coalition government's educational policy persisted. Joshi informed the Lok Sabha in monsoon 2001 that the National Curriculum Framework (NCF) on school education which he proposed to introduce was fully consistent with the National Education Policy guidelines formulated in 1986 and subsequently amended in 1992. For this reason, he did not consider it necessary to refer it to the Central Advisory Board on Education (CABE). This claim created a furore among some allies of the NDA and more so among some chief ministers. In fact, as a mark of protest, the Left Front chief minister of West Bengal, Buddhdev Bhattacharya, went to the extent of convening a meeting of non-BJP chief ministers. Though the Congress chief minister of Madhya Pradesh and the Congress-led UDF chief minister of Kerala did not attend the meeting, yet they did express their reservations about the HRD ministry's move.[66]

Another ministerial-cum-official intergovernmental mechanism is the meeting of members of the State Environment Committees (SEC). The SECs were set up in most of the states and union territories at the suggestion of the National Committee on Environmental Planning and Coordination (NCEPC) (established in 1972) with the purpose of seeking the active cooperation of both the state governments and union territories for the review of environmental issues of mutual interest and the constraints in tackling them. The chief minister generally chairs this Committee and the chief secretary of the state concerned is the member-secretary. For the first time, member-secretaries of the SECs met in the DST on 3 October 1978 to review their activities and suggest programmes of action for implementation. The meeting was attended by representatives from twelve states. Some of these committees made a good beginning, but most of them could not overcome teething troubles. An urgent need was felt for the SECs to be involved right from the stage of project formulation to avoid *ex-post facto* analyses of the project after its submission to the Planning Commission and subsequent reference to the NCEPC. It was also emphasized that the SECs could play an important role in setting up industries and incorporation of environmental safeguards for various developmental projects at the state level, apart from ensuring a close coordination between the government departments, research and educational institutions and industries.

Most of the members expressed the view that due to paucity of staff, it was difficult to give concrete shape to the plans chalked out earlier. The problem was further aggravated by the non-availability of efficient technical personnel for performing secretarial work pertaining to the environmental appraisal of projects. To make matters worse, some of the SECs did not even have financial support for setting up expert committees and meeting the expenses of their visits to project sites.[67]

The Chief Secretaries' Conference (CSC)

The conference of chief secretaries is presided over by the cabinet secretary in the central government. The first such conference held in 1965 focused on the law and order situation in the country. It was expected to become an annual feature and play an important role, but somehow this did not materialize and it has failed to be as effective as it should have been. The items included on the agenda of the CSC are sponsored both by the centre and the states. Maheshwari remarked:

> Like the USPC, this forum apparently finds nothing which it is prohibited from discussing, it is an open-ended conference. And, it is this 'open-endedness' which severely restricts its utility as a forum for meaningful discussion. As it is called upon to discuss the whole gamut of subjects concerning the states, it should either agree to meet for a much longer duration (which is unlikely) or the agenda of the conference may be broken up into functional components each to be explored in the appropriate functional secretaries' conference, rendering the chief secretaries' conference redundant.[68]

The main rationale for the existence of such a body is the directions it may provide to the USPC. To quote Maheswari: 'Its utility flows directly from the inevitable imperfection of the chief ministers' conference.'[69] In view of the fact that union–state premiers are not able to spare much time to discuss a particular issue, the same can be taken up (for discussion) at length at the CSC. Though organically the CSC is in no way linked with the USPC, the agenda of the former is completely independent of the USPC. Its meetings are timed with those of the latter. If they meet before the premiers and explore the issues to be discussed at their conference, the CSC can become a useful body for optimizing the performance of the USPC.[70] Another such meeting of union–state secretaries of tourism was held in New Delhi on 11 September 2001 to discuss the National Tourism Policy.

Zonal Councils

Another example of USPCs is the zonal councils set up on the basis of recommendations of the States' Reorganization Act, 1956. They are somewhat different from the former inasmuch as the zonal councils, as the name itself suggests, include the chief minister of only a particular zone, in addition to the union home minister. The reorganization of states on linguistic lines could ignite frenzied passions that could threaten the integrity of the country. Under the circumstances, zonal councils were thought to be the most suitable and necessary instruments of inter-governmental consultation and cooperation (mainly in social and economic fields) and also of keeping in check controversies and particularistic tendencies among the states.[71] Nehru was also convinced about the necessity of zonal councils as revealed in the following observation he made in the Lok Sabha:

> . . . the more I have thought about it, the more I have been attracted to something which I used to reject seriously . . . that is the division of India into four, or five or six major groups regardless of language. . . . We may have what I would call zonal councils, i.e. a group of 3, 4, or 5 states, as the case may be having a common council.[72]

Originally, the States' Reorganization Act provided for the setting up of five zonal councils, though today the country is divided into six zones—northern, central, eastern, north-eastern, western and southern. Each zonal council includes a union minister, the chief minister and two ministers from states in the zone, and two members from union territories in the zone.[73] It is assisted by advisers. The zonal councils began to function from mid-1957. For some time, the meetings were held on a regular basis where problems of mutual interest were discussed, but since 1967 the meetings have become less frequent and the states have preferred to discuss their problems directly with the central government.[74]

These councils are advisory bodies and can discuss any matter which is of interest to some states, or to the centre and a state in the zone. Some of their major achievements have been in the field of irrigation and power, development of backward areas, health schemes and reciprocal concessions related to domiciliary curbs on admissions. The allegation that these councils are no better than a fifth wheel in the administrative coach serving no purpose other than hindering efficiency can be refuted. To quote Pal:

> Rather these councils by providing a regular forum for discussing matters of common interest in different zones, have become clearing houses of ideas and not a mere device for registering agreements. So long as they enable the member states to understand one another's difficulties and needs, it would strengthen cooperation among states in the zone.[75]

The Sarkaria Commission recommended that the existing five zonal councils constituted under the States' Reorganization Act, 1956, and subsequently expanded into six, should be reconstituted under Article 263 of the Constitution. Further, the North-Eastern Council set up under the North-Eastern Council Act should function as the zonal council for the north-eastern states in addition to its existing functions. It also recommended that a chairman should be elected annually on rotation basis from amongst the chief ministers of the member-states as against the existing practice by which the union home minister acts as the chairman. Another suggestion made by the Commission was that the zonal council should meet at least twice a year in the state of which the chief minister is the chairman.

There is no denying the fact that zonal councils are useful agencies which facilitate first level discussions on regional and interstate issues, but they can be fully effective only when there is proper coordination between the zonal councils and the intergovernmental council coupled with objective leadership.[76]

It is often criticized that except for the North-Eastern Zonal Council (NEZC), by an large, zonal councils are defunct. This is presumably because the NEZC is embedded in an area that is perhaps the only 'natural' region in the country in geographical isolation and economic interdependence, at least more so than any other macro-region, e.g. north-west, Hindi-heartland, south India, etc.

INTER-STATE TRIBUNALS

There are many interstate rivers in India. The regulation and development of the waters of these rivers and river valleys has been a source of interstate tension. Article 262(1) of the Constitution provides: 'Parliament may by law provide for the adjudication of any dispute or complaint with respect to the use, distribution or control of the waters of, or in, any inter-state river, or river valley.' The Parliament also enacted the Inter-State River Water Disputes Act, 1956, that makes a provision for reference of such a dispute to tribunals on the receipt of an application from a state, when the union government is satisfied that the dispute 'cannot be settled by negotiations'. Most of the disputes relate to the sharing of waters of interstate rivers, and the interpretation or implementation of the terms of an agreement.[77] However, there are inordinate delays in the settlement of such disputes. Moreover, there is no provision for an adequate machinery to enforce the award of the tribunal.[78]

The union government has so far set up four tribunals under the Act: (*a*) the Narmada Tribunal, (*b*) the Krishna Tribunal, (*c*) the Godavari Tribunal, and (*d*) the Kaveri Tribunal. The entire process of setting up these tribunals was very cumbersome and time consuming. The Sarkaria Commission suggested that once an application is received from a state, it should be mandatory on the union government to constitute a tribunal within a period not exceeding one year from the date of receipt of the application of any disputant state, and that the Inter-State Water Disputes Act should be amended so as to empower the union government to appoint a tribunal, *suo motu*, if necessary. Further, there should be a provision in the Act that states shall be required to give requisite information for which purpose the tribunal may be vested with powers of a court. The Act should further be amended to ensure that the award of a tribunal becomes effective within five years from the date of the constitution of a tribunal, and that it should have the same sanctity as a decree of the Supreme Court.[79]

Tribunals have also often referred the matter to a commission chaired by a Supreme Court judge. If the tribunal as well as the commission fail, the matter is finally referred to the Supreme Court. Water disputes have so far been more or less amicably settled with the exception of disputes involving Punjab, Haryana and Rajasthan, and Tamil Nadu and Karnataka. Over the last few years, the Kaveri dispute has often found Tamil Nadu and Karnataka at loggerheads, especially during periods of drought. Failing all political negotiations, the matter has been provisionally settled by the Supreme Court's intervention. Recently, the Punjab government turned the heat on the sharing of waters from Ravi–Beas–Sutluj and Yamuna by terminating interstate agreements among riparian states signed in 1981, 1985 and 1994 by an Act of the state legislature. The union government has made a presidential reference to the Supreme Court under its advisory jurisdiction.

The recent proposal for interlinking all major rivers of India—if implemented—is likely to exacerbate such interstate conflicts in the future. The protagonists of the project argue that it would obviate the paradoxical occurrence of floods and droughts simultaneously in various parts of the country by a rational apportionment of water resources of the country. Ecologists, however, argue that it would disturb the ecological balance and bring natural calamities in its trail.

National Water Resources Council (NWRC)

Various bodies like the Irrigation Commission, the National Commission on Agriculture and the Rashtriya Barh Ayog emphasized the need for apex bodies to evolve national policies for the development and use of water resources in the pursuit of larger national interests. The National Development Council discussed the matter at a meeting held on 14 March 1982 and argued that a climate should be created in which national water plans are prepared keeping in view the national perspective as well as state and regional needs. It is in this context that the NDC welcomed the proposal of the Government of India for the setting up of the National Water Resources Council and the River Basin Commissions. It was decided by the government that the NWRC would be chaired by the prime minister, with the union minister of irrigation as vice-chairman, and key union ministers and all chief ministers of states as members.

The functions of the NWRC include the formulation of the national water policy and periodic review of the policy; examination and review of water development plans submitted to it by the National Water Development Agency, the River Basin Commissions, etc.; making recommendations for the acceptance of water plans with such modifications as may be considered appropriate and necessary, etc.[80]

The council is supposed to meet as often as may be necessary but at least once a year. It frames its own rules of business and procedure. The Ministry of Irrigation provides administrative or other assistance to it as per its requirements. The union minister of Water Resources is the vice-chairman and the secretary of the Ministry of Water Resources is the secretary of the NWRC. The Ministry of Water Resources provides the necessary assistance to the Council.[81] The regulations governing the Council were further amended by the Government of India resolutions of 21 January and 12 June 1987.

NATIONAL INTEGRATION COUNCIL (NIC)

The National Integration Council is a rather unique agency in the sense that it combines governmental as well as non-governmental representatives and is truly national in scope. Its intergovernmental nature is evident in its composition that includes union ministers as well as chief ministers. Its non-governmental aspect is reflected in its membership which includes leaders of various political parties, vice-chancellors, educationists, scientists, industrialists, and leading personalities from the fields of arts and letters, media and other walks of life.

The first conference of the National Integration Council was convened by Nehru in September-October 1961 with the purpose of finding ways and means of combating the evils of communalism, casteism and regionalism which threatened the country's unity and integrity. The statement made at the end of the conference recommended the launch of a national pledge campaign and dwelt upon matters related to education. code of conduct and economic development for the promotion of national integration. The National Integration Council was thus established with the purpose of reviewing all matters related to national integration and making recommendations. It was constituted and reconstituted as and when considered necessary.

Thc NIC met for the first time in June 1962 and set up two committees: Committee on National Integration and Regionalism and the Committee on National Integration and Communalism.

The need for the NIC receded into the background in the wake of the demonstration of solidarity at the time of the Chinese aggression. However, fissiparous tendencies and communal conflicts necessitated the reconstitution of the NIC in 1968. The NIC set up three committees to deal separately with the communal, regional and educational aspects respectively. It also set up a Standing Committee to ensure that satisfactory progress was made with regard to the implementation of its recommendations and other related matters. This was headed by Indira Gandhi in her capacity as the prime minister. It met four times between 26 October 1968 and 5 November 1970. The NIC and its committees, however, remained inactive since mid-1970. A Steering Committee of the Council met under the chairmanship of the prime minister on 24 August 1973 to discuss the role of the council in the future. It decided to ascertain the views of the chief ministers of states and political parties on the Council's recommendations. In March 1976, a number of groups were set up to consider various problems. The first group which met once on 27 November 1976 communicated its recommendations to the state governments for necessary action. The other group which operated under the administrative control of the Ministry of Education and Social Welfare could not complete its work and wound up in August 1978.

The NIC was reconstituted in 1980 and met twice in November

1980 and January 1984. At the meeting in November, it decided to set up three committees—the Standing Committee, the Committee on Caste and Communal Harmony, and the Committee on Education. The Standing Committee and the Committee on Caste and Communal Harmony functioned under the chairmanship of the home minister, whereas the Committee on Education functioned under the chairmanship of the education minister. The second meeting stressed the need for preserving the country's unity and integrity.

The NIC was again reconstituted in February 1986 and its first meeting was held in the Parliament Home Annexe on 7 April 1986 under the chairmanship of Rajiv Gandhi. The Council reviewed the question of national integration and communal harmony in the context of the volatile situation in Punjab. It also adopted a resolution by consensus calling upon the people of India, particularly Punjab, Haryana and the adjoining areas, to stand firm against acts of terrorism and extremism and to dissociate themselves from those who preached violence and secession. It appointed a 21-member Standing Committee under the chairmanship of Jagjivan Ram to function on a continuing basis and to formulate both short-term and long-term measures for preserving national integrity throughout the country. It also resolved to remain alert to the situation and to meet as often as necessary. The second meeting of the NIC was held on 12 September 1986 to review the welfare measures for the minorities during the course of which it was decided to set up a group of 3-5 members of the NIC to suggest further follow-up action.

The NIC was yet again reconstituted in February 1990 and at its first meeting held on 11 April 1990 is New Delhi issues such as the communal situation, increased use of violence by political secessionist activists, the situation in Punjab and Kashmir and Ram Janambhoomi–Babri Masjid imbroglio were discussed. It also adopted a unanimous resolution on the escalation of terrorist violence and communal tension in the country and for the setting up of a committee on the promotion of communal harmony and a spirit of camaraderie among people owing allegiance to different religious belief systems. It decided to convene at least three meetings of the NIC every year. In recent times, only P.V.

Narasimha Rao convened a few meetings of the NIC in the backdrop of pressing national problems related to the communal situation in the country and the highly volatile situation in Jammu & Kashmir and Punjab.

According to Vijapur, Singh and Suresh, 'the Council does not work as a continuing body, as originally envisaged, but lapses into inactivity periodically and is revived only when the communal situation or other conflict situation becomes very serious. As a matter of fact it is revived to serve as a 'crisis management mechanism'.[82]

It is rather pitiable that the immense potentialities of the NIC have not been fully exploited, particularly considering the fact that as compared to the ISC/NDC, it has the added advantage of having among its members the top brass and elite (from the non-governmental sector) from different walks of life. In this unique capacity, it can serve as a comprehensive forum that encompasses the combined advantages of both the top level governmental and non-governmental think tank.

National Commission on Population (NCP)

The National Population Policy (NPP) envisaged the setting up of a National Commission on Population (NCP) which was notified by the Government of India on 11 May 2000. While explaining the need for such a body, the resolution read:

> During the next two decades, the country will have to face the challenges and utilize the opportunity provided by the current phase of demographic transition to rapidly achieve both population stabilization and sustainable achievement in human development. There is an urgent need for planners, programme implementors and the people themselves to expedite this process by focusing on promoting synergy between demographic, educational, environmental and developmental programmes in order to achieve this goal. To provide overall guidance to this national effort, the Government of India has decided to constitute a National Commission on Population, as under, with immediate effect.[83]

The NCP is headed by the prime minister as the chairman and the deputy chairman of the Planning Commission as the vice-chairman. All chief ministers, concerned union ministers, all major political parties, specialists, NGOs, private sector and media representatives are the other members of the NCP. Its functions include: (*a*) to review, monitor and give directions for the implementation of the NPP; (*b*) to promote synergy between demographic, educational, environmental and developmental programmes so as to hasten population stabilization; (*c*) to promote inter-sectoral coordination in planning and implementation across government agencies to involve civil society and the private sector and to explore possibilities of international cooperation; and (*d*) most importantly, the Commission is to facilitate the development of a vigorous people's movement in support of this national effort.[84]

At the first meeting of the NCP in July 2000 in New Delhi concern was expressed to achieve population stabilization on an urgent basis. State governments and various parties present at the meeting showed strong political will and commitment. Some state governments elucidated their population policies and set up State Population Commissions under the chairmanship of their respective chief ministers. The experts, representatives of the media, the corporate sector, NGOs and civil society also offered their support for the cause of rapid population stabilization and human development.[85]

CENTRAL MECHANISMS WITH IMPLICATIONS FOR STATES

A number of union agencies vitally affect the governance in states, such as the prime minister's office, the National Security Council, the Ministry of Finance, the Planning Commission, the Finance Commission, the Election Commission, the Reserve Bank of India, the Comptroller and Auditor General of India, the Union Public Service Commission, para-military forces, the Central Bureau of Investigation, the Central Vigilance Commission, and the Central Electricity Authority. The functions performed by them are briefly described here.

PRIME MINISTER'S OFFICE (PMO)

What functioned as the Prime Minister's Secretariat (PMS) (since the Nehru era to the time of Indira Gandhi), was transformed and renamed as the Prime Minister's Office by Morarji Desai. The PMS considerably expanded under Indira Gandhi and became the hub of the highly centralized prime ministerial system during her reign. Under the lendership of Desai, the PMO was comparatively reduced in size, though it still continues to be a source of vast powers. To quote Dhar:

> The PMO works in different ways under different prime ministers and secretaries depending on their individual styles and the degree of collaboration with the cabinet secretary and the ministries. But it is most productive when it is able to mobilize its resources in conjunction with those available elsewhere in the system.[86]

NATIONAL SECURITY COUNCIL (NSC)

The idea of a National Security Council was first mooted, though not implemented, by the National Front government. It was set up by the BJP-led coalition government headed by Atal Behari Vajpayee in October 1998. It is chaired by the prime minister himself whose principal secretary serves as the National Security Advisor. The NSC is a three-tiered body consisting of the Strategic Policy Group, the National Security Advisory Board, and a secretariat represented by the Joint Intelligence Committee. The Strategic Policy Group (SPG) forms the nucleus providing interministerial coordination and support for the NSC. It comprises the cabinet secretary, chiefs of the three services (the seniormost among whom is the Chief of the Defence Staff), the foreign secretary, the home secretary, the defence secretary (Defence Production), the finance secretary, secretary (Revenue), the RBI governor, the director of Intelligence Bureau, secretary (Research and Analysis Wing), secretary of Department of Atomic Energy, Scientific Advisor to the Defence Minister, secretary (Space) and chairman, Joint Intelligence Committee (JIC). The National Security Advisory Board (NSAB) includes eminent personalities outside the government with expertise in areas like external security, strategic analysis, foreign affairs, defence, armed forces, internal security, science and technology and economics. Its function is formulation and direction of the nation's security policies.

PLANNING COMMISSION

When a national planning process was launched at the time of independence India opted for a mixed economy in which the public sector played an important role in 'guiding and directing the economy towards the objectives of growth, modernization, self-reliance and social justice'.[87]

A new era of systematic planning was ushered in with the setting up of the Planning Commission in March 1950. It was constituted through an Executive Order of the Government of India as an advisory body to make recommendations to the union cabinet. The resolution stressed the need for 'adequate coordination' between the development schemes initiated by the union and the states and for comprehensive planning based on a careful appraisal of resources and essential conditions of progress.[88] India adopted a strategy of five-year plans which were to be operationalized through successive annual plans. It was in this context that

> the principal task of the Planning Commission was to formulate the five-year and the annual plans for the most effective and balanced utilization of the country's material, capital and human resources, appraise from time to time, the progress in their implementation and suggest adjustment of policy and such other measures that were considered necessary in light of these appraisals.[89]

In discharging its function of investment planning of the economy, the Planning Commission focuses mainly on its planning and allocative functions. This means distribution of plan funds between the centre sector plan and central assistance to state plans as also across central ministries/departments.

The Commission works under the overall guidance of the National Development Council. The prime minister, in his capacity as chairman, participates and gives directions to the Commission on all major policy issues. Besides, it has a deputy chairman and full-time members who function as a composite body in detailed plan formulation.

The main criticism levelled against the Commission is that the union government has assumed a dominant role in the formulation of plans, even in areas which fall in the domain of the states. It has been observed that often the Planning Commission is ignored and not even given a chance to examine and render independent advice on developmental policies and programmes. There are allegations that sometimes the union ministries and departments try to use the Commission as a device to get the states to comply with their own way of thinking. This is done through frequent changes in the composition of the Commission which results in insecurity of tenure of its members.[90]

Therefore, the state governments desire that the Commission should not only work independently but also without being influenced or pressurized by the union government. To this end, the expert opinion has been that the Planning Commission should be transformed into a statutory institution so that it is more of a professional or expert body, less amenable to political influence. The proponents believe that as a statutory body the Commission would be under the NDC, and would be governed by distinguished experts with a fixed tenure. Consequently, they would be less prone to any political pressure. Moreover, the statutory status would make it mandatory for the union government as well as the state governments to take its advice and pay due regard to it.[91] A counter viewpoint is that if the commission is accorded a statutory status, it would lead to rigidity in its functioning. Some state governments are of the view that it should continue to remain an arm of the union government but discharge its functions in a federal spirit. Some experts have even talked about federating the Planning Commission. For instance, Kabra suggested that 'the practice of the centre appointing the members of the Planning Commission must be replaced by a system by which they are jointly appointed by the centre and the states'.[92]

The Sarkaria Commission report did not support the idea of transforming the Commission into a statutory body, but only suggested some procedural reforms. It said that the fact that the Planning Commission is headed by the prime minister and includes the union finance minister, not only gives it stature, but also ensures at a very early stage of plan formulation the commitment of the union to the policies, programmes and financial outlays, including levels of central assistance.[93]

In the context of the neo-liberal paradigm shift in public policy framework in the 1990s, the Planning Commission is afflicted with an identity crisis of sorts. It is searching for a new relevance and role in an economy that is witnessing privatization and globalization. The Commission so far has not only survived but also adapted to the reformed policy regime. To quote from a recent Planning Commission document:

> The Planning Commission has to go beyond undertaking more budgetary allocations, between the competing sectors and regions, for that alone would not be enough, and more towards ensuring policy harmonization over time and across space. This would require the Planning Commission to strengthen its role as a 'Think Tank'—a repository of expert knowledge—for the nation has to be strengthened.[94]

FINANCE COMMISSION

The Constitution provides for the setting up of an institution of a quasi-judicial nature, the Finance Commission, for advising the President, besides other things, on the division of certain tax revenues raised by the union between the union and the states. An important aspect is the allocation of resources which are transferred to the states with wide differentials in fiscal capabilities and requirements.

Article 280 of the Constitution requires the President to constitute a Finance Commission every five years to recommend to the President the patterns of distribution between the union and the states of the net proceeds of taxes which are to be, or may be, divided between them and the allocations among the states of the respective shares of such proceeds; the principles which should govern the grants-in-aid of the revenues of the states out of the Consolidated Fund of India; and any other matter referred to the Commission by the President in the interest of sound finance.[95]

In the US and Canada, the idea of an independent or regular agency for this purpose did not find acceptance. The Finance Commission in India, due to its constitutional status, forms a unique arrangement. The architects of the Constitution, by making it an expert body, have thereby excluded the devolution of resources from the arena of political bargaining. The role entrusted to the Commission is advisory. Its recommendations are not mandatory and the Parliament remains the supreme authority to ensure whether appropriate action has been taken by the union executive on the recommendations of the Finance Commission. This is guaranteed by requiring the union government to lay down before both Houses of Parliament every recommendation made by the Finance Commission along with an explanatory memorandum regarding the action taken thereon.[96]

The fiscal arrangement envisaged in the Constitution has been criticized on certain grounds: constraints imposed by the union on the Finance Commission by prescribing certain terms of reference; non-implementation of important recommendations of the Finance Commission by the union government; and problems arising out of the methodologies followed by the Finance Commission.[97]

Some state governments are of the view that the existing institutional arrangements are adequate, while others want its functions to be enlarged. They argue that since they are established periodically, their approach has been ad hoc, marked by a lack of continuity from one Commission to another. They have therefore suggested a more permanent set-up. Some of the important suggestions in this respect are: the functions of the Finance Commission be enlarged to include consideration of the Plan and other transfers and/or undertaking of comprehensive annual/periodical reviews of the financial performance of the union and state governments; the Finance Commission be made a permanent or standing body to cope with enlarged responsibilities; coordination between the Finance Commission and the Planning Commission be streamlined so as to ensure an integrated view on the flow of central assistance to the states; and the Finance Commission be provided a permanent and well-equipped secretariat to conduct studies and maintain operational continuity for the benefit of the subsequent Finance Commission.[98]

The Administrative Reforms Commission suggested that one member of the Planning Commission should also be nominated as a member of the Finance Commission. The Sarkaria Commission also proposed that the person in charge of financial resources in the Planning Commission should be a member of the two Commissions. This would enable the adoption of an integrated approach to the assessment of financial resources and needs of the states by the two Commissions.[99]

Regarding the composition of the Finance Commission, the Constitution provides that it should include a Chairman and four other members. The Expert Committee on Financial Provisions of the Constitution (1947) recommended that two members of the Commission should be selected from a panel of names drawn up by the states. This recommendation was based on to the apprehension that the states' case may go by default unless they are represented on the Finance Commission. The Sarkaria Commission, however, did not recommend any change in the composition of the Finance Commission.[100]

Election Commission of India (ECI)

The Constitution of India has set up a single central agency responsible for parliamentary, presidential, vice-presidential and state assembly elections. In the Constituent Assembly debates, the question of including elections in the chapter on Fundamental Rights (FR) was discussed. The Committee dealing with Fundamental Rights argued that in order to recognize the independence of elections and to avoid any interference by the executive in the elections to the legislature, it should be regarded as a fundamental right. However, when the matter was brought before the House, no objection was raised to it being treated as of fundamental importance but it was argued that it should appropriately be provided for in some other part of the Constitution and not in the chapter on Fundamental Rights. The Drafting Committee consequently deleted it from the category of fundamental rights and incorporated it in a separate part containing Articles 289, 290, etc. Thus, sub-clause (1) of Article 289 transferred the superintendence, direction and control of preparation of electoral rolls and of all elections from Parliament and legislatures of the states to a body outside the executive to be called the Election Commission.[101]

Sub-clause (2) says that there shall be a Chief Election Commissioner and such other Election Commissioners as the President may appoint from time to time. The original proposal in the Constituent Assembly under Article 289 recommended one Commission to handle elections to the central legislature, both the upper and lower houses, and a separate Election Commission for each province and each state, to be appointed by the Governor or head of the state. The present Article 289 radically differs from it. It proposes to centralize the election machinery in the hands of a single Commission to be assisted by Regional Commissioners, who would work under the superintendence and control of the Central Election Commissioners, not under the provincial government. This radical change was due to the fact that some provinces had a mixed population. Besides the original inhabitants or native people residing in a province, there were other people living there who were racially, linguistically or culturally different from the native people of that particular province. Both the drafting committee and the central government noted that in such provinces the provincial governments managed affairs in such a way that people who did not belong to the province racially, culturally, or linguistically were excluded from the electoral rolls. This was against the spirit of democratic norms. Therefore, a change was brought about whereby the entire election machinery was brought under the control of the Central Election Commission. It was alone entitled to issue directives to returning officers, polling officers and others engaged in the preparation and revision of electoral rolls so that no injustice was done to any citizen in India, who under the Constitution is entitled to be included on the electoral roll.[102]

This explains the rationale for entrusting the conduct of elections to an independent constitutional body, the Election Commission. In *T.N. Seshan* vs *Union of India and Others* (1995) 4 SCC 61, the Supreme Court observed:

> In order to ensure the purity of the election process, it was thought by our Constitution-makers that the responsibility to hold free and fair elections in the country should be entrusted to an independent body which would be insulated from political and/or executive interference. It is inherent in a democratic set-up that the agency which is entrusted with the task of holding elections to the legislatures should be fully insulated so that it can function as an independent agency free from external pressures from the party in power or executive of the day. This objective is achieved by the setting up of an Election Commission, a permanent body, under Article 324(1) of the Constitution.[103]

The Supreme Court in *M.S. Gill* vs *The Chief Election Commissioner of India* (1977) stated that where the enacted laws are weak or do not provide adequate provision to deal with a given situation in the conduct of elections, the Election Commission under Article 324 of the Constitution has the residuary powers to act in an appropriate manner.[104]

Initially, the Commission had only one Chief Election Commissioner but from 1 October 1993, the Election Commission has been made a three-member body (on a continuous basis), consisting of the Chief Election Commissioner and two Election Commissioners. It executes its work by convening regular meetings, circulation of papers and even on the telephone if the situation so demands. The findings are subsequently recorded. All the Election Commissioners have an equal say in decision-making. Some of the executive functions of the Commission are also entrusted to its officers in the secretariat. The Commission is supported by a separate secretariat at New Delhi with the strength of about 300 officials who are organized in a hierarchy. Deputy Commissioners, the seniormost officers in the secretariat, also render assistance to the Commission.[105]

With the 73rd and 74th Constitutional Amendments in 1992, the Parliament created State Election Commissions for independent control of panchayat and municipal elections. The Election Commission of India is of the view that it is the Commission's duty to support, assist and strengthen these State Commissions, because they organize and control elections to the first level of democracy, which forms the roots of the higher levels right up to the Parliament.[106]

A particular issue concerning union–state relations that has recently aroused a great deal of controversy as well as litigation in courts against the states and union government relates to the Commission's control over officers of the two orders of government deputed on polling duty during the time of the elections. The Election Commission of India has been particularly concerned about the mass transfer of officers for political reasons just prior to the polls and the casual attitude of governments towards complaints of the Commission against offending officers. The Commission has, therefore, demanded more consequential and effective powers over the poll duty officers.

The foregoing discussion reveals that the Election Commission of India is a unique union mechanism having far-reaching implications for the state governments. In other federations, the election scene is marked by a multiplicity of authorities under the federal and state governments, often resulting in chaotic administration of elections, as illustrated by the American Presidential election in 2000. The Indian Constitution has created an integrated election machinery which parallels the unified hierarchy of the judiciary in Canada and India. In this regard, the Canadian judicial system is similar to that of India but the Canadian election system is not to the same extent.

Reserve Bank of India (RBI)

The RBI was established on 1 April 1935 in accordance with the provisions of the Reserve Bank of India Act, 1934. Since its inception, its central office is located at Mumbai. Initially, it was owned privately, but consequent upon the nationalization of banks in 1949, it came to be fully owned by the Government of India. The Preamble to the Act prescribes the following objectives: '. . . to regulate the issue of Bank Notes and keeping of reserves with a view to securing monetary stability in India and generally to operate the currency and credit system of the country to its advantage'.[107]

The central board is nominated/appointed by the central government for a period of four years. It comprises official as well as non-official directors. Official directors include a full-time Governor and not more than four Deputy Governors. The non-official directors numbering ten are from various fields including one government official. In addition to these officials, there are four directors representing the four local boards whose function is general superintendence and direction of the Bank's affairs. The local boards cover four regions of the country—Mumbai, Kolkatta, Chennai and New Delhi. Their function is to advise the central board on local matters, to represent territorial and economic interests of the local cooperative and indigenous banks, and to perform such other functions as delegated by the central board from time to time.[108]

The main functions of the RBI are the formulation, implementation and monitoring of the monetary policy; prescribing broad parameters of banking operations within which the country's banking and financial system functions; managing the Foreign Exchange Management Act, 1999; performing a wide range of promotional functions to support national objectives; and performing merchant banking function for the central and sate governments and acting as their banker.[109] The RBI has twenty-two regional offices, most of them located in the state capitals. It also has six training establishments.

COMPTROLLER AND AUDITOR GENERAL OF INDIA (CAG)

The office of the CAG was created under the provisions of Articles 149 to 151 of the Constitution. In pursuance of Article 149, the duties, powers and conditions of the CAG have been ordained in (DPC) Act 1971 of Parliament.

The statutory duties of the CAG incorporate audit of revenue and expenditure of the union and state governments accounted for in the respective consolidated funds; transactions relating to contingency funds and public accounts; trading, manufacturing, profit and loss accounts and balance sheets and other subsidiary accounts maintained by any government department; accounts of stores and stocks in government organizations, government companies and government corporations whose statutes provide for audit by the CAG; authorities and bodies substantially financed from the Consolidated Funds of the union and the states, etc.[110] The audit reports of the accounts of the union and the states are submitted by the CAG to the President/Governor to be tabled in Parliament or the state legislatures.

After the founding of the Constitution in 1950, the CAG continued to be statutorily responsible for compiling the accounts of the union and states from the initial accounts rendered to him. However, he is relieved of this responsibility by the provisions of the 1971 Act. By the end of March 1987, only the union government and the governments of Goa, Diu and Daman, Pondicherry, Delhi and Andaman and Nicobar Islands had assumed this responsibility. In many states, the Indian Audit and Accounts Department handles entitlement functions like authorizing salaries to gazetted officers.[111]

The CAG also performs a fiduciary role in union–state financial relations by certifying the share assignable to the states out of the taxes collected by the union. The actual expenditure incurred by the states on programmes initiated and funded by the union is audited by the CAG and certified for the purpose of readjusting central assistance released on a provisional basis.[112]

In the discharge of his duties the CAG is authorized to inspect any office of the organizations subject to his audit; call for any books of account required during audit; and call for such information as required for the preparation of any account or report.[113]

The Constitution includes various provisions to ensure the independent functioning of the CAG:

1. He shall be removed from office only if each House of Parliament decides by majority of the total membership as well as a majority of not less than two-thirds of the members present and voting.
2. His salary and conditions of service cannot be varied to his disadvantage after his appointment.
3. He shall not be eligible for further office under the Government of India or of any state, after he demits office.
4. His administrative powers and the conditions of service of persons serving in his department shall be prescribed by rules made by the President only after consulting him.
5. The administrative expenses of his office shall be charged upon the Consolidated Fund of India.[114]

The CAG functions through the Indian Audit and Accounts Department. From its headquarters in New Delhi it controls and directs the activities of the various offices of the department.

UNION PUBLIC SERVICE COMMISSION (UPSC)

The UPSC was established after the founding of the Indian Constitution. It is a successor to the Public Service Commission set up in October 1926 under the provisions of the Government of India Act, 1919 and the Federal Public Service Commission. It was constituted under Article 315 of the Constitution to 'act as an independent and impartial body, charged with the responsibility of selecting the most suitable candidates from among the best talents available in the country for appointment as also providing to the government independent and expert advice on matters concerning the services'.[115] Since its inception, the UPSC has emerged as an impartial body restoring the confidence of the people in the creation of an efficient, clean and accountable administration.

The functions performed by the Commission are broadly divisible into two categories: (*a*.) the provisions of the Constitution and the Acts, Rules and Regulations made thereunder, and (*b*) the conventions and special orders issued by the Government. Under Article 320, the Commission is required to advise the government on various matters including: to conduct examinations for appointment to the services of the union of India; to recruit by selection through interviews; to advise on the suitability of officers for appointment or promotion as well as transfer/deputation; to advise on all matters relating to methods of recruitment to various services/posts; disciplinary cases relating to different civil services; and miscellaneous matters relating to the grant of extraordinary pensions, reimbursement of legal expenses, etc.[116]

Besides, the Commission has to be consulted in respect of proposals for amending the UPSC. Under Article 321, the Commission has to be consulted in the case of appointments to certain categories of posts under the Municipal Corporation of Delhi, the Employees State Insurance Corporation, and the Employees Provident Fund Organization. According to the UPSC's report of 31 March 1998, the Commission comprised the chairman and nine members against the stipulated strength of the chairman and ten members. This strength was fixed in 1986 by the President under Article 318 (vide Department of Personnel and Training, notification no. 39024/1/80-Estt-(B), dated 22 August 1986). A detailed examination of the work done by the Commission revealed that due to an increase in population in the intervening period of eleven years, the present strength was inadequate. Further, it was found that in order to handle the workload, it was necessary to increase the strength of its members from ten to thirteen.[117]

Each state of India has its own Public Service Commission, besides the UPSC, which enjoys the same constitutional status as the UPSC. The All-India Services, though recruited by the UPSC and trained by the union, work both for the union and the states. Also, there is a provision for promotion from State Services to the All-India Services.[118]

The union and state governments are generally expected to accept the recommendations of their respective Public Service Commissions whose reports are constitutionally mandated to be tabled in Parliament and the state legislatures. This provides an opportunity for legislative control of the executive in this matter.

PARAMILITARY FORCES

The maintenance of law and order is primarily a state subject and to achieve this goal each state has its own agencies and organizations. Apart from these, there are six agencies of the union government under the control of the Ministry of Home Affairs to assist the states in the maintenance of law and order—the Central Reserve Police Force (CRPF), the Border Security Force (BSF), the Central Industrial Security Force (CISF), the National Security Guard (NSG), the Indo-Tibetan Border Police (ITBP), and the Assam Rifles.

The CRPF is the main force to assist states to maintain law and order. It was raised on 27 July 1939 at Neemuch (Madhya Pradesh) as the 'Crown Representatives' Police'. After independence, it was renamed the CRPF. The present strength of the CRPF is 1,67,367 comprising 137 Battalions, 119 Executive Battalions, 10 Rapid Action Force Battalions, 2 Mahila Battalions, 5 Signal Battalions and 1 Special Duty Group, 30 Group Centres, 8 Training Institutions, 3 Base Hospitals, 7 Arms Workshops and 1 Central Weapon Store.[119] It is committed to ensuring the internal security of the country throughout the year and its personnel have rendered yeoman service by way of fighting terrorism, insurgency and militancy in Jammu & Kashmir and in the north-eastern region as well as Naxalilte/PWG in Bihar and Andhra Pradesh. A special wing of the CRPF called the Rapid Action Force (RAF) has been set up to deal with communal tensions.

The Assam Rifles is largely meant for the north-eastern states for guarding the borders, counter-insurgency operations and law and order duties. Its operational control is with the army. It was initially raised in Cachar Levy in 1835 and is the oldest para-military force in India. It has 31 Battalions, 1 Training Centre and School, 3 Maintenance Groups, 3 Workshops, 1 Signal Unit, 1 Construction Company and a few ancillary units and is organized in 7 Ranges. It was primarily raised for the maintenance of internal security in tribal areas and along the international border in the north-eastern region, though now it also operates in Punjab, Jammu & Kashmir and Sri Lanka in conjunction with the army. At present, it is engaged in intense counter-insurgency operations in Manipur, Nagaland and Tripura.[120]

The BSF and the ITBP are chiefly responsible for guarding the borders of the country. Taking over from the various State Police Forces guarding the Indian border, the BSF was raised in 1965 with a strength of 25.5 Battalions. At present, its strength is 157 Battalions, 20 Artillery Battalions, 3 Premier Training Institutions, 9 Subsidiary Training Centres, 2 Combat Training Schools, 1 Water Wing, 1 Air Wing, 1 Signal Regiment and 9 Special Units to guard the 7,411 km long border. It is the duty of the BSF to prevent trans-border criminal activities like smuggling, infiltration/exfiltration and other illegal operations.[121]

The ITBP was established on 24 October 1962 in the wake of the Chinese aggression for reorganizing the frontier intelligence and security set up along the 2,115 km long Indo-Tibet border. It was restructured in 1978, comprising 9 Service Battalions with 4 Specialist Battalions and 2 Training Centres. From time to time, it has been assigned additional duties like security of banks in Punjab during the period of militancy in the state, fighting terrorism in Jammu & Kashmir and VIP security. At present, the strength of the ITBP is 25 Service Battalions, 4 Specialist Battalions and 3 Training Centres.[122]

The CISF was set up in 1968 for providing security and protection to public sector undertakings (PSU). It has a sanctioned strength of over 95,000 and is inducted in 236 public sector undertakings. During 1999-2000 (up to December 1999), the CISF detected 4,238 cases of theft from the PSUs involving property (recovered from stolen goods) worth Rs 5.49 crore. Being a central armed force, it has been pressed into service wherever necessary to provide assistance to the civil administration.[123]

The NSG is a special force set up as a federal contingency force in 1984 to counter terrorism and anti-hijacking operations. Its present strength is 7,357. It has also been entrusted with the responsibility of providing mobile security to 'Z' plus category VIPs.[124]

During the 1998 and 1999 elections, special provisions were made to equip the central paramilitary force to assist the state police forces in terms of weaponry and equipment. To meet the large requirements of these forces, a separate procurement wing has been in operation in the Ministry of Home Affairs since 1992-3.

The maintenance of 'parallel' agencies by the union government is a very 'unusual' feature of the Indian federal system. The states argue that since public order is a subject included in the state list in the Constitution, the setting up of central police forces is an encroachment on their jurisdiction. The union, however, contends that these forces are required to protect the union government's properties and installations. In the late 1960s there was a serious conflict between the union and the states on the issue of deployment of the CRPF units in Kerala and West Bengal. However, in more recent years, the states have got accustomed to the encroachment on the part of the union government by way of deployment of the Central Police Forces even for basic law and order duty, to say nothing of special occasions such as election duty, natural disaster and communal riots.

There are two viewpoints on the expanding size of these forces. On the one hand, some liberals as well as Marxists like Rajni Kothari and Manoranjan Mohanty perceive in the expanding size of these forces a threat to human rights and fundamental rights in terms of illegal detention, torture, custodial rape, and encounter deaths occasioned by the police and paramilitary forces. The mounting evidence of human rights violation by the police and security forces shows that they seek to justify their actions on the ground that such steps are necessary to maintain law and order. Explaining this trend, Marwah wrote:

> After independence the basic role of the police and its structure did not undergo any change, even though the demands of the police increased. The emphasis still remains on 'order' rather than the 'law'. The heart of the matter is that the Indian police system is not accountable to the people, it is not a service, it is a force, and finally it is one of the most unfortunate British legacies which the democratic India has retained

and strengthened with all the characteristics of a repressive colonial force.[125]

The number of complaints registered in the National Human Rights Commission (NHRC) during the years 1996-7 and 1997-8 was 16,823 and 31,299 respectively. It rose to 54,236 in 1999. Complaints ranging from simple to odious against the police and the security personnel constitute more than half of the total number of complaints received by the commission.[126] On the other hand, neo-conservatives like Atul Kohli and M.P. Singh seem concerned, and rightly so, about the growing crisis of ungovernability in India.

Central Bureau of Investigation (CBI)

The CBI was set up in April 1963, by a resolution of the union government

> . . . for investigation of crimes formerly handled by the Delhi Special Police Establishment (DSPE) as also important cases under the Defence of India Act and Rules, particularly hoarding and blackmarketing in Essential Commodities having repercussion and ramification in several states; for collection of intelligence relating to certain types of crimes; for participation as the National Central Bureau in the work connected with the International Criminal Police Organisation; for maintenance of crime statistics and dissemination of information relating to crime and criminals for the study of the specialized crimes of particular interest to the Government of India or crimes having All India, Inter-State importance and for the coordination of laws relating to the crime.[127]

Thus over the years, the CBI has been looked upon as an agency entrusted with the responsibility of investigating crimes of national importance as well as a variety of important cases referred to it by the state governments. Its assistance is available to state police forces on request for investigation of interstate crimes and other difficult cases, which otherwise would fall under the jurisdiction of the local or state CID, on account of expediency of public demand, legislative opinion or direction of superior courts.[128]

By the 1990s, there was much controversy surrounding the autonomy of the CBI from the union executive. In 1997, in *Vineet Narain and others* vs *Union of India* (1997), the Supreme Court on 18 December delivered a key judgement with regard to the Jain Hawala case. The court order addressed the key issue of autonomy for the CBI and the Enforcement Directorate (ED), the agencies that are charged with dealing with the recent spate of cases involving corruption in high places, and the nexus between politicians, bureaucrats and criminals. The order abolished the 'single directive' of 1969—a union government directive that prevented the CBI from investigating officers above the rank of Joint Secretary without the prior permission of their respective ministries. All these orders were interim in character, 'to operate till such time as they are replaced by suitable legislation'.[129]

The order seemed to rewrite drastically section 4(1) of the CBI's Parent Act, the Delhi Special Police Establishment Act of 1946 which says: 'The superintendence of the Delhi Special Police Establishment shall vest in the central government.'[130] In an effort to remove the CBI's superintendence from the Prime Minister's Office, the Supreme Court ordered that henceforth the CBI would operate under the superintendence of the Central Vigilance Commission (CVC). The court had asked Parliament to grant statutory status to the CVC, which had hitherto been a peripheral body. The judgement said:

> . . . while the government shall remain answerable for the CBI's functioning, to introduce visible objectivity in the mechanism for overviewing the CBI's functioning, the CVC shall be entrusted with the responsibility of superintendence over the CBI's functioning. The CBI shall report to the CVC about cases taken up by it for investigation; progress of investigations; cases in which charge-sheets are filed, and their progress. The CVC shall review the progress of all cases moved by the CBI for sanction of prosecution of public servants which are pending with the competent authorities, specially those in which sanction has been delayed or refused.[131]

But this direction is problematic. If the government remains answerable for the CBI's functioning, it would logically follow that it must have at least some powers to regulate that functioning. However, the court's direction on the CBI that immediately follows its orders on superintendence by the CVC deals with this issue. It mandates that the 'Central Government shall take all measures necessary to ensure that CBI functions effectively and efficiently and is viewed as a non-partisan agency'.[132] This innocuous power was routinely used by the government in defence of its constant interference in CBI investigations. Reconciliation of the conflicting mandates given by the Supreme Court and the CVC would be a tough task since the order dealt with the idea of 'superintendence' only in passing, principally to exclude the process of investigation, a statutory exercise of power, from its ambit. The government also argued that the CBI could not be made accountable to the CVC without amending the Delhi Special Police Establishment Act. This meant a truly independent CVC. Though the Court advised that it should be given a statutory status, the Parliament could be forced by the judiciary to pass or not pass a piece of legislation. Forestalling the charge of infringement on Parliament's domain, the Court contended that since the executive was not granting autonomy to the CBI, the judiciary had to step in. 'In a catena of decisions of this court', the bench noted, 'this power has been recognized and exercised, if need be, by issuing necessary directions to fill the vacuum till such time (as) the legislature step in to cover the gap or the executive discharges its role.'[133]

The court order did not prescribe a fixed tenure for the Central Vigilance Commissioner, who heads the CVC, or safeguards against coercion and removal from office. It said that the Central Vigilance Commissioner be selected by a 'committee comprising the prime minister, the home minister and the leader of opposition from a panel of outstanding civil servants and others'—a prescription Parliament is free to reject.[134] The Commissioner would head a committee with the home secretary and secretary (personnel) as members and make recommendations for the appointment of the Director of the CBI. The Committee would draw up a panel of IPS officers on the basis of their seniority, integrity, experience in investigation and anti-corruption work. The final selection would be made by the Appointments Committee of the Cabinet (ACC) from the panel recommended by the Selection Committee. If none among the panel is found suitable, the reasons thereof shall be recorded and the Committee asked to draw up a fresh panel.[135]

The tenure of the CBI Director would be of two years, regardless of the date of his superannuation, to ensure that an officer suitable in all respects is not ignored merely because he has less than two years left for his superannuation from the date of his appointment.[136] Despite this, even when the CVC is made a statutory body and becomes truly independent, the CBI would continue to have an uncomfortably close linkage with the government. It would not have either the authority or the incentive to monitor regularly the probity of people in public life. The fact, however, remains that the CBI has not gained full autonomy.

Central Vigilance Commission (CVC)

The CVC was set up in 1964 by a resolution of the Ministry of Home Affairs in pursuance of the recommendations made by the Committee on Prevention of Corruption under the chairmanship of K. Santhanam. It was established for evolving and applying common standards in deciding cases involving lack of probity and integrity in administration. The Commission was conceptualized 'as an apex body for exercising general superintendence and control over vigilance matters in administration and ensuring probity in public life'. The role of the Commission is advisory and it enjoys the same degree of independence and autonomy as the UPSC in the discharge of its powers and functions.[137] Home Minister Lal Bahadur Shastri, while tabling the scheme of the CVC in Parliament, observed that the Commission was to be a fearless champion to the man of integrity and a source of terror to the corrupt officer. The sole purpose of setting up the CVC was to improve the 'Vigilance Health' of the country. Since the CVC is not a statutory body like the CAG, the UPSC and the Supreme Court, its jurisdiction and functions can be amended by a government order.

Among the basic powers and functions assigned to the Commission by the Government of India are to undertake an inquiry into any transaction in which a public servant under the Government of India is suspected or alleged to have acted for an improper purpose or in a corrupt manner; tender independent and impartial advice to the government on cases having vigilance angle at different stages of investigation, inquiry, appeal, review, etc.; scrutinize and approve proposals for appointment of Chief Vigilance Officers in various organizations and assess their work;

and organize training courses for them, and other vigilance functionaries in central government organizations.[138]

Till 1998, the Commission existed as a body authorized by an administrative order and did not have any statutory status. However, the Supreme Court in Vineet Narain case (Jain Hawala case) directed that the CVC should be accorded a statutory status. Consequently, the CVC Ordinance 1998 was passed, and a Bill, the Central Vigilance Commission Bill, was introduced in Parliament. It could not be passed and the initial Ordinance expired. Another fresh Ordinance, the CVC Ordinance 1999, was issued with effect from 8 January 1999. The Lok Sabha passed the CVC Bill 1999 on 15 March 1999.

Central Electricity Authority (CEA)

The setting up of the Central Electricity Authority to coordinate with State Electricity Boards is another interesting trend of the federalization process in India. The CEA is a statutory organization constituted by the central government under Section 3(1) of the Electricity (Supply) Act, 1948. The Ministry of Power is supported by the CEA in all technical, financial and economic matters. The CEA is responsible for technical coordination and supervision of programmes and is also entrusted with a number of statutory functions. It is headed by a chairman, who is an ex-officio secretary to the Government of India and has six full-time members, who are of the rank of ex-officio additional secretaries to the Government of India. Their expertise include areas of Thermal, Hydro, Economic and Commercial, Power System, Planning, Grid and Operation. The CEA also has five part-time members, including a legal member.

The functions and duties of the CEA are prescribed under the rules framed in Section 4B(1) of the Electricity (Supply) Act, 1948, or by issue of written directions in matters of policy involving public interest under Section 4A(1) of the said Act.[139]

Its 'most important function is to develop a sound adequate and uniform national power policy, formulate short-term and perspective plans for power development and coordinate the activities of planning agencies in relation to the control and utilization of national power resources'.[140] It also acts as an arbitrator between the state government or the board and a licensee.

Under the provisions of the Electricity (Supply) Act, 1948, the union government has further added a few more functions such as coordination of research and development in the field of power generation; evaluation of financial performance of the State Electricity Boards (SEB) constituted under section 5; techno-economic appraisal of power projects; and promotion of interstate and joint sector power projects.[141] Besides these functions, the CEA is involved in the design and engineering of power projects in order to develop in-house technical expertise and also to help the SEBs, generating companies and state authorities requiring such aid under Section 3(1)(v) of the Electricity (Supply) Act, 1948.[142]

Another body is the Central Electricity Regulatory Commission (CERC), which is an independent statutory body with quasi-judicial powers. It was constituted on 25 July 1998 under the Electricity Regulatory Commission Act, 1998. Some of its important functions are:

1. To regulate the tariff of generating companies owned or controlled by the central government.
2. To regulate interstate transmission including tariff of the transmission entities.
3. To regulate interstate bulk sale of power, etc.[143]

Some of the important orders issued by the Commission are the Availability Based Tariff Order (ABT) and the Indian Electricity Grid Code (IEGC).

Prasar Bharati

For a long time, there has been an ongoing debate to make the government-owned All India Radio and Doordarshan autonomous corporations. Their functioning as a government department/ministry had aroused a great deal of dissatisfaction with the attempt of the ruling parties to run the radio and television in a partisan manner. To this end, the Prasar Bharati Act, 1990, was enacted by the National Front government, but for some reasons the Act was not implemented. For the first time, Prime Minister I.K. Gujral tried to reorganize the electronic mass media in terms of this Act. The successive NDA government also appointed a committee chaired by N.R. Narayanamurthy to carry out a comprehensive review of the Prasar Bharati. The committee recommended in its report that Prasar Bharati as the public broadcaster must play 'an important and critical role in determining the direction and thrust of broadcasting in India by setting standards through programmes that are meaningful, absorbing, diverse in content, innovative in design, and of the highest quality'.[144]

It further recommended an amendment to the Act to the effect that the Prasar Bharati and its constituents—Doordarshan and All India Radio—must be autonomous and completely free to make their own operational and tactical decisions. It would be a desirable amendment from the perspective of union–state relations for the party in power in New Delhi has often tried to control the government media to subserve its partisan interests.

Independent Regulatory Authorities

Since the onset of economic liberalization in 1991, several semi-judicial independent regulatory authorities have been set up in important policy areas under Acts of Parliament, such as power sector, telecommunication, information technology, company affairs, corporation. Chaired by a Supreme Court judge and experts as members, these mechanisms are meant to replace direct administrative control by government departments in various policy areas which have implications for states as well.[145]

There is a vast proliferation of central and intergovernmental mechanisms in Canada and India. Both countries bear the imprint of their highly centralized Constitutions, despite the fact that Canada has since become incredibly more federal and India considerably more federalized. Yet by all available indicators, India continues to be relatively more centralized than Canada. The result of this difference is that intergovernmental relations are much more vigorous in Canada than in India. None the less, one observes with a certain degree of irony that the cabinet system in Canada works with a greater degree of collective responsibility under the effective leadership of the prime minister compared to the coalitional/minority cabinets in India in which the prime minister's authority has often been put under conflicting pressures of a large assortment of parties in the union coalition cabinet.

To conclude in the words of comparative federalist Watts, 'Ultimately, the design of intergovernmental co-ordinating councils will need to find a balance between shared goals, provincial autonomy, political stability, democratic transparency and accountability, equity, efficiency and innovative flexibility. Difficult choices and value trade-offs will therefore be unavoidable.'[146]

NOTES

1. David Cameron, 'The Structure of Intergovernmental Relations', *International Social Science Journal* (Federalism), no. 167, UNESCO Blackwell Publishers, March 2001, p. 121.
2. 'Executive Federalism' in the sense that these forums bring the Executive Heads of the two orders of government together for policy formulation and implementation.
3. As Brian R. Opeskin citing Sharman, observed: 'The executive plays a major role in intergovernmental relations in all federations. This role is pre-eminent in countries with Westminster style systems of government because of the dominance of the executive over the Parliamentary process' ('Mechanisms for Intergovernmental Relations in Federations', *International Social Science Journal* [Federalism], no. 167, UNESCO Blackwell Publishers, March 2001, p.130]. It may be added that this is particularly true in the case of one party government. This does not however always happen in conditions of minority and coalition governments as the Canadian experience with the former and the Indian experience with the latter illustrate.
4. Cameron, 'The Structure of Intergovernmental Relations', op. cit., p. 126.
5. Hamish Telford, 'Federalism in Multinational Societies: Switzerland, Canada and India in Comparative Perspective', doctoral dissertation, Department of Political Science, University of British Columbia, 1999.
6. John Porter, *The Vertical Mosaic: An Analysis of Social Class and Power in Canada*, Toronto: University of Toronto Press, 1965, p. 379.
7. Ibid., p. 380.
8. See Garth Stevenson, *Unfulfilled Union: Canadian Federalism and National Unity*, Toronto: Gage, 1989.
9. Ronald L. Watts, 'Federalism in Canada', typescript, 1996, p. 61.
10. Interview with Richard Simeon, University of Toronto, 8 February 2000.
11. Interview with Thomas Crouchene, School of Policy Studies, Queen's University, 9 February 2000.

12. Ibid.
13. David Cameron, 'Intergovernmental Relations in Canada', in *Intergovernmental Relations in Federal Countries*, ed. J. Peter Meekison, Forum of Federations, n.d., p. 14.
14. Robert F. Adie and Paul G. Thomas, 'Federalism and the Administrative State', a chapter in their book, *Canadian Public Administration: Problematical Perspectives*, Scarborough: Practice Hall, 1987, p. 446.
15. Ibid.
16. James Ross Hurley, 'Executive Federalism', in *Public Administration and Public Management: Experiences in Canada*, ed. Jacques Bourgault, Maurice Demers and Cynthia Williams, Quebec: Les Publications du Quebec, 1997, p. 117.
17. Richard Simeon, *Federal Provincial Diplomacy: The Making of Recent Policy in Canada*, Toronto: University of Toronto Press, 1972, p. 134.
18. Ibid.
19. Adie and Thomas, op. cit., p. 447.
20. Ibid.
21. John W. Langford, *Transport in Transition: The Reorganization of the Federal Transport Portfolio*, Montreal: McGill-Queen's University, 1976, pp. 194-5.
22. Simeon, *Federal Provincial Diplomacy*, op. cit., p. 136.
23. Stuart Mackinnon, 'First Ministers' Conferences', paper presented at the Fifth Conference on Public Policy and Administrative Studies, University of Guelph, 22 April 1988, pp. 20-1.
24. J.H. Aitchison, 'Inter-Provincial Co-operation in Canada', in *The Political Process in Canada: Essays in Honour of R. MacGraegor Dawson*, ed. J.H. Altchson, University of Toronto Press, Toronto, 1963, p. 155.
25. Richard Simeon, *Federal Provincial Diplomacy*, op. cit., pp. 137-8.
26. Ibid., p. 138.
27. Ibid.
28. Mackinnon, 'First Ministers' Conferences', op. cit., pp. 21-2.
29. Ibid.
30. Personal communication, 5 October 2004.
31. Internet: http://www.council of the federation.ca.
32. Hurley, 'Executive Federalism', op. cit., pp. 118-19.
33. Interview with Evert A. Lindquist,University of Victoria, Victoria, 24 December 1999.
34. A.A. Lomas, 'The Council of Maritime Premiers: Report and Evaluation after Five Years', in *Canadian Federalism: Myth or Reality*, ed. J. Peter Meekison, Toronto: Methuen, 1977, pp. 353-63.
35. Adie and Thomas, op. cit., pp. 447-8.
36. Mackinnon, 'First Ministers' Conferences', op. cit., p. 24.
37. Simeon, op. cit., p. 142.

38. *The New Face of Government*, Ottawa: Ministry of Supply and Services, 1994.
39. *The History of the Bank of Canada: Who Needs a Central Bank?*, Canada Year Book 1999 on CD-ROM Statistics, Canada, 1999.
40. Bank of Canada, http://www.bank banque. ca/english/histor-htm., ibid.
41. Finance and Services 3, ibid.
42. *Shaping Canada's Future Together Proposals*, Ottawa: Ministry of Supply and Services, 1991, Appendix, para. 17, p. 57.
43. Auditor General of Canada, *Canadian Federal Government Handbook*, Globe Information Services, 1995, pp. 21-2.
44. Ibid., pp. 407-8.
45. Document 58: CBC, Journalistic Policy, July 1982, 1-38 in *Documents of Canadian Broadcasting*, ed. Roger Bird, Ottawa: Carleton University Press, 1988, p. 588.
46. Ibid., pp. 588-9.
47. *Shaping Canada's Future Together Proposals*, para. 21, p. 57.
48. Privy Council Office, *Decision-Making Process and Central Agencies in Canada, Ottawa: Federal, Provincial and Territorial Practices*, Information and Research Centre, 1998, pp. 3-7.
49. Watts, op. cit., p. 50.
50. 'Maintaining the Right', *Canada Year Book, 1999* on CD-ROM Statistics, Canada, 1999.
51. Ibid.
52. J.R. Mallory, *The Structure of Canadian Government*, Toronto: Macmillan, 1971, pp. 302-3.
53. David Cameron, 'Intergovernmental Relations in Canada', in *Intergovernmental Relations in Federal Countries*, ed. J. Peter Meekison Forum of Federations, n.d.
54. Government of India, Lok Sabha Secretariat, *Constituent Assembly Debates*, Book 5, vols. X-XII, 3rd rpt, New Delhi: Lok Sabha Secretariat, 1999, pp. 990-1.
55. The term Chief Ministers' Conference in this context is a misnomer. For the Conference does not include only the CMs but also the PM and some key Union Ministers. A new name—Union-State Premiers' Conference (USPC)—is, therefore, suggested and hereafter the same shall be used for what is typically referred to as the Chief Ministers' Conference in India.
56. S.R. Maheswari, 'The Centre-State Consultative Machinery in India: Union-State Relations', *Indian Journal of Public Administration*, February 1984, p. 45.
57. Ibid.
58. Navroz K. Dubash and Sudhir Chella Rajan, 'Power Politics: Process of Power Sector Reform in India', *Economic and Political Weekly*, vol. XXXVI, no. 35, 1-7 September 2001, p. 3383.

59. For background, see *Asian News Digest*, 2-8 September 2000, p. 565.
60. This new term is suggested for what in India is generally called the Governors' Conference. This is because such conferences include, in addition to the Governor, the President of India, who is actually its chairman. Its meetings are generally convened at the union government's initiative. The states, of course, may propose the convening of the CCHUS.
61. Maheswari, 'The Centre-State Consultative Machinery in India: Union-State Relations', op. cit., p. 41.
62. Ibid., pp. 41-2.
63. Ibid.
64. *The Times of India* (Bombay) and *The Hindu* (New Delhi) in *Indian Recorder*, 5-11 February 1996, p. 1750.
65. 'Taking Hindutva to School', *Frontline*, 20 November 1998, pp. 4-9.
66. *Frontline* (Madras), vol. XVIII, no. 18, 1-14 September 2001, pp. 4-11.
67. Garima Bhatnagar, 'Party Politics and Intergovernmental Relations in Indian Federalism (1977-1989): A Study of Changing Political Configuration and Relationships in Functional Areas', M. Phil. dissertation, New Delhi: Jawaharlal Nehru University, Centre for Political Studies, School of Social Sciences, 1991, pp. 170-2.
68. Maheswari, 'The Centre-State Consultative Machinery in India: Union-State Relations', op. cit., p. 46.
69. Ibid.
70. Ibid.
71. *Lok Sabha Debates*, vol. I, 23 December 1955, p. 880.
72. *Lok Sabha Debates*, vol. X, pp. 3513-14.
73. Chandra Pal, 'Co-operation through Statutory Bodies', a chapter in his book, *Centre-State Relations and Co-operative Federalism*, Delhi: Deep & Deep, 1983, p. 206.
74. Ibid.
75. Ibid., p. 232.
76. H.A. Gani, *Centre-State Relations and Sarkaria Commissioni*, Delhi: Deep & Deep, 1990, p. 108.
77. *Commission on Centre-State Relations, Report*, Part I, p. 487.
78. Ibid.
79. Ibid.
80. Ministry of Irrigation, *Resolution Dated 10 March 1983, Constituting National Water Resources Council and Amendments Thereto, No. 611179-PP*, New Delhi.
81. Resolution no. 611179-PP, dated 14 October 1985, New Delhi.
82. Abdulrahim P. Vijapur, Ajay Kumar Singh and Kumar Suresh, 'Evaluation of the Role and Working of National Integration Council' a chapter in their book, *Pluralism, Minorities, National Integration: Problems and Prospects*, Delhi: South Asian Publishers, 1997, p. 148.

83. Government of India, Planning Commission, No. A-43011/17/2000-Admn. I, Yojana Bhawan, New Delhi, dated 11 May 2000.
84. Government of India, *National Commission on Population*, typescript New Delhi, n.d. p. 2.
85. Ibid., p. 3.
86. P.N. Dhar, 'The Prime Minister's Office: Seeing through the Mystique', *The Times of India* (New Delhi), 24 February 1989, p. 8.
87. Planning Commission, *Indian Planning Experience: A Statistical Profile*, New Delhi, January 2001.
88. *Commission on Centre-State Relations*, *Report*, Part I, p. 362.
89. Planning Commission, *Indian Planning Experience: A Statistical Profile*, op. cit.
90. *Commission on Centre-State Relations*, *Report*, Part I, p. 362.
91. Ibid.
92. K.N. Kabra, 'Federating the Planning Commission', *The Hindu*, 2 July 1996.
93. *Commission on Centre-State Relations*, *Report*, Part I, p. 362.
94. Planning Commission, *Indian Planning Experience: A Statistical Profile*, op. cit.
95. *Commission on Centre-State Relations*, *Report*, Part I, p. 282.
96. Ibid.
97. Ibid.
98. Ibid.
99. Ibid.
100. Ibid.
101. V.S. Rama Devi and S.K. Mendiratta, *How India Votes: Election Laws, Practice and Procedure*, Delhi: Butterworths India, 2000, pp. 173-6.
102. Ibid.
103. Ibid.
104. Election Commission of India, *Landmark Judgements on Election Laws*, vol. I, New Delhi: Election Commission of India, 1999, p. 486 and Election Commission of India, *Fifty Years of the Election Commission of India, Golden Jubilee Celebrations*, New Delhi: Nirvachan Sadan, 17 January 2001, p. 2.
105. Ibid.
106. Election Commission of India, *Elections in India: Major Events and New Initiatives 1996-2000*, New Delhi: Nirvachan Sadan, 2000.
107. Internet, RBI website address http://www. rbi.org.in/ rbi profile. html.
108. Ibid.
109. Ibid.
110. Indian Audit and Accounts Department, *Activity Report, 1996-97*, CAG of India.

111. Indian Audit and Accounts Department, *Activity Report, 1986-87*, CAG of India.
112. Ibid.
113. Ibid.
114. Ibid.
115. Union Public Service Commission, *48th Annual Report, 1997-98*, New Delhi: UPSC, 1 April 1997-31 March 1998, p. 1.
116. Ibid.
117. Ibid.
118. R.B. Jain, 'The UPSC and the SPSCs in India in Union-State Relations', *Indian Journal of Public Administration*, February 1984, pp. 168-9.
119. Ministry of Home Affairs, *Annual Report, 1999-2000*, New Delhi: Department of Internal Security, Jammu & Kashmir, States and Home, Government of India, Chap. XI.
120. Ibid.
121. Ibid.
122. Ibid.
123. Ibid.
124. Ibid.
125. Ved Marwah, 'The Sub-Culture', *Seminar*, October 1977.
126. Sankar Sen, 'Complaints against the Police—Investigatory Role of the National Human Rights Commission', *The Indian Police Journal*, vol. XLVII, no. 4, October-December 2000, p. 50.
127. H. Bhisham Pal, *Central Police Forces of India*, New Delhi: Government of India, Ministry of Home Affairs, Bureau of Police Research and Development, p. 97.
128. Ibid., p. 99.
129. 'Empowering Investigative Agencies', *Frontline*, 9 January 1998, p. 26.
130. [The] Delhi Police Establishment Act, 1946, p. 465.
131. 'Empowering Investigative Agencies', *Frontline*, p. 26.
132. Ibid.
133. Ibid.
134. Ibid.
135. Central Bureau of Investigation (CBI) and Central Vigilance Commission (CVC), 272, Articles 32, 142, 141 and 144, *Supreme Court Annual Digest*, 1988.
136. Ibid.
137. Central Vigilance Commission, *Annual Report*, New Delhi, 31 March 1998, p. 1.
138. Ministry of Home Affairs, Resolution no. 24/7/64-AVD, dated 11 February 1964.
139. Ministry of Power, *Annual Report, 2000-2001*, p. 36.
140. The Electricity (Supply) Act, 1948, as amended by Electricity Laws

(Amendment) Act, 1998, Bare Act 2001, Allahabad: Law Publishers (India) Pvt. Ltd., pp. 8-9.

141. *Annual Report*, pp. 36-7.
142. Ibid., p. 37.
143. Ibid.
144. Website address: http://www.mib.nic.in/nicpart/ pbmisn. htm.
145. For a detailed discussion, see M.P. Singh, 'Economic Liberalization and Political Federalization in India : Mutually Reinforcing Responses to Global Integration', in *The Impact of Global and Regional Integration on Federal Systems: A Comparative Analysis*, ed. Harvey Lazar, Hamish Telford and Ronald L. Watts, School of Policy Studies, Queen's University, McGill–Queen's University Press, 2003, Chap. 6.
146. Watts, 'Intergovernmental Councils in Federations', *Constructive and Cooperative Federalism*, IIGR, Queen's University and IRPP, Montreal, 2003(2).

CHAPTER 6

First Ministers' Conferences in Canada

One of the most important federal institutional innovations in Canada that initially began as a convention of the Constitution before it became incidentally entrenched in the constitutional text in 1982 is the First Ministers' Conference (FMC). The original Constitution did not provide for it presumably because it was thought that the two orders of government had demarcated jurisdictions and an intergovernmental conflict could be resolved by the federal executive's power of disallowance of provincial legislations. However, provincial powers tended to increase following favourable interpretation by the Judicial Committee of the Privy Council and gradual decline of the power of disallowance by Ottawa.[1] The FMC has now emerged as a unique policy instrument intended to provide a forum for consultation and coordination between the federal and provincial governments. It has been essentially episodic but has tended to take place on a fairly regular basis: without this instrumentality of 'Executive Federalism', it is difficult to comprehend the working of the Canadian federal system.

In a way, the emergence of the FMCs would appear to be an inevitable development in retrospect. For in a parliamentary federal system, it is the executive that could have emerged as the focal point of intergovernmental relations. The Second Chamber, which is supposed to be a federal house, cannot be regarded as a forum for decisively reconciling intergovernmental issues because the Senate in Canada is appointed by the federal government of the day and is inefficacious. According to Opeskin, 'Executive Federalism' develops naturally in countries with Westminster style parliamentary federal systems like Canada and Australia.[2] This pattern of intergovernmental relations is largely a matter of convention rather than a written constitutional provision. Thus, the prime minister and the premiers in Canada have automatically become the natural forum for the conduct of intergovernmental relations. In contrast to Opeskin's opinion, Papillon and Simeon, who adopted an idealistic or prescriptive view, observed that a Westminster style parliamentary federal system premised on the governments' responsibility to their respective legislatures implies that 'executive summits are bound to have a limited decision-making role'.[3] Reality, however, bears out Opeskin's view.

Ironically, the Canadian Constitution Act, 1867, does not make any reference to the FMC. Yet, as mentioned earlier, FMCs have become an indispensable intergovernmental mechanism. This is due to a number of reasons. First, the division of powers between the federal and provincial governments, especially in the classical Canadian Constitution written in an age when the doctrine of dual sovereignty was the prevalent idea, creates divided jurisdictions that cannot be functionally sustained in any political system. This functional imperative was felt at an early stage which is evident from the fact that officials from the two orders of government had to meet within a year of the founding of the Confederation, though the first ministers themselves first met in 1906, nearly forty years after the Constitution became effective. Second, the Constitution also envisaged shared jurisdiction between the two levels of government which can be functionally operated only through intergovernmental cooperation. Such shared jurisdictions in Canada in fact expanded enormously later outside the framework of the Constitution on the basis of intergovernmental agreements, largely through the mechanism of the FMCs, even though initially these agreements were laboriously worked out at the level of official and ministerial negotiations. Indeed, the bulk of fiscal federal arrangements in Canada are the outcome of intergovernmental negotiations and compacts. In fact, the Constitution also entrusted major responsibilities in fields like health, education and welfare to provincial governments but the federal government monopolized most of the fiscal, bureaucratic and political resources. This necessitated intergovernmental collaboration.[4] Third, the need for intergovernmental relations was most acutely felt with the emergence of new policy areas that were not visualized by the Constitution, such as environment, energy, ecology, international treaties and trade, especially in a world that is rapidly becoming more globalized and regionally integrated. Meekison offered two justifications for the existence of FMCs: (*a*) for provincial interest to be reflected in federal policy making; and (*b*) for the federal and provincial governments to work together for pursuing common interests in areas where they would like to cooperate despite divided jurisdiction. The National Energy Policy is a good example of this where the two levels of government were required to work together.[5]

The foregoing developments have put increasing emphasis on intergovernmental relations. Besides fiscal federalism, the development of the post-Second World War welfare state in Canada has been a by-product of what came to be known as cooperative federalism replacing the classical federal doctrine of divided sovereignties. Finally, even in the era of neo-liberal economic policy reforms emphasizing market forces instead of the state, the importance of intergovernmental cooperation has not waned. In recent years Canada has successfully replaced the welfare state by a new Social Union Framework consistent with a paradigm shift to a new economic order with greater accent on 'globalization—a recognition of globalizing and localizing pressures that have simultaneously impacted the central federal state'. As Meekison observed, 'by the beginning of the 1970s, the First Ministers' Conference had become recognized, important, and permanent part of the political process in Canada'.[6]

The abortive Victoria Charter of 1971 provided, among others, 'A conference of Canada and the first ministers of the provinces shall be called by the prime minister of Canada at least once a year unless, in any year, a majority of those composing the conference decide that it shall not be held'.[7] The communique issued after the Annual Premiers' Conference held in Toronto in 1974 'urged the prime minister of Canada to invite the provincial premiers to a private discussion prior to the next federal budget', with the purpose of considering 'ways for the provinces and the federal government to take cooperative action on the major economic issues facing Canada today'. The Premiers' Conferences invariably leave some issues to be authoritatively taken up by the FMC in the final instance. The final constitutional recognition of this body which was earlier lacking, came to be incorporated in Section 49 of Part V of the Constitution Act, 1982, which envisaged a constitutional conference of the prime minister of Canada and the first ministers to be convened by the former within fifteen years after the new constitutional provisions went into effect to 'review the provisions' of Part V.

The FMC has emerged as a major instrument of 'executive federalism' in the Canadian political system to deal with any emergent problem of national magnitude affecting both orders of government.

Another possible alternative for federal representation of regional interest in Canada was sought to be found in the federal cabinet. By convention the prime minister provides a definite representation to each region in Canada in the cabinet and the ministers are, in fact, expected to speak out for their regions in cabinet deliberations.

Yet the cabinet has not truly evolved into an intergovernmental institution for the simple reason that the cabinet ministers are an integral part of the federal government and they cannot really claim to authoritatively speak for the provincial governments. This is particularly true when different parties are in power at the two levels of government. Even if the same party happens to be in power in Ottawa and a provincial capital, the Canadian party system is so much regionalized that the two orders of government are generally not unanimous in their views on the same issues and policies.

Because of these factors, neither the senate nor the federal cabinet has been able to eclipse the FMC as an intergovernmental mechanism. Mackinon, Secretary, Canadian Intergovernmental Conferences, aptly observed in this connection:

> Not only do the eleven First Ministers represent the totality of the executive power in Canada, as leaders of the majority party in their respective legislatures, they usually have effective control over those legislatures. In a sense, then, the FMC represents the concentration of the executive and legislative powers in Canada.[8]

Issues discussed at the FMCs between 1906 and October 2004, cross-tabulated with the various prime ministers are presented in Table 6.1. A total of 75 FMCs was convened during this period, of which 19 dealt with economy and fiscal federalism; 22 with constitutional reforms; 3 with economy, fiscal federalism and

TABLE 6.1: FIRST MINISTERS' CONFERENCES BETWEEN 1906 AND OCTOBER 2004: ISSUES DISCUSSED UNDER DIFFERENT PRIME MINISTERS

Prime Minister	*Cat.* 1	*Cat.* 2	*Cat.* 3	*Cat.* 4	*Total*
Laurier	1	–	–	–	1
Borden	–	–	–	1	1
King	2	–	–	3	5
Bennett	1	1	–	2	4
Laurent	1	2	–	3	6
Diefenbaker	3	–	–	1	4
Pearson	–	2	1	6	9
Trudeau	7	11	–	5	23
Clark	1	–	–	–	1
Mulroney	1	6	2	3	12
Campbell	–	–	–	1	1
Chretien	2	–	–	5	7
Martin	–	–	–	1	1
Total	19	22	3	31	75

Notes: Cat. : Category.
Category 1: Economy and Fiscal Federation.
Category 2: Constitution.
Category 3: Economy and Fiscal Federalism, Constitution.
Category 4: Economy, Constitution and/or More Diverse Issues, Social Security.

Source: Information collected from Intergovernmental Conference Secretariat and Parliament Library in Ottawa and tabulated by the author.

Constitution; and 31 with a diverse assortment of issues like economy, Constitution, and social security. Among the prime ministers, Trudeau and Mulroney were the most inveterate users of the FMC as a forum for intergovernmental negotiation, co-operation and coordination. Of 23 such meetings chaired by Trudeau, 11 dealt with the constitution; 7 with economy and fiscal federalism, and 5 with a more diverse set of issues. During Mulroney's premiership, 12 FMCs were held, 6 of which focused on the constitution; 1 on economy and fiscal federalism; 2 on economy, fiscal federalism and constitution; and 3 on more diverse concerns. During Pearson's regime 9 FMCs were held, 6 dealt with diverse issues; 2 with the constitution; and 1 with eonomy, fiscal federalism and constitution. Under Chretien, there was a definite decline in the frequency with which such meetings were held: with his third back-to-back majority, only 7 FMCs were held until the summer of 2003. His successor, Paul Martin, convened the first FMC meeting on healthcare in September 2004, and the question of constitutional reforms that had dominated the FMC agenda in the 1980s, was held in abeyance as had happened during Chretien's term in office.

In the initial phase between 1906 and 1929, only three FMCs were held. Their frequency appreciably increased between the 1930s and 1940s when 8 FMCs were convened. This increase is explained by the Great Economic Depression and the Second World War. During the 1950s 7 such conferences were held, in the 1960s 15, in the 1970s 16, and in the 1980s 13. The phenomenal increase in their frequency is explained in terms of the growing importance of fiscal federalism, economy, constitutional reforms and ecology. A decline in their frequency since the 1990s may be attributed to the repeated failure to make further headway in constitutional reforms at Meech Lake and Charlottetown and the resultant fatigue and lull on this front. However, economy, fiscal federalism and, to an extent, social security still recognize the necessity and importance of the first ministers' meetings even during this phase. Papillon and Simeon perceived a shift from FMCs (more formal conferences) to first ministers' meetings (FMMs marked by less formality and more flexibility) in the post-Meech Lake/Charlottetown period.[9]

What are the factors that affect the success or otherwise of the FMCs? It is difficult to give a precise answer to this question as a number of factors are involved. Among the more important ones, are the typical issues or interests that have produced enduring cleavages in federal–provincial relations, personalities of the prime ministers and premiers, secrecy or publicity surrounding such meetings, and repeated success or failure that may encourage the first ministers to convene more such meetings or dampen their spirits to continue their labour.

A close examination of the efficacy of the FMC as an intergovernmental mechanism reveals that a contingent relationship among at least five important factors determines the final outcome. These are: (*a*) issues, identities and ideological climate of the

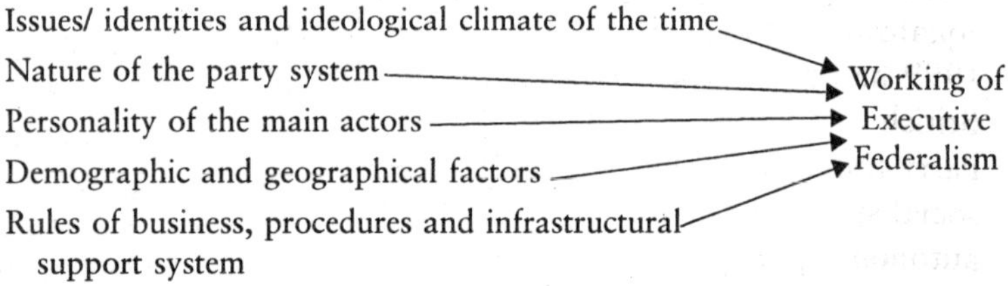

FIGURE 6.1: FACTORS AFFECTING THE WORKING OF FMC AS AN INSTRUMENT OF EXECUTIVE FEDERALISM IN CANADA

time; (*b*) the nature of the party system; (*c*) personality of the main actors involved; (*d*) demographic and geographical factors characterizing the federating units; and (*e*) rules of business, procedures and infrastructural support system (see Figure 6.1).

In a country of subcontinental dimensions, bicultural and a multicultural mosaic, regionalism as a factor is both a cause and an effect in federal politics. Obviously, the working of executive federalism through the FMC is deeply influenced by regional diversities and the line-up at any federal–provincial conference. Besides Quebec's separatism, other regional configurations that determine the line-up of political forces at the FMCs are the fiscal dominance of the federal government, the economic dominance of Central Canada or St. Lawrence Valley, the Maritimes' discontent, and the alienation of the Western Provinces. These cleavages, with the exception of Quebec, are usually not mutually reinforcing; rather they are cross-cutting in their mutual interaction. For this reason party divisions cannot fully account for the alignment of political forces in the FMCs, for example, even though the poorer provinces are generally more likely to agree with Ottawa, left–right divide does not matter as much in Canada as in some European countries. Historically, poorer provinces like Quebec and those in the Maritimes/Atlantic often sided with the federal government and the poorer among the Prairies/Western Provinces were generally more persistently opposed to the federal government. In addition, more recently, Quebec seems to have drifted out of the federal orbit on an enduring basis. Moreover, poorer provinces are overly concerned about equalization payments from the federal government. Three rich provinces—

Ontario, British Columbia (BC) and Alberta—do not receive any equalization payments. Of the three, Ontario and Alberta in 1999 had right-of-centre governments that advocated tax cuts. British Columbia, which had a socialist National Democratic Party (NDP) government, did not want tax cuts and supported social spending. Provinces are generally very protective of their autonomy but there are differences among them. For instance, BC supported the National Energy Policy (NEP) as did Manitoba but Saskatchewan held the middle ground. Premier Davis of Ontario strongly supported the NEP but Premier Peter Laugheed of Alberta vehemently opposed it. Trudeau's NEP purported to introduce greater federal control over Canada's oil resources: Ontario being the most industrialized province was bound to benefit from it, while Alberta with the richest oil resources would stand to lose. Going against Trudeau's NEP, oil producing provinces like Alberta and Saskatchewan expressed the view that oil resources was a provincial subject under the Constitution. This was disputed by other provinces like Ontario because the latter's industries need oil. Quebec had its own reasons to support provincial jurisdictional claims because it produces a substantial amount of hydroelectricity power and desires a distinct society status for itself on cultural grounds. This also explains why the Western Provinces want a greater share in federal power through such constitutional reforms as the Triple 'E' Senate (Equal, Effective and Elected).

Further, BC's relations with the federal government have been strained regardless of which party was in power in that province or in Ottawa. For instance, Victoria and Ottawa did not agree even when the Social Credit Party, a conservative political formation, was in power in BC and the Progressive Conservative Party in Ottawa. Another example is Alberta—a province that has for some time allied with Quebec advocating more power for the provinces. Even when the Conservatives were in power both in Alberta and Ottawa, the situation did not change. Today when the Conservatives are in power in Alberta and the Liberals have formed a minority government with the outside support of the NDP in Ottawa (winter 2004), the situation remains more or less the same. Party ideology, therefore, does not shed much light on federal–provincial relations and alignments. Moreover, Liberals in Quebec sometimes distance themselves from Liberals at the federal level. Likewise, on the NEP, the Conservatives in Ontario supported the Liberals in Ottawa against the Conservatives in Alberta. Public opinion on the NEP generally supported the federal initiative. Similarly, when the federal government proposed medicare in the 1960s, several provinces opposed it. Since there was a strong public opinion in favour of it, the federal government persisted with its policy of medicare and finally succeeded in giving effect to an agreement with the provinces to institute it. Also, provincial governments at times soften their opposition to a particular policy when they realize that the public opinion is in favour of it.

There could be federal–provincial and interprovincial differences on cultural policies as well, for example, language rights. In more recent times, Quebec and Newfoundland wanted annulment of constitutional provisions relating to language rights within their provincial jurisdictions. These rights are entrenched in the case of Quebec in the BNA Act, while in the case of Newfoundland these were incorporated in 1949 when that province joined the Confederation. Over time, they have become more region-oriented and for this reason they wanted minority language rights to be revoked within their provincial jurisdictions.

Fiscal issues have given rise to federal–provincial friction, and cost-shared programmes (for example, Canada Health and Social Transfer Programme [CHST] 1995) what are often referred to as 50:50, that is, if the provinces spend a dollar, the federal government also matches it by a dollar. When the federal government began to put a cap on it by excluding the wealthier provinces, the provincial governments were alarmed. This is because the share of richer provinces like Alberta, BC and Ontario, which was earlier 50 per cent for each was reduced to 5 per cent.[10]

Recently, another highly debated issue was the development and distribution of the federal infrastructure fund. Ontario wanted the per capita criterion to be adopted because it has a large number of taxpayers and would be able to generate more funds that way. The federal government, as a matter of policy, wanted a larger share for the poorer provinces. On a similar controversial issue relating to the basis of federal healthcare funding, Finance Minister Paul Martin (who is presently the PM) changed it and opted for the per capita criterion. This method benefited the populous provinces, but the smaller provinces were placed in a disadvantageous position and were, therefore, dismayed.

Another crucial factor that affects the deliberations at the FMC is the ideological climate of the time. Developments in the Canadian political system in the last half century or so point to at least two major ideological shifts with an intermediate phase intervening between the two. After the Second World War, Canada followed a strategy of development with an emphasis on Keynesian economic policies based on State intervention (in the economy) to institute a welfare state. Under the leadership of Mackenzie King and St. Laurent the framework of social securities underlying the State was put in place from the 1940s to the 1960s. The trend of centralization of the Canadian political system under the impact of the Great Economic Depression and the Second World War thus continued unabated after the war in terms of setting up a welfare state with federal initiative and its fiscal dominance. This was the period of enormous expansion of federal finances and powers, even though judicial interpretation and the consequent heightened provincial consciousness could not completely obliterate the federal political framework of Canada. If anything, there was a slow and steady expansion of provincial jurisdiction and resources that was to come to fruition at a later stage. Against this backdrop, it is easy to understand that the ideological temper of the time favoured federal leadership in the Canadian political system. It is also understandable that even with a less forceful personality as the prime minister during this phase, the ideological momentum of the times would have easily favoured the dominance of the federal government in intergovernmental relations.

Beginning with the 1980s, Canada, as also the rest of the world, witnessed a major ideological paradigm shift under the impact of the neo-liberal policy package emphasizing economic liberalization and privatization. In other words, the change was from a welfare state to a more privatized economy with greater scope for market forces. But this major shift was preceded by an interregnum during which federal dominance in the polity continued with a greater concern for cultural issues. These were the Trudeau years spanning from 1968 to the early 1980s. With the welfare state already in place and the Quiet Revolution in

Quebec having taken place in the 1960s resulting in the emergence of a French–Canadian bourgeoisie, the attention was increasingly focused on bicultural and multicultural concerns, French–Canadian susceptibilities, partition of the Constitution from London to Ottawa and the renewal of the Constitution with an Amending Formula and the Charter of Rights and Freedoms. This period simultaneously witnessed continued federal dominance in Canadian politics under Trudeau's leadership as also gradual assertion of provincial identities and power including Quebec's separatism. Accounts of the FMCs during this period clearly reveal the continued federal dominance under Trudeau.

Since the 1980s, pressures for decentralization at home and economic globalization, which in the Canadian context primarily mean North American continentalism, have fundamentally altered economic and political structures. Two processes—federalization and globalization—have been simultaneously at work. The net effect of these far-reaching changes has been manifested in the form of downsizing both the federal government and the welfare state. Typically, federalism as well as the welfare state in Canada have been geared to national power grid and national economic production machine. Globalization has weakened the national federal state as also the organization of productive forces at the national level. Economic globalization and information revolution have created an atmosphere conducive to the free play of multinational and market forces. As Courchene aptly observed:

> With the increasing shift toward north-south, rather than east-west trade, all provinces except PEI now export more to the rest of the world than to the rest of Canada. . . . One obvious challenge arising from this is that our east-west transfer system must now be superimposed over an increasingly north-south trading system. Another is the resulting pressures for greater decentralization (and presumably enhanced asymmetry) that are mounting in the face of this shift from domestic to international markets. Finally, but hardly exhaustively, Canada's fiscal (debt/deficit) overhang is leading to a significant downsizing and decentralization of Ottawa's powers, especially in the social policy arena.[11]

In the changed ideological environment, there is a palpable decline in the will and ability of the federal government to continue the trend of federal domination of the FMCs. Thus, the rationale for convening FMCs for constitutional reforms and welfare policics has become weak. This is, however, not to suggest that FMCs have become redundant; there are other reasons for their continued relevance.

The Social Union Framework Agreement (SUFA) signed at the 1999 FMC aptly illustrates the new pattern of social policies and fiscal federalism that is emerging after the retreat of the welfare state. This new programme was launched with provincial rather than federal initiative which was the case with the earlier pattern of Ottawa-dominated welfare spending. Ontario played a leading role in initiating the programme. The first policy framework of the social union was decentralized reflecting provincial preferences, but when the federal government was finally invited to join the programme, it took the position that since Ottawa was putting more money on the table, its own perspectives must also be accommodated. But in any case, it was a federal–provincial programme that was less top-down and more bottom-up.

Another example of the extension of the FMC to a rather innovative use in the changed ideological climate was Chretien's idea of Team Canada trade missions to foreign countries, including one to India. The first ministers travel together in the same plane and generally stay together in the same hotel. Thus, they get a rare opportunity to develop a close rapport that facilitates good interactions with a greater degree of assurance. But closer contacts may also at times breed antipathies. For instance, one federal civil servant divulged the information (in Toronto on 8 February 2000) on the condition of anonymity that he knew about a particular Team Canada's visit to China from which at least one premier returned with a very low opinion about one of his colleagues. From available accounts, it becomes amply clear that Team Canada has been a tremendous success in terms of its impact on both intergovernmental and trade relations.

According to Courchene, it is a positive development because it reflects 'the growing influence of provincial governments in the area of international trade. It is an experiment in cooperative federalism in the area of trade relations in a nation which is becoming more decentralized and where the influence of the provincial governments is increasing'.[12] But this experiment may not be uniformly successful in all policy areas, for example, on the constitutional question which ended in deadlock. Harvey

Lazar rightly cautioned that on more difficult and intractable issues, only good interpersonal relations would not suffice. Trade is a different matter, because irrespective of whether one is a federalist or a sovereignist, more trade is always desirable. As far as trade is concerned, for which Team Canada is basically designed, it does help.[13]

An important issue that the FMC had to settle in the early years of the present century was related to the huge federal surplus Canada accumulated after successfully reducing its deficit of the past. To this end, in the past decade, Canada had cut spending on social programmes and some other areas of government expenditure. Financing the government's debt—which in the past had become unmanageable—constituted a substantial portion of the country's annual budget. By the turn of the century, it was more or less under control, thanks to the economic prosperity that had created the surplus; but the dilemma was what to do with so much surplus!

There has developed a huge debate about this large federal surplus, especially when provinces are all running deficits. This has fuelled increases in federal contributions to healthcare, and a major debate about 'fiscal imbalance' raising the issue that Ottawa has more money than it has responsibilities, and provinces more responsibilities than money. So, some argue that there should be a fundamental readjustment of fiscal federalism.[14]

The right wing in Canada—and Premier Harris of Ontario who was an ardent advocate of that—wanted that the government's surplus should be used for tax reductions. Tax reductions in Canada, like the United States, mainly help those who are financially better off. The left wing in Canada, on the other hand, wanted the money to be utilized for social programmes. The premiers were divided in their support to the right and left wing candidates, and so was the Liberal Party's caucus. This sort of division in the Liberal Party was historically one of its greatest strengths because it was linked to two main groupings in the population—those concerned about social justice and those focusing on wealth. This, coupled with its other octopus-like spread across parts of the body politic, allowed the party to capture a major share of votes in Canada, and an even larger share of seats in the House of Commons, making it in the process, over a period of time, a 'government party'.

The nature of the party system is another important factor impacting the working of executive federalism in Canada. The confederalization or bifurcation of national parties with greatly autonomous provincial units implies that party discipline is more characteristic of parliamentary proceedings rather than the proceedings of the FMCs. This means that the prime minister and the premiers are mainly governed by federal or provincial considerations while making known their respective stands at the meetings.

The nature of the party system affects intergovernmental relations in yet another way. As long as the system of two major parties and one minor party in Parliament was prevalent, the matter was less complicated. Since 1993, the federal party system has become a multi-partisan configuration and the Liberal Party (inclusive of the 1993 elections) continued to hold fort for three consecutive elections to the House of Commons, and in the fourth one in 2004, it won again but had to contend with a minority government. So far the impact of the party system transformation has been rather limited both in the parliamentary and intergovernmental arenas (with special reference to executive federalism). But given the present political scenario characterized by hung parliament, the impact of the change in the party system on federal as well as parliamentary arenas may become more pronounced in the years to come.

Another factor that impinges on the efficacy of the FMC as an instrument of executive federalism is related to the charisma and respect commanded by the main actors at these conferences. The vast resources at the disposal of the federal government coupled with the fact that the prime minister chairs the meetings and plays a major role in setting the agenda substantially influence the deliberations (at such meetings), but one must not overlook the fact that the prime minister can neither unilaterally convene such meetings nor set their agenda without taking the premiers into confidence. To quote Franks:

> This process of agenda setting and issue defining is hugely complicated, and usually takes a long time on important issues. What goes on at the first ministers' meetings is often only the icing on the cake, or as I would

describe it in canoeing terms, the froth on the water at the end of the rapids.[15]

The first ministers are the glamorous tips of icebergs with most of spadework done by the ministers and civil servants, both federal and provincial. Convening a FMC may mean months and often years of groundwork done behind the scenes by the ministerial staff. Both personalities and political processes together determine the success or failure of the FMCs.

By available indicators, prime ministers like Mackenzie King, Lester Pearson, Pierre Elliot Trudeau and Brian Mulroney were exceptionally active on the FMC front. When Trudeau became the prime minister in 1968 in the wake of a massive 'Trudeau mania', he added a new dimension to federal–provincial relations by virtue of his dynamic leadership style. Trudeau was more interested in national unity, English–French relations, French language concerns, and far less concerned about the economy. He was a French–Canadian federalist who abhorred provinces that advocated separatism. His initial years as prime minister were largely devoted to issues such as healthcare, tax reforms and other related matters, but subsequently his impact was most intensely felt on constitutional issues. His premiership was marked by intense and sustained negotiations that resulted in the patriation of the original Constitution from London to Ottawa and the adoption of the 1982 Constitution Act that included for the first time the Charter of Rights and the Amending Formula. Trudeau and Rene Levesque of Quebec and Blakeney of Saskatchewan were involved in an intense debate on the Charter. Finally, Trudeau had his way, and full credit goes to him for the inclusion of the Charter. By virtue of his mass appeal and charismatic personality, he was confident that his position was absolutely secure. Despite being aggressive in his approach, he was interested in intellectual pursuits. He had a unique way of dealing with the provinces, for example, if his proposal of contributing something to the cause of healthcare and education met with opposition from some provinces, he had the temerity of telling the people that the federal government had good intentions but could not do much as the provinces failed to extend their cooperation. However, despite his influence, federal–provincial relations during his regime were more tension-ridden than during Pearson's. The latter was a diplomatic prime minister who adopted a conciliatory rather than a combative approach.

Mulroney was a shrewd politician whose negotiating skills were such that he succeeded in reaching an agreement in principle on Quebec's endorsement of the 1982 Constitution—an issue which had been in the doldrums. Yet, a subsequent change in political circumstances conspired to undo the Meech Lake Accord for lack of ratification by some provinces. At the time of the Accord, the premier in Newfoundland was a Conservative who went along with Mulroney, also a Conservative. Subsequently, at the time of ratification, there was a change of government in the province that brought Clyde Wells, a liberal to power, who forcefully articulated his views against the consensus.

Mulroney's approach to governance was to buy loyalty—an approach which no doubt has its own drawbacks, for instance, if one buys loyalty in a region, another one is displeased and vice versa. It is prudent to adopt a policy based on equity and justice. Ironically, he was not completely oblivious of this, as is evident from his model of labour–capital relations.

Prime Minister Jean Chretien was rather combative without ceasing to be pragmatic—a trait comparable partly with Trudeau and partly with Mulroney. In principle, he was less open to the idea of federal–provincial collaboration and was therefore perceived to be combative, but it may be indicative of the changed ideological climate which emphasized rightsizing the federal government and spending. He was a minister in the Trudeau Cabinet, and both had a more or less a similar style of functioning. He was the one who had mooted the idea of Team Canada trade missions abroad. Chretien's successor, Prime Minister Paul Martin is much more accommodating to the provinces generally, and Quebec in particular, than was Chretien. He seems to be more sympathetic to asymmetrical federalism.[16]

In a similar vein, Cameron remarks:

> The departure of Chretien from the political stage marks the emergence of a new generation of political leadership for whom Quebec nationalism is no longer the single most important defining element of their world-view. Paul Martin, though a federal politician, is far more comfortable with Quebec nationalism than is his predecessor, just as Premier Jean

Charest of Quebec is far more comfortable with Canada and Canadian federalism than Bernard Landry, the man who preceded him.[17]

Apart from the charisma of the prime minister, the presence of influential provincial premiers with a mass appeal is also a deciding factor, as has already been indicated. Trudeau and the Quebec Parti Quebecois (PQ) Premier, Rene Levesque, did not share a particularly good rapport with each other. The Progressive Conservative (PC) Premier of Alberta, Peter Laugheed (also of the Trudeau period), was a strong individual, who enjoyed a great deal of influence as also other premiers like Bouchard of Quebec, Welsh of Newfoundland and Blakeney of Saskatchewan. In contrast, Premier Davis of Ontario and Liberal Premier Bourassa of Quebec adopted a more conciliatory and accommodating attitude. Harris was more influential and believed in bridging the gap between the federal and regional Governments. Today, who ever heads Quebec is not only combative, but also wields a great deal of influence at the FMCs, as Quebec is a large minority province crucial to the fortunes of the government. Prime ministers often grudge the emergence of provincial premiers as national leaders through the forum of the FMC, as the open sessions are televised and watched by people all over the nation. Fortuitous stopgap prime ministers like Kim Campbell (PC) were also inclined to use the forum of the FMC to present themselves as national leaders surrounded by provincial premiers. In fact, Premier Bob Rae of Ontario refused to attend the FMC convened by her as he was convinced that she should have waited until she got the people's mandate in the forthcoming parliamentary elections. Also, the federal government often decries the tendency of provincial premiers to speak to the galleries or to the constituents in their provinces while using the forum of the FMC. This may work both ways. A popular prime minister like Trudeau took advantage of his mass appeal for putting pressure on reluctant premiers to fall in line with a federal policy.

On balance, publicity is prohibitive of serious negotiation and success. By experience, serious negotiators generally prefer behind the scene activity which is perceived to be more conducive to giving effect to some kind of agreement. Generally, secrecy is criticized by the media as undemocratic and elitist.

Influence at the FMC is also a function of the agenda. If economic issues are on the agenda, Ontario is likely to wield greater influence for the simple reason that its contribution to the national economy, particularly the industrial sector, is by far the most substantial. On fiscal issues, Alberta with its rich oil resources and agricultural production, tends to be influential on issues relating to cultural policies and constitutional reforms and Quebec carries clout by virtue of it being a French-majority province in a nation with an English-speaking majority. The separatist movement in Quebec is keenly watched by the whole country. Influence also depends on the line-up at the Conference. If provincial governments remain firmly united, they can exert much pressure on Ottawa. However in such an eventuality, Ottawa may become paranoiac and disinclined to convene a meeting. Federalists often shudder at the thought of a situation where provinces gang up against the federal government. However, the latter is in a position to exercise a certain degree of influence in case Ottawa succeeds in driving a wedge between the provinces. An example of Social Union Framework Agreement illustrates the point elaborated above. The characteristic feature of this was that the initiative came from the provinces, and practically all the provincial governments—with the exception of Quebec that came in late—were united on this issue. The result was that ultimately Ottawa was persuaded to participate in this programme. It even made available federal funds on the basis of which it was able to put forth its point of view with a certain degree of authority in the programme that finally shaped up.

Demographic and geographical factors also enter into the executive federalism equation. For example, the premiers of Ontario and Quebec for most of Canada's history carried much clout due to the sheer size of population of these two largest provinces as well as due to the size of Ontario's economy. With the growing population of the Western Provinces and vast natural resources of Alberta and British Columbia, the influence commanded by Alberta in particular and the Western Provinces in general has become more pronounced in the FMCs over the years. The smaller size in geographical as well as demographic terms of the Atlantic Provinces as also of their smaller economies implies that they do not carry the same weight as Ontario, Alberta and Quebec.

Another important factor impinging on executive federalism relates to the rules of business, procedures and infrastructural support system. At the FMCs, agreements are generally reached before the actual meetings are convened. If bureaucrats have drafted a proposal on which the politicians agree, the deal is clinched. The officers meet on several occasions before the FMC to do the spadework. In the second stage, if a particular province does not agree with the federal proposal, it would initiate talks with the other provinces to win them over to its point of view. Similarly, the federal government, in its efforts to line up its allies for this purpose, turns to the provinces that are fiscally dependent on Ottawa such as the four Maritime provinces and one of the Prairie provinces—Saskatchewan. These poorer provinces are more likely to extend support to Ottawa. These line-ups are typical over fiscal matters. On constitutional issues, Ontario is more likely to be an ally of the federal government.[18] The groundwork done before the FMC is largely the work of two sets of committees. First, the Continuing Committee of Ministers in the policy issue area that is going to be discussed, and second, the Continuing Committee of offices dealing with the policy issue area. For example, before the FMC in September 1980, these two sets of committees met during summer to negotiate the matter and prepared a draft of the consensus reached for the meeting of the first ministers who finalized the federal–provincial policies in the area concerned. The issue was constitutional reforms which was broken down into fourteen components. When the first ministers met there was little to be done for areas of agreement and disagreement and the contents thereof had already been identified and worked out by the two sets of committees that preceded the FMC. This illustrates that closed door negotiations or low profile meetings work much better than high-powered FMCs in the glare of media publicity.[19]

The staff meets all the time, intense briefings take place, and papers are circulated. If there is an agreement, then they prepare a communique.[20] The officials also play a very important role in these meetings. For instance, those in the prime minister's office discuss the matter with officials in the premiers' office and prepare the agenda of the meetings keeping in view the respective policies and aspirations of both. Both the prime minister and the premier are thoroughly briefed by their respective officers with regard to the issues to be discussed, what would be the likely position of the other government, and what position their government may take in the matter. If the question pertains to finance, the prime minister has the option of asking the finance minister, or any other minister who is involved in the matter at hand, to accompany him. The same is true for the provinces as well. Occasionally, if there is a difficult question the first ministers discuss the issue among themselves rather than in the presence of other ministers and officials, as had happened during the Meech Lake negotiations. After the meeting, the delegates go into the details of the discussions held (on that day) so as to chalk out the strategy to be adopted for the next day.[21]

These meetings appear to be mere discussions at the informal level, but the fact remains that at times they do read to agreements like the Social Union Framework Agreement, the Meech Lake and Charlottetown Accords. At times, the conference forms a working group of ministers from among themselves and asks them to report back to the next conference. Occasionally, when the report has been prepared the first ministers may say, 'keep that in, we are going to discuss it in the next meeting'.[22]

Negotiations lead to agreements but they do not have any legal status until they are placed before Parliament and Provincial Legislatures for approval/ratification.[23] On a constitutional issue, a certain specified majority/unanimity is required. On some issue, the consent of seven provinces and the prime minister is necessary, while on others the consent of all the ten premiers and the prime minister is mandatory. Consensus generally means compromise and softening positions to reach an agreement. If no agreement is reached, the first ministers can either agree to disagree or else the prime minister may take a unilateral action as was done by Trudeau in 1980 when he took the constitutional issue to London for necessary action by the British Parliament and finally, by 1981, most of the provinces (with the exception of Quebec that refused to be a party to the Constitution), the federal government and the rest of Canada fell in line and gave their consent to his proposal.[24]

The process of the FMC is facilitated by the institutional support of the Canadian Intergovernmental Conference Secretariat (CICS) initially set up in February 1968 as the Secretariat of the Constitutional Conference, but transformed and broadened in 1973 as an agency that provides administrative services for the planning and conduct of federal–provincial and interprovincial conferences. It is a neutral intergovernmental body whose budget is supported by both levels of government; and its staff is selected from both governments.

The task becomes easier when Ottawa is the venue: the old railway station in the heart of the town is transformed into an intergovernmental conference facility with a hall for public conferences, smaller rooms for private meetings and space for individual government delegation headquarters, support services, media services and delegate lounges.[25]

The FMC as an exercise has often been criticized on various grounds. The most common criticism is that it is not democratic. This is primarily because of the allegation that it is an elitist body where 'eleven men in suits' decide behind closed doors on behalf of the whole nation. Moreover, the legitimacy of the meetings is often questioned—by journalists rather than by academics—on the ground that they are not amenable to open deliberations and public scrutiny. Watts conceded that the FMC is a body of elites, but it should not be forgotten that they are elected by the people to their respective legislatures and they are there as the executive heads of their respective governments. The pressure groups in his opinion have no right to be there any more than as audience or citizens. If the first ministers take a wrong decision, they are accountable for it to the electorate, while the pressure groups are self-elected.[26] After the Meech Lake Accord, an attempt has been made to broaden the ambit of public opinion and pressure group inputs either prior to the conferences or at the time when they are held. Some observers suggested greater public participation in these, including holding joint sessions of Parliament and Provincial Legislatures (much in advance of such meetings) and inviting the leaders of the opposition parties to attend the Conference. Some effort toward greater non-governmental participation, though not to the extent suggested earlier, was made at the time of the abortive Charlottetown Accord and the eminently successful Social

Union Framework Agreement. Sicdle mentioned other policy areas, for example, Children's Agenda where round table meetings of representatives of different groups are held and whose suggestions are passed on to the federal and provincial departments concerned.[27] Some commentators, however, argued that if the first ministers are forced to decide in the glare of media publicity, decisions may become extremely difficult to reach.[28]

In Gordon Smith's view, considerable productive work is done both at the level of ministerial meetings and at the level of officials. For instance, meetings of finance ministers are more crucial whereas ministerial/official level meetings are more elaborate and successful because they are less politicized.[29]

Another concern is related to what may be called the expertise problem. Sometimes the executive heads taking decisions on certain issues are not necessarily specialists in the policy area concerned, especially if it calls for technical expertise. For example, environment is an area which requires inputs from a wide range of sciences and arts. There is no guarantee of expert representation in the decision-making area unless the political executives are sensitive enough to expert opinion. In such a situation, the expert and assertive viewpoints may get sidetracked politically.[30]

A third major criticism of intergovernmental relations pertains to the lack of institutional status. None of the procedures regarding the FMC are outlined anywhere in the Constitution or law. Everything is left to the decision makers, especially the prime minister. There has been no attempt to codify decision-making rules as is done in Parliament and provincial legislatures. If anything, the decisions are informal (by consensus or unanimity) and there have been occasions marked by controversies because of unilateral action taken by a prime minister, a glaring example being that of Trudeau on the patriation of the Constitution. Viewed from this perspective, the process may appear to be lacking in legitimacy and accountability. However, Watts strongly defended their informal and flexible nature. This leaves much scope for evolving workable mechanisms in an area where flexible negotiations and procedures are much better than any codified constitutional rule.[31]

The Meech Lake and Charlottetown Accords represent two efforts to lay down some basic rules and procedures for the FMCs going beyond the mere reference to these conferences in the 1982 Constitution, though not with any success. George Anderson, deputy minister in the Federal Ministry of Intergovernmental Affairs in Ottawa, informed that Canadians are not really in the business of creating new organizations at the level of the FMCs.[32] Following the establishment of the Secretariat of Intergovernmental Conference, other support organizations in some technical fields have also been set up, for example, the Canadian Institute of Health Research and Science (in the area of healthcare) and a common secretariat to coordinate the work of various orders of government (in the field of climate change).

According to Lazar, there could be a stronger Intergovernmental Secretariat and an annual FMC similar to the Annual Premiers' Conference which would go a long way in promoting cooperative federalism in the new era.[33]

Segal proposed some other reforms. For example, the budgetary process could be improved through executive federalism. He wondered why so much secrecy surrounds the budget in Canada or in India when the economic trends in the present-day world are common knowledge. It would be more beneficial if the federal and provincial finance ministers got together to prepare the budget. If the chairman of the Bank of Canada held a meeting with all the finance ministers on an annual basis, there could be a better coordination of federal–provincial policies leading to greater fiscal stability. Identifying other areas needing more effective federal–provincial collaboration, he added that the process could be used to reform the healthcare system of Canada which is a universal service that is based on 75 per cent provincial contribution. The system has not been significantly reformed for the last twenty-five years. Another area that deserves the attention of the first ministers in his view is Canada–US relationship which could use creative interventions to reconcile Canadian nationalism with globalism.[34]

Looking ahead, it can be surmised that the FMCs and other aspects of intergovernmental relations will continue to be used as mechanisms of federal–provincial consultation and harmonization in the Canadian federal system. In all probability, noted Mackinon,

> there will be a continued attempt to use the FMC as a venue for the development of broad national economic policies, an aspect that can be

seen emerging as a significant feature of FMCs on the economy. Also, from time to time one might expect, even with an annual FMC on the economy with a broad agenda, that situations amounting to national emergencies may continue to warrant the holding of a separate FMC devoted to that issue. Past examples can be found in the discussions arising out of the energy crisis in the 1970s or earlier conferences in the 1930s concerning unemployment relief.[35]

With the issue of constitutional reforms in Canada having been held in abeyance by the Liberal Governments led by Chretien and Martin (at least till, winter 2004), intergovernmental relations have reached a deadlock. Nevertheless, Executive Federalism in Canada is still necessary to manage the economy and ecology which continue to be on the agenda even after constitutional reforms have been put on the back burner. Canadians have moved ahead on the course of privatizing the Crown Corporations and replacing one of the most well-developed welfare states in the world by a renegotiated Social Union Framework of securities and national integration under a reworked system of cooperative federalism. There is a lull on the issue of Quebec's separatism but federalists and sovereignists are working through the existing constitutional framework. This standoff cannot continue in this state of uncertainty indefinitely. The Canadian political system will have to address the question of constitutional renewal to the satisfaction of all Canadians.

In conclusion, it is useful to refer to the viewpoint of Papillon and Simeon who believe that FMCs are an essential, though a weak link in the Canadian parliamentary federal institutional chain.[36]

NOTES

1. Martin Papillon and Richard Simeon, 'The Weakest Link? First Ministers' Conferences in Canadian Intergovernmental Relations', typescript, pp. 5-6 (in *Canadian Federalism, Canada: The State of the Federation 2002*, ed. J. Peter Meekison, Hamish Telford and Harvey Lazar, Kingston: IIGR/Montreal: McGill Queen's University Press, 2004, pp. 113-40.
2. Brian R. Opeskin, 'Mechanism for Intergovernmental Relations in Federations', *International Social Science Journal*, no. 167, UNESCO: Blackwell Publishers, March 2001, p. 130. One may add that this is particularly true in situations of one party governments. This does not,

however, always happen in conditions of minority and coalition governments as the Canadian experience with the former and Indian experience with the latter illustrate.

3. Papillon and Simeon, op. cit., p. 3.
4. Ibid., p. 8.
5. Interview with J. Peter Meekison, Victoria, 20 December 1999.
6. J. Peter Meekison, 'First Ministers' Conferences in the Canadian Federal System', in *Ottawa and the Provinces: The Distribution of Money and Power*, ed. Thomas J. Courchene, David W. Conklin and Gail C.A. Cook, Ontario Economic Council Special Research Report, Federal Provincial Relations Series, Ontario Economic Council, Toronto, 1985, vol. 2, p. 168.
7. Section 48.
8. Stuart Mackinon, 'First Ministers' Conferences', paper presented at the Fifth Conference on Public Policy and Administrative Studies, University of Guelph, 22 April 1988, p. 3.
9. Papillon and Simeon, op. cit., pp. 25-8.
10. Personal Communication with Richard Simeon, Toronto, November 2004.
11. Thomas J. Courchene, 'ACCESS: A Convention on the Canadian Economic and Social Systems', working paper prepared for the Ministry of Intergovernmental Affairs, Government of Ontario, August 1996, p. 1.
12. Interview with Thomas J. Courchene, School of Policy Studies, Queen's University, 9 February 2000.
13. Interview with Harvey Lazar, IIGR, Queen's University, 7 February 2000.
14. Personal Communication with Richard Simeon, University of Toronto, Toronto, November 2004.
15. C.E.S. Franks, personal communication, dated 20 August 1999.
16. I am thankful for this observation to the veteran Canadian scholar, Richard Simeon, op. cit.
17. David R. Cameron, 'Canada', *The Federal India*, Centre for Policy Alternatives and the Forum of Federations with Support of the Canadian Intergovernmental Development Agency and Foreign Affairs Canada, Browns Beach Hotel, Negombo, 3-5 April 2005, p. 28.
18. Interview with Hugh Segal at the School of Policy Studies, Queen's University, 12 November 1999.
19. Interview with James Ross Hurley in Ottawa, 23 November 1999.
20. Interview with Hugh Segal, op. cit.
21. Interview with Ronald L. Watts, IIGR, Queen's University, 15 February 2000.
22. Interview with James Ross Hurley, op. cit.

23. Interview with Richard Simeon, University of Toronto, 8 February 2000.
24. Interview with Stuart Mackinon, CICS, Ottawa, 23 November 1999.
25. James Ross Hurley, 'Executive Federalism', in *Public Administration and Public Management Experiences in Canada*, ed. Jacques Bourgault, Maurice Demers and Cynthia Williams, Quebec: Les Publications due Quebec, 1997, p. 118.
26. Interview with Ronald L. Watts, op. cit.
27. Interview with Leslie Siedle, 19 January 2000.
28. Ibid.
29. Interview with Gordon Smith, Victoria, 21 December 1999.
30. Interview with Richard Simeon, op. cit.
31. Interview with Ronald L. Watts, op. cit.
32. Interview with George Anderson, 2 February 2000.
33. Interview with Harvey Lazar, op. cit.
34. Interview with Hugh Segal, op. cit.
35. Mackinon, 'First Ministers' Conference', op. cit., p. 28.
36. Papillon and Simeon, op. cit.

CHAPTER 7

National Development Council and Inter-State Council in India

The need for an intergovernmental mechanism in a federal system for coordination of relations between the two orders of government is fairly obvious today. In the early phase of federal constitution-making, the framers (for example, those who drafted the British North America Act, 1867) did not, however, visualize this need, presumably because they were swayed by the classical notions of dual sovereignty in a federal political order. Nevertheless, at a later stage of federal constitution-making, say, in the post-Second World War period, the idea was more readily recognized.

In contrast to the classical parliamentary federal Constitution of Canada, the Indian Constitution was alive to the necessity of an intergovernmental mechanism for union–state relations, as is evident from a provision to this effect under Article 263. Despite these differences in the constitutional provisions of Canada and India, the early major intergovernmental forums were initiated informally outside the framework of the Constitution in both countries. The First Ministers' Conference (FMC) in Canada, the National Development Council (NDC) and the Inter-State Council (ISC) in India are cases in point.

NATIONAL DEVELOPMENT COUNCIL

In the Constitution, state governments have been accorded a primary role in developmental concerns such as agriculture, local government, education, economic and social planning, public health and irrigation. These subjects are either included in the state list or in the concurrent list. The most elastic revenue resources like corporate and personal income tax and customs are allocated primarily to the union, though some of these are subsequently shared by the states. The states have jurisdiction over agricultural income tax and sales tax (now in the process of being phased out by Value Added Tax—VAT), but these are either inelastic in a slow developing/stagnant economy or the state governments are reluctant to tap them for fear of unpopular reaction by significant segments of the electorate. By and large, states do not have resources commensurate with their developmental responsibilities. However, there is a provision for transfer of resources from the union to the states on the advice of the Finance Commission. Thus, the Constitution envisages a system in which the union and the states must work in cooperation. It is here that the role of the NDC assumes significance as the key intergovernmental forum for union–state negotiations and cooperation.

Significantly, the NDC emerged in the context of the introduction of development planning in the Nehru era. As K.N. Kabra aptly observed: 'The recognition of the multi-level character of the planning process in our federal polity, continental sized, diverse and many-tiered economy and a highly differentiated society was an inevitable blow for the forces of centralism.'[1] The multi-level federal character of the Indian political system was further strengthened by the 73rd and 74th Constitutional Amendments in the early 1990s that placed the Panchayati and Nagar Raj institutions on a constitutional footing with more regular elections and autonomous and devolved revenue resources to the local bodies. In a letter to the Andhra Pradesh Chief Minister, Chandrababu Naidu (dated 27 April 2001), Prime Minister A.B. Vajpayee emphasized the importance of Panchayati Raj as the third tier of government in India's federal polity. He deplored 'the tendency of many state governments to create parallel structures, which marginalized Panchayati Raj institutions'.[2]

Though the accelerated pace of neo-liberal economic reforms in India since 1991 necessitated some change in the nature of economic policies and planning processes, yet the important role of the NDC in union–state relations hardly diminished. If anything, with the increasing federalization of the Indian polity and assertion of state autonomy, localism and ethnic identities, its role in India's cooperative federalism is likely to become even more crucial.

BACKGROUND

When the Interim Government set up the Advisory Planning Board in 1946 under the chairmanship of K.C. Neogy the benefit of a consultative body representing the provinces, the princely states and other interests to advise the Planning Commission was pointed out. Consequently, the NDC came into being with the object of ensuring 'uniformity of approach and unanimity in its working'.[3]

In the Draft Outline of the First Five-Year Plan, the Planning Commission recommended,

> In a country of the size of India where the states have, under the Constitution, full autonomy within their own sphere of duties, it is necessary to have a forum such as National Development Council, at which from time to time, the prime minister of India and the chief ministers of states can review the working of the plan and its various aspects.[4]

The NDC was set up in August 1952 'to strengthen and mobilize the effort and resources of the nation in support of the five-year plans, to promote common economic policies in all vital spheres and to ensure the balanced and rapid development of all parts of the country'.[5] The Council was assigned the following functions:

1. To review the working of the National Plan from time to time.
2. To consider important questions of social and economic policy affecting national development.
3. To recommend measures for the achievement of the aims and targets set out in the National Plan, including measures to secure the active participation and cooperation of the people, improve the efficiency of the administrative services, ensure the fullest development of the less advanced regions and sections of the community and, through sacrifice borne equally by all citizens, build up resources for national development.[6]

The study team of the Administrative Reforms Commission (ARC) in its interim report observed that in the future set-up of planning in the country, the NDC would have to play an increasingly dynamic role. It pointed out that in the emerging political situation in the country, the NDC had to be developed as the most important instrument for ensuring all-India support for the National Plan. As the supreme political body offering advice on the formulation of the Plan, the Council would have to operate ceaselessly (without interruption) and its working would have to be more systematized than in the past.[7]

The ARC also supported this and recommended that the NDC should be reconstituted to include the prime minister, the deputy prime minister, ten ministers of the central cabinet in charge of major ministries, chief ministers of all the states and members of the Planning Commission. In a note of dissent, H.V. Kamath, one of the members of the ARC, expressed concern that a plethora of ministers would make the NDC too unwieldly. He was of the view that besides the prime minister and the deputy prime minister, only ministers of finance, home affairs, agriculture, industry and irrigation and power should be included as members of the council. He further proposed that in view of the rapidly changing political landscape, the chief ministers of the union territories and the chief executive councillor of Delhi should invariably be invited to attend the meeting of the Council.[8] The ARC also recommended that the functions of the NDC be redefined. The most important change suggested was that the NDC should be specifically required 'to prescribe guidelines for the formulation of the National Plan'.[9]

The government considered the recommendations of the Commission and decided to reconstitute the NDC and redefine its functions. To this effect, a Resolution was passed on 7 October 1967. The revised functions of the NDC were:

1. To prescribe guidelines for the formulation of the National Plan, including the assessment of resources for the Plan.
2. To consider the National Plan as formulated by the Planning Commission.
3. To consider important questions of social and economic policy affecting national development.
4. to review the working of the Plan from time to time and to recommend such measures as are necessary for achieving the aims and targets set out in the National Plan, including measures to secure the active participation and cooperation

> of the people, improve the efficiency of the administrative services, ensure the fullest development of the less advanced regions and sections of the community and, through sacrifice borne equally by all citizens, build up resources for national development.[10]

The reconstituted NDC would comprise the prime minister, union ministers of all states and union territories and members of the Planning Commission. Delhi Administration would be represented in the Council by the Lt. Governor and the Chief Executive Councillor, and the remaining union territories by their respective administrators. It further provided that other union ministers could be invited to participate in the deliberations of the Council. The Secretary of the Planning Commission would act as secretary to the NDC and the Planning Commission would provide administrative and other assistance for the smooth functioning of the Council. It also required the Council to meet 'as often as may be necessary and at least twice in each year'.[11]

Initially, when the NDC comprised the prime minister, the chief ministers of states and members of the Planning Commission, it was considered too unwieldly for an effective discussion of problems.[12] To facilitate more effective deliberations, a Standing Committee was set up in 1954 with members of the Planning Commission and chief ministers of nine states. It served a useful purpose at the time of formulation of the Second Five-Year Plan but met only twice subsequently—in 1957 and 1958—and thereafter in 1963. The Standing Committee, henceforth, became almost defunct. Over the years, in addition to regular members, a large number of central and state ministers were invited, thus making the body too unwieldly. Against this background, the ARC study team recommended the continuance of the earlier composition of the NDC. Also, to make the NDC operationally more effective, it suggested that 'sub-committees of the NDC may be appointed from time to time, and especially at the time of formulating a five-year plan'.[13] It further recommended the constitution of counterparts of these NDC committees at the official levels 'so that there is adequate consultation, communication, and therefore mutual understanding and cooperation between the states and the union in all matters pertaining to

Planning'.[14] Regarding the effective utilization of the subcommittees as recommended by the Commission, the question of constituting a subcommittee of the NDC to examine the principles and patterns of central assistance was duly considered by the NDC in May 1968, but the exclusion of any chief minister from the subcommittee was found impracticable. Only the central cabinet ministers were excluded from the subcommittee. A number of subcommittees, of a purely ad hoc nature, were appointed from time to time to investigate problems of national importance, for example, the Mehta Committee in 1957 to evaluate the performance of the Community Development Programme. Unfortunately, the recommendations of these committees were not faithfully followed by the central government, thus defeating the very purpose of their establishment. As a reaction to the lack of action on these recommendations, Biju Patnaik, the chief minister of Orissa, who was also the chairman of the Austerity Committee, tendered his resignation in 1992.[15] The official level committees for regularly discussing and examining plan problems had also not been set up, though in the past meetings were held to discuss particular problems between the Planning Commission and officials of the state government such as Planning Secretaries. Two working groups were appointed under the auspices of the NDC in 1968 to examine and make recommendations on certain problems of interstate disputes.[16]

The study team of the ARC also noted that the measures of consultation and examination of issues by the Council were 'inadequate' because certain aspects of perspective planning and possible alternatives were not placed before the Council in sufficient detail. It highlighted the shortcomings in its conferencing procedures: short duration of meetings, delays in the circulation of agenda papers, use of the Council as 'a forum for the ventilation of individual grievances rather than for collective discussion of principles and polity', etc., and suggested a more systematic and in depth involvement of the Council in all basic questions of planning policy, particularly those pertaining to goals and objectives, alternative frameworks, strategy and crucial sectors, and assistance in arriving at a national consesus. It was further suggested that the Council should be assisted by a Standing

Advisory Committee consisting of official advisors from each state, concerned central ministers and the Planning Commission.[17]

The Sarkaria Commission on union–state relations also highlighted some of the shortcomings of the Council: the NDC meets only at the initiative of the Planning Commission which determines its agenda; the Council approves the Approach Paper and the draft Plan but does not keep track of the progress of the Plan (for instance, consideration of other policy questions affecting national development which is one of its stated functions has been infrequent and insufficient); the frequency and duration of its meetings are inadequate; the Planning Commission does not always place before the Council alternative sets of perspectives, strategies and targets along with the assumptions made to enable it to decide among the choices available; the conferencing procedure consists of set speeches made by the chief ministers with very little mutual discussion; the summing up of deliberations often does not reflect the diversity of views; the time given to states for crystallizing their views is not enough; and the Standing Committees and the Special Committees are not formed or convened on a regular basis for in depth analysis and consideration of issues.[18]

Due to these reasons, the NDC was perceived as a forum deficient both in effective participation and systematic deliberation of alternatives. As a policy making body it was not able to guide the Planning Commission and also failed to carry out a critical appraisal of the implementation of the plans and policies. This sorry state of affairs led to a review of the reorganization of the NDC. It was suggested that a constitutional or a statutory status would improve the functioning of this body. These reappraisals suggested, among other things, the following: the NDC should exercise greater control over the Planning Commission and have a say in determining the composition of the Planning Commission as well; some even supported the idea of representation of experts on this body. According to one view, there should be experts on the Planning Commission and the role of the NDC should be political decision-making and laying down national guidelines on planning; another view was that the NDC should express its opinion on all matters of national development and should be actively involved in evolving policies of industrial development, trade and commerce, prices, etc.; and one state government even proposed that the NDC should approve the guidelines for the preparation of the plans, the Approach Paper to the five-year plan, and the quantum and allocation of central assistance for state plans.[19]

In its final analysis, the Sarkaria Commission made the following recommendations: the NDC should function more effectively and emerge as the highest political level of intergovernmental body for giving direction and thrust to planned development of the country. Being the supreme intergovernmental body for all matters related to socio-economic development, it should be renamed and reconstituted as the National Economic Development Council (NEDC) by a Presidential Order under the provisions of Article 263 so as to have moorings in the Constitution; the NEDC should be involved in the formulation of plans right from the beginning. Selection of studies and setting up of various working groups should be done under the guidance of the Standing Committee of the NEDC; the draft Approach Paper containing all relevant data and alternative strategies should be circulated to the States at least two months prior to the meeting of the NEDC to consider the same; a preparatory meeting should be convened by the Planning Commission with deputy chairman and/or Secretaries of the State Development Boards two weeks prior to the NEDC to consider the Approach Paper/draft five-year plan for identifying the main issues and firming up the agenda for the meeting of the NEDC; deliberations in the NEDC should be so structured as to facilitate meaningful discussions on each item of the agenda; the NEDC or its Standing Committee should meet regularly to discuss economic issues of national significance in addition to the usual developmental issues; the NEDC should formulate its own procedures to enable it to discharge its responsibilities; the Secretary of the Planning Commission should serve as Secretary of the NEDC and the Planning Commission should provide such administrative or other assistance for the work of the Council as may be required; and a Standing Committee of the NEDC should be constituted consisting of the prime minister, the finance minister, three other union ministers nominated by the prime minister, deputy chairman of the Planning Commission and Governor, Reserve Bank of India, and six chief ministers, one from each zone selected on the basis of rotation or consensus. This Standing Committee should be constituted under Article 263 along with the NEDC. It may, however, set up other committees or subcommittees to advise it or the Standing Committee on special issues.[20]

WORKING OF THE NDC UNDER VARIOUS REGIMES

The Nehru Premiership

The Nehru era ushered in the first formative phase of governance during which the NDC was constituted and its procedures and rules of business were devised. A textual factor during this phase was that there were at least two forums that more or less mirrored each other in terms of composition: one was the Congress Working Committee, a party forum that included the most influential union ministers and state chief ministers along with other party functionaries, and the second was the NDC that included key union ministers and all chief ministers. Since the Congress party was a dominant political force in New Delhi as well as in practically all states, these two forums had more or less a similar party political configuration. The relevance of this fact of union–state relations is that either of the two forums could be used for union–state policy making and harmonization. Yet, the very fact that the NDC was set up underlined its essential intergovernmental character, authoritatively representing the two orders of government in the Indian federation. None the less, it would appear that a certain air of superfluity would be inevitable in the case of the NDC which would tend to get partially eclipsed not only by the apex party forum but also by Parliament to an extent. This was because in the period of one-party dominance under a charismatic prime minister, the Parliament would naturally shine with a more authoritative glow of power, especially at a time when the travails of the nationalist movement were over and the centre of political gravity had shifted from the movement to the party in power, and from the latter to the government.

Brecher, Nehru's political biographer, rightly acknowledged Nehru's role in the planning process:

Firstly, he stands at the decision-making structure by virtue of his position as prime minister, chairman of the Planning Commission and chairman of the NDC—and because he is Jawaharlal Nehru. He is the link between the planning agencies and the government and is brought into any matter requiring cabinet approval, notably broad decisions concerning targets, aims and priorities. Secondly, because of his multiple positions and personal prestige he is the central focus of attention for all pressure groups. . . .[21]

Nehru regarded the NDC as an apex democratic institution in the field of planning. At the eighth meeting of the NDC in December 1956, he declared that he attached great importance to the NDC because it enabled them to develop an integrated outlook on the problems faced by them. The central government, viewed India in a rarefied atmosphere and it was necessary to lead it to reality through the more practical knowledge and experience of the chief ministers. On the other hand, the chief ministers may think only of their respective states rather than the whole of India.[22] He wrote letters to the chief ministers every fortnight giving them details of policy decisions taken by the central government from time to time. He asserted that the questions for consideration by the NDC were important and weighty. The chief ministers met in some respects as custodians of interests of the states, but even more in the capacity of members of the NDC, looking at India as a whole and realizing that the health of the whole was absolutely important for any part to be healthy. He stressed on the *whole* of which they were separate parts and the emphasis was to be on the progressive health of the country. He, therefore, pleaded with the chief ministers to think in terms of the interest of the nation as a whole and not in terms of individual states.[23]

Further, Nehru stressed that the NDC was a working council, not a debating body. Though it was inescapable that the chief ministers would be concerned about the affairs of their respective states, the main purpose of the council was to evolve an all-India outlook. Normally, particular schemes of the states were discussed in the Planning Commission than in the council. The relevant subjects of discussion in the council were those affecting all the states and sometimes significant specific issues.[24] Nehru exhorted the chief ministers to abandon their narrow outlook and to focus on issues of national importance.

A survey of Nehru's inaugural addresses at the NDC meetings provides a glimpse of his vision as well as strategy of economic development. It appears that he espoused a model of modernity in which the main emphasis was on the building up of heavy industry with the state/public sector playing the leading role in the process of development, though the existence of the private sector was not altogether ruled out. Though his conception of planning was essentially centralized under federal tutelage, yet he greatly emphasized the participation and commitment of the state governments, the community and the grassroots in the developmental process. His rhetorical speeches highlighted the crucial importance of education and agricultural development, but latter-day observers or commentators lamented the lopsided educational and agricultural growth in India's development strategy whose initial foundations were led by the Nehru government. Even during his premiership, critical views were expressed in the NDC by the first leftist chief minister of Kerala, K. Thanu Pillai, who complained that in the last two plans, Kerala had received relatively smaller central assistance than other states. It was for the Planning Commission to identify which industries could be located in Kerala. Though Kerala was the largest producer of rubber in the country, yet no rubber factories were located in the state.[25]

Nehru's objectives of establishing a 'socialistic pattern of society' and planned economic development were to come to grief under his successors who succumbed to the pressures of populist politics and revised the socialist dream in favour of a market-oriented vision of capitalist development on the debris of state and planning failures.

The Shastri Premiership and the Early Indira Gandhi Years

The brief tenures of Lal Bahadur Shastri and Indira Gandhi as prime minister between 1964 and 1971 were more or less a continuation of the trend of union–state relations in the preceding Nehru era. However, the period witnessed the growing importance of regional party leaders and state chief ministers in the early post-Nehru period. A series of catch-all non-Congress coalition governments were formed in all major north Indian states, but since they included political parties of all hues ranging from the right centre to the left, they failed to establish a stable and effective front of non-Congress state governments against the Congress dominated centre. Indeed, the Congress party at the centre misused its overriding constitutional powers to destabilize the fractious non-Congress coalition governments in the states![26] Nevertheless, rumblings were heard when the Congress still provided the main common political framework in the country either as the ruling party or in the opposition. Hence, the political repercussions of these changes were felt within the Congress party itself that developed a more collective leadership rather than a politically differentiated federal framework in terms of different political parties ruling in New Delhi and the state capitals.[27] Two factors put additional pressure on the declining Congress party to close ranks and manage its internal differences within the house rather than outside. First was the Chinese aggression in 1962. For example, at the twenty-second meeting of the NDC held on 6 September 1965, the chief ministers wanted that at a time when the country was facing external aggression, the Council should not waste time discussing the various aspects of the Plan. Instead, they left it to the prime minister's discretion to reorient, alter or amend the Plan (as and when necessary) to meet the emergent situation and safeguard the country's security and long-term interests. It may be noted that in 1964-5, there was a severe drought and food crisis in the country.

The second factor was the growing internal division within the Congress party which was resolved amicably by the Congress Working Committee dominated by regional party bosses under Congress President, K. Kamraj, who successfully coordinated Shastri's succession from Nehru and Indira Gandhi's succession from Shastri. The expanded Congress Working Committee including most union and state chief ministers virtually became what Brecher called the 'grand federal Council' of the Indian Republic.[28] By the end of 1969, despite the growing external challenge from opposition parties, unity in the Congress finally ruptured as Indira Gandhi decided to take on the dominant party bosses (using her entrenched position in the government and the Congress Parliamentary Party) and ousted the right wing old guard Syndicate leadership from the party.[29]

The fourth general elections in 1967 altered the parameters of politics in the country by unseating the Congress government in half of the states. Despite the fact that most of these non-Congress state governments—barring the left wing coalition in Kerala and the right wing coalition in Orissa—were unstable, a new federal ferment was conspicuously evident: the new political scenario required a renegotiation of union–state relations as well as a review of the planning machinery, as revealed by the following observation:

> The situation has changed radically since the last elections. While the states continue to be financially dependent on the centre, several of them have assumed different enough political colours to feel the need for planning organizations of their own, especially since credit for planning at the centre tends to be monopolized by the Congress. Congress-ruled states are not to be left behind either, they now have much greater political leverage at the centre and would like to have developmental autonomy commensurate with that leverage. Still, to get anywhere near influencing the planning decisions, the states need to do a lot of home work and programming. This, as the recent meeting of the National Development Council showed, the chief ministers are not yet prepared to do. Hence the reluctance to tax agriculture, procure food-grains or take decisions with the long run in view.[30]

In this changed context, the need for an adequate planning machinery was acutely felt by political analysts. The report of the ARC (1957) also underlined this point. In fact, the deputy chairman of the Planning Commission, D.R. Gadgil, held similar views. 'He would like to fix the Central Assistance (which forms roughly 50 to 60 per cent of the states' plan outlays) according to Plan priorities and let the states decided the size of their plans on the basis of their resources.'[31] The *Economic and Political Weekly* appropriately commented:

> Each state must have a development pattern suited to its resource endowments. The dictation and all-pervasive intervention from above and subsequent horse-trading with states, encourages them to put up as many unbaked developmental schemes as they can devise, in the hope that Central Assistance would be elastic to their ambitions. This behaviour pattern is reproduced between the state and its districts. In this scramble to formulate schemes which would qualify for and fit into anticipated financial allocations, resources and priority requirements of region are often ignored.[32]

Nevertheless, a perusal of the speeches of the chief ministers during these years in the NDC reveals that the opinions expressed did not strictly follow major party lines, especially the Congress/non-Congress cleavage. If the non-Congress chief ministers were critical of the draft Fourth Plan prepared by the Central Planning Commission, some Congress chief ministers, too, were not sparing in their critical comments.

Indira Gandhi's Premiership from 1971 to 1977

It is important to examine the context in which union–state relations developed during this phase. Four contextual aspects need to be considered. First, internal politics in the Congress party was in turmoil as indicated by the fact that the brief phase of collective leadership under Shastri and the early years of Indira Gandhi were gradually replaced by the latter's dominance at the culmination of a round of factional politics that resulted in the decisive split of the Congress towards the end of 1969. Second, politics in major north Indian states was marked by unstable non-Congress coalition governments that provided an opening for federal forces by giving the non-Congress opposition parties an opportunity to enjoy power at the state level. Third, pluralistic and federal tendencies unleashed by the foregoing two contexts could not develop into a long-term trend as these possibilities were thwarted by the assertion of leadership claims (on her behalf) by Indira Gandhi who not only managed to oust her factional opponents in the Congress party in the 1969 split, but also managed to bring about political mobilization in the country in the 1971 mid-term Lok Sabha elections which she fought on the slogan of *garibi hatao*. Facing a challenge from her right wing Syndicate opponents in the party, she took a series of populist pro-poor measures such as nationalization of fourteen major commercial banks, abolition of privy purses for the Maharajas, promises of bank credits and jobs to the unemployed and the poor, and speedy land reforms. These policies yielded rich dividends and she was voted back to power with a thumping majority which enabled her to checkmate her opponents both within the national Congress party and in the north Indian states that were lost to the Congress since 1967. Fourth, though Indira Gandhi emerged as the dominant political leader in the Congress party and the country in the electoral legislative arenas, she had to contend with a new development in the larger arena of mass politics. The Nav Nirman movement launched by the Congress (O) leader, Morarji Desai, in Gujarat, and the anti-corruption movement triggered off by the youth in Bihar—which drew Jayaprakash Narayan from virtual political retirement to provide leadership to both these movements—posed a challenge to her. Thus, even with massive legislative majorities, she found it difficult to govern and claim larger democratic legitimacy. This contradiction of parliamentary and mass politics eventually culminated in the proclamation of Internal Emergency in June 1975 with large scale arrests of leaders of the mass movements and opposition parties.

These conditioning factors naturally affected the working of the NDC as a major intergovernmental forum. For example, no meeting of the NDC was held between 27 March 1970 and 28 May 1972. Another major gap is noticeable during the pendency of Internal Emergency—the period between the thirtieth meeting in December 1973 and the thirty-first meeting in September 1976. With the kind of political dominance Indira Gandhi was able to command in the country during this phase, it was obvious that the central government had the upper hand both in the formulation of the plans and in the NDC meetings. However, a survey of speeches delivered in the NDC indicates that critical voices were not entirely silenced. Interestingly, criticism of the Plan documents was not only from the non-Congress chief ministers but even the Congress chief ministers expressed reservations against the Plans presented for the approval of the NDC. It may be seen that issues of underdevelopment and regional disparities did not find expression strictly along party affiliations.

The Janata Phase: Morarji Desai's Premiership

The post-Emergency 1977 Lok Sabha elections proved to be a turning point in Indian politics because it altered the parameters of politics in the country, especially in terms of union–state relations. The Janata Party that was hastily formed on the eve of the elections with the improper merger of major non-Congress and non-Communist opposition parties, came to power in major north Indian states. It was essentially a confederal political configuration that formed government in New Delhi as well as in Uttar Pradesh, Bihar, Madhya Pradesh, Haryana, Himachal Pradesh, Rajasthan, Gujarat, Orissa, etc. It emerged victorious in those areas that had been the worst affected by the excesses of the Emergency. The Congress-ruled states in the south re-elected the Congress party except in Tamil Nadu where one of the regional parties was victorious again. The political scenario in the country was fairly variegated with the Janata Party in power at the centre and a broad spectrum of parties ruling in the states. After 1967, this was another major opening for the state-level political forces to experience a more federalized context than before. A crude index of this federalization is that the NDC meetings were regularly convened annually in contrast to the preceding periods during which its meetings were not held for years. Also, the fiscal federal policies and centrally-sponsored schemes were seriously reviewed at these meetings.

However, as the Janata Party did not succeed in the south, the full extent of federal possibilities could not materialize. This could be attributed largely to the existence of the overarching unity in the Janata Party, primarily a north Indian party, because of the painful memory of suffering together under the emergency authoritarians, and the moderating presence of JP until his death.

The thirty-second meeting of the NDC held in March 1978 and chaired by Prime Minister Morarji Desai was in sharp contrast to the preceding meetings under Congress prime ministers. Commenting on the meeting, an analyst observed:

> The NDC is no longer a rubber-stamping body which would promptly accept any 'consensus' dictated by the central government from time to time. The present political landscape and the alignment of forces precludes that happening. If anybody in the central government or the Planning Commission entertained the idea of going through with the conventional pattern of obtaining the old type of consensus, he must have become much wiser after the event.[33]

Commenting on the same meeting of the NDC, Romesh Thapar made a perceptive observation:

> The meeting had been one of the most positive sessions of the National Development Council. The dramatic dimension of the Plan had been

endorsed, Prime Minister Desai had been most responsive to the suggestions of chief ministers—even including in the Plan document a whole bunch of points advanced by Jyoti Basu of the CPI(M)!—and there had been a generally agreeable discussion about the need to decentralize powers, although it had been pointed out quite firmly that the NDC could not turn itself into a Constitution-making body.

Between now and October, state Plans will be worked out, but significantly, there is every reason to believe that the states will be encouraged to do this solid work themselves. Indeed, it would not be an exaggeration to say that this session of the NDC reflected a very healthy attitude by the centre to the pressure from the states for greater self-reliance in handling the resources allotted to them.[34]

Indira Gandhi's Restoration

The return to power of the Congress under Indira Gandhi in 1980 ushered in a new phase of Congress dominance. However, this dominance was with a difference. To begin with, a mellowed Mrs Gandhi came to power who had learnt some lessons from the Emergency and its aftermath. Sanjay Gandhi's premature death in an air crash also precluded some of her proclivities for personal and familial rule, though she attempted to fill this void by inducing her reluctant elder son Rajiv Gandhi to join politics. Second, from the early 1980s, the Congress party began to lose in popularity in a number of states which was amply reflected in the assembly elections. However, the Congress party continued to rule until the end of the decade, first under Indira Gandhi and subsequently under Rajiv Gandhi. During this phase, Indira Gandhi faced a number of electoral defeats at the state level; she also had to contend with growing regional ethnic mass movements led by the Akali Dal in Punjab and the sons of the soil movement in Assam. The dominant feature of this phase of Indira Gandhi's rule was an enhanced degree of regional assertion on the part of non-Congress parties and mass movements. This enlarged opening for federal forces in the political system is also reflected in the meetings of the NDC during this period. It met four times in five years with rather agendas that included the Sixth Five-Year Plan, Approach Paper to the Seventh Five-Year Plan, Indira Gandhi's new 20-point programme, law and order situation, river water disputes, finances of the states and Plan implementation.

Rajiv Gandhi's Premiership

Rajiv Gandhi succeeded Indira Gandhi as prime minister in the wake of the latter's assassination. So severe was the distorting impact of this calamity on the political process that President Zail Singh swore him in the prime minister's office in unseemly haste—even before the Congress party had formally elected Rajiv Gandhi as its leader. In the past, President S. Radhakrishnan had opted for a provisional appointment of the seniormost cabinet colleague as the prime minister, pending the election of the Congress Parliamentary Party leader, for example, Shastri's succession to Nehru and Indira Gandhi's to Shastri. On both occasions, Gulzari Lal Nanda acted as the provisional prime minister before the regular incumbent assumed control.[35]

Rajiv Gandhi's approach to federal politics was somewhat different in the sense that even though he followed Indira Gandhi's centralizing approach in the Congress-ruled states, he was more amenable to regional demands in non-Congress states: he signed a series of ethnic accords with the dominant regional parties in Punjab, Assam and Mizoram.

The tempo of NDC meetings seen in the immediately preceding phase remained more or less unchanged during this period as well. Three meetings were convened during Rajiv Gandhi's premiership and at these meetings the draft Seventh Five-Year Plan, the New Education Policy and the mid-term appraisal of the Seventh Plan were discussed. A review of the proceedings of NDC meetings during this phase reveals that this was by far the most vigorous articulation of the critical views of state governments, presumably because almost half of the states were ruled by non-Congress parties.

At the meeting in November 1985, the draft seventh plan was approved as well as criticized by chief ministers and Lieutenant Governors. Commenting on this meeting, Romesh Thapar, noted 'the unreality of the two-day ritual of the National Development Council' where 'there was no discussion whatsoever on the interventions of S. Barnala, N.T. Rama Rao, R.K. Hegde and Jyoti Basu'. Thapar went on to record: 'When substantial matters are raised, either an uncomfortable silence prevails or the exchanges are designed to evade the issues raised.'[36]

A number of chief ministers drew attention to the problems faced by their states and made impassioned appeals to those present to accept their suggestions.[37] They pleaded for more central assistance as they were unable to mobilize additional resources to the extent desired by the Planning Commission. They sought structural changes in the pattern of assistance to take care of the special needs of the states.[38] There was also a reference to the heated exchange between the prime minister and the Congress-I chief ministers on the issue of greater financial autonomy for state governments.[39] Consequently, a 16-member committee of the NDC was set up to examine the future of centrally-sponsored schemes. The committee was to examine the recommendations of the Ramamurti Committee on three schemes, review the criteria laid down by the NDC in 1979 for pursuing such schemes, and suggest modifications in the criteria or additional criteria that should govern such schemes in the future.[40]

At the meeting held in March 1988, chief ministers from both the Congress-I and the non-Congress-I ruled states demanded greater central assistance for the mid-term appraisal of the Seventh Plan. The chief ministers of the latter states, however, were critical of the central government's continued encroachment on powers of the states. Most of them 'asked' for their legimitate due of central assistance.

Rajiv Gandhi introduced a new style in the conduct of the meeting which was held after a gap of two years in March 1988. He insisted that the chief ministers should speak impromptu for the allocated time of 10 minutes. The chief ministers initially agreed but soon became disillusioned as they were neither allowed to make lengthy speeches nor permitted discussions on the points raised by them.

The chief minister of Andhra Pradesh, N.T. Rama Rao, stayed away from the proceedings of the NDC after the main speeches were made because he thought that the atmosphere was not conducive to free and frank discussion. On being 'asked to abruptly conclude his speech by Mr. Rajiv Gandhi who reportedly looked at the watch when he was addressing the meeting and even hinted that he should conclude', Rama Rao questioned: 'why should we go all the way to the NDC if we were not allowed to speak our difficulties?'[41]

Jyoti Basu also faced hostility from the dais for raising political issues by criticizing the appointment of governors without taking the chief ministers into confidence. He was castigated for criticizing the planning process as well.[42] Infuriated by Rajiv Gandhi's repeated pointing to his watch, Basu abruptly ended his speech and asked the prime minister sarcastically as to why he was reducing the NDC meeting to the level of being a 'mere formality'.[43] Some opposition chief ministers expressed the view that the NDC meeting had become an object of ridicule as it had neither been allowed to set goals nor give thought to proper implementation.[44]

The last meeting of the NDC during Rajiv Gandhi's premiership was marked by unseemly and restive demeanour on the part of the prime minister and unusually disparaging comments by the non-Congress chief ministers. A commentator described the meeting as 'a disaster'. The observer added,

> It should make everyone sit up that an institution like the NDC, which has all the time since its establishment been held up as a forum for centre-state and inter-state dialogue, in place of the Inter-State Council envisaged under the Constitution, is proving to be so very ineffective.[45]

The acrimonious marathon meeting (which lasted for almost 9 hours) appeared to be an exercise in futility and the nadir of dysfunctionality for the NDC as the premier forum for inter-governmental relations.

Post-1989 Phase

The 1989 Lok Sabha elections was a turning point in Indian politics, especially in union–state relations and patterns of federal politics. The year witnessed the transformation of one party dominance into a multiparty system. The Congress party, whose fortunes were gradually declining over the 1980s, was decisively routed. It yielded power to a multiparty federal coalitional formation comprising the Janata Dal, some major regional parties, and major Communist Parties. The communist group was part only of the legislative coalition, as it did not join the cabinet. An unlikely parliamentary ally of the ruling coalition was the right wing Hindu nationalist party, the BJP, which decided to reluctantly support the coalition government with the motive of keeping the Congress out of power. The National Front Government headed by V.P. Singh was thus a minority coalition government dependent on the outside support of the right and left wings of the party system. This new political dispensation in New Delhi and a variety of political parties in power in different states fundamentally altered the parameters of federal politics in India. The changed political configuration occasioned a renegotiation of union–state relations in which the union for the first time felt the compulsion for a new strategy of accommodating state governments and regional political forces. Some regional and national parties in power at the state level also had direct representation in the federal coalition cabinet. This enormously increased the influence of regional political parties in the government at the centre. As a result of these developments, a major avenue was opened for the operation of federal forces and tendencies in the political system.

Another dimension of increased federalization during this period was a more differentiated or variegated pattern of party representation in the election of the President of the Republic. Until then, the presidency and the union cabinet overlapped in terms of party representation in such a manner that the head of the state and the head of the government and the cabinet generally belonged to the same party. In the 1990s, this pattern changed. In the initial years of the decade, with the exception of the term of the Rao's Congress government, the presidency continued to be occupied by Congress nominees whereas the union cabinet was formed by non-Congress coalition governments. In the later years of the decade, cabinets were formed by left of centre or right of centre non-Congress coalitions, but a former Congressman, K.R. Narayanan, was elected to the presidency with an all-party consensus. These new trends engendered a tendency towards activist presidency or at least a more unrestrained and open expression of differences between the prime minister and the President. Although there was no radical departure from the strictly constitutional construction of presidential power, there were occasions when the President had a final say on some issues as the union cabinet chose not to press its point of view. Around the same time, there was evidence of greater discretion in the exercise of the Governor's power and some other constitutional offices like the Election Commission of India. There was also a radical shift in judicial behaviour inasmuch as the Supreme Court for the first time in the *S.R. Bommai case* established a judicial review of proclamation of President's Rule in states in 1994.

This naturally had an impact on intergovernmental relations and mechanisms. For one thing, the NDC diversified in terms of party representation. This was so because of both the coalitional nature of the cabinet at the centre and parties of different hues forming governments in the states. For another, the V.P. Singh government, in pursuance of the National Front election manifesto, proceeded to appoint for the first time the ISC under Article 263 of the Constitution in 1990. Thus, instead of a single intergovernmental mechanism in the NDC, there was another—the ISC.

During the rule of the National Front government, two meetings of the NDC were convened (in June and October 1990) to discuss the approach paper to the Eighth Five-Year Plan, distribution of central budget support for the states' plan expenditure, issues relating to right to work and impact of the gulf crisis on India's balance of payments.

At the 42nd meeting of the NDC in October 1990, it was unanimously agreed to modify the Gadgil formula for resource allocation among the states. The amendment reduced the weightage given to population and increased that to per capita income. Under the Dandavate formula, devolution of resources for non-special category states was 55 per cent on the basis of population; 25 per cent on the basis of per capita income; 5 per cent on the basis of fiscal management; and 15 per cent on the basis of special development problems.[46] The criteria set by the Gadgil formula for resource allocation was population, 60 per cent; per capita income, 20 per cent; tax effort, 10 per cent; and special problems, 10 per cent. Tax effort was redefined as 'fiscal management', including both revenue and expenditure. Thus, the NDC took a collective view that the performance of each state in this area should be evaluated in the light of a variety of related indices and not just taxation effort. The new formula widened the criterion of 'special problems', by calling it *special developmental problems*. These included coastal areas, special environment issues like flood and drought prone areas, exceptionally sparse or thickly populated areas, special difficulties for achieving minimum reasonable plan size, desert problems and problems of slums. The government thus ensured that even the developed and non-special category states did not suffer at all.[47] The revision added a measure of equity to the formula. However, the prime minister's assertion that none of the non-special category states would gain or lose more than 7 per cent in their proportion of assistance under the existing formula continued to prevail. This would put a limit on the transfer of resources and could lead to a fresh controversy.[48]

Under the new formula, the 25 per cent per capita income criterion would be applied with 20 per cent under the existing formula based on the national average and the remaining 5 per cent would be through the distance criterion—the distance between the per capita income of the state and the highest per capita income.[49] The revised formula would then be applicable to the non-special category states for apportioning of funds left after the special requirements specified had been met from the overall provision of central assistance for states.[50] Funds required for centrally-aided schemes from the total central assistance would be allocated on the same basis as was done earlier. Separate amounts for special area programmes for hill, tribal and border areas would be set apart. Further, 30 per cent of the balance would be allocated to special category states inclusive of the North-Eastern Council. The Gadgil formula would be applied to the non-special category states after these needs had been met. The NDC decided to appoint a committee to suggest lasting solutions to the financial problems of all special category states.[51] It was further decided that the same grant–loan ratio (90:10) would be applicable to Assam and Jammu & Kashmir as to other special category states. The non-special category states received grants and loans in the ratio of 30:70.[52]

The P.V. Narasimha Rao government was partly in tune with the general tenor of politics during the 1990s and partly differed. It was initially formed as a one party minority government dependent on parliamentary support of some other parties but gradually transformed itself halfway through its term into a one party majority government through accretion of support as a result of favourable election results in Punjab and manipulative realignment of political parties in Parliament. It convened four meetings of the NDC—in December 1991, May 1992, April 1993 and September 1993. The agenda of these meetings included the Approach Paper and the final document of the Eighth Five-Year Plan, review of centrally-sponsored developmental schemes, distribution of central assistance and open market borrowings among the states during the Eighth Plan, population control policy, consideration of the NDC committee reports on austerity, population, employment and illiteracy, micro level planning, etc.

The Rao regime was succeeded by two shore-lived United Front governments headed by H.D. Deve Gowda and I.K. Gujral respectively. Deve Gowda called the 47th meeting of the NDC in January 1997. The Gujral government did not convene any meeting, presumably because much of its attention was focused on foreign policy concerns as also because of its short duration.

The premature termination of the United Front regime was followed by two BJP-led coalition governments under the leadership of Atal Behari Vajpayee. The new government held the 48th meeting of the NDC in February 1999 after a gap of over two years. The delay was apparently caused by the fall of the two United Front governments in 1997 and 1998. This led to a delay in finalizing the Ninth Plan. The draft Ninth Plan was provisionally kicked off pending its subsequent approval by the NDC which could be done only at the 1999 meeting.

The second meeting of the NDC under Vajpayee's premiership was held on 1 September 2001 in New Delhi during the course of which the draft approach paper to the Tenth Five-Year Plan (that envisaged an 8 per cent annual growth in the next five years) was unanimously approved. It was also decided at the meeting that the prime minister and all the chief ministers would have a 'Davos-type informal retreat to mull over the future of economic reforms'.[53]

Commenting on the proceedings of this meeting of the NDC, S. Swaminathan ruefully dubbed them as 'monologues' and remarked:

> It is indeed a sad comment that centre–state equations have become so skewed that many state governments have simply degenerated as financial dependents on the centre for day-to-day survival instead of leveraging the opportunities for socio-economic development opened up by the

process of decentralization of decision-making. Even if the NDC is to remain a ceremonial make-believe of consultation, it cannot be too strongly argued that for viable development to benefit the poor, centre–state coordination and synergy ought to become integral elements in governance.[54]

The third NDC meeting (which was the NDC's 50th meeting) was convened by Vajpayee on 23 December 2002 in New Delhi. On the occasion of Golden Jubilee of the NDC meetings, the prime minister in his opening address emphasized the need to push ahead with the economic reforms programme and announced the setting up of four subgroups of the NDC to work out the modalities to improve governance, implement policies and programmes, remove barriers to internal trade, create an investor-friendly climate and provide more resources to the Panchayati Raj institutions.[55]

After the formation of Congress-led United Progressive Alliance (UPA) government in New Delhi in May 2004, the NDC convened its 51st meeting in June 2005. Preparatory to this meeting, the Planning Commission had held discussions with union and state governments to conduct mid-term appraisal of the Tenth Five-Year Plan launched by the previous government. Previous negotiations on the mid-term appraisal document had revealed some disagreements over the contentious issue of disinvestments, particularly between the Congress and the Left parties. However, the matter did not figure in the speeches of the prime minister and the deputy chairman of the Planning Commission. The 8.1 per cent rate of growth targeted by the NDA government was marginally lowered to 7 to 8 per cent. There were exhortations galore from the union's side urging the state governments to double agricultural output in ten years, overcome electricity shortage by attracting public and private sector investment, streamline state electricity agencies, raise additional resources, and minimize expenses.[56]

Analysis

The NDC serves—and with certain reforms it can serve even better—as a useful instrument of intergovernmental relations in matters pertaining to economic development and fiscal policy related issues in the Indian federal set-up. For it provides a unique forum for bringing together the executive heads of the two orders of governments in the country.

Since 1952, the NDC has met 51 times until June 2005. In the realm of development planning, the NDC has been more functional with a concrete agenda than Parliament. Admittedly, the Rajya Sabha as a federal chamber can claim to represent the interests of the states but its composition is not intergovernmental as that of the ISC and the NDC. A member of the Rajya Sabha clearly represents the people or legislators of a state rather than the government of the state, whereas the NDC/ISC represent the executive heads of the union and the state governments respectively.

During thirty-seven years of one party government (Congress dominance and Janata Party government rule), the NDC held 40 meetings, i.e. an average of 1.1 per year. In fifteen years of multiparty coalition/minority governments since November-December 1989, it held eleven meetings, i.e. an average of 0.73 per year (see Table 7.1). It may seem paradoxical that the frequency of meetings between the two phases declined by 30 per cent in terms of averages. One would have expected a higher frequency during the latter phase given the greater commitment and representation of state level political parties in the union government as indicated by a more differentiated group of parties in power in the union and in the states since 1989. However, this paradox may be explained by two factors. First, coalition and minority governments have been unstable and short-lived, resulting in delays in the launching of plans. Second, different groups of parties, including the regional ones, ruling in the states, have been partners in the federal coalition governments. This has provided them direct access as well as opportunity for representation of their views in the union cabinet. In this political set up the chief ministers have enjoyed considerable political clout and influenced decisions at the federal level informally rather than through formal channels like the NDC. The union government found itself dependent on their support but chief ministers had their own vested interests and viewpoints. Their influence on the federal government would, therefore, ultimately depend on realpolitik.

TABLE 7.1: NDC MEETINGS FROM 1952 TO JUNE 2005

Government	*No. of Years*	*No. of Meetings*	*Average per Year*
One Party Dominant Phase 1			
Jawaharlal Nehru (1952-64)	12	20	1.67
Lal Bahadur Shastri (1964-6)	1.5	2	1.33
Indira Gandhi (1966-77)	11	9	0.82
Janata Interregnum			
Morarji Desai (1977-9)	2.5	2	0.8
One Party Dominant Phase II			
Indira Gandhi (1980-4)	4	4	1.0
Rajiv Gandhi (1984-9)	5	3	0.6
Multiparty Coalition/Minority Governments Phase I			
V.P. Singh (1989-90)	1	2	2.0
One Party Congress Minority Government			
Narasimha Rao (1991-6)	5	4	0.8
Multiparty System Phase II			
Deve Gowda (1996-7)	1	1	1.0
Atal Behari Vajpayee (1998-2003)	5	3	0.6
Manmohan Singh (2004-)	1	1	1.0

Source: Information collected from Plan Coordination Division, Planning Commission of India, New Delhi and tabulated by the author.

A content analysis of the issues on the agenda of 51 NDC meetings from 1952 to June 2005 (see Table 7.2) reveals the preoccupation of this key intergovernmental mechanism. Of the 153 items discussed at the meetings, the highest frequency (69) was of planning process related issues. The second highest pertained to food, agriculture, power, irrigation and related issues (19), followed by rural development, public participation and related issues (14). Social sector—health, employment and education—numbered 13, macroeconomic issues 9, centrally sponsored schemes 6, land reforms 5. The miscellaneous items included in the residual category number 16.

In the context of the frequency of the meetings, it is relevant to remember that the NDC's organization and role were renegotiated

TABLE 7.2: FREQUENCY DISTRIBUTION OF ISSUES

	Issues	*No. of Times*
1.	Land reforms and related issues	5
2.	Food, agriculture, power, irrigation and related issues	19
3.	Rural development and related issues	14
4.	Social sector (health, employment and education)	13
5.	Planning process related issues	69
6.	Macroeconomic issues	9
7.	Centrally-sponsored Schemes (CSS)	6
8.	Miscellaneous*	16

Note: * The category 'Miscellaneous' includes various items river water disputes, administration related issues, law and order situation, particularly atrocities perpetrated against the weaker sections, 1982 as the year of productivity, the new 20-point programme, some aspects of forest policy, management of State Road Transport Undertakings, rehabilitation of displaced persons from Pakistan, the National Cadet Corps, land for displaced persons from East Pakistan, progress report of research programmes committee, arrangement for deployment of surplus personnel in major projects in the public and private sector, etc.

by a government resolution in October 1967 which stated that it should meet 'as often as may be necessary and at least twice in each year'. At that time, non-Congress governments were in power from Chandigarh to Calcutta. However, the 1967 coalition experiments were rather short-lived. In 1971, Indira Gandhi came back to power with a thumping majority; the actual impact of non-Congress governments was, therefore, not considerable.

According to one point of view, the NDC has convened a meeting whenever there has been an issue that needs to be specifically discussed by it. In defence of this argument, it may be stated that the 48th meeting of the NDC was called urgently by the prime minister (at a very short notice) at the request of some chief ministers to discuss, among other things, the approval of the Plan Document, increase in the administered price of food grains, etc.[57] Apologists of this point of view argue that the NDC has nothing to lose if it does not have a constitutional or statutory status. Being directly under the prime minister who is its chairman imparts to it a special status in the government.[58]

Due to the fact that the NDC does not have any constitutional or statutory status, plans are invariably launched without the stamp of its formal approval; its meetings are not held for considerable periods of time. For instance, the draft Ninth Five-Year Plan proposal prepared by the Planning Commission and provisionally implemented in 1997, was belatedly approved by the NDC in 1999, after a lapse of two years.[59] It is precisely for this reason that the Sarkaria Commission recommended that the NDC should be reconstituted as the NEDC by a Presidential Order under the provisions of Article 263 so as to have moorings in the Constitution.

For a proper understanding and explanation of the role and relevance of the NDC, it is necessary to examine its working not only in the context of union–state relations, but also in the context of the strategy of economic development in the country. Development planning was launched in the Nehru era. In order to be more effective, it is imperative that it adapts itself to the changed contexts and policy shifts. These changes began to be reflected from the Fourth Five-Year Plan onwards. On the one hand, a new kind of politics has emerged which may be referred to as 'populist' politics in which politicking has elbowed out rational economic planning. Vested interests of particular classes, especially those who are influential politically, have adversely affected the planning process. On the other hand, policy shifts due to economic liberalization have changed the context of planning in the country. In the initial stages of development planning expansion, emphasis was on public investment; the bulk of investments came from the state. Subsequently, public investment began to decline in size and made way for private investment. The planning process ought to be reoriented keeping in view the needs of the economy in which the role of the private sector is constantly expanding. According to one school of thought, there is no place for state planning in a liberalized economy. Yet, in the rethinking about the strategy of economic development, planning continues to be relevant in a developing country like India, and the process of planning must be adjusted to the changed economic structure. In other words, the planning process needs to be geared to the restructuring of the economy. In view of the expanding private sector there is a need for some sort of indicative planning for this sector which must be different from planning for the state sector. In the entire process, the NDC has emerged as a key agency, especially in the new setting where the importance of the state governments and the private sector is increasing. Earlier, the Planning Commission was engaged in planning mainly for the union including plans for the states as well, which easily fell in line. However, exception was made in the case of West Bengal which, because of its different (leftist) ideological leanings, has a somewhat different perspective on planning. State Planning Boards/Commissions have been set up in all states, with the exception of Sikkim. Some states have also established district planning units. Besides the State Planning Boards and Commissions, other development departments and agencies (such as Directorates of Economics and Statistics, research institutions and universities, finance corporations and voluntary agencies[60]) are also involved in the planning process.

Most states have expressed their displeasure at not being given due opportunity to participate in national planning. At present, states are consulted only after the broad features of the five-year plans have been decided. Though the majority of state planning boards lack expertise, yet the states are now politically more assertive and desire a greater say in the planning process. On the basis of a suggestion made by one state government, the Sarkaria Commission recommended, 'State Planning Boards should perform functions for the state governments as the Planning Commission does at the national level. . . . The chief minister should be the chairman of the State Planning Board as his active involvement would be necessary for the success of the state level planning'.[61]

Following the 73rd and 74th Amendments on Panchayati and Nagar Raj, the third tier of government, that is, the grassroots level, has become relevant for political and developmental processes. The question that arises is: how to involve the zila parishads, block level and gram panchayats in the process of planning right from the stage of plan formulation, determining priorities, arranging resources, devising implementation strategies, review or appraisal of plan implementation and feedback of these exercises into the planning process. The Sarkaria Commission also stressed the need for strengthening institutions like zila parishads and elected municipal corporations both financially and functionally. It further emphasized the necessity of regular elections and sessions of these institutions and added that the means for ensuring these in all the states uniformly should be evolved by the union government in consultation with the NEDC.[62]

There is a need to correlate macroeconomic indicators and the ground realities at the grassroots level. States vary in many respects. Some states are relatively more developed than others. In economically developed states, there is a class of industrial bourgeoisie; in agriculturally advanced states, a class of agrarian capitalists exists. Also, some states have a larger tribal population or other backward classes. Since state level and grassroots level situations vary, the planning process should take into account these variations. Different classes have vested interests; those which are politically influential attempt to influence political and economic processes. What is important is that the processes of politics and economic planning should coordinate these differential needs and aspirations. On the one hand, states should aggregate local level factors into a cohesive framework of policies and on the other hand, the national or federal political process should aggregate diversities and disparities among states. Hence, politics can play a creative role in the entire process. Needless to say, the NDC is a crucial intergovernmental mechanism in all these processes.

The planning process has assumed another dimension, i.e. it has become more bargain-oriented in nature. The states believe that if the Finance Commission fails to fulfil their aspirations, an effort could be made to achieve their objectives through the Planning Commission. This accent on the bargaining process has projected the NDC as the principal bargaining forum.

The planning discourse has taken a quantum leap, but India continues to remain wedded to the obsolete development discourse concerned with issues such as GDP-based thinking, growth, investment, savings, capital-output ratio, in other words, purely economistic planning. It is not concerned with development disparities and their implications for the state, society, administration, quality of life, human development indicators, etc. The NDC and its role should be reconceptualized within these altered parameters of planning. In this context, Kabra visualized two circles of planning: the inner and the outer. The NDC is located as a pivotal agency in the inner circle (of planning), but it should be sensitive to and concerned about the implications of planning for the outer circle, such as the impact of globalization on agriculture, industry, backward regions and poorer sections, and of central pay revisions on the finances of the state governments. The NDC as an important intergovernmental mechanism can play an ingenious political role in the planning as well as political processes. The NDC can facilitate a process of multi-level planning—planning for the central government, the state governments, local levels and indicative laying out of the framework for the private sector.[63]

The NDC is pre-eminently a political body where divergent and conflicting politics of development and planning are reconciled. The work of the Planning Commission is a highly technocratic exercise which does not adequately reflect conflicting interests, aspirations, etc. The NDC has evolved into a forum where political conflicts are resolved in such a manner that the consensus that emerges is realistic and effective and has a close bearing on its implementation. This is the most important role of the NDC.

The NDC with a permanent secretariat and a permanent Finance Commission should serve as the key intergovernmental mechanism, where a diversity of perspectives is debated, conflicting interests are articulated, and different preferences are aggregated into a coherent policy framework of public policies.

The role envisaged for the NDC is more in the future than in the past. The lack of a constitutional status is a drawback which ought to be corrected to enable it to actualize the potentialities projected. Indeed, as has been argued later, it would be more appropriate to merge the NDC with the ISC and provide adequate infrastructural support. In fact, this merger could be brought about without any formal amendment either in the Constitution or the Presidential Order setting up the ISC under Article 263.

For neither the Constitution nor the Presidential Order exclude the specific functions assigned to the NDC in the domain of economic development and planning by the 1952 Cabinet Resolution.

INTER-STATE COUNCIL

In India, an intergovernmental mechanism was clearly recognized by the Government of India Act, 1935, as well as the 1950 Constitution. Ironically, despite the existence of a constitutional provision for such an intergovernmental mechanism, it was not pressed into service by the Indian political elite immediately after the promulgation of the Constitution. A constitutionally entrenched Inter-State Council was first used by the National Front government headed by V.P. Singh much later in 1990 by a Presidential Order.

ORIGIN AND CONTEXT

Article 246 of the draft Constitution which addressed the problem 'of coordination between states' was adopted without any debate or amendment and was finally accepted as Article 263 of the Constitution. The consensus on this Article, that provided for the establishment of the Inter-State Council for intergovernmental coordination if the President considered it in 'the public interests', was probably facilitated by the existence of a similar provision in the Government of India Act, 1935 (Article 135), for the constitution of an Inter-Provincial Council.[64]

Article 263 of the Constitution provides that

> if at any time it appears to the President that the public interest would be served by the establishment of a Council charged with the duty of—(*a*) inquiring into and advising upon disputes which may have arisen between states; (*b*) investigating and discussing subjects in which some or all of the states, or the union and one or more of the states, have a common interest; or (*c*) making recommendations upon any such subject and, in particular, recommendations for the better coordination of policy and action with respect to that subject, it shall be lawful for the President by order to establish such a Council, and to define the nature of the duties to be performed by it and its organization and procedure.

Even before Independence, the Government of India Act, 1935, had made a reference to the establishment of an Inter-Provincial Council for facilitating interprovincial cooperation. Article 135 of the 1935 Act reads:

If at any time it appears to His Majesty upon the consideration of representations addressed to him by the Governor-General and the public interests would be served by the establishment of the Inter-Provincial Council charged with the duty of—(*a*) inquiring into and advising upon disputes which may have arisen between Provinces; (*b*) investigating and discussing subjects in which some or all of the Provinces, or the Federation and one or more of the Provinces, have a common interest; or (*c*) making recommendations upon any such subject and, in particular, recommendations for the better coordination of policy and action with respect to that subject, it shall be lawful for His Majesty in Council to establish such a Council, and to define the nature of the duties to be performed by it and its organization and procedure.

Markandan drew attention to the fact that Article 263 of the Constitution relating to the Inter-State Council emerged from two preceding stages in slightly different versions.[65] In the draft of the Article (then numbered 193) prepared by B.N. Rau, the Legal Advisor to the Constituent Assembly, the caption was 'Cooperation between States', and clauses A and B of the Article referred to the regional governments as 'units' and to the Government of India as the 'federation'. Markandan noted that when the Drafting Committee of the Constituent Assembly discussed this Article at its meeting held on 28 January 1948, the caption was left unchanged but the words 'units' and 'federation' were changed to 'states' and 'union'. Further, in the Draft Constitution submitted by the Drafting Committee to Dr Rajendra Prasad, the President of the Constituent Assembly, the word 'cooperation' in the caption was replaced by 'coordination' to make it consistent with the body of the Article where the word 'coordination' was used. On the basis of this evidence, Markandan offered an essentially unitary or parliamentary interpretation of the functions of the ISC. According to him, coordination is given effect to by a higher authority for administrative convenience, while cooperation takes place among equals. He concluded,

Inter-State Council is not a forum wherein issues like retention or otherwise of state autonomy, use and misuse of Article 356 or the nature of the framework could be placed and discussed. These are matters for Parliament to discuss. In any case, the Council is not the forum for discussing matters with a view to seeking states' cooperation.

Extending his argument further, Markandan criticized the Sarkaria Commission report for having taken for granted that the framers of the Constitution had envisaged a federal framework and recommended that the ISC be developed into a forum for a 'Bargaining Federation'. It may be argued that Markandan's interpretation of the Constitution does not stand close scrutiny. First, although Markandan is aware of the fact that the Rau draft was inspired by Article 135 of the Government of India Act, 1935, he does not, as a matter of convenience, take note of the fact that even in the 1935 Act, the caption is 'Inter-provincial cooperation'. If anything, this imperial Act can be construed to mean an instrument of administrative convenience much more than the 1950 Constitution. Thus, his quibbling over the difference between 'coordination' and 'cooperation' in this context would appear to be rather misplaced. Second, Markandan glosses over one missing link between the Draft Constitution finalized by the Drafting Committee and the one submitted to the Constituent Assembly. He argued,

> The dichotomy in the use of the word 'cooperation' in the heading and 'coordination' in the body was rectified in the Draft Constitution submitted to the President of the Constituent Assembly on 21 February 1948, not by using the word 'cooperation' in the body instead of 'co-ordination' but by substituting the word 'coordination' in the heading to accord with the use of the word 'coordination' in the body.

The question arises: who made this verbal alteration? An examination of the minutes of the Drafting Committee (dated 28 January 1948), and the appendix to it that contains the text of the Draft Constitution as approved by the Drafting Committee reveals that the caption 'Cooperation between States' was left unchanged but the Draft Constitution submitted by the Chairman of the Drafting Committee to the President of the Constituent Assembly on 21 February 1948 mysteriously uses the phrase 'Coordination between states', which is also found in the final text of the Constitution as approved by the Constituent Assembly. Dr Ambedkar made this change, but he did not refer the matter back to the Drafting Committee and seek its approval. This, indeed, would have been the valid procedure.[66]

In any case, Markandan's quibbling over the words 'cooperation' and 'coordination' and subscribing to an archaic administrative and unitary interpretation of the functioning of the ISC is not only based on a questionable construction of the jurisprudence of the original intentions of the founding fathers, but also turns the clock back on the work of the Sarkaria Commission and several Supreme Court judgements that have interpreted the Indian Constitution as federal, albeit with a strong parliamentary centre.[67]

The Administrative Reforms Commission was well aware of the informal and ad hoc conferences of labour, food, finance and chief ministers, etc., which were designed to coordinate the policies of the central and state governments relating to these areas. These conferences were not held regularly and the agenda was decided by the concerned union ministry unilaterally. The ARC perceived these conferences as inadequate for resolving interstate conflicts as well as for coordinating national and state policies. It, therefore, recommended the creation of the ISC as a standing body to achieve policy coordination.[68]

Comparing the recommendations of the report of the study team and those of the ARC with regard to the structure and functions of the ISC, Lawrence Saez made an interesting point: whereas the former conceptualized it as a 'super-cabinet with prime minister and all chief ministers as members', the latter recommended it as an 'Ad-hoc conference of prime minister, all central ministers, zonal council and key opposition leader representatives' with the addition of chief ministers as invitees. Further, the study team recommended the appointment of a permanent body whereas the ARC wanted it on a purely temporary basis—for a trial period of two years. The role of the recommended body was advisory according to both the study team and the ARC.[69]

The Rajamannar Committee set up by the DMK government of Tamil Nadu in 1969 also recommended the establishment of an ISC comprising 'the chief ministers or their nominees, all the states having equal representation, with the prime minister as the chairman. No other minister of the union cabinet should be a member of the Council'.[70] The ARC's study team, however, suggested that it should comprise the prime minister, the union ministers for finance, home, labour, food, chief ministers 'or their nominees' and invitees. The ARC recommended the inclusion of the prime minister, the finance and home ministers and a representative of each of the zonal councils.[71]

Though both the ARC and the Rajamannar Committee recommended the establishment of the ISC, they differed with respect to its composition and functions. The ARC proposed a composition that ensured a balanced representation of both the centre and the states, whereas the Rajamannar Committee emphasized the dominance of the states in the Council by excluding the union ministers other than the prime minister. Likewise, the ARC envisaged an advisory role for the ISC in resolving interstate conflicts. The Rajamannar Committee advocated that it should be invested with important legislative and executive powers. The committee intended to transfer some of the powers (at that time exercised by the centre) to the Council which under the recommended composition would be dominated by the chief ministers.[72]

The Sarkaria Commission also suggested that a permanent ISC (called the Inter-Governmental Council—IGC) should be set up under Article 263 of the Constitution. It should be entrusted with the duties set out in clauses (b) and (c) of Article 263 other than socio-economic planning and development. The Council should evolve guidelines for the identification and selection of issues to be brought before it and ensure that only such matters of national importance relating to subjects of common interest are discussed in it.

The Council would consist of a general body assisted by a smaller Standing Committee. The general body would include the prime minister, all chief ministers and union cabinet ministers, or all union ministers dealing with subjects of common interest both to the union and the states. The Standing Committee would include the prime minister, six chief ministers, one from each zone selected annually, and six union cabinet ministers to be nominated by the prime minister. The general body of the IGC shall meet at least twice a year and the Standing Committee at least four times a year. The meetings of the general body would be held in camera and the proceedings would be conducted in a manner similar to that of the union cabinet meetings. Practices and procedures laid down for cabinet meetings may also be followed by the general body. Matters proposed to be referred to the general body would be first discussed by the Standing Committee. Normally, only such matters as referred to by the Standing Committee would be taken up for discussion by the general body. All other matters would be normally considered and disposed of at the level of the Standing Committee. The IGC and its Standing Committee should set up ad hoc subcommittees to investigate important issues. The procedure adopted for the Standing Committee would be the same as that followed for cabinet subcommittee meetings. Also, the council should have a permanent secretariat.[73]

The Constitution empowers the government to set up such a mechanism of consultation and cooperation as and when the need arises to facilitate the smooth working of the system as a whole. Since the Constitution does not make it mandatory for the government to set up such a Council, successive central governments did not see the need to do so.

During the first two decades after independence, the Congress party dominated the political scene and was in power both at the centre and in the states, centre–state disputes could easily be resolved at the party forum. Moreover, there was a lack of will to develop an institutional device which would be useful in promoting coordination among the states. Under Nehru's leadership such conflicts were amicably resolved across the table, thanks to his charisma and the dominance of the Congress party. The situation dramatically changed after the 1967 elections when non-Congress Governments were formed in various states, even though the Congress continued to remain in power at the centre.

Consequently, differences between the two levels of government surfaced. Despite this, the ISC was not set up presumably because of the unstable and weak coalitional governments in most states, with the exception of Tamil Nadu. Following the strengthening of the Congress party at the centre and its return to power in most states in 1971-2, the need for the formation of such a Council was relegated to the background. Even the Janata Party under Morarji Desai's premiership did not consider the need for setting up such a Council. This was because the Janata Party was not only in power in New Delhi but also in major north Indian states; and in view of the fact that the Congress and the DMK continued to dominate the southern states, the Janata at the centre might have had apprehensions that such a forum would provide the non-Janata political forces an opportunity to confront its power at the centre. When Indira Gandhi replaced the Janata dispensation in the 1980 elections, she also did not relish the idea of such a Council. Nor, for that matter, did her successor Rajiv Gandhi evince any interest in such council. In the phase of multiparty coalition governments at the end of the 1980s, regional parties began to play a prominent role, leading to a definite tilt in favour of greater federalization of the erstwhile highly centralized system. In the light of the changed political scenario, the National Front government of V.P. Singh realized that the task of setting up of the ISC should be accomplished on a priority basis. Thus, the ISC was duly established in 1990.

The reason for the National Front becoming a staunch supporter of the Council could partly be attributed to the initiative taken by the opposition parties and non-Congress governments during the premierships of Indira Gandhi and Rajiv Gandhi. The states were aggrieved at the arbitrary manner in which the centre dealt with them in the matter of imposing President's Rule on unconstitutional grounds. They also resented the discriminatory manner in which the non-Congress governments appointed governors, judges, etc. The prerogative to make such appointments lay with the centre. However, this authority was not intended to override the federal character of the Constitution.[74] In the process of declaring most industries, mines and other assets of the states as of national importance and claiming exclusive authority for the exercise of legislative and administrative authority over them, the centre had encroached on the states' autonomy in vital areas. The states had registered their protest against this through periodic representations to the centre and also in their memoranda to the Sarkaria Commission.[75]

Chief ministers like R.K. Hegde and N.T. Rama Rao promoted the idea of greater coordination among the non-Congress(I) states, besides emphasizing the need for a constitutional provision enabling the centre and the states to amicably resolve their differences. Commenting on the centre's overbearing attitude Jyoti Basu said,

> The unity of our country has been subjected to considerable strain during the last few years. This has been caused mostly by an overbearing, and if I may add, obsessive preoccupation on the part of those who were in authority at the centre to concentrate all powers and responsibilities in their hands.

These views became deep-rooted over the years, and the non-Congress (I) states collectively evolved a strategy to protect themselves against encroachments by the centre. The idea of the ISC was thus an inevitable by-product of the States' new thinking.[76]

On 13 January 1990, V.P. Singh wrote to the chief ministers of all states and Lt. Governors of union territories seeking their views on the recommendations of the Sarkaria Commission on the setting up of the ISC and its composition, duties and procedures.[77] In his letter he reiterated his government's commitment to set up the ISC in its election manifesto. The government also formed a Cabinet Committee consisting of the home minister (Mufti Mohammad Sayeed), the finance minister (Madhu Dandavate), the information and broadcasting minister (P. Upendra) and the deputy chairman of the Planning Commission (R.K. Hegde) to consider the recommendations of the Sarkaria Commission.

The Institutional Set up

The ISC was finally established by a Presidential Order notified on 28 May 1990. It said:

> There shall be an Inter-State Council consisting of the prime minister, chief ministers of all the states, chief ministers of union territories having a Legislative Assembly and Administrators of union territories not having a Legislative Assembly, and six ministers of cabinet rank in the Union Council of ministers to be nominated by the prime minister. Other ministers and minister of state having independent charge may also be invited when any item related to a subject under their charge is to be discussed. The prime minister shall be the chairman of the Council and shall preside over its meetings. In his absence, he may nominate any union minister of cabinet rank to preside over the meetings. The Council

shall be a recommendatory body and in that capacity, shall perform the following duties: (*a*) investigating and discussing such subjects, in which some or all of the states or the union and one/or more of the states have a common interest, as may be brought up before it; (*b*) making recommendations upon any such subject and in particular recommendations for the better coordination of policy and action with respect to that subject; and (*c*) deliberating upon such other matters of general interest to the states as may be referred by the chairman of the Council.[78]

The procedure to be followed in the conduct of its business was outlined: the Council shall adopt guidelines for identifying and selecting issues to be brought up before it; it shall meet at least thrice every year and at such time and place as the chairman may appoint in this behalf; the meetings shall be held in camera; ten members (including the chairman) shall form the quorum for a meeting of the Council; all questions shall be decided by consensus and the decision of the chairman as to the consensus shall be final; and in the conduct of its business, the Council shall observe such other procedure as it may, with the approval of the central government, lay down from time to time. The Council shall have a secretariat consisting of such officers and staff as the chairman may deem fit to appoint.[79]

An amendment was made in clause 2 of the Inter-State Council Order 1990. It added:

Provided that where a Proclamation: issued by the President under article 356 of the Constitution of India in relation to any state; or issued by the Governor of Jammu & Kashmir under section 92 of the Constitution of Jammu & Kashmir is in force the Governor of that State shall be invited to attend the meetings of the Council.[80]

At its second meeting held on 15 October 1996, the ISC recommended that there should be a Standing Committee of the Council for continuous consultation and processing of matters for the consideration of the Council. The Ministry of Home Affairs in a notification said that the Standing Committee would comprise ministers of home, finance, industry, defence, human resource development, besides the chief ministers of Orissa, Rajasthan, West Bengal, Andhra Pradesh, Maharashtra and Assam.

The functions of the Standing Committee would include continuous consultation and processing matters for consideration of the Council; reviewing and updating the recommendations of the Sarkaria Commission, especially the vital question of devolution of financial powers from the central government to state governments; examining the changes required in Article 356 of the Constitution; considering the current views of the state governments on 179 recommendations on which there was consensus in the subcommittee as well as 12 items on which there was no consensus; processing all matters pertaining to centre–state relations before they are discussed in the ISC; monitoring the implementation of decisions taken on the recommendations of the Council; and considering any other matter referred to it by the Chairman/Council. The Standing Committee would submit its report on items (2) and (3) mentioned above within three months. It may also invite, if necessary, experts and persons eminent in specific fields to have the benefit of their views while deliberating upon the related subjects.[81]

In accordance with the recommendations of the Sarkaria Commission on setting up ad hoc committees to investigate special matters, the ISC's Standing Committee, at its meeting held on 9 December 1998, approved a subcommittee to be set up under the convenorship of the union defence minister to discuss and reach a consensus on amending Article 356 of the Constitution in the context of discussions held at the earlier meetings of the Standing Committee, the ISC and the judgement of the Apex Court in the Bommai case.[82]

At the meeting held on 22 January 1999, the ISC approved a set of amendments to the guidelines of 28 May 1990 with regard to identifying issues to be brought before the Council. These amendments provide a relatively more open procedure for identification of issues to be discussed in the Council. Previously, the chairman (i.e. the prime minister) was authorized to identify an issue to be discussed by the Council. Under the new dispensation, any member or chief minister could raise any issue of concern to them in the Council, but the chairman has the authority to approve whether a particular issue falls within the purview of the duties of the Council or not.[83]

These guidelines envisage that

> if majority of the members of Inter-State Council propose the discussion of an issue or keeping in view the importance of a particular issue which is considered desirable to do so, the Council may consider such an issue with the approval of the chairman in terms of provisions of clause 4(c) of the Presidential Order dated 28 May 1990.[84]

The guidelines also specify matters that may legitimately be discussed in the Council: (*a*) national appraisal of the measures taken to implement the Directive Principles of State Policy incorporated in Part IV of the Constitution; (*b*) any matter in the union list, the concurrent list or the state list of the Constitution of India: (*i*) in respect of which, there exists a common interest as referred to in clause (*a*) of paragraph 4 of the said order or a need for better coordination as referred to in clause (*b*) of the paragraph, or as the case may be, it is a matter of general interest as referred to in clause (*c*) of that paragraph, or (*ii*) in respect of which the adoption of an uniform policy with regard to legislation or executive action is desirable in the national interest; (*c*) proposal for legislation by the union or a state on any matter in the concurrent list, including amending legislation; and (*d*) cooperation and assistance by the state in the implementation of laws enacted by Parliament and in the exercise of executive powers of the union in the state.[85]

The new guidelines provide that the following issues, 'as far as may be expedient, may not be brought up before the Council': (*a*) a matter that can be resolved between the centre and the states at the official or ministerial level; (*b*) issues slated to be discussed by the NDC, the NIC, the Finance Commission, the Planning Commission or any other body of such nature; (*c*) any issue being discussed in Parliament; (*d*) any issue allocated by the Constitution to 'a specified authority other than the central government such as the Election Commission or the Supreme Court, etc.'; (*e*) any issue likely to 'create discord between the states or otherwise be against the public interest or against the sovereignty or integrity of India, the security of the state, friendly relations with foreign state or public order'; and (*f*) any issue constitutionally falling within the exclusive jurisdiction or special responsibility of the union or under an act of Parliament.[86]

WORKING OF THE ISC UNDER VARIOUS REGIMES

National Front Government

The format of the first meeting of the ISC held in October 1990 under the leadership of V.P. Singh was similar to that of the NDC. The prime minister agreed to institutionalize the procedure for regular consultation between the states and the centre in order to review centre–state relations on a periodic basis. In view of the persistent demand of all the state governments and political parties that the consultation procedure between the states and the union be institutionalized, the best way to achieve this was by establishing the ISC under Article 263 of the Constitution.

The first item on the agenda was a discussion of the recommendations of the Sarkaria Commission on centre–state relations. Singh emphasized that the relations between the centre and the states should keep pace with the changing needs of the people in India's federal polity, and invited the state governments to freely express their views on any aspect of the Sarkaria Commission's recommendations.[87]

The Council proposed to meet thrice a year. Apart from discussing the Sarkaria Commission report, it took note of various kinds of taxation and duties, the setting up of special courts for economic offences, resource mobilization, rural development, irrigation and interstate water disputes, aspects of the Governor's power, recommendations of the Mandal Commission, etc. He added that a subcommittee of the ISC would be set up to consider the various issues involved in centre–state relations and to make concrete suggestions in this respect.[88]

At its meeting held in September 1992, the subcommittee of the ISC approved the guidelines for the selection of issues to be considered by the ISC. The subcommittee noted and approved the recommendations on the setting up of the ISC. However, it did not favour the recommendation of the Sarkaria Commission that zonal councils should be recreated under Article 263. It approved the proposal that the north-eastern council be given additional responsibilities, similar to those of zonal councils. However, this issue needed to be examined in its various dimensions.[89]

Congress Minority Government

During the rule of the Congress government under P.V. Narasimha Rao, no meeting of the ISC was convened. This is not to suggest that intergovernmental affairs were not discussed during this period, but to point out that the forum of the ISC was not used. There could be two explanations for this. It was presumably a veiled rebuff of the Congress government directed at V.P. Singh's National Front government which had earned the distinction of setting up the ISC. In contrast, the Congress governments for nearly four decades had avoided instituting this constitutional forum. Moreover, Rao did convene a number of meetings of the National Integration Council set up by Nehru in the 1960s where issues of interstate as well as national concern were discussed.

United Front Governments

After a hiatus of six years, the second meeting of the ISC was convened by the United Front (UF) government headed by H.D. Deve Gowda on 15 October 1996. The meeting was necessitated by the assurance held out by the UF government in its Common Minimum Programme (CMP) that it was committed to ensuring a strong institutional framework for centre–state consultations. During the intervening six years, a subcommittee of the ISC met and examined the recommendations of the Sarkaria Commission on centre–state relations.

In his inaugural speech, Deve Gowda said that the centre would not hesitate to decentralize decision-making wherever it served the national interest. He expressed the centre's willingness to devolve more powers to the states and to consider more areas where the states could take independent decisions.[90] Advocating 'cooperative federalism' in the Indian context, he added that it meant a strong centre, a strong state and strong local government institutions, and that the UF government had introduced a new style of governance in which consultation with the states was accorded prime importance.[91] He noted that 'the most important requirement of a healthy centre–state relationship is frequent interaction. This would ensure that both sides are in a position to appreciate each others' problems and arrive at responsible decisions'.[92] According to him, 'a system of decision-making, which does not provide for adequate consultation, is bound to lead to distrust and needless tensions. There is, therefore, clearly a need for an institutionalized system of regular consultations between the centre and states.' This system, referred to as 'cooperative federalism', would help both the centre and the states.[93] Deve Gowda stated that cooperative federalism would recognize the fact that in their respective spheres of action, the centre and states were both supreme, but in areas where their interests overlapped, there had to be a system of continuous and sincere consultations and joint decision-making.[94] He cautioned that there would be areas where conflicts could arise between the centre and the states. But the interest of the country and the people at large was of paramount importance.[95] A parochial, confrontationist approach based on the protection of interests of either the centre or the states in his opinion would only weaken the fabric that had held together independent India. He said: 'We have to rise above narrow perspectives and strengthen the forces of democracy and unity.'[96] The centre requires a continuous system of consultation with the states so that the country's scarce and precious resources are utilized in an optimum manner and that the centre and the states are in a position to jointly solve the wide array of economic, social and political problems. He added, 'the Inter-State Council had become even more important today, when we have a coalition government with a number of parties participating'.[97] Emphasizing the need to make the ISC a more effective organization, he said, 'We must ensure that its meetings are convened at regular intervals. We also need to establish a system by which major national issues are discussed.'[98]

The Council decided to set up a Standing Committee to examine the structure of centre–state fiscal relations with a view to promoting decentralization. An 11-member Standing Committee of the ISC was constituted with Indrajit Gupta as chairman, four central ministers and six chief ministers.[99]

The third meeting of the ISC was held on 17 July 1997 when second UF government headed by I.K. Gujral was in power. After several rounds of inconclusive discussions during the previous year, the UF government finally decided to shelve the proposal to amend Article 356 in order to prevent its misuse. The meeting failed to arrive at a consensus on any of one suggested amendments. The Council, however, ratified the consensus reached by the Standing Committee on devolving 29 per cent of the central pool of taxes to the states as per the provisions of the Ninth Finance Commission w.e.f. 1 April 1996. Addressing the chief ministers, Gujral said that a 'give-and-take' approach between the centre and states was necessary to evolve a consensus on major issues, but cautioned against any move to weaken the federal spirit.[100]

On 28 November 1997, the fourth meeting of the ISC was held. The Council which met amid reports of Congress withdrawing support to the UF government, did not take up the issue of Article 356 of the Constitution and the role of the Governor, and dealt mainly with financial matters.[101] The Council approved 29 recommendations of the Sarkaria Commission on the sharing of central duties, royalties, cooperative taxes and functioning of the Finance Commission.[102]

BJP-led Coalition Governments

The fifth meeting of the ISC was held on 22 January 1999 during the premiership of Atal Behari Vajpayee. It had a tough agenda on its hands: how should the emergency provisions under Articles 355 and 356 of the Constitution be handled?[103] Another important issue that was expected to come up during discussions pertained to granting more powers to the ISC to take up 'sensitive' matters. According to the existing guidelines, several matters were out of bounds for the ISC such as those pending in Parliament or before the Planning Commission.

On 20 May 2000, the sixth meeting of the ISC was held during the tenure of the NDA government, again led by Atal Behari Vajpayee. Some of the chief ministers were of the view that the meetings should be convened at regular intervals, at least once a year, so that no policy issue impinging on centre–state relations was settled unilaterally by the centre. The centre, on the contrary, was in no mood to make any such commitment. Several chief ministers strongly disapproved the arbitrary manner in which an additional term of reference (TOR) had been entrusted to the

Eleventh Finance Commission (EFC) without prior consultation with the states.

An important decision taken at the seventh meeting of the ISC on 16 November 2001 was that in the appointment of Governors consultation with the chief ministers was made obligatory. For this, a constitutional amendment could be made. Another important decision was to allow the centre to retain the power to institute a commission of inquiry against any minister of state government, but with appropriate safeguards to prevent its misuse.

Article 356 dominated the Council's deliberations at the eighth meeting held in August 2003 in Srinagar. There was a 'unanimous' agreement on the question of amending Article 356 in accordance with the *Bommai judgement* of the Supreme Court. The objective was to incorporate the case law into the text of the Constitution.[104] Ironically, such consensus had been reached in the past as well, but action on it is still awaited.

Congress-led United Progressive Alliance Government

The ninth meeting of the ISC was chaired by Prime Minister Manmohan Singh in June 2005, coinciding with the NDC meeting. There were three items on the agenda: (*a*) blueprint of action plan on good governance, (*b*) disaster management-preparedness of states to cope with disasters, and (*c*) implementation report on decisions taken by ISC on the recommendations of the Sarkaria Commission.[105] The prime minister emphasized the importance of ensuring a caring police force, effective law enforcement, and efficient service delivery by the government agencies. He urged the chief ministers to initiate measures for disaster mitigation and integrate disaster management into development planning. He also stressed the role of community and Panchayati Raj institutions, and the corporate sector in this venture. Several chief ministers reminded the union government to set up a constitution review commission to look into the entire gamut of union state relations as promised in the UPA Common Minimum Programme. Almost all chief ministers used the occasion to highlight problems of their own concern going beyond the agenda items.[106]

Analysis

Data on the meetings of the ISC and its Standing Committee since its inception in 1990 are presented in Table 7.3. During this period, only nine meetings of the Council were convened which is rather surprising in view of the fact that this period saw a paradigm shift in union–state relations. This is also in contravention to the notification that considered desirable for it to meet three times a year. A document of the ISC reports that out of 247 recommendations of the Sarkaria Commission, 62 were not accepted, 179 were implemented and 6 were under implementation. Out of 62 items not implemented, the largest number related to administrative, financial, and economic relations (24 items each). Out of 179 items implemented, by far the largest number of items concerned financial and economic relations. Out of six items under implementation, four refer to legislative relations and one each to administrative relations, food, agriculture and environment.[107] In the Srinagar meeting, it was decided that the ISC in future would become the forum to sort out important issues of political and socio-economic concerns of cooperative federalism.

During this period, the Standing Committee of the Council met ten times. Its subcommittees met more frequently to prepare the groundwork for the Council meetings.[108] The Council met only once during the tenure of the NF government, not even once during the Rao Congress regime, three times under the UF government, four times under the BJP-led coalition government, and once during the Congress-led UPA government. Common issues were discussed at these meetings: recommendations of the Sarkaria Commission report covering the entire gamut of centre–state relations; Article 356; interstate river water disputes; greater autonomy to states; centrally-sponsored schemes; devolution of financial powers to the states and Panchayati Raj; the Governor's role; consideration of state legislation reserved by Governors for presidential assent; resource mobilization; good governance, disaster management; etc.

In fact, on most crucial issues, any substantial consensus in the Council has been conspicuous by its absence. Discussions on Article 356 and the role of the Governor clearly illustrate this

TABLE 7.3: INTER-STATE COUNCIL MEETINGS SINCE 1990

Government	*Full Council*	*Standing Committee*	*Sub-committee*	*Issues*
National Front (NF)	1	–	4	Recommendations of the Sarkaria Commission
Congress	–	–	–	
United Front (UF)	3	5	–	Sarkaria Commission's recommendations, interstate river water disputes, greater autonomy to states, centrally-sponsored schemes, devolution of financial power President's Rule role of Governor
National Democratic Alliance (NDA)	4	1	–	Articles 356, 355, consideration of provincial legislation reserved for President's assent, devolution of financial power, TOR for the Eleventh Finance Commission
United Progressive Alliance (UPA)	1			Good Governance disaster management and Sarkaria Panel

Notes: 1. When the Congress government under Rao was in power, two meetings of the subcommittee were held, but since they were formed by an ISC meeting during the NF government, these meetings are included under the NF government in the table.

2. The UF formed two governments headed respectively by H.D. Deve Gowda and I.K. Gujral. Likewise, the BJP-led coalition formed two governments during the period under review, one after the 1998 elections and the other after the 1999 polls. The 13-day minority government formed by the BJP after 1996 is not accounted for in the table for obvious reasons.

point. If any concrete decision was taken by the ISC, it pertains to the guidelines laid down by it concerning procedures and rules of business of the Council and its committees. Some sort of consensus on devolution of finances to the states and various Finance Commissions' recommendations are also evident.

This monumental failure of the ISC to emerge as an active intergovernmental forum in the Indian federal system calls for an explanation. With the growing federalization of the Indian parliamentary federal polity, it was expected that the ISC would come into its own as a useful forum of intergovernmental relations. However, this was not so. The reasons for this need to discussed in terms of two phases:

1. The first four decades of the Indian federation during which the ISC was not formally set up under Article 263 of the Constitution.
2. The period since its institution in 1990.

As mentioned earlier, the Nehru government preferred to set up the NDC in 1952 for intergovernmental clearance of the five-year plans specifically. But the NDC was not set up under the Constitution, the reason being that its less formal organization (by a Cabinet Resolution) makes it more amenable for the centre to manage intergovernmental affairs in its own way without the constraints of a constitutionally entrenched body. The broad spectrum of intergovernmental relations was left out of its purview. This may be for two reasons. In the first place since the Congress party was dominant at the national and state levels, by and large, intergovernmental issues were discussed across the table at the Congress party forums. So where was the need for setting up of the ISC? Economic planning being a more complex issue necessitated the creation of the NDC.

The successive governments preceding the NF government elected in 1989 continued this tradition. The Sarkaria Commission recommended the setting up of the ISC under Article 263, but at the same time reduced its importance by recommending the continuation of the NDC as a separate intergovernmental mechanism with constitutional entrenchment. The NDC continues to exist, but it is yet to be given constitutional entrenchment under Article 263.

The continued existence of these two separate mechanisms has meant the dominance of the NDC in the more salient area of economic federalism and the simultaneous eclipse of the ISC in the political domain where its importance is further reduced because of the presence of coalition governments in New Delhi (since 1989) in which state and/or national parties are directly represented. Since parties advocating state autonomy are often directly represented in the federal coalition governments, they hardly need the alternative intergovernmental forum of the ISC to articulate their interests.

Because of these reasons, the ISC could not acquire the functional relevance visualized by the makers of the Constitution. This did not happen even after 1989 when one party dominance at the centre as well as in the states yielded place to a more diversified party system in which it was expected that the ISC would emerge as an important forum of intergovernmental negotiations and policy making. However, in the absence of a more vigorous ISC, the union cabinet itself has become impregnated with unmediated regional pressures and pulls by the ruling parties at the state level which are also partners in the coalition governments in New Delhi. This has not only vitiated the collective responsibility of the cabinet, but has also eroded the coordinating and arbitrating authority of the prime minister's office. For this reason, it would appear that the basic structure of parliamentary government in India has at least partly lost its functional coherence and institutional integrity. There is a need to deliberate on how to correct the prevailing state of affairs. In the wider context of growing federalization, Douglas Verney talked about the need of promoting the idea of responsible federalism comparable to the notion of 'responsible parliamentary government'. To this end, he proposed modifications in the existing ISC in which the President replaces the prime minister as the chairman of the general body of the Council, while the prime minister continues to chair its Standing Committee. 'The full President-in-Council could then act as a federal buffer between the union cabinet and the Governors. President's rule would initially be via the President-in-Council and not the Home Ministry'.[109] Its recommendations may then be made to the Executive Committee of the ISC for submission to the union cabinet. It would lend greater legitimacy to the exercise of presidential power under Article 356.[110]

Singh and Saxena,[111] however, pointed out that it may lead to a serious division of parliamentary authority and executive power and the union government so as to alter the basic nature of the parliamentary/cabinet government at the centre. Nothing comparable to it exists either in a parliamentary or presidential government. The idea of a permanent and sharp divergence of political opinion between the President-in-Council and Parliament, on the one hand, and the Steering Committee of the Council on the other, may lead to a friction/deadlock in the system. In any case, in a parliamentary cabinet system, the ultimate responsibility and authority of the union executive for proclamation of President's Rule cannot be compromised in favour of the President-in-Council or its Steering Committee. A politically diverse body like the President-in-Council may be too cumbersome and lacking in cohesion to perform an emergency executive job like recommending proclamation of President's Rule in a state. Over a period of time, the existing system may adjust to the changed expectations and the political climate. Any hasty adventure in constitutional restructuring may neither be necessary nor desirable.

There is another aspect to the two existing interstate agencies in the NDC and the ISC. Singh asked whether there is a need for two separate intergovernmental mechanisms, the NDC and the ISC.[112] The existence of two separate bodies is at least partly based on the rationale that the ISC would deal with political problems whereas the NDC would be involved in formulating plans and macroeconomic policies. This would keep politics out of economic policies. The actual experience hardly corroborates this expectation. 'This purely rational, administrative mode of thought', Singh argued, 'is counter-productive for a federal society of subcontinental proportions. For it denies the critical and creative role of federal politics in creating national consensus through sub-national or regional autonomy.' He, therefore, proposed the merger of the NDC and the ISC into one constitutional forum for intergovernmental negotiations and policy making, much like the FMC in Canada that deals with political problems, economic policies as well as constitutional reforms.

There is justification in this proposition. In Canada, the basic groundwork of creating a federal consensus is done by numerous federal–provincial official and ministerial conferences whose recommendations are finally approved by the apex conference of the first ministers. Canadians have also institutionalized an annual Provincial Premiers' Conference to reach an interprovincial consensus for their dealings with the federal government. The Canadian experience suggests that the merger of the ISC and the NDC into a common intergovernmental forum may be a good model for India to experiment with.

Lloyd Rudolph and Susanne Rudolph[113] persuasively argued that economic liberalization in India since 1991 has gradually created a federal market economy with a more meaningful sharing of decision-making powers between the centre and the states. This new liberal policy shift has granted a measure of economic sovereignty and decentralized autonomy to the states and the chief ministers now bear the burden of managing economic growth in their respective states. They are required to negotiate a path of economic development with private capital as well as to avoid undue capitulation to unwarranted populist political pressures. They also have to coordinate their governance and economic management with the centre's new role as a regulator and fiscal disciplinarian and contend with hard budgetary constraints imposed by the faceless international lending and credit rating agencies. In this new economic and political environment both the centre and the states would find their respective interests and compulsions at cross-purposes and would therefore require more than ever before common intergovernmental forums to reconcile contradictions and harmonize their policies.

Returning to the analysis of the present working of the NDC and the ISC, an effort has been made to examine and delineate factors that influence the effectiveness of these mechanisms using the explanatory model presented in Figure 7.1.[114] This model brings out six major factors in the given order of importance.

The party system appears to be an important factor which affects the functioning of intergovernmental mechanisms. When the Congress party was in power under Jawaharlal Nehru, Indira Gandhi and Rajiv Gandhi, the NDC was overly dominated by the centre. In fact, the process of planning itself was highly

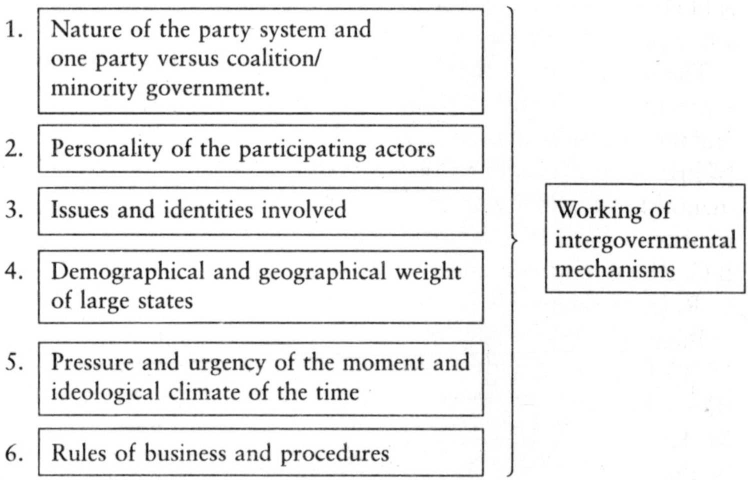

FIGURE 7.1: FACTORS AFFECTING THE WORKING OF NDC AND ISC IN INDIA

centralized. The five-year plans prepared by the Planning Commission which was chaired by the prime minister were seldom questioned by the chief ministers, especially during the premiership of Nehru and Indira Gandhi, and until the late 1970s. It was only thereafter that Indira Gandhi and Rajiv Gandhi had to contend with the critical views of opposition chief ministers, either individually (the Left Front chief minister Jyoti Basu since 1977) or collectively (southern non-Congress chief ministers' Conference convened by the Janata Dal chief minister R.K. Hegde in the early 1980s). Towards the end of his premiership, Rajiv Gandhi, faced a walkout from the NDC by the TDP chief minister N.T. Rama Rao. With the transformation of one party dominance into a more competitive party configuration during the Janata government's interlude in the late 1970s and since 1989, there has been a perceptible change in the working of the NDC and the ISC. Even though the frequency of meetings of the NDC and the ISC has declined in the era of multiparty system and coalition governments, diverse and variegated shades of political opinions are represented in these bodies than was the case earlier. Thus, the degree of discussion and debate in an intergovernmental forum is likely to be more intense in a fragmented party system than in a one party dominance system.

The second factor that influences the functioning of intergovernmental mechanisms is the personality of the prime minister and the chief ministers concerned. Prime ministers like Jawaharlal Nehru, Indira Gandhi and Rajiv Gandhi dominated intergovernmental forums in a way that is unimaginable under other prime ministers. Similarly, eminent State leaders like chief ministers B.C. Roy (Congress) and Jyoti Basu (Left Front) of West Bengal, C. Rajagopalachari (Congress) of Madras, S.K. Sinha (Congress) of Bihar, Morarji Desai (Congress) of Bombay, R.K. Hegde (Janata Dal) of Karnataka, Biju Patnaik (Janata Dal) of Orissa, N.T. Rama Rao and Chandrababu Naidu (TDP) of Andhra Pradesh, M. Karunanidhi (DMK) and J. Jayalalitha (AIADMK) of Tamil Nadu, Laloo Prasad Yadav (RJD) of Bihar and S.M. Krishna (Congress) of Karnataka enjoyed more clout in the deliberations of intergovernmental mechanisms than others. However, personality alone may not always be a decisive factor. For instance, even a strong-willed and domineering prime minister like Morarji Desai was hamstrung by the factional feud in the Janata Party (that was virtually a *de facto* coalition government as the constituent parties that hurriedly merged to form it on the eve of the 1977 Lok Sabha elections could never carry forward the process of integration in the new party to its logical conclusion). Besides, some prime ministers of minority coalition governments (like I.K. Gujral, Narasimha Rao, A.B. Vajpayee, and Manmohan Singh) have been more conciliatory and accommodative than V.P. Singh, who conducted himself like a one party majority prime minister. Among the chief ministers endowed with conciliatory skills were Jyoti Basu, the late R.K. Hegde, Chandrababu Naidu, etc. Hence, the stronger the personalities involved on both sides at an intergovernmental forum, the less likely are the chances of a consensual outcome.

Another factor that impacts the effectiveness of intergovernmental mechanisms is issues and identities in question. For instance, issues like development planning have been more amenable to resolution than contentious issues like Article 356, the role of the Governor and devolution of financial powers to the states. Similarly, where strong regional identities are involved, a consensus is difficult to achieve such as the question of increased autonomy for some states, treaty making power of the union government, communalism, and interstate river water disputes. In fact, most of these issues are generally not included in the agenda of formal intergovernmental mechanisms and are sought to be tackled by the Union State Premiers' Conferences (USPC), semi-judicial tribunals, National Integration Council, etc. It may be surmised that developmental and other non-controversial issues are more likely to be resolved at an intergovernmental forum than issues dealing with major constitutional matters.

Moreover, demographic and geographical factors also influence the differential in the political weight of the larger states in comparison to that of the smaller ones. However, one perceptible change in this regard is that the political influence of non-Hindi rimland states like those of the south, Punjab and West Bengal has increased in the coalition era as compared to that of the Hindi belt like UP, Bihar, Madhya Pradesh, Haryana and Rajasthan in different phases of Congress dominance. Thus, the demographical and geographical weight of larger states is likely to count more in one party government, whereas under coalition governments, a group of other states may also acquire influence to countervail the weight of larger states.

Further, intergovernmental consensus is sometimes possible under the pressure and urgency of the moment and the ideological climate of the time. For example, governments have generally been more accomodative in arriving at a workable understanding on developmental plans and fiscal federalism than on constitutional amendments relating to federal provisions and constitutional division of powers between the union and the states. The urgency of an issue at an intergovernmental forum is likely to facilitate political expediency in favour of consensus resolution. The changed ideological climate following economic liberalization explains why consensus has been more feasible on economic reforms in the same way as consensus on development planning was in the Nehru era.

Finally, rules of business and procedures pertaining to intergovernmental mechanisms contribute to their success. It may be added that the rule of decision by consensus as determined by the prime minister may be regarded as the sheet anchor of workability of these mechanisms. If decision by majority had been the *modus operandi*, these bodies would have permanently got stuck in the mire of conflict, particularly in the multipartisan and coalition phase of governance. From a democratic point of view, this may be perceived by some observers as an undue limitation on the powers of the chief ministers. This is probably a precondition for their ability to take a decision that does not lead to permanent conflicts and crafts a decision worthy of continued commitment of all parties concerned. This naturally demands an open mind on all sides and a democratically accommodative leadership on the part of the prime minister. At present, the agenda is determined by the prime minister after prior consultation with the chief ministers. The meetings are held in camera and the press is briefed at the end of the meetings. This is for the good as it facilitates dispassionate discussion away from the limelight of the media. The chief ministers often complain that the agenda papers are sent to them late, giving their officials little time to do the necessary homework. This can easily be taken care of. The quality of decision can be considerably improved if affected interests and policy groups in the government and the civil society have opportunities of greater representation and participation in the process prior to these meetings. Therefore, the more political actors at an intergovernmental forum are prepared and well briefed in advance about the agenda, the more likely they are to bring dispassionate and rational discussion to the table.

To sum up, the NDC and the ISC have emerged as two apex intergovernmental mechanisms of great importance, but they have hardly realized their full potential. To this end, they need to be constitutionally entrenched and functionally streamlined, especially in a climate when the Indian political system is charted on a course of growing federalization that is still working the process out to its denouement. It has been suggested here that these two mechanisms should be merged into one key apex intergovernmental forum.

NOTES

1. Kamal Nayan Kabra, *Development Planning in India: Exploring an Alternative Approach*, Delhi: Sage, 1997, p. 14.

2. *Panchayati Raj Update*, Institute of Social Sciences, vol. VIII, no. 6, June 2001, p. 3.
3. S.R. Sen, 'Planning Machinery in India', *Indian Journal of Public Administration*, vol. VII, no. 3, July-September 1961, p. 233.
4. Planning Commission, *Draft Outline, First Five-Year Plan*, New Delhi, 1952, p. 253.
5. National Development Council, Cabinet Secretariat, Resolution No. 65/15/CF-67, dated 7 October 1967.
6. National Development Council, Cabinet Secretariat, Resolution No. 62/CF/50, dated 6 August 1952.
7. H.K. Paranjape, *The Reorganised Planning Commission: A Study in the Implementation of Administrative Reforms*, New Delhi: Indian Institute of Public Administration, 1970, pp. 7-8.
8. Ibid.
9. Ibid.
10. National Development Council, Cabinet Secretariat Resolution No. 65/15/CF-67, dated 7 October 1967.
11. Ibid.
12. Paranjape, *The Reorganised Planning Commission*, op. cit., p. 9.
13. Administrative Reforms Commission, *Report of the Study Team on Centre-State Relation*, vol. I, New Delhi: Government of India, Ministry of Home Affairs, 1967, p. 11.
14. Ibid.
15. Geetanjali Das, 'National Development Council and Regional Development: A Study of Its Role and Functional Dimensions in Indian Federal Polity', doctoral dissertation, Orissa: Berhampur University, 1997, pp. 75-8.
16. Paranjape, op. cit., p. 10.
17. Administrative Reforms Commission, *Report of the Study Team on Centre-State Relations*, op. cit., pp. 100-7.
18. *Commission on Centre-State Relations, Report*, Part I, pp. 380-1.
19. Ibid.
20. Ibid.
21. Michael Brecher, *Nehru: A Political Biography*, London: Oxford University Press, 1959, p. 523.
22. Speech by Nehru at the eighth meeting of the NDC held in December 1956, p. 23.
23. Ibid., p. 2.
24. Government of India, Planning Commission, Speech by Nehru at the Ninth Meeting of the NDC held on 3 June 1957, *Summary Report*, New Delhi: Planning Commission, p. 1.
25. Speech by Thanu Pillai at the Sixteenth Meeting of the NDC held on 12 September 1960, p. 31.

26. Paul Brass, 'Coalition Politics in North India', *American Political Science Review*, vol. LXXII, December 1968.
27. Michael Brecher, *Nehru's Mantle: The Politics of Succession in India*, New York: Praeger, 1966; M.P. Singh, *Split in a Predominant Party: The Indian National Congress in 1969*, Delhi: Abhinav Publications, 1981.
28. Brecher, *Nehru's Mantle*, op. cit.
29. Singh, *Split in a Predominant Party*, op. cit.
30. 'Planning from the Base', *Economic and Political Weekly*, vol. II, no. 50, 23 December 1967.
31. Ibid.
32. Ibid.
33. *Economic and Political Weekly*, 25 March 1978, p. 542.
34. Romesh Thapar, 'Into Janata's Second Year', *Economic and Political Weekly*, vol. XIII, no. 13, April 1978, p. 565.
35. Brecher, *Nehru's Mantle*, op. cit.; Singh, *Split in a Predominant Party*, op. cit.
36. Romesh Thapar, 'Two Nations or One?', *Economic and Political Weekly*, vol. XX, nos. 45, 46 and 47, November 1985, p. 1901.
37. *The Hindustan Times*, 9 November 1985.
38. *Business Standard*, 9 November 1985.
39. *Financial Express*, 30 November 1985.
40. Ibid., 26 April 1986.
41. *Indian Express*, 21 March 1988.
42. Ibid., 23 March 1988.
43. Ibid., 22 March 1988.
44. Ibid.
45. *Economic and Political Weekly*, vol. XXIII, nos. 14 and 15, 2-9 April 1988, p. 668.
46. *Economic Times*, 12 October 1990.
47. Ibid.
48. *Business Standard*, 12 October 1990.
49. Ibid.
50. Ibid.
51. Ibid.
52. For a detailed account of the proceedings of the meeting, see Government of India, Planning Commission, *Summary Record* of the Forty-second Meeting of the NDC held in October 1990, New Delhi: Planning Commission.
53. *The Hindu*, 2 September 2001.
54. Ibid., 5 September 2001, p. 14.
55. Internet: http://www.hinduonnet.com/2002/12/22 Stores/2002 122204160100.htm

56. *The Hindu*, 28 June 2005 and *The Times of India*, 29 June 2005, both Delhi editions.
57. Interview with Rajeev Malhotra, Deputy Advisor, Planning Commission, New Delhi, August 2001.
58. Ibid.
59. Prime Minister's Foreword to the *Ninth Five-Year Plan, 1997-2002*, vol. I, *Development Goals, Strategy and Policies*, New Delhi: Government of India, Planning Commission.
60. *Commission on Centre-State Relations, Report*, Part I, op. cit, Chap. XI.
61. Ibid.
62. Ibid.
63. Interview with K.N. Kabra, Indian Institute of Public Administration, New Delhi, August 2001.
64. The text of the Draft Constitution in B. Shiva Rao, ed., *The Framing of India's Constitution: Select Documents*, New Delhi: Indian Institute of Public Administration, vol. 3, *Constituent Assembly Debates*, Book 3, vol. VIII, p. 819.
65. K.C. Markandan, 'Bargaining Federation?', *The Pioneer*, 6 July 2000.
66. Minutes of the Meeting of the Drafting Committee held on 28 January 1948 and the Appendix containing the B.N. Rau draft are incorporated in B. Shiva Rao, ed., *The Framing of India's Constitution*, op. cit., pp. 447-54. Dr. Ambedkar's letter of 21 February 1948 forwarding the text of the Draft Constitution is also contained therein.
67. I benefited by my discussions with M.P. Singh on this point.
68. *Deccan Herald*, 8 January 1990.
69. Lawrence Saez, *Federalism without a Centre*, Delhi: Sage, 2002, p. 108.
70. *Rajamannar Report on Centre-State Relations, Madras: Inquiry Committee*, Government of Tamil Nadu, 1971.
71. *Indian Express*, 9 May 1990.
72. B.L. Maheshwari and R. Ram Mohan Rao, 'The Rajamannar Report: A Survey of Reactions in Centre-State Relations', in *Centre-State Relations in the Seventies*, ed. B.L. Maheshwari, Calcutta: Minerva Associates, 1973, p. 305.
73. *Commission on Centre-State Relations, Report*, Part I, Delhi: Government of India Press, 1988.
74. *The Statesman*, 1 July 1990.
75. Ibid.
76. P. Tharyan, 'Inter-State Council: A Constitutional Need', *The Hindustan Times*, 19 February 1990.
77. *The Hindu*, 14 January 1990.
78. Inter-State Council Order 1990, notified on 28 May 1990, F. No. IV/11017/3/90-CSR, New Delhi: Ministry of Home Affairs, 28 May 1990.
79. Ibid.

80. Inter-State Council [Amendment] Order 1990, notified on 19 July 1990, Ministry of Home Affairs, Notification no. IV/11017/3/90-CSR.
81. Ministry of Home Affairs, Inter-State Council Secretariat, New Delhi, 5 December 1996, Notification no. 7/4/96-ISC.
82. Ministry of Home Affairs, Inter-State Council Secretariat, Notification no. 7/2/2000-ISC, New Delhi, 26 April 2000.
83. *Guidelines for Identifying and Selecting Issues to be brought before the Inter-State Council*, Inter-State Council Secretariat, 22 January 1999, Section I, Clauses (i) and (ii).
84. Ibid., last para.
85. Ibid., Section 2.
86. Ibid., Section 3.
87. *The Hindu*, 11 October 1990.
88. *The Economic Times*, 11 October 1990.
89. *The Times of India*, 16 September 1992.
90. Ibid.
91. *Business Standard*, 16 October 1996.
92. Ibid.
93. Ibid.
94. Ibid.
95. Ibid.
96. Ibid.
97. Ibid.
98. Ibid.
99. *Financial Express*, 12 December 1996.
100. *The Hindustan Times*, 19 July 1997.
101. *Deccan Herald*, 29 November 1997.
102. *Financial Express*, 29 November 1997.
103. *The Indian Express*, 21 January 1999.
104. *The Hindu*, 29 August 2003.
105. Information collected from ISC Secretariat, Vigyan Bhavan Annexe, New Delhi.
106. *The Hindu*, 29 June 2005.
107. Government of India, *Inter-State Council Secretariat*, Ministry of Home Affairs, n.d., p. 19.
108. For a detailed account of these meetings, see Rekha Saxena, doctoral dissertation, op. cit.
109. Douglas V. Verney, 'Responsible Government and Responsible Federalism: Parliamentary Government in Plural Societies', typescript, 1990, Department of Political Science, York University, Toronto, p. 14.

110. 'Reframing Continuity', Rekha Saxena's interview with Douglas Verney, *The Pioneer*, 5 April 2001.
111. M.P. Singh and Rekha Saxena, 'India Independent: The First Half Century of Political Development and Decay', *The Indian Historical Review*, vol. XXVI, July 1999, pp. 155-6.
112. M.P. Singh, 'Inter-State Council: Why It Continues to be the Fifth Wheel in the Intergovernmental Car?', paper submitted to the National Commission for the Review of the Working of the Indian Constitution, typescript, 2001.
113. Lloyd Rudolph and Susanne Rudolph, 'Iconisation of Chandrababu: Sharing Sovereignty in India's Federal Market Economy', *Economic and Political Weekly*, vol. XXXVI, no. 18, 5-11 May 2001, pp. 1541-52.
114. Rekha Saxena, 'Strengthening Federal Dialogue: Role of NDC and ISC', *Contemporary India*, vol. 1, no. 3, July-September 2002.

CHAPTER 8

Summary and Conclusions

In 1867 Canada was the first modern government to seek to combine the parliamentary principle with the federal principle with a strong parliamentary centre which some theorists of federalism have called parliamentary federalism. In 1950, India adopted more or less a similar Constitution. Social and regional diversities in the two countries coupled with the British colonial heritage evolved into this constitutional denouement.

Over the years, the First Ministers' Conferences in Canada and the National Development Council and Inter-State Council in India have emerged as effective apex organs of intergovernmental relations. The FMC has the final responsibility of federal–provincial policy making in Canada in vital areas of governance like economy, ecology, energy, tax sharing and harmonization, constitutional reforms, promotion of interprovincial and international trade and commerce. Groundwork is done at the ministerial or deputy ministerial conferences but the FMC has the ultimate responsibility for intergovernmental negotiation, approval and announcement. Agreements reached still require the sanction of the Parliament and provincial legislatures, which may also be involved in the process by the respective first ministers in the earlier stages of negotiation through briefings and consultations.

Between 1906 and October 2004, 75 FMCs were held. Of these, 19 dealt with economic and fiscal federalism, 22 with constitutional reforms, three with economy and fiscal federalism and constitutional reforms, and 31 with more diverse assortment of issues like economy, constitution and social security. During the post-Second World War period, the frequency and importance of the FMCs' decisions enormously increased. The maximum number of meetings were held during the tenures of Pearson (9), Trudeau (23), Mulroney (12) and Chretien (7). The sudden increase in the number of FMC meetings between the 1960s and the 1980s is largely attributable to the fact that constitutional reforms were in the forefront of the Canadian political system. For example, 11 out of 23 FMC meetings during Trudeau's and 6 out of 12 during Mulroney's premiership focused on the Constitution. Both these premiers in post-War period sought to resolve Canada's constitutional dilemma. In this endeavour, Trudeau was relatively more successful than Mulroney. Trudeau's major achievements were the patriation of the Constitution from London to Ottawa and the formalization of the 1982 constitutional compact with the Charter of Rights and Freedoms and an Amending Formula. Despite his intent, vigour and persistence, Mulroney failed to bring Quebec back into the constitutional consensus both at Meech Lake and Charlottetown.

There was an evident decline in the frequency of FMCs during the term of Chretien's Government, which seemed to have put the issue of constitutional reforms on the backburner, taking cue from the repeated failures of his predecessor. The same is true of the first FMC convened by Prime Minister Paul Martin (Liberal) in September 2004. It should be emphasized that the FMC continues to serve as the top executive federal forum for decision-making in areas such as economy, fiscal federalism and social security.

A common criticism of the FMC as a mechanism of federal–provincial decision-making is its elitist character and unrepresentative credentials. It has been said that 'eleven men in suits' deciding for the whole nation is a strange spectacle of democracy. This criticism reflects that the legacy of British constitutionalism and representative theory is being questioned by some Canadians. The un-English influence in the realm of constitutionalism in Canada is also reflected in recourse to referendums which is a feature of post-revolutionary constitutionalism, say, France and Switzerland. Those who defend the FMC on this count argue that it is perfectly legitimate and democratic for the executive heads of the two orders of government to meet and decide on behalf of their respective governments as they are duly elected and accountable to their parliamentary and provincial electorates. Decisions of the FMC are at least in principle subject to approval by the Parliament and provincial legislatures.

However, noted observers of the Canadian system like Franks[1] argued that the decisions of the FMC are not always duly referred to and approved by Parliament. Provincial premiers may also bypass their provincial legislatures in this matter. However, this can be corrected. Incidentally, a recent development in Canadian politics has been the ambivalence of the governments of Quebec and Canada to refer contentious constitutional issues to referendums. From a conservative perspective, this may appear to be inconsistent with the Canadian tradition of governance. From a liberal democratic perspective, however, it may be a step in the direction of participatory democratic politics. The choice for Canadians is not an easy one, given the fact that these unconventional developments threaten to destroy the Canadian Federal Union or undo a laboriously negotiated constitutional consensus like the one arrived at Charlottetown in 1992.

India's experience with its two intergovernmental mechanisms—the NDC and the ISC—has not been as successful as Canada's with the FMC. This may be indicative of the fact that the working of the Indian political system is less federal than the Canadian polity. Neither the NDC nor the ISC can match the FMC as an intergovernmental forum of federal–provincial bargaining and decision-making. It was expected that this would change when the one party dominance under the Congress gave way to a multi-party system and coalition and minority governments in 1989. However, this did not, happen. During the era of Congress dominance at the centre as well as in most states, the Congress Working Committee (which comprised most powerful union ministers and chief ministers) eclipsed the NDC and atrophied the necessity of establishing the ISC. Even the NDC was set up informally by a Cabinet Resolution rather than under the relevant constitutional provision.

The Sarkaria Commission report underlined the importance of strengthening intergovernmental forums like the NDC and the ISC by granting them constitutional status. However, its recommendation to continue these two forums as separate bodies—one for planning and economic development and the other for political matters—contained the possibility of the contining eclipse of the ISC by the NDC. The Government of India set up the ISC in 1990 under the Constitution, but did not invest the NDC with a constitutional status. Therefore, neither the NDC nor the ISC could emerge as an important forum of intergovernmental relations. The reasons for this are not far to seek. Lack of constitutional status continued to debilitate the NDC, while the ISC even with its constitutional status languished because the parties ruling at the state level with their direct representation in the federal coalition cabinet did not require the ISC to express their viewpoints. Their representatives in the federal coalition could directly convey their views to the prime minister and the dominant coalition partners in the union government.

Thus, even during the phase of greater federalization in Indian politics, the early promise of the ISC emerging as an important intergovernmental forum was not realized. Over the decade since its inception, it has met only nine times, though its subcommittees have met more frequently. The ISC has worked on the sidelines, and there is hardly any substantial consensus and action stemming from it that can be said to be a significant contribution of it. For example, though it has discussed the Sarkaria Commission report for a long time, yet this has not been followed by any action or implementation of more important issues of constitutional amendments. The same is true of Article 356 which has been discussed threadbare and there have been certain points of agreement for amending it. But there has been no action or amendment.

It would not be appropriate to write off the ISC. For its relevance as an intergovernmental forum with certain reforms is unquestionable. In the changed future context, its importance in the political system may increase. For example, if the present trend of mushrooming of regional political parties gives way to a more structured set of federal political parties and the federal cabinet functions with greater institutional autonomy and collective responsibility, the need for an intergovernmental forum like the ISC may become urgent. The National Commission for the Review of the Working of the Constitution (NCRWC) recommended in its report in 2002 that 'in resolving problems and coordinating policy and action, the union as well as the state should more effectively utilize the forum of Inter-State Council'.[2]

Even the Common Minimum Programme (CMP) of the United Progressive Alliance (UPA) stressed the need for making 'the

National Development Council a more effective instrument of cooperative federalism', and 'reactivation of the Inter-State Council'.[3]

Canada offers an interesting comparative illustration of this point. The party system in Canada has peculiarly adapted itself to the institutional logic of the parliamentary federal system there. Over the years even the national parties have evolved as organizations that are doubly sensitive to the federal as well as provincial institutional requirements. With the possible exception of the National Democratic Party, the Liberal as well as Conservative parties in Canada are so organized that the federal and provincial wings of the same party function more or less independently of each other. The federal Liberals, for example, function within the institutional imperatives of politics in Parliament whereas provincial Liberals are largely guided by their provincial institutional matrix. The two levels of politics are thus relatively insulated from the disruptive effects emanating from the other level. Moreover, the prime minister commands enormous power, patronage and influence as the executive head of the federal government. This helps him ensure a disciplined group of party loyalists behind his leadership in Parliament. Provincial premiers have similar resources at their disposal within their respective domains. The efficacy of the FMC as an intergovernmental forum can be largely understood within this institutional framework.

Despite its lack of constitutional status, the NDC has been the most important apex intergovernmental forum in India. This is not to suggest that its functioning has been ideal, and that it has realized its full potentialities as a constitutional federal forum. If anything, it would appear that there is a need for desirable reforms and immense possibility of its growth as a grand federal council of the Indian Republic.

In over 50 years of existence since 1952, to date (June 2005), it has held 51 meetings, i.e. an average of at least one meeting a year. This cannot, however, be interpreted to mean actual annual meetings as there are wide gaps between one meeting and the other. For example, the 49th meeting in September 2001 took place after two and a half years. As Swaminathan observed:

That nearly thirty months had lapsed after the last meeting of the NDC in February 1999 is enough to show how apathetic the centre had remained to the need to convene NDC meetings earlier to orchestrate developmental schemes throughout the country from time to time, so that ridiculous failure of governance of the type which has manifested itself recently in Orissa in starvation deaths in a country which has hoarded foodgrain stocks of the magnitude of 60 million tonnes, no longer maligns a democratic order.[4]

Swaminathan expressed his dissatisfaction with the procedure and mood of the 49th meeting:

Belated as it was, the NDC meeting appears to have followed the beaten track, with the prime minister delivering an ex parte expatiation on practically every area of decision-making where, over the past two years, vacillation, equivocation and sloppiness of governance, have done duty for energetic policy response and implementation.[5]

However, it may be said in the union's defence that the delays are mainly attributable to the vast architecture of the NDC's composition, difficulties in ensuring the availability of all the members, instability of governments at the centre and in the states, and intervening elections at various levels.[6]

One thing that can be definitely said about the NDC is that it has not been as idle and inconsequential as the ISC appears to be. Its agenda has often included crucial issues of intergovernmental significance. Issues related to the process of planning have been the most important preoccupation 69 items out of a total of 153 were discussed between 1952 and June 2005. Other issues in descending order of frequency counts for the same period are: food, agriculture, power, irrigation and related issues 19; rural development and related issues 14; social sector, including health, employment and education 13; centrally-sponsored schemes 6; land reforms 5; and miscellaneous 16. Credit for the initiation of development policies and dynamics of union–state relations goes to the NDC. However, a detailed analysis reveals that much is left to be desired as far as the frequency and procedures of NDC meetings and the process of plan formulation and implementation are concerned.

However, before making a critique of executive federalism in Canada and India and offering suggestions for reforms, it may be worthwhile to examine the factors that impinge on the working of intergovernmental mechanisms in these countries. It is not easy to measure and evaluate the effectiveness of these mechanisms in clear-cut terms. Models of organizational effectiveness cannot be uncritically applied here as these mechanisms are neither a close bureaucratic system nor a highly institutionalized and a regular political organization like a Parliament with well established structures and procedures. They are more of an informal gathering with minimal rules of business. Given this fact, only open system approaches to organizational study can be used in this context. To this end, Caplow's multivariate model of organizational effectiveness may be employed here.[7] In his estimation, four factors impinge on organizational effectiveness in an open system: stability of structure, integration of interactional intercourse, voluntarism or non-coercive decision, and achievement of goals. The first three factors contribute to the fourth factor in different ways, i.e. 'net result of the organization's activity'. This model can be employed in a generalized way to evaluate the effectiveness of intergovernmental mechanisms in Canada and India.

In absolute terms, Canadian scholars may be dissatisfied with the manner in which executive federalism operates in their country, but in comparative terms this model of federal–provincial executive decision-making appears to be a remarkable success. In the light of the discussion so far, it may be argued that the structure and process of intergovernmental relations in Canada are fairly characterized by stability of structure, integration of interactional intercourse, voluntarism and non-coercive decision, and achievement of goals in various areas of governance, including to an extent, constitutional renewal. It is only since the 1990s that there has been an impasse on constitutional reforms.

As far as the practice of Executive Federalism in India is concerned, it may be said that both the NDC and the ISC reasonably satisfy the first three indicators of stability, integration and voluntarism. In view of the fact that organizational structures are defined by executive orders, the NDC and the ISC can increase the frequency of their meetings and consciously try to promote internal harmony and reduce conflict. Decisions at these forums are taken by consensus as considered appropriate by the prime minister. As far as achievement of goals is concerned, these bodies, especially the NDC, have been fairly successful in keeping the union–state negotiations and decisions going in the realm of intergovernmental relations.

The foregoing analysis of the data on the FMC, the NDC and the ISC attests that even though these bodies may not have met frequently and are occasionally marked by overt disagreements, they have been able to fulfil the minimal criterion of keeping union–state conflicts within bounds of manageability, though there may be unanswered questions about a rigorous test of their effectiveness measured against some abstract or comparative standard.

CRITIQUE AND SUGGESTIONS FOR REFORMS

To a certain extent, recent trends in the working of intergovernmental mechanisms in Canada and India are broadly similar. These mechanisms show a declining graph in the urgency or frequency of their meetings. The reasons for this, of course, vary. In Canada, the decline is attributable to the growing hiatus between Canadian federalism and Quebec nationalism. Initiatives for reconciling this growing contradiction in the FMC through constitutional reforms have recurrently failed, with the result that the various prime ministers have been reluctant to convene an FMC on constitutional reforms.

In India, the NDC has played an important role in federal policy making in the arena of economic development and planning. This trend continued unabated during the period of planned economic development. Following plan holidays and economic liberalization, the role of planning in the economy diminished. For one thing, liberalization and privatization deregulated the economy and, for another, the quantum of public investment declined to nearly one-third compared to what it was in the era of rigorous economic planning.[8] Even though the planning process has survived, its role and rigour have diminished. It is in this context that the NDC has suffered an erosion, if not an eclipse. On the other hand, when the ISC was set up in 1990, it was a reflection of the growing diversity of the state and union governments in terms of party affiliations. However, once it was set up, the expectation that it would emerge as a major forum of intergovernmental relations was belied. The reason was partly the instability of successive coalition/minority governments and the fact that the major regional parties in government or opposition in the states had direct representation in the federal cabinet coalitions. Hence, there was no need for the ISC as a forum for representation in federal decision-making. Both the NDC and the ISC did not gain in importance even during the phase of greater federalization.

Bodies like the FMC, the ISC and the NDC can be criticized on the ground that they are too elitist to be considered fully democratic and participative consistent with the temper of the times. Executive federalism is too executive or statist to allow legislative inputs and participatory space to institutions of civil society such as the press, NGOs and other professional and associational organizations. Moreover, publicity focused on the top executives from the two orders of government meeting in a forum encourages them to speak to the galleries/constituents back home rather than to the negotiating parties around the table. Further, the non-statutory nature of these agencies (barring the ISC in India) leads to irregular periodicity of their meetings and non-circulation of agenda papers sufficiently in advance as well as lack of adequate time for debate, especially in India. Like the FMC, the NDC and the ISC can ensure that their proceedings are more open and participative by making provisions for conference-eve consultations and representations with affected interests and organizations in civil society.

Suggestions for reforming these apex forums must go beyond procedural matters to substantial issues of restructuring. The experience so far has revealed that even though the FMC has been incidentally mentioned in the Constitution in the context of constitutional review and amending formula, the body for other practical purposes remains largely non-statutory. Hence, the prime minister may avoid convening a meeting if he does not consider it necessary, even if the provincial premiers feel otherwise. Realists may find this latitude and flexibility good, but this may not be true of those who take a sympathetic view of provincial or state autonomy. Another objection to the idea of having a constitutionally or statutorily entrenched intergovernmental mechanism is that it may establish a parallel centre of power in opposition to the federal union cabinet. That this apprehension is unfounded is amply demonstrated by the fact that the constitutionally sanctioned ISC has not posed any such threat to the union cabinet. This is partly because strong regional parties have direct representation in the union cabinet itself, so that the need for the alternative forum of the ISC to articulate their regional demands was not really felt. But the problem with this in India is that the union cabinet itself becomes internally fractured along deeply divisive regional lines, and that the regional party chiefs influence the union ministers through remote control that undermines the authority of the prime minister. This also vitiates the principle of collective responsibility of the cabinet to the Parliament. In the light of this experience, it appears reasonable to argue that a constitutional intergovernmental forum would create a federal council alongside the federal or union cabinet which would have a meaningful demarcation of jurisdiction and well understood rules and conventions of working. Thus, the idea of creating constitutionally entrenched apex intergovernmental mechanisms is appropriate.

In the Canadian context, Papillon and Simeon suggested that it would be desirable to link the FMC more directly to the federal parliamentary and provincial legislative processes to ensure accountability and reduction of tension between the FMC and legislatures at the two levels of government. For the same reasons, this reform could be recommended for the NDC and the ISC.[9]

Canada has such a body in the FMC which is the clearing house for all intergovernmental affairs diligently worked out by the myriad of deputy ministerial and ministerial conferences. India, too, has operated through two such apex intergovernmental forums—the NDC (since 1952) and the ISC (since 1990). The Sarkaria Commission report recommended the continuation of both these bodies with constitutional entrenchment.

In India, the idea of merging the NDC and the ISC could be given a serious consideration because of several reasons: first, it would avoid unnecessary bifurcation of the apex intergovernmental body with the same membership in the NDC and the ISC. The creation of two separate bodies was rationalized on the ground that it would keep politics out of the process of planning. The experience, however, has been different. In any case, politics cannot really be separated from economic decision-making. In fact, a certain degree of political contestation is necessary to inject a doze of democratic bargaining to remove the distortions of an imposed consensus that may really conceal an unjust political order. Second, this artificial separation also results in narrow construction of policy areas not only along economic and political issues but also in the proliferation of a large number of national councils for a variety of policy areas that lack integrated high power status to lend weight to their recommendations. These national councils may continue as bodies of technocrats, whose recommendations should be considered by a top-level intergovernmental agency representing the executive heads of the two orders of government. Moreover, there is no constitutional obstacle to the merger of the NDC and the ISC as Article 263 of the Constitution does not restrict the functions of the ISC to any specific limitation in terms of economic or political decision-making. The division of work between the two is specified only in the cabinet resolution which led to the establishment of the NDC.[10]

If this proposed merger becomes a reality, the secretariat of the ISC can serve the newly created union–state council or federal council. The Planning Commission that serves as the secretariat of the NDC may continue as an agency of think tank and planning in the new federal order with certain modifications. For instance, the Planning Commission is the creation of the union executive, lacking any statutory or constitutional status. From a central agency it should be transformed into a federal agency. This can be done by replacing the present procedure of appointment by the union cabinet through nomination by the union–state/federal council and appointment by the union cabinet. The nomination of the members of the Planning Commission by the union–state council would allow the state governments to have a say in the matter along with the union government. However, the union–state council would also be plagued by the problem pointed out by the Sarkaria Commission in relation to the NDC. As a body, it is too large to be able to go into the minute details of the matter under consideration. To rectify this, the union–state/federal council should have, as recommended by the Sarkaria panel, in the context of the NDC, a Standing Committee comprising the prime minister, some key union cabinet ministers nominated by the prime minister, deputy chairman of the Planning Commission, the Governor of the RBI, and six chief ministers, one from each zone selected on the basis of rotation or consensus.

In order to refute the allegation of it being an elitist body, the FMC has often resorted to the practice of holding larger consultation with affected groups and organizations in civil society on the matter under consideration before the meeting of the first ministers. Governmental and non-governmental observers are also invited to express their views at the FMC without, however, having any voting right. A similar practice aimed at wider democratic consultation and participation can be recommended in the Indian context to refute the charges of democratic deficit in the Indian parliamentary federal system. It is here that India can benefit from the Canadian federal experience.

Canada may find the Indian experience with union–state planning of some interest and relevance. India is a leading federal system in the Commonwealth, and the Third World generally, that has experimented with democratic planning for economic development—a technique that originated with the socialist experiment in the USSR.

In the wake of neo-liberal economic liberalization since the early 1990s, the Planning Commission has been partly sidelined in the new context in which public investment has gradually yielded place to private investment in the economy. Yet, the Planning Commission has survived and adapted itself to the new public policy climate. In fact, if the economic situation does not significantly improve to ensure a reasonable measure of equity and justice, there may be a demand for a renewed role of the state in the economy which would lead to greater relevance of the Planning Commission. This is because developments in the Third World have amply demonstrated that market is a good instrument but a bad master. The Indian experience may be relevant to Canada which has often found its public economic policies riddled with federal–provincial confrontations and wasteful use of natural resources. The governments in Canada have been alive to this problem. For example, the Trudeau government in the early 1970s established three systems of incipient planning—the Privy Council Office, the Treasury Board and the Department of Finance. Besides, every department had its own planning staff. As a senior, Canadian academician pointed out, 'instead of coherence and efficiency we got confrontation, bureaucratic infighting and a draining of morale'.[11] Taking off from this experience, Thorburn advocated 'a process of institutional innovation in which a federal–provincial economic development commission would be created'.[12] He concluded:

> There must be an overall, master plan within which the lower levels of economic planning fit as part of a whole. First, one must decide what the unit is: Canada, a province, a region, an industry, or what? Then the plan must be elaborated, and it must be sold to those elites both within and outside government who are expected to carry it out, and whose lives will be deeply affected by it. The process is one of developing coherence.[13]

This aptly describes the process of planning in India!

Yet, going by the paradigm shift to neo-liberal economic reforms in recent decades in both Canada and India, there can be no gainsaying that in the prevailing policy regime, the State has been constrained to yield more space to the market and civil society. None the less, the State continues to play an important role in managing the transition in both countries and a new model of interface between the State, the civil society and market needs to be renegotiated.

NOTES

1. C.E.S. Franks, 'A Continuing Canadian Conundrum: The Role of Parliament in Intergovernmental Relations and National Unity', in Rekha Saxena (ed.), *Mapping Canadian Federalism for India*, Delhi: Konark, 2002, pp. 42, 175-92. See also the editorial 'Introduction'.
2. *Report of the National Commission to Review the Working of the Constitution (NCRWC), 2002*, Chap. 8, para 8.12.4.
3. *Common Minimum Programme of the United Progressive Alliance (UPA)*, May 2004, New Delhi.
4. S. Swaminathan, 'NDC-Monologues Prevail', *The Hindu* (New Delhi), 5 September 2001, p. 14.
5. Ibid.
6. Discussion with Rajeev Malhotra, Deputy Advisor, Planning Commission, New Delhi, 6 September 2001.

7. Theodore Caplow, *Principles of Organization*, New York: Harcourt, Brace and World, 1964, pp. 121-4.
8. Discussion with Rajeev Malhotra, op. cit., May 2001.
9. Martin Papillon and Richard Simeon, 'The Weakest Link? First Ministers' Conferences in Canadian Intergovernmental Relations', in *Canadian Federalism, Canada: The State of Federation 2002*, ed. J. Peter Meekison, Hamish Telford and Harvey Lazar, Kingston: IIGR and Montreal: McGill Queen's University Press, 2004, pp. 113-40.
10. Rekha Saxena, 'Role of Intergovernmental Agencies', *The Hindu*, 29 January 2002.
11. H.G. Thorburn, *Planning and the Economy: Building Federal-Provincial Consensus*, Toronto: James Lorimer and Company, published in association with the Canadian Institute for Economic Policy, 1984, p. 243.
12. Ibid., p. xv.
13. Ibid., p. 243.

Bibliography

PRIMARY SOURCES

GOVERNMENT OF INDIA AND OTHER PUBLICATIONS

Administrative Reforms Commission, *Report of the Study Team on Centre-State Relations*, vol. I, New Delhi: Government of India, Ministry of Home Affairs, 1967.

Central Vigilance Commission, *Annual Report*, New Delhi, 31 March 1998.

Commission on Centre-State Relations, Report, Parts I and II, Nasik: Government of India Press, 1987-88 (Chair Justice R.S. Sarkaria).

Common Minimum Programme, United Progressive Alliance (UPA), New Delhi, May 2004.

Constituent Assembly Debates (CAD), 6 books, New Delhi: Lok Sabha Secretariat, 1999.

Constitution of India 1950, as amended to date.

Delhi Police Establishment Act, 1946.

Election Commission of India, *Elections in India: Major Events and New Initiatives 1996-2000*, New Delhi: Nirvachan Sadan, 2000.

———, *Fifty Years of the Election Commission of India, Golden Jubilee Celebrations*, New Delhi: Nirvachan Sadan, January 2001.

———, *Landmark Judgements on Election Laws*, 2 vols., New Delhi: Election Commission of India, 1999.

Finance Commission, *Report of the Tenth Finance Commission (for 1995-2000)*, New Delhi: Ministry of Finance Press, 1994.

Government of Tamil Nadu, Rajamannar Report on Centre-State Relations, Madras: Inquiry Committee, Government of Tamil Nadu, 1971.

Guidelines for Identifying and Selecting Issues to be Brought Before the Inter-State Council, Inter-State Council Secretariat, 22 January 1999.

Gwyer, Maurice and A. Appadorai, eds., *Speeches and Documents on the Indian Constitution 1921-27*, vol. 2, London: Oxford University Press, 1957.

Indian Audit and Accounts Department, *Activity Report 1986-87*, CAG of India.

———, *Activity Report, 1996-97*, CAG of India.

Lok Sabha Debates, New Delhi: Lok Sabha Secretariat.

Ministry of Finance, *First Report of the Ninth Finance Commission (for 1989-90)*, New Delhi: Ministry of Finance Press, July 1988.

———, *Report of the Eleventh Finance Commission (2000-2005)*, New Delhi: Ministry of Finance Press, June 2000.

Ministry of Home Affairs, *Annual Report, 1999-2001*, New Delhi: Department of Internal Security, Jammu & Kashmir, States and Home, Government of India.

———, Inter-State Council Order 1990, notified on 28 May 1990, File No. IV/11017/3/90-CSR, New Delhi, 28 May 1990.

———, Inter-State Council Secretariat, New Delhi, 5 December 1996, Notification no. 7/4/96-ISC.

———, Resolution no. 24/7/64-AVD, dated 11 February 1964.

———, *Administrative Reforms Commission, Centre-State Relations*, New Delhi: Ministry of Home Affairs, 1969.

Ministry of Irrigation, Resolution dated 10 March 1983, *Constituting National Water Resources Council and Amendments Threats*, Resolution no. 611179-PP, New Delhi.

———, Resolution no. 611179-PP, dated 14 October 1985, New Delhi.

Ministry of Health and Family Welfare, *National Population Policy, 2000*, New Delhi: Government of India, Department of Family Welfare, Nirman Bhawan.

Ministry of Labour, *Annual Report, 1993-94*, Part I - Labour.

Ministry of Power, *Annual Report 2000-2001*.

National Commission to Review the Working of the Constitution, NCRWC, 2002.

National Commission on Population, New Delhi: Government of India, n.d.

National Development Council, Cabinet Secretariat, Resolution no. 62/CF/50, dated 6 August 1952; 65/15/CF-67, dated 7 October 1967.

Planning Commission, *Annual Report 2000-2001*, New Delhi: Yojna Bhawan.

———, *Draft Outline, First Five-Year Plan*, New Delhi, 1952.

———, *Indian Planning Experience: A Statistical Profile*, New Delhi, January 2001.

———, *Mid-Term Appraisal of the Ninth Five Year Plan (1997-2002)*, New Delhi, October 2000.

———, *Ninth Five-Year Plan, 1997-2002*, vol. I, *Development Goals, Strategy and Policies*, New Delhi: Government of India, Planning Commission.

———, *Summary Records of National Development Council Meetings*, 1952-2005.

———, *Pradhan Mantri Gramodaya Yojana (PMGR)*, New Delhi: Rural Development Division.

———, No. A-43011/17/2000-Admn. I, Yojana Bhawan, New Delhi, 2000.

Report of the National Commission to Review the Working of the Constitution (NCRWC), 2002.

Shiva Rao, B., ed., *The Framing of India's Constitution: Select Document*, 5 Vols, New Delhi: Indian Institute of Public Administration, 1967.

S.R. Bommai vs *Union of India and Others*, *All India Reporter*, Supreme Court Section, 1994.

States Reorganization Commission, *Report*, Delhi: Government Printing Press, 1955.

The Electricity (Supply) Act, 1948, as Amended by Electricity Laws (Amendment) Act, 1998, Bare Act 2001, Allahabad: Law Publishers India Pvt Ltd.

Union Public Service Commission, *48th Annual Report, 1997-98*, New Delhi: UPSC, 1998.

GOVERNMENT OF CANADA PUBLICATIONS (INCLUDING PROVINCIAL GOVERNMENTS)

A Project for Quebec: Affirmation, Autonomy and Leadership—Final Report, Montreal, Quebec: Quebec Liberal Party, October 2001.

Auditor General of Canada, *Canadian Federal Government Handbook*, Globe Information Services, 1995.

Canada Constitution Acts 1867 and 1982.

Canada Inter-governmental Conference Secretariat, *News Release*, Ref. 830-718/004, Canada Year Book 1999 on CD-ROM Statistics, Canada, 1999.

Canada Year Book, 999 on CD-ROM Statistics, Canada, 1999.

Communique of First Ministers' Conferences, Canadian Inter-governmental Conference Secretariat, Ottawa.

Courchene, Thomas J., 'ACCESS: A Convention on the Canadian Economic and Social Systems', Working Paper prepared for the Ministry of Intergovernmental Affairs, Government of Ontario, August 1996.

Courchene, Thomas J. et al., eds., *Ottawa and the Provinces: The Distribution of Money and Power*, Toronto: Ontario Economic Council Special Research Report, Federal Provincial Relations Series, 1985.

Dominion-Provincial First Ministers' Meetings from 1927-1980, typescript, Canada: Library of Parliament.

Federal-Provincial First Ministers' Conferences 1906-1985, Canadian Inter-governmental Conference Secretariat.

First Ministers' Meeting on the Constitution: Final Consensus Report on the Constitution, Document 8002-032/001, Charlottetown: P.E.I., 27-28 August 1992.

First Ministers' Meeting on the Economy, Outcome of Discussions, Toronto: Ontario, 24-25 March 1992, Document 800-030/017.

First Ministers' Meeting, A Framework to Improve the Social Union for Canadians, Ottawa, Ontario 4 February 1999, Document 800-037/001.

First Ministers' Meeting, Communique on Early Childhood Development, News Release, Canadian Inter-governmental Conference Secretariat, Document 800-038/005.

First Ministers' Meeting, Communique on Health, News Release, Canadian Inter-governmental Conference Secretariat, Document 800-038/004.

Grodzins, Morton, *U.S. President, Commission on National Goals, Goals for Americans.*

Hurley, James Ross, *The Canadian Constitutional Debate: From the Death of the Meech Lake Accord of 1987 to the 1992 Referendum*, Ottawa Ministry of Supply and Services, 1994.

Joint Steering Committee, *Blueprint for the Canadian Federal Inspection System*, 1994.

Maintaining the Right, Canada Year Book, 1999 on CD-ROM Statistics, Canada, 1999.

Office of the Prime Minister, *News Release*, Canada, 18 July 1994.

Press Release, Communique, Document 800-036/006, Joint Communique First Ministers' Meeting, Ottawa, 12 December 1997.

Privy Council Office, *Decision-making Process and Central Agencies in Canada, Ottawa: Federal Provincial and Territorial Practices*, Information and Research Centre, 1998.

Reviewing the Canadian Federation: A Progress Report, Background Document for the First Ministers' Meeting, 20-21 June 1996, Government of Canada, Library of Parliament, 4 July 1996.

Royal Commission on Aboriginal Peoples, *Report of the Royal Commission on Aboriginal Peoples*, vol. 5, Ottawa: The Commission, 1996.

Royal Commission on Electoral Reform and Party Finance, *Final Report*, vol. 4, Ottawa: Ministry of Supply and Services, 1991.

Shaping Canada's Future Together Proposals, Ottawa: Ministry of Supply and Services, 1991.

Sustaining Economic Growth, Background Document for the First Ministers' Meeting, 20-21 June 1996, Government of Canada, Library of Parliament.

Statute of Westminster, 1931.

Task Force on Canadian Unity, Coming to Terms: The Words of the Debate. February 1979.

The Canadian Charter of Rights and Freedoms, Ottawa: Ministry of Supply and Services, 1987.

The History of the Bank of Canada: Who Needs a Central Bank?, Canada Year Book 1999 on CD-ROM Statistics, Canada, 1999.

The New Face of Government, Ottawa: Ministry of Supply and Services, 1994.

The Quebec Reference Judgement, 1998.

WEBSITE ADDRESSES

Bank of Canada, http://www.bank banque. ca/english/ histor-htm.bjp.org/ today

CICS webmaster.scics.gc.ca

hinduonnet.com

Internet, RBI websisite address http://www.rbi. org. in/rbi profile. html.

Internet, http://www.mce.gouv.qc.ca/v/html/v4061001.html.

News Releases - APC 2001, website address www.gc.ca.

Prasar Bharati, website address http://www.mib.nic. in/nic part/pbmisn. htm.

SECONDARY SOURCES

BOOKS

Adie, Robert F. and Paul G. Thomas, *Canadian Public Administration: Problematical Perspectives*, Scarborough: Prentice Hall, 1987.

Arora, Balveer and Douglas V. Verney, eds., *Multiple Identities in a Single State: Indian Federalism in Comparative Perspective*, Delhi: Konark, 1995.

Austin, Granville, *Working a Democratic Constitution: The Indian Experience*, Delhi: Oxford University Press, 1999.

Austin, Granville, *The Indian Constitution: Cornerstone of a Nation*, Bombay: Oxford University Press, 1966.

Beard, Charles, *An Economic Interpretation of the Constitution of the United States*, New York: Free Press, 1965.

Blindenbacher and Arnold Koller, eds., *Federalism in a Changing World: Learning from Each Other,* Montreal & Kingston: McGill-Queen's University Press, 2003.

Bird, Roger, ed., *Documents of Canadian Broadcasting*, Ottawa: Carleton University Press, 1988.

Bombwall, K.R., *Foundations of Indian Federalism*, Bombay: Asia Publishing House, 1967.

Bourgault, Jacques et al., eds., *Public Administration and Public Management Experiences in Canada*, Quebec: Les Publications, 1997.

Brass, Paul R., *The Politics of India Since Independence: The New Cambridge History of India*, 2nd edn., Cambridge: Cambridge University Press, 1994.

Brecher, Michael, *Nehru: A Political Biography,* London: Oxford University Press, 1959.

Breacher, Michael, *Nehru's Mantle: The Politics of Succession in India*, New York: Praeger, 1966.

Brock, Kathy L., *A Mandate Fulfilled: Constitutional Reform and the Manitoba Task Force on Meech Lake*, project sponsored by the University of Outreach Fund, December 1990.

Burgess, Michael and Alain G. Gagnon, eds., *Comparative Federalism and Federation*, Toronto: University of Toronto Press, 1993.

Caplow, Theodore, *Principles of the Organisation*, New York: Harcourt, Brace and World, 1964.

Chadda, Maya, *Ethnicity, Security and Separatism in India*, Delhi: Oxford University Press, 1997.

Chakrabarty, Bidyut, ed., *Centre-State Relations in India*, Delhi: Segment Book Distributors, 1990.

Deutsch, Karl W., *Nationalism and Alternatives*, New York: Alfred A. Knopf, 1969.

Deutsch, Karl W. et al., *Political Community and the North Atlantic Area*, Princeton: Princeton University Press, 1957.

Dikshitar, V.R., *Maurayan Polity*, Madras: University of Madras, 1932.

Dua, B.D. and M.P. Singh, *Federalism in the New Millennium*, Delhi: Manohar, 2003.

Dua, B.D. *Presidential Rule in India 1950-1974*, Delhi: S. Chand, 1979.

Elazar, Daniel L., *Federalism: An Overview*, Pretoria: HSRC, 1995.

Elazar, Daniel L., ed., *Federal System of the World: A Handbook of Federal, Confederal and Autonomy Arrangements*, 2nd edn., Harlow: Longman Corp. Ltd., 1994.

Elazar, Daniel L., *Exploring Federalism*, Tuscaloosa, Alabama: The University of Alabama Press, 1987.

———, *American Partnership: Intergovernmental Cooperation in the Nineteenth Century United States*, Chicago: University of Chicago Press, 1962.

Friedrich, C.J., 'New Tendencies in Federal Theory and Practice', mimeograph, 1964.

Gani, H.A., *Centre-State Relations and Sarkaria Commission*, Delhi: Deep & Deep, 1990.

Grewal, J.S. and Hugh Johnston, eds., *The India-Canada Relationship: Exploring the Political Economic and Cultural Dimensions*, Delhi: Sage, 1994.

Griffiths, Ann L., *Handbook of Federal Countries, 2002*, Forum of Federations, Montreal & Kingston: McGill-Queen's University Press, 2002.

Hamilton, Alexander, Jay John and Madison James, *The Federalist* (with an Introduction by Edward Mead Earle, dated 14 May 1973), New York: The Modern Library College Editions.

Heesterman, J.C., *The Inner Conflict of Tradition: Essays in Indian Ritual, Kingship, and Society*, Delhi: Oxford University Press, 1985.

Jackson, Robert J. and Doreen Jackson, *Politics in Canada: Culture, Institutions, Behaviour and Public Policy*, Scarborough: Prentice-Hall/ Allyn and Bacon, 1999.

Kabra, Kamal Nayan, *Development Planning in India: Exploring an Alternative Approach*, Delhi: Sage, 1997.

———, *Planning Process in a District*, Delhi: Indian Institute of Public Administration, 1977.

Khan, Rasheeduddin, *Federal India: A Design for Change*, Delhi: Vikas, 1992.

———, *Rethinking Indian Federalism*, Shimla: Indian Institute of Advanced Study, 1997.

Kincaid, John and G. Alan Tarr, eds., *A Global Dialogue on Federalism: Constitutional Origins, Structure, and Change in Federal Countries*, vol. 1, published for Forum of Federations and IACFS, Montreal & Kingston, London-Ithaca: McGill-Queen's University Press, 2005.

King, Preston, *Federalism and Federation*, London: Croom Helm Ltd., 1982.

Kohli, Atul, *The State and Poverty in India: The Politics of Reform—South Asian Studies*, Cambridge: Cambridge University Press, 1987.

Kothari, Rajni, *State Against Democracy: In Search of Humane Governance*, Delhi: Ajanta Publications, 1988.

Kulke, Hermann, ed., *The State in India 1000-1700*, Delhi: Oxford University Press, 1995.

Kurian, K. Mathew and P.N. Verghese, eds., *Centre-State Relations*, Delhi: Macmillan, 1981.

Langford, John W., *Transport in Transition: The Reorganization of the Federal Transport Portfolio*, Montreal: McGill-Queen's University Press, 1976.

Leslie, Peter M., *Federal State, National Economy*, Toronto: University of Toronto Press, 1987.

Livingston, William S., *Federalism and Constitutional Change*, Oxford: Clarendon Press, 1956.

Maheshwari, B.L., ed., *Centre-State Relations in the Seventies*, Calcutta: Minerva Associates, 1973.

Majeed, Akhtar, ed., *Coalition Politics and Power Sharing*, Delhi: Manak Publications, 2000.

———, *Constitutional Nation-Building: Half a Century of India's Success*, Delhi: Manak Publications, 2001.

———, *Federalism within the Union: Distribution of Responsibilities in the Indian System*, Delhi: Manak Publications, 2004.

———, *Federal India: A Design for Good Governance*, New Delhi: Manak Publications, 2005.

Mallory, J.R., *The Structure of Canadian Government*, Toronto: Macmillan, 1971.

Manor, James, ed., *Nehru to the Nineties: The Changing Office of Prime Minister in India*, Delhi: Viking, 1994.

March, J.G. and J.P. Olsen, *Rediscovering Institutions*, New York: Free Press, 1989.

Mathew, George, ed., *Status of Panchayati Raj in the States of India*, Delhi: Concept, 1994.

May, Ronald J., *Federalism and Fiscal Adjustment*, Oxford: Oxford University Press, 1969.

McNaught, Kenneth, *The Penguin History of Canada*, London: Penguin Books, 1988.

Meekison, J. Peter, ed., *Canadian Federalism: Myth or Reality?*, Toronto: Methuen, 1968.

Meekison, J. Peter, *Intergovernmental Relations in Federal Countries*, n.d.

Menon, V.P., *The Transfer of Power in India*, Bombay: Orient Longman, 1957.

Mohan, Chandra, *Regionalism in Canada: A Multidisciplinary Approach*, Delhi: Allied Publishers, 1995.

Mukarji, Nirmal and Balveer Arora, eds., *Fedralism in India: Origin and Development*, Delhi: Vikas, 1992.

Olling, R.D. and M.W. Westmacott, eds., *Perspectives on Canadian Federalism*, Scarborough: Prentice Hall, 1988.

Pal, B.H. Bhisham, *Central Police Forces of India*, New Delhi: Government of India, Ministry of Home Affairs, Bureau of Police Research and Development.

Pal, Chandra, *Centre-State Relations and Co-operative Federalism*, Delhi: Deep & Deep, 1983.

Papillon, Martin and Simeon, Richard, 'The Weakest Link? First Ministers' Conferences in Canadian Intergovernmental Relations', in *Canadian Federalism, Canada: The State of the Federation 2002*, ed. J. Peter Meekison, Hamish Telford and Harvey Lazar, Kingston: IIGR and Montreal: McGill Queen's University Press, 2004.

Paranjape, H.K., *The Reorganized Planning Commission: A Study in the Implementation of Administrative Reforms*, New Delhi: Indian Institute of Public Administration, 1970.

Porter, John, *The Vertical Mosaic: An Analysis of Social Class and Power in Canada*, Toronto: University of Toronto Press, 1965.

Pylee, M.V., *Constitutional Amendments in India*, Delhi: Universal Law Publishing Co., 2003.

———, *Constitutional History of India (1600-1950)*, Delhi: S. Chand, 1984.

Rama Devi, V.S. and S.K. Mendiratta, *How India Votes: Election Laws, Practice and Procedure*, Delhi: Butterworths India, 2000.

Ray, Ansal, *Tension Areas in India's Federal System*, Calcutta: World Press, 1970.

Richards, John F., *The Mughal Empire: The New Cambridge University of India*, Delhi: Foundation Books, 1993.

Riker, William H., *Federalism: Origin, Operation, Signifiance*, Boston: Little Brown and Company, 1964.

Roger, Bird, ed., *Documents of Canadian Broadcasting, Ottawa*, Canada: Carleton University Press, 1988.

Rudolph, Lloyd and Susanne Rudolph, *In Pursuit of Lakshmi: The Political Economy of the Indian State*, Delhi: Orient Longman, 1987.

Russell, Peter H., Rainer Knopf and Ted Morton, *Federalism and the Charter*, Ottawa: Carleton University Press, 1990.

———, *Leading Constitutional Decisions: Cases on the BNA Act*, Toronto: McClelland and Stewart, 1973.

Saez, Lawrence, *Federalism without a Centre*, Delhi: Sage, 2002.

Sawer, Geoffery, *Modern Federalism*, London: C.A. Watts and Co. Ltd., 1969.

Saxena, Rekha, ed., *Mapping Canadian Federalism for India*, Delhi: Konark, 2002.

Saxena, Rekha, *Indian Politics in Transition*, Delhi: Deep & Deep, 1994.

Sharma, Ram Sharan, *Aspects of Political Ideas and Institutions in Ancient India*, Delhi: Motilal Banarsidass, 1991.

Simeon, Richard, *Federal Provincial Diplomacy: The Making of Recent Policy in Canada*, Toronto: University of Toronto Press, 1972.

Singh, M.P., *Split in a Predominant Party: The Indian National Congress in 1969*, Delhi: Abhinav Publications, 1981.

Singh, M.P. and Rekha Saxena, *India at the Polls: Parliamentary Elections in the Federal Phase*, Delhi: Orient Longman, 2003.

Singh, M.P. and Rekha Saxena, guest eds., *Political Science Annual 1997*, Delhi: Deep & Deep, 1998.

Singh, M.P. and Rekha Saxena, eds., *Ideologies and Institutions in Indian Politics*, Delhi: Deep & Deep, 1998.

———, *India's Political Agenda: Perspectives on the Party System*, Delhi: Kalinga Publications, 1996.

Smiley, Donald V., *The Federal Condition in Canada*, Toronto: McGraw-Hill Ryerson Ltd., 1987.

Stevenson, Garth, *Unfulfilled Union: Canadian Federalism and National Unity*, Toronto: Gage Publishing Limited, 1982.

Swainson, Donald, ed., *Oliver Mowat's Ontario*, Toronto: Macmillan, 1972.

Thapar, Romila, *Asoka and the Decline of the Maurayas*, Delhi: Oxford University Press, 1997.

———, *From Lineage to State: Social Formations in the Mid-first Millennium B.C. in the Ganga Valley*, Bombay: Oxford University Press, 1984.

———, *A History of India*, vol. 1, Harmondworth: Penguin, 1966.

Thorburn, H.G., *Planning and the Economy: Building Federal-Provincial Consensus*, Toronto: James Loriner and Company, published in association with the Canadian Institute for Economic Policy, 1984.

Verma, Meera, Mrinal Mehta and Rumki Basu, eds., *Essays on Indian Government and Politics: A Continuing Review*, Delhi: Jawahar, 1999.

Vijapur, Abdulrahim P., ed., *Dimensions of Federal Nation Building—Essays in Memory of Rasheeduddin Khan*, Delhi: Manak Publications, 1998.

Vijapur, Abdulrahim P., Ajay Kumar Singh and Kumar Suresh, *Pluralism, Minorities, National Integration: Problem and Prospects*, Delhi: South Asian Publishers, 1997.

Vile, M.J.C., *Constitutionalism and the Separation of Powers*, Oxford: Clarendon Press, 1969.

———, *The Structure of American Federalism*, London: Oxford University Press, 1961.

Watts, Ronald L., *Comparing Federal Systems*, Montreal and Kingston: McGill-Queen's University Press, 1999.

———, *New Federations, Experiments in the Commonwealth*, Oxford: Clarandon Press, 1966.

Wheare, K.C. *Federal Government*, London: Oxford University Press, 1963.

Wildavasky, Aaron, ed., *American Federalism in Perspective*, Boston: Little Brown and Company, 1967.

Young, Robert, ed., *Stretching the Federation: The Art of the State in Canada*, Kingston: Institute of Inter-governmental Relations, 1999.

Articles: Journals/Newspapers/Typescripts

Adie, Robert F. and Paul G. Thomas, 'Federalism and the Administrative State', *Canadian Public Administrations: Problematical Perspectives*, Scarborough, Ontario: Prentice Hall, 1987.

Arora, Balveer, 'Negotiating Differences: The Challenges of Federal Coalitions', *Denouement*, January-February 1999.

Aitchison, J.H., 'Inter-Provincial Co-operation in Canada', in *The Political Process in Canada: Essays in Honour of R. MacGraegor Dawson*, ed. J.H. Attchison, Toronto, 1963.

Bhatia, Ravi, 'Federalism in India and the Supreme Court Ruling', in *Federalism in the New Millennium*, ed. B.D. Dua and M.P. Singh, Delhi: Manohar, 2003.

Bhatnagar, Garima, 'Party Politics and Intergovernmental Relations in Indian Federation (1977-1989): A Study of Changing Political Configuration and Relationships in Functional Areas', M. Phil. dissertation, New Delhi: Jawaharlal Nehru University, School of Social Sciences, Centre for Political Studies, 1991.

Birch, A.H., 'Approaches to the Study of Federalism', *Political Studies*, vol. XIV, no. 1, February 1966.

Brass, Paul, 'Coalition Politics in North India', *American Political Science Review*, vol. LXXII, December 1968.

Brass, Paul R., 'The Strong State and the Fear of Disorder', paper presented at the conference on Democracy and Transformation: India Fifty Years After Independence, sponsored by UPIASI, New Delhi, 16-19 November 1997.

Cameron, David, 'Canada', *The Federal Idea*, The Centre for Policy Alternatives and the Forum of Federations with the Support of the Canadian International Development Agency and Foreign Affairs, Canada, Browns Beach Hotel, Negombo, Sri Lanka, 2005.

———, 'Intergovernmental Relations in Canada', in *Intergovernmental Relations in Federal Countries*, ed. Peter Meekison, Forum of Federations, n.d.

———, 'The Structure of Intergovernmental Relations', *International Social Science Journal*, no. 167, UNESCO: Blackwell Publishers, 2001.

Cairns, Alan C., 'The Judicial Committee and Its Critics', *Canadian Journal of Political Science*, vol. IV, no. 3, 1971.

Cody, Howard, 'Evolution of Federal Provincial Relations in Canada', *American Review of Canadian Studies*, vol. VII, no. 1, 1977.

Das, Geetanjali, 'National Development Council and Regional Development: A Study of Its Role and Functional Dimensions in Indian Federal Polity', doctoral dissertation, Orissa: Berhampur University, 1997.

Davis, Rufus, 'The Federal Principle Reconsidered', in *American Federalism in Perspective*, ed. Aaron Wildavasky, Boston: Little Brown and Company, 1967.

Dawson, Mary, 'The Quebec Secession Reference', typescript, Library of Intergovernmental Relations, Queen's University, Kingston, n.d.

Dhar, P.N., 'The Prime Minister's Office: Seeing through the Mystique', *The Times of India*, 24 February 1989.

Dhavan, Rajeev, 'Indian Federalism and its Discontents: A Review', 1996, typescript.

Dikshit, Ramesh D., 'Military Interpretations of Federal Constitutions: A Critique', *Journal of Politics*, vol. XXXIII, February 1971.

Dua, B.D., 'The Prime Minister and the Federal System', in *Nehru to the Nineties: The Changing Office of Prime Minister in India*, ed. James Manor, Delhi: Viking, 1994.

———, 'A Study in Executive-Judicial Conflict: The Indian Case', *Asian Survey*, vol. XXIII, no. 4, April 1983.

Dua, B.D. and M.P. Singh, 'Wither Indian Federalism: The Sarkaria Commission Report and Beyon', *Monthly Commentary*, August 1989.

Dubash, Navroz K. and Chella Rajan Sudhir, 'Power Politics: Process of Power Sector Reform in India', *Economic and Political Weekly*, vol. XXXVI, no. 35, 1-7 September 2001.

Elazar, Daniel J., 'Using Federalism Today', *International Political Science Review*, vol. XVII, no. 4, 1996.

Elton, David, 'Federalism and the Canadian West', in *Perspectives on Canadian Federalism*, ed. R.D. Olling and M.W. Westmacott, Ontario: Prentice Hall, 1988.

Fletcher, Martha, 'Judicial Review and the Division of Powers in Canada', in *Canadian Federalism*, ed. Peter J. Meekison, Toronto: Methuen, 1977.

Franks, C.E.S., 'A Continuing Canadian Conundrun: The Role of Parliament in Intergovernmental Relations and National Unity', in *Mapping Canadian Federalism for India*, ed. Rekha Saxena, Delhi: Konark, 2002.

Gould, Harold A, 'The Second Coming: The 1980 Elections in India's Hindi Belt', *Asian Survey*, vol. XX, no. 6, June 1980.

Greenstein, Fried I. and W. Polsby Nelson, eds., *Handbook of Political Science: Governmental Institutions and Processes*, vol. 5, Massachusetts: Addison-Wesby Publishing Company, 1975.

Hodgins, Bruce W., 'Disagreement at the Commencement: Divergent Ontarian Views of Federalism, 1867-1871', in *Oliver Mowat's Ontario*, ed. Donald Swainson, Toronto: Macmillan, 1972.

Hueglin, Thomas O., 'Federalism in Comparative Perspective', in *Perspectives on Canadian Federalism*, ed. R.D. Olling and M.W. Westmacott, Scarborough, Ontario: Prentice Hall, 1988.

Hurley, James Ross, 'Executive Federalism', in *Public Administration and Public Management Experiences in Canada*, ed. Jacques Bourgautt, Maurice Demers and Cyntina Williams, Quebec: Les Publications du Quebec, 1997.

Jain, R.B., 'The UPSC and the SPSCs in India in Union-State Relations', *Indian Journal of Public Administration*, February 1984.

Kabra, K.N., 'Federating the Planning Commission', *The Hindu*, 2 July 1996.

———, 'Towards Participative Union-State Relations', *Mainstream*, 27 January 1996.

Kaviraj, Sudipta, 'Indira Gandhi and Indian Politics', *Economic and Political Weekly*, vol. XXI, nos. 38 and 39, 20-27 September 1986.

Kincaid, John, 'From Cooperative to Coercive Federalism', *The Annals of American Academy*, May 1990.

Kothari, Rajni, 'Integration and Exclusion in Indian Politics', *Economic and Political Weekly*, 22 October 1988.

Kymlicka, Will, 'Federalism and Nationalism in Canada: A Comparative Perspective', in *Mapping Canadian Federalism for India*, ed. Rekha Saxena, Delhi: Konark, 2002.

Lindquist, Evert A., 'Efficiency, Reliability or Federation: The Art of the State in Canada', in *Stretching the Federation: The Art of the State in Canada*, ed. Robert Young, Kingston: Institute of Inter-governmental Relations, 1999.

Livingston, William S., 'A Note on the Nature of Federalism', *Political Science Quarterly*, vol. LXVII, no. 1, March 1952.

Lomas, A.A., 'The Council of Maritime Premiers: Report and Evaluation after Five Years', in *Canadian Federalism: Myth or Reality*?, ed. J. Peter Meekison, Toronto: Methuen, 1977.

Mackinon, Stuart, 'First Ministers' Conferences', paper presented at the Fifth Conference on Public Policy and Administrative Studies, University of Guelph, 22 April 1988.

Maheshwari, S.R., 'The Centre-State Consultative Machinery in India: Union-State Relations', *Indian Journal of Public Administration*, February 1984.

Maheshwari, B.L. and R. Ram Mohan Rao, 'The Rajamannar Report: A Survey of Reactions in Centre-State Relations', in *Centre-State Relations in the Seventies*, ed. B.L. Maheshwari, Calcutta: Minerva Associates, 1973.

March, J.G. and J.P. Olsen, 'The New Institutionalism: Organizational Factors in Political Life', *American Political Science Review*, vol. 78, 1984.

Majeed, Akhtar, 'Coordinating Ethnic Pluralities', *Indian Journal of Federal Studies*, vol. II, no. 1, 2001.

———, 'The Federal Muddle in Tamil Nadu: Constitutional Issues', *Indian Journal of Federal Studies*, vol. II, no. 2, 2001.

Mallory, J.R., 'The Five Faces of Federalism', in *Canadian Federalism: Myth or Reality*?, ed. J. Peter Meekison, Toronto: Methuen, 1977.

Markandan, K.C., 'Bargaining Federation?', *The Pioneer*, 6 July 2000.

Marwah, Ved., 'The Sub-Culture', *Seminar*, October 1977.

Mathew, George, 'India: (Republic of India)', *The Federal Idea*, Centre for Policy Alternatives and the Forum of Federations with the Support of the Canadian International Development Agency and Foreign Affairs, Canada, Browns Beach Hotel, Negombo, Sri Lanka, 2005.

Meekison, J. Peter, 'First Ministers' Conferences in the Canadian Federal System', in *Ottawa and the Provinces: The Distribution of Money and Power*, ed. Thomas J. Courchene, David W. Conklin and Eail C.M. Coole, Ontario Economic Council Special Research Report, Federal Provincial Relations Series, Ontario Economic Council, Toronto, 1985.

Opeskin, Brian R., 'Mechanisms for Intergovernmental Relations in Federations', *International Social Science Journal*, no. 167, UNESCO: Blackwell Publishers, March 2001.

Pelletier, Benoit, 'A Call into Question of the Foundations of the Federal Spending Power', speech delivered at the conference on Redistribution within the Canadian Federation, University of Toronto, Faculty of Law, 6 February 2004.

Pal, Chandra, 'Co-operation through statutory Bodies', in *Centre-State Relations and Co-operative Federalism*, Delhi: Deep & Deep, 1983.

Papillon, Martin and Simeon, Richard, 'The Weakest Link? First Ministers' Conferences in Canadian Intergovernmental Relations', in *Canadian Federalism, Canada: The State of the Federation*, ed. J. Peter Meekison, Hamish Telford and Harvey Lazar, Kingston: IIGR and Montreal: McGill-Queen's University Press, 2004.

'Planning from the Base', *Economic and Political Weekly*, vol. II, no. 50, 23 December 1967.

Ramasubramanian, K.A., 'State Autonomy and National Integration', in *Centre-State Relations in India*, ed. Bidyut Chakrabarty, Delhi: Segment Book Distributors, 1990.

Rudolph, Lloyd and Rudolph, Susane, 'Iconisation of Chandrababu: Sharing Sovereignty in India's Federal Market Economy', *Economic and Political Weekly*, vol. XXXVI, no. 18, 5-11 May 2001.

Russell, Peter, 'The End of Mega-constitutional Politics in Canada'?, *Political Science and Politics*, vol. XXVI, no. 1, 1993.

———, 'The Political Purposes of the Canadian Charter of Rights and Freedoms', *The Canadian Bar Review*, vol. 61, no. 1, March 1983.

Saxena, Rekha, 'Indian Model of Federation', *The Federal Idea*, the Centre for Policy Alternatives and the Forum of Federations with the support of the Canadian International Development Agency and Foreign Affairs, Canada, Browns Beach Hotel, Negombo, Sri Lanka, 2005.

———, 'Introduction', in *Mapping Canadian Federalism for India*, ed. Rekha Saxena, Delhi: Konark, 2002.

———, 'Recent Trends in Parliamentary Federal Systems: India and Canada', *Indian Journal of Federal Studies*, vol. 1, 2003.

———, 'Strengthening Federal Dialogue: Role of NDC and ISC', *Contemporary India*, vol. 1, no. 3, July-September 2002.

———, 'Role of Intergovernmental Agencies', *The Hindu*, 29 January 2002.

———, 'Reframing Continuity', interview with Douglas Verney, *The Pioneer*, 5 April 2001.

———, 'Party System Transition and Electoral Turning Points in India', *Trends in Social Science Research*, vol. V, no. 1, June 1998.

———, 'Political Regionalisation', *The Pioneer*, 26 February 1998.

———, 'Federalization of Predominantly Parliamentary Regimes', in *Political Science Annual 1997*, guest ed. M.P. Singh and Rekha Saxena, New Delhi: Deep & Deep, 1998.

Shastry, Sandeep, 'Representing the States at the Federal Level: Role of the Rajya Sabha and the Inter-State Council', paper presented at the International Conference on Transforming a Federation: India's Experience, Organized by the Centre for Advanced Study of India, University of Pennsylvania, Konrad Adenauer Foundation, New Delhi, and Forum of Federation, Ottawa, 16-19 February 2003, New Delhi.

Sathyamurthy, T.V. 'Impact of Centre-State Relations on Indian Politics: An Interpretative Reckoning, 1947-87', *Economic and Political Weekly*, vol. XXIV, no. 38, 23 September 1989.

Saez Lawrance and Rekha Saxena , 'Mandate 2004', *Mainstream,* Annual No., January 2005.

Sen, Abhijit and C.P. Chandra Shekhar, 'Elections Analysis: Verdict 91', *Frontline*, vol. VIII, no. 14, 6-19 July 1991.

Sen, S.R., 'Planning Machinery in India', *Indian Journal of Public Administration*, vol. VII, no. 3, July-September 1961.

Shastry, Sandeep, 'Indian Federalism and National Integration', *Indian Journal of Political Science*, vol. 48, no. 2, 1986.

Savoie, Donald J., 'The Atlantic Region: The Politics of Dependency', in *Perspectives on Canadian Federalism*, ed. R.D. Olling and M.W. West Macott, Ontario: Prentice Hall, 1988.

Singh, M.P. and Rekha Saxena, 'Lok Sabha Elections 2004: Change with Continuity', *Think India*, vol. 8, no. 1, January-March 2005.

Singh, M.P., 'Federal Division of Responsibilities in India', *Indian Journal of Federal Studies*, vol. I, 2004.

———, 'Economic Liberalization and Political Federalization in India: Mutually Reinforcing Responses to Global Integration', in *The Impact of Global and Regional Integration on Federal Systems: A Comparative Analysis*, ed. Harvey Lazar, Hamish Telford and Ronald L. Watts, Queen's University, School of Policy Studies, Montreal: McGill-Queen's University Press, 2003.

———, 'Inter-State Council: Why It Continues to be the Fifth Wheel in the Inter-governmental Car?', paper submitted to the National Commission for the Review of the Working of the Indian Constitution, typescript, 2001.

Singh, M.P. and Rekha Saxena, 'India Independent: The First Half Century of Political Development and Decay', *The Historical Review*, vol. XXVI, July 1999.

———, 'Accommodating Regionalism: Federal Constitutional Discourses in Canada and India', in *Regionalism in Canada: A Multidisciplinary Approach*, ed. Chandra Mohan, New Delhi: Allied Publishers, 1995.

———, 'Indian State: Historical Context and Change', *The Indian Historical Review*, vol. XXI, nos. 1-2, January 1995.

———, 'India: The Constitution and Consensus', in *The India-Canada Relationship: Exploring the Political Economic and Cultural Dimensions*, ed. J.S. Grewal and Hugh Johnston, Delhi: Sage, 1994.

———, 'From Centrist Predominance to Polarized Pluralism: The Post-1989 Party System in India', *Punjab Journal of Politics*, vol. XVI, nos. 1-2, 1992.

Swaminathan, S., 'NDC-Monologues Prevail', *The Hindu* (New Delhi), 5 September 2001.

Stein, Michael, 'Federal Political System and Federal Societies', *World Politics*, vol. XX, July 1968.

———, 'Taking Hindutva to School', *Frontline*, 20 November 1998.

Telford, Hamish, 'Federalism in Multinational Societies, Switzerland, Canada and India in Comparative Perspective', doctoral dissertation, Department of Political Science, University of British Columbia, 1999.

Thapar, Romesh, 'Two Nations or One?', *Economic and Political Weekly*, vol. XX, nos. 45, 46, 47, November 1985.

———, 'Into Janata's Second Year', *Economic and Political Weekly*, vol. XIII, no. 13, April 1978.

Tharyan, P., 'Inter-State Council: A Constitutional Need', *The Hindustan Times*, 19 February 1990.

Verney, Douglas V., 'From Quasi-Federation to Quasi-Confederacy? The Transformation of India's Party System', *Publius*, The Journal of Federalism, vol. 33, no. 4, Fall 2003.

———, 'Are All Federations Federal? The United States, Canada and India', in *Multiple Identities in a Single State: Indian Federalism in Comparative Perspective*, ed. Balveer Arora and Douglas V. Verney, New Delhi: Konark, 1995.

———, 'Responsible Government and Responsible Federalism: Parliamentary Government in Plural Societies', typescript, Department of Political Science, York University, Toronto, 1990.

Vijapur, Abdul Rahim et al., 'Evaluation of the Role and Working of National Integration Council', in *Pluralism, Minorities, National Integration: Problems and Prospects*, Delhi: South Asian Publishers, 1997.

Watts, Ronald L., 'Intergovernmental Councils in Federations', *Constructive and Cooperative Federation*, Kingston: IIGR, and Montreal: McGill Queen's University, 2003.

———, 'Models of Federal Power Sharing', *International Social Science Journal*, vol. 167, UNESCO: Blackwell Publishers, March 2001.

———, 'Intro: Federalism in an Era of Globalization', *International Social Science Journal*, no. 167, UNESCO: Blackwell Publishers, March 2001.

———, 'Federalism in an Era of Globalization', *International Social Science Journal*, no. 167, UNESCO: Blackwell Publishers, March 2001.
———, 'Federalism, Federal Political System and Federations', *Annual Review of Political Science*, no. 1, 1998.
———, 'Federalism in Canada', Kingston: Queen's University, Institute of Inter-governmental Relations, March 1997, typescript.
———, 'Canada: Three Decades of Periodic Crises', *International Political Science Review*, vol. XVII, no. 4, 1996.

NEWSPAPERS

Asian News Digest
Asian Recorder
Business and Political Weekly
Business Line
Business Standard
Deccan Herald
Edmonton Journal
Financial Post
Guardian
Indian Recorder
Leader-Post
National Post
Ottawa Citizen
Ottawa Letter
Ottawa Sun
St. John's Evening Telegram
Telegraph Journal
The Citizen
The Economic Times
The Financial Express
The Gazette
The Globe and Mail
The Hindu
The Hindustan Times
The Indian Express
The Pioneer
The Statesman
The Times of India
The Tribune
Toronto Star
Vancouver Sun
Windsor Star
Winnipeg Free Press

Index